Larry Gwin
Ramon "Tony" Nadal
Joe Marm
Robert Jeanette
Bill Beck

d "Doc" Johnson
Kevin MacCauley
Kreig Lofton
Kenneth Pipes
Ralph "Doc" Danielle
Mike Hill

nk Llewellyn
Kent Miller
James F. McCoy
Bill Purcell
Bob Ruth
Carey Spearman
Richard Lyons

G. "Fred" Platt
Rip Van Winkle
John Frescura
Craig Lansing
Bob Donoghue
Jon R. Cavaiani

ohn McCain
Paul Galanti
Fred Cherry
Wayne Coe
Chuck DeBellevue
Steve Ritchie

erry Berry
Colin Broussard
Toby Haynsworth
Harry Summers
John Valdez
Major Jim Kean

THE
SOLDIERS' STORY

— AN ILLUSTRATED EDITION —

an imprint of Quarto Publishing Group USA Inc.
142 West 36th Street, 4th Floor
New York, New York 10018

WELLFLEET PRESS and the distinctive Wellfleet Press logo are trademarks of
Quarto Publishing Group USA Inc.

Text © 2015 by Ron Steinman
Produced by Hourglass Press LLC

Creative direction & graphic design: Coral Communications & Design
Photo research, photography & graphic design: Carol R. Guzowski
Photo research & graphic design assistant: Maria Tubil
Photography retouching & graphic design assistant: Osei A. Boasiako
Front cover design: Osei A. Boasiako
Research and preliminary design: Kamil Wierciszewski
Historical consultant: Stephen Lee, PhD.
Photo credits: Brittany Ffrench

Special thanks to the photography department at the National Archives, College Park, Maryland.
Special thanks to Charlie Snyder for allowing us to photograph part of his collection.

The publisher has attempted to verify all names and facts herein;
any changes or ommissions will be corrected in future editions.

ISBN-13: 978-1-57715-108-1

Printed in China

2 4 6 8 10 9 7 5 3 1

www.quartous.com

THE SOLDIERS' STORY

AN ILLUSTRATED EDITION

VIETNAM IN THEIR OWN WORDS

With historic images from the NATIONAL ARCHIVES

EXPANDED EDITION, INCLUDES PREVIOUSLY UNPUBLISHED MATERIAL

RON STEINMAN

WELLFLEET
PRESS

TABLE OF CONTENTS

INTRODUCTION

This book is about the Vietnam War as seen and felt by the young men who were there. During their tour of duty, some battled aggressive North Vietnamese regulars in the Ia Drang Valley. Some lived under siege in Khe Sanh. Some joined in fierce combat with the Viet Cong and North Vietnamese in and around Saigon and Hué during the Tet Offensive. They bombed North Vietnam, rescued downed pilots, and sometimes became prisoners of war. They conducted secret operations in Laos and Cambodia. And, finally, they witnessed the end of the war when Saigon fell in 1975.

U.S. Marines (in 1965), armed with M14 rifles. Although the first Marines deployed to Vietnam carried the heavy and obsolete M14, by 1967 Marine units were armed with the new M16 rifle.

We conducted extensive interviews for the six-hour documentary series *The Soldiers Story*, produced by ABC News for The Learning Channel. Our mandate for the television series was to let these men tell stories of their life in battle: under siege at Khe Sanh, in ambush at the battle of the Ia Drang Valley, and during the Tet Offensive, the air war, the secret war, and the Fall of Saigon. Of the more than 150 men we talked to on and off camera, 76 are in this book. Unlike a documentary film, which allows very little time for an individual to be heard, a book has the luxury of length. Here, in these pages, these men can and do express themselves fully. This is their personal story, not a formal or complete history of their lives in Vietnam or the Vietnam War.

Combat is never precise. It is confusing, frightening, deadly—an unexpected hell. This book does not discuss strategy and tactics, though right or wrong decisions at the command level in significant moments did seriously affect the lives of every one of these men. Rather than the battle plans conceived by generals in their air-conditioned offices far from the front, what mattered most to the soldier in the field was getting over the next hill, plowing safely through the next rice paddy, getting through the day. The so-called "big picture" was of little consequence to the average GI.

After only a few short weeks in South Vietnam, these ordinary soldiers learned that in war there are no winners or losers. Fatalism quickly emerged as the centerpiece of their existence. Mainly, these men experienced the discomfort of life in a strange land from the first hour they landed in South Vietnam until the day they departed.

One Marine says he and his buddies lived only for "Semper Fi," always faithful to the basic precept of one for all, all for one. Every man in the book echoes that thought. Soldiers helped each other because they knew they would get help in return. It was neither crass nor calculating. It was genuine, real, meaningful. They learned to trust each other as their only salvation. Along with that sense of duty, a responsibility to and for each other, however, they often had a feeling of helplessness, particularly when under fire. We should never forget that these were men in war. Their experience of battle was direct, mostly raw, filled with emotion. They had a sense of the waste of life and of time.

Clearly, they left feeling a terrible sadness about Vietnam and the war's horrors. Their memories of a distant time that no longer exists are not only sad, but desolate, recalling an experience that was in many ways often formless. Except on the battlefield, their lives had no pattern, no constant. These young men who had never been away from home, were now thousands of miles away from the drive-in and football field, in an atmosphere and environment that said, "This is the Twilight Zone." In South Vietnam, a place of unusual customs, peoples, ideas, languages, and religions for American soldiers, danger was everywhere. The inexplicable was the only constant. Their life was the camps, foxholes, sandbags, bunkers, hooches, tents, jungles, swamps, rice paddies, snakes, rats, and even tigers. For the most part, though, war was mundane and boring, the everyday. But no one ever wanted it to become too familiar. Troops kept their spirits up in spite of the routine of their jobs. Some semblance of normalcy was necessary. Yet the men in this book found it impossible to lead normal lives. In their interviews, they rarely, if ever, talk about being heroes, seeking glory, or acting with courage, though they do describe heroism and courage as a matter of course. Their way of surviving was to rise to extraordinary spiritual and physical heights without thumping their chests.

After the Vietnam War ended, many thought it may have been the last American war where courage and individual acts of heroism were still possible. Men in small units going up against an aggressive, battle-savvy enemy had been the norm. In some cases after a firefight, American troopers gained a grudging respect for their Communist foe. Sooner than anyone thought, however, America found itself immersed in the first Gulf War, then the wars in Iraq and Afghanistan. Despite the development of new, high tech weapons that played a big role in those two wars, American combatants still had to go into battle on the ground to seek, find, and destroy the enemy. Individual heroism did not die because of advanced technology. In a sense, it flourished because the only way to root out the foe was usually on foot in one on one battles between small units.

Marines patrolling the rice paddies. Soldiers and Marines in Vietnam needed to be particularly careful of where they walked, as Communist forces were adept at the use of booby traps and land mines.

From what I read and hear, the thoughts and testimonies of the men (and now the women) who saw combat in Iraq and Afghanistan are a perfect match for what readers will see of Vietnam, as described in this book. Some things never change—mainly what troops, in whatever war they may be in, experience in combat.

In Vietnam, I was present for many of these battles, though as a journalist, not a soldier.

In 1965, a few months before going to Vietnam to serve as Saigon bureau chief for NBC News, I produced a network feed for NBC News from Dover, Delaware, late one November afternoon. The day was brutally cold. Angry black clouds filled the sky in twisted masses, as if nature were planning revenge for all those unnecessary deaths. NBC had two cameras at the Air Force base to cover dead soldiers returning home from a still little-known war. We saw the Air Force cargo plane appear in the distance, land, and taxi to a stop. Its rear cargo doors opened. Plain wooden boxes rolled out of the cargo bay. Inside the boxes were the remains of young Americans in black polyurethane body bags. Historians like to give war a "face." There was no face to war that anyone recognized that day. These were the dead coming home for a proper burial.

Though the fighting had stepped up in Vietnam, the war had not yet taken hold in the public mind. It was not the overpowering force it would soon become in 1966. But someone at NBC News had decided body bags arriving from Saigon in plain pine boxes would interest our audience. I do not know how many people watched our feed that day, but I am sure the simple, dignified ceremony was touching and moving to our viewers. As Pentagon officials saluted the dead, other young men removed the caskets one box at a time. Dignitaries and families were there to claim the returning bodies. Mothers, fathers, sisters, and brothers of the dead soldiers cried, often uncontrollably. There were a few short speeches. The event ended, and we journalists went on to other stories—for the moment.

Less than six months later, I was in Saigon as bureau chief seeing the war for myself, learning how men survive and succeed in the most adverse situations. For all I know, some of those dead that gloomy day might have been returning from the fierce and unexpected battle in the Ia Drang Valley in early November between American Air Cavalry and North Vietnamese regulars, an intense fight not immediately understood as a powerful portent of things to come.

For many, as with me, arriving at Saigon's Tan Son Nhut Airport was a journey into another dimension. The week before I left New York for my first trip to the Far East, there were long and sometimes tearful farewells with friends and family. During the flight there was too much wine and too many cigarettes. Apprehension from lack of sleep combined with fear of the new made me feel restless during the long trip. My passage aboard the crowded Pan American jet finally ended when I arrived in a war zone that I would call home for more than two years and would remain part of my life for many decades to come. When the cabin doors opened, the blast of heavy heat nearly overwhelmed me. I was unable to absorb all the sights and sounds that instantly invaded my body and soul. I found it impossible to process the new information until hours, days, weeks, perhaps even years later.

The feeling inside the huge terminal, with its hangar-like high ceiling was otherworldly. There were very few American faces—almost no other Western faces except for construction workers, diplomats, or journalists like myself. I thought American troops would be everywhere inside the building. We were at war. It was Saigon. But the only American soldiers I saw were military police, patrolling uneasily through the bustling crowds with their counterparts in the South Vietnamese Army (ARVN), wary, I assumed of a sudden terrorist attack. They were also wary of each other—generally the Americans toward the Vietnamese, whom they did not trust as soldiers nor as people. As I traveled into the city, I saw even fewer American soldiers. Again, though, there were the ubiquitous MPs in Jeeps, or on guard in front of American installations and living quarters.

Marine cameramen outside of I Corps headquarters, Da Nang. As in WWII and Korea, the American military cameramen were everywhere in Vietnam.

During the Tet Offensive, American MPs handled the brunt of the fighting in Saigon. Under an agreement with the South Vietnamese government, regular American troops were not stationed in Vietnamese cities. During my years in Saigon, I had my share of dealings with military police in all the services. Most were pleasant, nothing out of the ordinary. We always thought MPs were only cops in khaki uniforms with steel pots on their heads, carrying sidearms and wearing fancy bands on their arms. MPs, in fact, were men with tough jobs, taking care of drunks, working the occasional drug bust, and investigating robbery, rape, and murder. Their patrols were always tense, and Vietnamese and all Westerners looked on them with suspicion. In any language, they were cops. When the Tet Offensive broke loose without warning, in Saigon, these were the men in combat on the ever-moving, always dangerous front lines in the narrow, cluttered city streets. Though not specifically trained for combat, they more than held their own against battle-hardened North Vietnamese and Viet Cong troops, and they tell remarkable stories of combat and courage under fire. They did what they had to do, handled the unexpected, and fought bravely for as long as it took to secure victory.

Until the Tet Offensive, almost all the news stories on American television were of combat outside the cities—in jungles, over hills, on mountains, with soldiers slogging through rice paddies and mud. Most American troops never set foot in a Vietnamese city unless they were on a three-day pass or moving through a town. Their experience was in the bush, in hamlets and villages, not in the many small, low-slung, ugly towns that then dotted the country, some of which are still a part of a landscape that never seems to change.

Khe Sanh was one of those godforsaken places. Khe Sanh happened on my watch as a bureau chief. It made me angry then, and it still does now. A forced siege and one of the most controversial battles of the war, it was, I thought, a complete waste of time and men. Launched before the Tet Offensive and continuing past Tet's end, it was a brilliant diversion by the North Vietnamese lasting seventy-seven days in all. The siege succeeded in pinning in place some of the very best American combat troops in the country.

Two Navy A-6 Intruders provide close air support over rice paddies in South Vietnam unloading their bombs on the enemy positions.

Khe Sanh caught the fancy of my editors in New York and, according to them, the public. It was a good story that deserved coverage, but in my opinion it never deserved its enormous play. Getting film crews in and out of Khe Sanh was difficult and dangerous. I never believed the risk was worth the sameness of the stories that came back. Producers in New York reprimanded me for not providing more Khe Sanh stories. I disagreed then and do now. Each time I put a team into Khe Sanh, it meant I had one less crew to cover other more significant stories of the war. Camera crews sustained wounds from shrapnel. They twisted their ankles and wrenched their backs jumping onto the airstrip from still moving C-130 cargo planes. It was not always worth the effort. Ultimately my staff came first, and I doubted the necessity of sacrificing them for a story that hardly changed from day to day.

The value of Khe Sanh is heard in the pages of this book through the voices of the men trapped there, under orders they did not understand then or now, all these years later. Those combatants—Marines, army gunners, medics, and helicopter pilots—did their duty in spite of being puzzled and came away forever changed, feeling they achieved almost nothing except the devastation of a once beautiful landscape. To a man, they still wonder why they walked away from the base after they did so little as soldiers and gave so much of themselves in return.

The tales these men tell sometimes resemble exploding canisters of emotion, starbursts of memory. In middle age, these men have become reflective. During the war, they hardly had time to think. Indeed, if a soldier spent too much time in contemplation, he could not do his job. In Vietnam, the so-called romance of war did not exist or faded quickly. There were, however, always exceptions. Much of this book is a story of endurance in conditions so foreign as to make them dreamlike. At best, life in war is unreal. Survival lies in facing down the terror and fear of death. Survival becomes physical, always moving, and elusive, like mercury. And it always creates psychological scars. There are a few who rise beyond the rest—those who succeed under terrible conditions because their preordained mission might be to last longer than anyone else.

I met one such man in late 1966 on a flight from Japan to Saigon with an intermediate stop in Hong Kong. We sat next to each other, he by the window, I along the aisle. At first we said nothing. Then, over drinks we talked. He took one of my Camels, eleven cents a pack at the PX, and lit it. His name was Jim.

"What do you do?"

"I'm the bureau chief for NBC News in Saigon. You?"

"I sell powdered milk in Southeast Asia, mainly in Vietnam, Cambodia, and Thailand."

"Why powdered?"

"Refrigeration barely exists. This way they get nutrition, especially for babies. But they must boil the water first. That's the hardest thing to explain in the villages."

"You go to the villages?"

He smiled. "All the time. Most of my work is in the bush. I live in the boonies."

"Do you go anywhere you want?"

He smiled again. "I go where I want, as often as I want."

I looked at him out of the corner of my eye. Cigarette smoke made my eyes tear. His hair was very short. He had callused, strong hands with very short fingernails. There did not seem to be an ounce of fat on him. Milk salesman? I tried again.

"Do you really sell milk?"

"Yes, and one or two other things along the way. I don't carry a catalogue, but I can make myself understood."

He told me he spoke good Vietnamese and could make himself understood in several Montagnard dialects. That caught my attention, but I could tell from his face not to pursue it. We talked some about the war, and then he fell asleep. When we arrived in Saigon and started on our way inside the terminal, I lost track of my friend, the "powdered milk salesman."

Some months later I ran into Jim coming out of Cheap Charlie's, a Chinese Restaurant behind the Caravel Hotel. It was dusk in Saigon. Heat waves drifted off the pavement. He was in civilian clothing, but the unmistakable shape of a handgun protruded from beneath his bush jacket. We greeted each other as effusively as if we were best friends.

"How's the milk business?"

"Fair. Just fair."

"How come?"

"They didn't want milk as much as they wanted new toys."

"Toys?"

"It got so bad that I moved on to other things."

"Like what?"

"Selling ice to the Eskimos." He laughed.

"Sure. In Vietnam. You should be supplying your friends in the villages with something more substantial."

"I do. I do. Toys are substance. Because of my friends and me, whole villages now have the latest in all sorts of needed equipment. It makes their lives better and healthier." He looked at me and smiled. "My job is improve their quality of life. Surely you know what I'm saying."

I did. I knew when we were on the plane, and I knew on that Saigon street that he was with the Special Forces, a LRRP, a long-range patrol guy. He was someone who lived his life in the jungle at great risk and peril. Over the years I ran into him in all the expected places and some of the unexpected. He frequented Brodard, a Vietnamese coffee shop for underground dissidents and intellectuals in Saigon. He took too many meals at La Pagode, a third-rate spaghetti and pizza joint, reputedly run by a branch of the Corsican Mafia.

Cavalry troopers deplaning at Phu Bai during the units movement to Camp Evans. Traditionally the domain of horse soldiers and then armored vehicles, cavalry in Vietnam mostly rode into battle in helicopters. These units would be called Air Cav.

The last time I saw him was on the airstrip in Dak To in the Central Highlands. I had been with Premier Ky on an outreach trip to Montagnard tribes in that nearly isolated region. Ky was late and he had not returned from yet another "important" meeting. He owned the airplane, a battered C-130, so we had to wait for him to take us back to Saigon. Across the airfield, I spied my friend sitting casual at ease in a rundown Jeep. He had a communist AK-47 lying across his lap (he did not trust the standard issue M16), a bush hat on his head, and no insignia sewn on his shoulders. A Rhade tribesman was at his side.

I walked over the muddy field and said hello. He did not appear surprised to see me and greeted me warmly. He said he had not been back to Saigon for some months. He asked about the bars on Tu Do Street and wondered if the wine from Algiers had improved. I told him what I knew of Tu Do Street and said the Algerian red was still awful. He said he had come out to see the excitement and perhaps add a bit of protection if needed.

"All of you have been in our sights for hours," he said.

Just then Premier Ky's small, dusty motorcade of battle-worn Jeeps pulled up to the airplane. It was time to go. My friend and I shook hands and said good-bye. He smiled warmly. I turned, walked away, and did not look back. I never saw him again. For me he will always be one of those who made history but never thought about it. Above all, he was a survivor, as he moved lightly and surprisingly gently in and out of my life.

During the war, when I talked to soldiers they rarely if ever wanted to talk about the battles they had been in, the fighting they had seen, the death that was everywhere. Soldiers always thought more of the mundane, despite the heat, dirt, peril, fear of strange customs, and the anxiety of living in even stranger surroundings. Their minds were on girls, music, food, home, mom, dad, even apple pie. It was their way to keep going through many difficult days. Ultimately, each man formed his own truth about Vietnam.

Most American soldiers arrived in Vietnam aboard Boeing 707s charted by the American military from commercial airlines. Soldiers rarely departed from the United States in groups or with their unit. They usually flew alone. On arrival at Saigon's Tan Son Nhut Air Base, or up north in Da Nang, another entry point, or even by ship at Cam Ranh Bay, they would find their unit and settle in, if we can call it that, for the next twelve months, or until wounds or disease caused the premature end of their tour. At the end of that tour, they picked up their demobilization papers, arranged a flight home, and departed. Rarely did they look back—that would come later. Just as there were no marching bands to send them off, as we so well know now, there were no marching bands to welcome them home when they returned.

Many books measure the war in statistics. In those valuable works, we may, however, lose the personal meaning of battle for those who have seen combat. Statistics cloud reality. This book is, in its way, an attempt to bridge the gap between the theorists and those who served. In this book we do use some statistics. More than fifty-eight thousand died in the war. The wounded numbered better than three hundred thousand, and their wounds are still a constant reminder of the trauma of war. But the emphasis is on the overpowering, shattering experience of constant, life-threatening combat, a wounding that goes beyond the physical. Each man in combat, emerging from a war zone, undergoes a profound transformation that stays with him forever.

During my stay in Vietnam through much of 1966, all of 1967, and most of 1968, I would often cross the wide street separating my bureau office at 104 Nguyen Hue and enter the building known as JUSPAO (the Joint United States Public Affairs Office). There, in a large, plain auditorium, I would hear about the war's progress from military and civilian officers at their daily briefings, known as the Five O'Clock Follies. Here, statistics ruled. Briefings included enemy body counts, the killed and wounded, the number of days or weeks of a military operation, and the start or finish of an operation. The statistics measuring the effects of the air war were always more difficult to interpret for the public: flights, sorties, BDAs (bomb damage assessments), B-52s, Thailand, close-air support, A-7s, F-104s, flak, MiGs, rescue missions, enemy planes downed, helicopter gunships, Jolly Green Giants.

One Saturday afternoon on a particularly quiet day, a call came in from a navy briefing officer. He had two navy pilots who had just arrived from a strenuous bombing run, successfully attacking a fleet of junks in the South China Sea near the demilitarized zone (DMZ). They were fly-boys—air jockeys, cocky, gung-ho, fuzzy-cheeked youth, the elite. It was an opportunity to see them up close and talk with them one on one. My Saturday in-town crew was sitting in the bureau playing cards. I said, "Get a twelve-hundred footer, three lights, and let's go across the street for an interview." Twelve hundred feet of film is about thirty-three minutes of continuous run without changing magazines. It would be more film than we would need. We set up on the stage in the auditorium. The young, weary, though relaxed, navy pilots came out still dressed in their flight suits. Their faces haggard, they were in need of shaves. We sat down to talk. At last statistics were about to come to life.

The pilots, like all fighter pilots, laconic in the extreme, probably wishing for a beer, were only as forthcoming as the briefing officer allowed. They could not give us precise details, such as coordinates, but they could tell us almost everything else we wanted to know. Their flight was a routine mission looking for enemy movement in and around I Corps, in the northern part of South Vietnam where the Marines worked. There was not much activity. On their way back to the carrier they spotted a fleet of slow-moving junks and small, flat cargo boats off the coast of the DMZ, the line separating South Vietnam from North Vietnam. There were too many of them clustered together to be there for anything but something bad.

When the pilots started shooting at the junks they received heavy return fire. That indicated, without doubt, that those were no ordinary ships. The pilots destroyed most of the fleet. Ships were in flames. Debris was everywhere. Bodies clawed at pieces of wreckage over a wide area. The American fliers completed their mission without injury or damage to their airplanes and returned to base. The pilots made good copy on a slow day. The interview allowed us to put a face on the war in the skies, a part of the war where we rarely had access. We shipped the film; it appeared on the weekend news, and in that way we helped make the air war real. As the war continued, enemy gunners shot many of these pilots out of the sky. American fighters and bombers crashed over friendly territory and, more often, over enemy territory. Brave helicopter crews saved many downed pilots. Many pilots died. Captured airmen became POWs for more years than they could have imagined. The remarkable resolve of the prisoners and the American code of conduct prevailed over the radically different ideals of their jailers. Torture and beatings were commonplace. The battle for the hearts and minds of the POWs was a unique cultural war, a battle of sensibilities between two strong-willed peoples.

Interior of Ward #5 (Medical) - 91st Evacuation Hospital (Chu Lai), located at the headquarters of the Americal division. Formally the 23rd Infantry Division, which was activated immediately after the attack on Pearl Harbor hence the Hawaiian flag and Coat of Arms of the Kingdom of Hawaii hanging on the back wall.

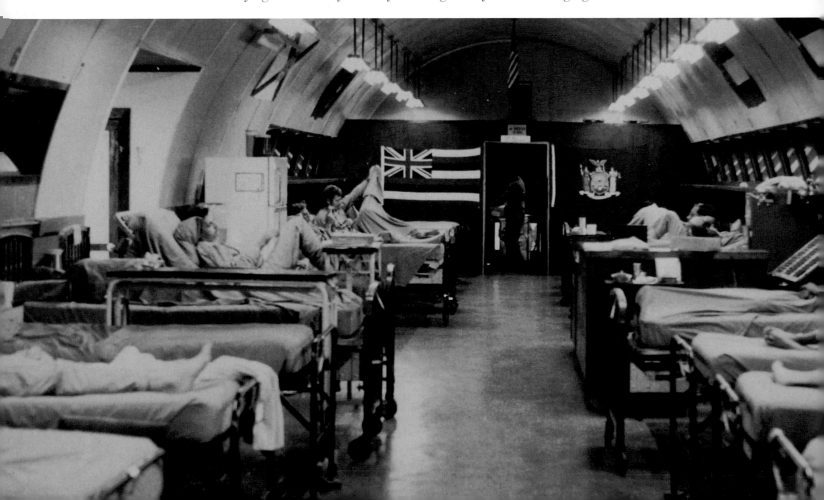

I must admit I had then, and still do a great empathy for the troops who served in Vietnam. Much of the time, tedium dominated their constricted lives. During Tet in Saigon and Hué, wherever Americans came under attack, especially at Ia Drang, where the action was so intense that it defied reason and in Khe Sanh where the siege went on for nearly three months, tedium was hardly the problem. But most GIs spent little of their time in combat. Many battles were short and intense, filled with confusion, terrible noise, and smoke, the smell of burning cordite and the loss of one's senses because of overpowering and inescapable fear. It was then that tedium set in again.

In 1967, one of my cameramen was recovering from an attack of malaria in the Third Field Hospital at Tan Son Nhut Air Base. While I was visiting him and getting an opinion on his progress, a medic asked if I was available to help feed the men on his ward. As usual, the army was short of hospital staff. As we spoke, doctors, medics, and nurses were on the incoming ramp outside the hospital, receiving a large number of severely wounded men who had just arrived from an ambush near the Cambodian border.

It was lunchtime, the hour to feed the men. The medic brought me to the kitchen door. He gave me a small trolley loaded with

Aerial view of cargo ship off-loading barges in Da Nang Harbor.

food and handed me a list of names to go with each tray. He then started me down a wide aisle with a long row of beds on each side. The place felt like the inside of a World War II Hollywood movie—only this was real. One row of beds ran along the outside wall, which had large windows with white adhesive tape in crisscross patterns to prevent flying glass if bombs or rockets hit the building. The other row lined up against the inside wall, with a seriously wounded man in each bed. I planned to open their tray table, swing it up, around, and over their prone bodies, hand them the tray, and walk away. That proved unrealistic. Some of these men had no hands, no arms, no legs. They had so many serious wounds, they could not eat without help. It was the middle of 1967. I had been in Vietnam more than a year, and I had seen my share of horror. But being in the presence of so many wounded in one place was very difficult. As I marched down the aisle distributing trays of food, I saw that I had to feed many of the men. Some were patient; others were not. One man, more a boy of less than twenty, his body swathed in white bandages, lay unmoving. But his eyes were bright—they burned with life's fire. And he could talk.

"Hey, man, over here. Don't ignore me!"

I stopped and turned to look at him. There seemed to be so little of him left, but he was still alive. Here was a young man who had held out for life when faced with almost certain death. The futility surrounding his future would come much later in his recovery. Now he was in charge, and he demanded service.

"Get that food over here. I'm hungry. I want to eat. Feed me."

I moved over to him, unwrapping the tray as I approached his bedside. Wrapped in bandages and a plaster cast from his head to his toes, he resembled a mummy from a 1930s film. There were two black holes for his eyes, two black holes for his nostrils. His mouth was a larger black hole in his white bandaged head. So I fed him. One spoonful at a time. Spoon by spoon. Slowly.

"More," he said.

"Faster," he said.

He demanded attention, and I readily complied. Then his tray was empty. There was no more food. His glass of water was empty. He could suck nothing more through his straw. There was nothing more for him to drink.

"Good, man," he said.

He sighed deeply and was quiet. I moved away and distributed the rest of my trays. This was gut-real. War is mostly what is in front of you at the moment. War for me then was the seemingly hopeless situation of that blond-haired youth. But he was not helpless. I learned that, though badly wounded, their individual spirits were strong, and that these young men had an enormous gusto for life, just as the men who speak in these pages do.

More than 2.7 million Americans served in South Vietnam itself. More than 3.7 million men served in the Vietnam theater of war, including Thailand, Guam, the Philippines, and in the South China Sea. A tour of duty was one year, but those who wanted to could sign up for additional tours. Some did re-up. Most did not. The average age in the Vietnam War was under 20 years, 19.2 years to be exact. The average age in Korea was 24 years. In World War II, the average age was 26 years. As in other wars, most of the men who served accepted the soldier's role as their duty. They usually supported the war because they grew up believing in and supporting their country. None of these men ever thought they lost the war, though many did question what they were doing in Vietnam and wondered about Washington's philosophy for fighting it.

As the war recedes from memory, fewer people know today what it meant to be in combat in Vietnam, to fight and stay alive in what at that time would become America's longest war. Society is always slow to recognize the price the soldier pays. The American public may never understand the personal experiences of combat these men knew so well. These voices should help rectify that for future generations. The battles these veterans describe were for them intense, powerful, and unforgettable … and through this book, can be for us as well.

By 1975, the only American military in the country was a detachment of Marine Special Security responsible for guarding the Americans who still remained in South Vietnam. In Saigon, until the very last days of the war, the only Vietnamese men you saw were the very young and the very old. Boys in their late teens and men through middle age were in the military, usually for the duration without relief, unless you call desertion, being wounded, or death relief of a sort. The young were away at war, out of the city for the most part, fighting elsewhere, usually far from home.

That all changed in early 1975 when North Vietnam launched its final offensive. To the surprise of everyone and, in retrospect, to the surprise of no one, South Vietnam collapsed more quickly than anyone thought.

Marine airlift of Vietnamese Army personnel during an airstrike against Viet Cong guerrillas.

What the few U.S. Marines who remained in the country saw, though expected and predictable, was still shocking: a country crumbled. It's only prop, the United States, rudely wrenched itself away from its one-time ally in its hour of greatest need. These young Marines, the last of America's fighting men in South Vietnam, saw, as did we at home, an army in disarray, refugees in flight, panic everywhere, a country in defeat. At the time of Saigon's fall, I was back in New York producing special broadcasts for NBC News. We frequently cut into Johnny Carson's Tonight Show at 11:30 P.M. and delayed the start of his monologue to the dismay of the show's staff, those who ran the network, and particularly those who counted the network's hard-earned dollars. Tired of Vietnam, NBC's entertainment executives thought there had been too much war coverage anyway, so why show more. We had our instructions from NBC News, though, not the entertainment side. Every opportunity we had, we filled the air with special broadcasts, ranging from five minutes to as long as an hour, which graphically described the crumbling country and the war's dramatic end. Fortunately, we in news prevailed, continuing to show the disintegration of South Vietnam in all its ungainly glory. The public deserved that much after witnessing the war for so many years on television.

The most lasting impressions I have of the men in Vietnam are their faces, almost all young. Many had not yet run a razor across their cheeks. Most had never been away from home, whether from a small farm town or a big city. Some were high-school graduates; others were dropouts and runaways. Few had any education beyond high school. Many were poor.

In every war, the very young always fight to satisfy some need in the very old. Now those once-young soldiers have their chance to speak. For many of these men, this is the first time they have talked in public about events that took place in their lives decades ago. We hear their voices and we see their faces, men in middle age. Scrolling back so many years, though, these are again young men, undiluted by the ravages of time. Their memories reach us mostly unspoiled, not yet altered by the realities of their later life. I see so much youth in their faces, despite their years, that it borders on fantasy. War has the terrible effect of changing everyone. The face of the war is not always the face you see in front of you. When I sat before these men during the interviews for the documentary series, I could see flashes of youth in their now middle-aged faces. When they reached back into their memory, I could see the vigor that once was so much a part of their lives, and for many of them, still remains.

POST-TRAUMATIC STRESS DISORDER

In Vietnam, when an American unit went into combat, each soldier, Marine, or sailor was at risk. Every American in war is a potential victim of psychological stress and a candidate for PTSD, post-traumatic stress disorder. The military teaches men, mainly the young, how to fight, how to kill, even how to survive under extreme pressure, but it rarely supports them if they are unable to maintain their stability after the trauma of combat. In a war zone, the military often stigmatizes any trooper for being unable to perform in combat, especially if he comes forward to report his concerns. Soldiers must feel free to let their superiors know they have problems, but most do not because it is a difficult thing for them to do.

There is strong anecdotal evidence that as many as one third of all Vietnam veterans have at one time or another suffered from PTSD. Today the estimate is that as many as 300,000 Vietnam veterans, perhaps as high as 11 percent, still suffer from PTSD. For them, the war never ends. PTSD manifests itself in nightmares, flashbacks while awake, heightened emotional intensity, drug and alcohol abuse, a higher rate of divorce, and possibly a major source of suicide among veterans. I personally know many soldiers who still suffer from PTSD and who will continue to do so with little hope of recovery.

The military, by its very nature, is macho and cannot tolerate weakness. If a soldier said he had a problem in war, his superiors considered it a flaw in his character. Reluctant or unmanageable soldiers were often in serious trouble with their superiors if they showed any sign of fragility. It is difficult to know precisely why PTSD was so rampant for returning Vietnam veterans. Some think it may be guilt, the shame of combat and the harm inflicted on the enemy and civilians alike that causes the syndrome. It took many years and many studies after Vietnam ended before the civilians in our government, the military, and doctors of every discipline, recognized that PTSD, labeled shellshock in earlier wars, was a genuine problem, but I do not believe they really understand it or have the desire to do much about it. The American military found it beyond its understanding that men suffer in combat. It still feels that way for those who served in Iraq and Afghanistan.

First, come back in time with me for a moment, because it is important that we understand trauma induced by stressful situations. Starting in the late 19th century and into the 20th century, medicine and the military called "stress-induced trauma" shellshock. The military and medical world usually shunted the malady aside as some sort of excuse for not going into combat. Officials in every country termed men who lacked the desire to continue fighting and killing "malingerers" Never considered a clinical problem by the military or doctors, shellshock made its way silently into every part of society, rattling around in the minds of lost men for years. From anecdotal evidence, we now recognize that severe floods, fires, and storms have had the same effect on men and women as did war.

Then there was a breakthrough in 1917 during World War I, when British doctors started to seriously study the psychological effect of the war on soldiers. A psychiatrist, Dr. William Rivers at the Craiglockhart War Hospital, worked with men returning from the front whom their superiors classified as "mentally unsound." Under orders, he tried to restore these men to normalcy and get them back to the trenches. One of his most famous patients was Siegfried Sassoon, a distinguished poet and decorated war hero who eventually decided he would no longer serve as an officer in the British Army. Rivers' conclusions, though important, almost fell between the cracks. In time, disillusioned with the scant acceptance of his research, he pursued other endeavors that took him far from his studies.

The findings of Dr. Rivers, mostly ignored when he was interacting with returning British soldiers, spread slowly through the medical community. For years, he was truly a lone voice that spoke clearly to war neurosis induced by the trauma of combat. But, as with many pioneers, his ideas had little effect on those in power. The attitude of the military was simple. Soldiers fight. They do not run from the enemy. They cannot have problems if the nation is to be victorious. In World War I, orders were to return these men to the front as soon as possible to face the horror of the terrible war in the trenches—a concept foreign to the way we now fight war where front lines hardly exist.

Rivers' return to prominence came toward the end of the last century in a remarkable trilogy of award-winning novels by the English writer Pat Barker written in the 1990s but set in World War I. Reading these books can give us a deeper understanding of stress-related trauma, and one that is easier to comprehend than anything found in scientific journals. In each of her three books, "Regeneratio", "Eye in the Door", and "Ghost Road", Pat Barker delves deeply into the theories of Dr. Rivers and into the minds of Siegfried Sassoon and the young poet Wilfred Owens. Sassoon lived a long life, producing many volumes of poetry and novels, but Owens was killed in action one week before the armistice that ended the war. Barker's style is sparse, her writing clear and spare, her ideas powerful. Her understanding of shellshock is remarkable. W.R. Rivers, now long dead, is her muse as well as her source. These books will help lead us on our search for answers not only to what causes stress in war, but also to why and how, more often than not, many in positions of power ignore it.

Change might be coming, but it appears to me that it is only cosmetic. Recently retired Army Vice Chief of Staff, General Peter Chiarelli, a man deeply concerned about the mental health of everyone in the military, wants to change the name of PTSD to erase the stigma he believes goes with the term post-traumatic stress disorder. He wants to call what some troops suffer post-traumatic stress injury. He hopes that by changing the name from PTSD it will help "reduce the stigma that stops troops from seeking treatment." General Chiarelli believes that "no 19-year old kid wants to be told he has a disorder." But his efforts have not lowered the high suicide rates either in the army or among veterans. Despite his caring, General Chiarelli still leaves behind a poorly trained staff of behavioral professionals to counsel soldiers in trouble.

How we describe the mental wounds of war will not alter what happens to the person who suffers from PTSD. As much as many do not like it, it seems the United States might be fighting wars of one kind or another for years to come. Men and women will die. Men and women will suffer lifelong physical and mental wounds. Lives will never be the same again. It means we must work diligently to understand and solve the problems that war brings to those who fight them. If not, we will have a group of permanently mentally debilitated veterans.

Once America's proud boots on the ground, many returning Vietnam veterans struggled to find a place in a society often blind to who they were and where they were. The major problem with the military in America and America itself is that we have successfully created a new underclass, the professional soldier. It is a caste of men and women in uniform to whom most people in our country have no connection. Many people who are not part of its ethos cannot identify with men and women in uniform. They cannot see them, touch them, or experience the life they led in the war zone. That is for the soldier's immediate family, their neighborhood, their hometown, their base, and their often tight-knit world. At home and out of uniform, they disappear from view so swiftly many of us do not know they are among us.

In Vietnam, the drafted filled the ranks of the military. Today, volunteers make up our fighting force. As a nation, we are good at filling young troopers' minds with the idea of sacrifice, of heroism, of patriotism. But none of that rhetoric matters to returning vets if they cannot find work and peace at home. If when the soldier comes home, he or she cannot find a viable place in society, these men and women might question what they were doing in war in the first place. In any case, the war never ends for some of the men who served in Vietnam. When you think about PTSD, what you are about to read also applies to those who served multiple deployments in Iraq and Afghanistan. We must deal with this as a nation and come to grips with the effects of war on the men and women who do the fighting. We must also learn how it affects everyone at home, something that took too many years after Vietnam for us to begin to understand.

This is not a book composed of battle reports, though it is about men in battle. Battle reports are mostly about numbers and positions, the names of units, their size, the deployment of men and weapons, the loss or gain of territory. The "Vietnam War" as an idea evades them. Men make judgments in the moment, in an action, not in advance, and troops in the field base their attitude on their immediate experience.

As you hear these veterans talk, they quickly open a window through which we can now peer—into their souls, hearts, and minds. We then become part of the moments they knew, moments large and small. This book is about soldiers in combat, on patrol, under siege, when wounded, as prisoners, flying jets and helicopters, and seeing them after battle, always after battle. It is how they lived and persevered. Their words and memories recall an often-difficult past they sometimes have refused to accept. Now years later, they still cling to these troublesome memories from an ever-increasing distance.

In some ways, Vietnam is a never-ending story. Anyone seeking complete understanding about the war will encounter enormous disappointment. Facts are not always facts. For some veterans the war is the nightmare of their life. For others, it is their seminal experience. For most, it is a monumental tragedy. These men tell specific stories of their life in the war. No more, no less. One GI says with feeling and wonder that speaks for anyone who served in Vietnam, "We survived. That is all that matters." That is sometimes tribute enough.

This, then, is a book about men who lived through the Vietnam War, soldiers' stories, heartfelt, direct, unfiltered ... but it also offers larger universal truths. Ultimately this is about men in war, men at war, men whose lives changed because of war, from their point of view, with their emotions showing. These men fought often gallantly and bravely, no matter what they thought about the war. If the battlefield transforms all men, then these men have come out the other side, very much themselves. Scholars, politicians, historians, and generals may argue about the war, but these men lived it. These are stories that could apply to any war at any time. Then they were teenagers in battle; today they are men. Here, I am grateful to help as they tell their stories in their words.

WHAT THEY CARRIED

As the Vietnam War fades into distant memory, it is worth knowing something about the many men who served, who they were, where they came from, how they suffered, and how they survived. Though the war ended many years ago and people tend to let it fade from our collective memory, the men who were in Vietnam should forever be in our sight.

U.S. Army issue helmet for Vietnam, with an M16 rifle, which was the standard weapon of infantry throughout the war with a Memorial American Flag.

2,709,918 Americans served in the military during the Vietnam War. Many of those, at one time or another, were in Vietnam. Of that number, between 1 million and 1.6 million actually saw combat. Some were in artillery units. Others served in the air—in helicopter gunships, medevacs, and troops transports. Many support troops not in the field were regularly under attack from enemy fire. We know that 58,220 Americans died in the war. Their names are engraved on the Vietnam Veterans Memorial Wall in Washington, D.C. The average age of those killed was 23 years. The oldest killed was 62, and there were three men who were only 16 years old when they died. More than 60 percent of those killed were under 21 years old with many of them only 20 years old. There were 303,644 wounded; one of every ten men in Vietnam became a casualty.

Though there was a draft, only 25 percent of the troops were draftees. The rest were volunteers, who made up about 70 percent of those who died in action. Draftees accounted for about 30 percent of those killed in action. Eighty-eight percent of the men were Caucasian. Eleven percent of the men were black. More than three quarters of the troops were working class Americans or of low income. Some were from the lower middle class.

Men in the field on military operations in Vietnam saw an average of 240 days of combat, a number far higher than soldiers experienced in World War II.

And through it all, there were, 248 Medal of Honor winners in that ever-dangerous and difficult war.

US M18A1 claymore, detonator and cord. Soldiers on patrol would carry claymores as part of their standard kit, along with mortar shells and machine gun belts.

The smallest unit was the squad, what veterans call "leg infantry." An army squad had ten men. Each squad had three fire teams. A staff sergeant led the squad, and he might have had two sergeants leading one of the three fire teams. The squad usually had two M79 grenade launchers and sometimes an M60, belt-fed machine gun, as well as a radio operator and the heavy radio he had to carry. Early in the war, men carried the M14 automatic rifle. Then the military command switched to the M16, a weapon that had serious problems with jamming and keeping the weapon clean, especially because of the heat, humidity, rain, and mud. Despite these problems, soldiers learned to live with the M16, often making the best of an undependable weapon. In the war's later years, an updated and more reliable version of the M16 became available and worked fairly well, though the men who used the M16 were always skittish. They never knew what to expect.

Army squadrons did not usually have medics attached, but a rifleman took that on when needed, which was often. Medics trained for 16 weeks and learned how to handle wounds and the resulting trauma that went with them. The medic wore no distinguishing marks so as to not to make themselves easy targets. Assigned mostly on the company and platoon level, much of what they did took place on medevac helicopter flights from action on the ground until they arrived at the nearest field hospital.

U.S. Marine uniform shirt

The job of squad-sized patrols was to search and destroy the enemy.
Most squads never had a full complement of men. The squad usually operated 20 percent to 30 percent below official strength. This meant it was seriously undersized. Sickness, men on leave, casualties, and replacements that were late in arriving were some of the reasons why those in command never solved this problem.

Marine squads had a somewhat different structure. Their squads moved with 13 men, divided into three fire teams with a full time medic, a Navy Corpsman, attached to the unit. Along with the riflemen, and its radio operator, also a rifleman, a Marine squad might carry a 60mm or 80mm mortar, a 3.5 rocket launcher, and the M79 grenade launcher.

The military likes to think in threes. A platoon has 3 squads and usually 30 to 40 men, led by a First Lieutenant. A company might have as few as 100 men and as many as 190, usually composed of three platoons and a heavy weapons unit, all led by a captain. An infantry battalion liked to have around 900 men that included three or four rifle companies, a headquarters company, and artillery. Marine battalions tried to have between 1000 and 1100 men. A Lieutenant Colonel was in charge. A brigade was even bigger. Composed of three battalions, it had between 2,500 and 3,000 men commanded by a full colonel. Finally, a division had three brigades, a desired roll of 15,000 to 20,000 men, but divisions in Vietnam were rarely that big. A major general usually commanded a division. The Marines had a similar command structure.

A trooper arrived in Vietnam with only the clothes on his back and maybe his duffel bag with a change of clothing and a few personal items. It did not take long for the quartermaster to outfit the average infantry man, Army or Marine, for combat. Issued two sets of

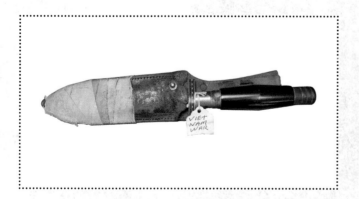

Dagger carried as a secondary weapon.

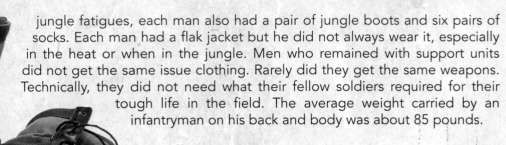

jungle fatigues, each man also had a pair of jungle boots and six pairs of socks. Each man had a flak jacket but he did not always wear it, especially in the heat or when in the jungle. Men who remained with support units did not get the same issue clothing. Rarely did they get the same weapons. Technically, they did not need what their fellow soldiers required for their tough life in the field. The average weight carried by an infantryman on his back and body was about 85 pounds.

Old boots

Starting with a typical squad, an infantryman had his M16 rifle. He may have been the operator of the M60, belt-fed machine gun or the M79 grenade launcher. If a medic was in the unit, he also carried an M16 but more likely he had a .45 pistol attached to his waist because it was less weight for him to carry. A few men might have a shotgun and some even had a personal handgun, a revolver, or a .45. Attached to his shirt were three to five fragment grenades and one or more smoke grenades. Some men in the squad also had a claymore mine.

The RTO, Radio Telephone Operator, was a special case. When on patrol, along with his usual pack, he had a specially designed communications package that weighed almost 24 pounds. He had to stick close to the squad leader. Without his presence, the squad could not receive information nor send information necessary to the success of the mission. His position was one of constant danger. His radio package sported a high antenna, which when raised to its full height, made the operator an easy target for enemy soldiers.

Each man wore a standard uniform made of cotton poplin and what the army called a "rip-stop" fabric. Loose fitting, the uniform provided ventilation, the ability to wick moisture out of the shirt or jacket, and, hopefully, dry fast after a rain storm. The clothing he wore helped keep insects out, the sun from becoming too hot, and protected the soldier from the everyday struggle in the jungle. He had a poncho and a poncho liner, and a bottle of what he called bug juice or insect repellent attached to his M1 steel pot helmet. The rucksack he carried, known as a backpack to civilians, had a round edged aluminum frame to ease the way the pack laid on his back.

What the infantryman really carried often was more than what was in his rucksack. On his body, he had an

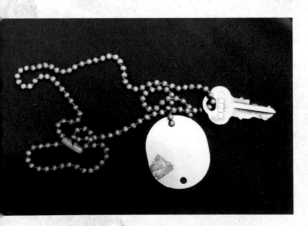

Keychain and worn out dogtag

The ALICE lightweight rucksack

Green plastic canteen and metal canteen cup

M1 steel pot helmets with different covers and interoir gear.

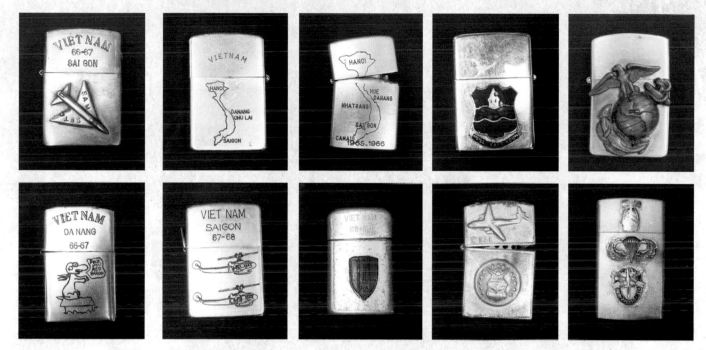

The essential Zippo® lighter with personal touches, from the Charles Snyder collection.

average of six, one quart, green plastic canteens and usually one metal canteen cup that he used for heating food or water, if necessary. Some men had as many as ten canteens of water, always at a premium, as they walked in extreme heat and humidity through jungle, up hills, and over mountains. Water weighed the most and for some men they had to weigh the amount of ammunition they lugged against the water they needed. It was a delicate balance and never achieved to satisfaction. Attached to his jacket or shirt were three to six hand grenades and possibly a bayonet and a machete. If he was toting a 21 pound machine gun, the M60, he had 100 to 200 rounds of ammunition. He usually had two to four bandoliers of M16 ammo. There were seven magazines on each bandolier and each magazine held 18 rounds.

He also had cigarettes, his Zippo® lighter, matches, and an extra pair of socks, which was almost more necessary than anything else he carried. His pair of high jungle boots had webbing to allow the water to spill out when the jungle or the streams he crossed filled the boot with water and made his feet wet. The terrain always determined how and where the troops moved. Along with the usual insects and leeches, more often than not punji sticks, sharp fragments of wood, bamboo, or metal buried in the ground and covered in excrement could penetrate the toughest boot, and were as dangerous as the enemy hiding in a jungle redoubt. Quick work by a medic usually saved the soldier from serious injury.

      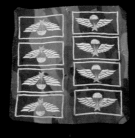    

  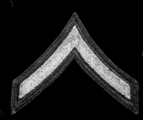   

RANGER
c8 75

4
3

USS BLUE RIDGE
LCC-19

21st FIGHTER SQUADRON
GAMBLERS

HEADHUNTERS
219th AVN CO

CCS WEATHER

52

TACA
VIETNAMESE
HUNTING CLUB
FINGERPRINT 32

C H C V

VIET-NAM
DEATH BEFORE
716
DISHONOR
SAIGON

CASPER
PLT.
ARMY
173RD ABN BDE

RED HORSE

FLYING 58TH

MEDEVAC
CO
SO THAT OTHERS MAY LIVE

SON TAY RAIDER
21 NOVEMBER 1970

3
BN
0
6th MARINES

UNITED NATIONS
NATIONS UNIES

AIRBORNE
11

5

OFFICIAL U.S. WAR
CORRESPONDENT

V

OFFICIAL U.S. ARMY
PHOTOGRAPHER

4

AA
2 HUNDRED MISSIONS
VIETNAM

19th

3 3
3

A

19th FASS
FAC
BIEN-HOA

★ CHAPTER 1 ★

THE BATTLE OF IA DRANG VALLEY

The Ia Drang Valley was a remote and inaccessible region in the Central Highlands of South Vietnam, a place of mostly scrub bush, nearly no clearings, deep ravines, and sun-baked termite hills, which American soldiers called ant hills, as tall as a man. Hanoi had decided in 1964 that its regular army troops, trained and equipped in the North, would enter the battle against the South. Hanoi's goal was to cut South Vietnam in two by driving across the middle of the country. First they had to get their troops down the Ho Chi Minh Trail into the South. The Ia Drang Valley in the Central Highlands was one of North Vietnam's destinations.

The U.S. Army decided to stop North Vietnam by sending in assault helicopters, quickly, efficiently, and ready for action when they landed. So 430 troops of the 1st Battalion, 7th Air Cavalry, Airmobile, 1st Cavalry Division, loaded on UH-1 helicopters, known as Hueys, and went on a search-and-destroy mission. They dropped into what seemed to be an unoccupied landing zone, designated Landing Zone X-Ray, a clearing as large as a football field. There they met a large force of more than two thousand North Vietnamese troops already in hiding. The American soldiers suddenly ran into unexpected resistance. Engaging in hand-to-hand fighting, where American and North Vietnamese saw each other's faces for the first time, and though badly battered, the Air Cavalry acquitted itself with valor despite being badly outnumbered. Helped by heavy artillery and air support, including unusually close strikes by B-52 bombers, the American forces inflicted heavy casualties on its well-trained enemy. Later the North Vietnamese surrounded and cut off an American platoon that had been walking through the jungle on its way to another landing zone (LZ Albany), where they hoped to then return to their base.

Intense, brutal fighting ensued. Days later, when the Air Cavalry broke through to the battered platoon, they found 21 dead and 29 wounded. Both sides suffered extremely heavy casualties. After four days of unrelenting fighting in one of the bloodiest battles of the war, 240 Americans had died and nearly 300 were wounded. However, American forces had killed approximately 1,800 North Vietnamese and wounded an untold number of their enemy.

The battle was the first major engagement between North Vietnamese regulars and the United States armed forces as both sides quietly escalated the war. It would take years for the United States command to understand the significance of the bloody fighting over those four days in November 1965. In 1975, Hanoi's strategy came full circle when the North Vietnamese successfully cut South Vietnam in two and finally ended the war.

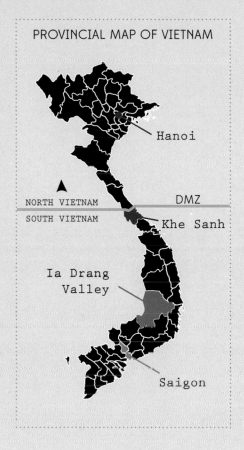

PROVINCIAL MAP OF VIETNAM

Hanoi

NORTH VIETNAM
SOUTH VIETNAM

DMZ

Khe Sanh

Ia Drang Valley

Saigon

The Ia Drang Valley is a valley located about 32 miles south west of Pleiku in the Central Highlands of Vietnam. The word "ia" is a word of the Montagnard, meaning river.

CLINTON POLEY

Assistant Machine Gunner 2nd Platoon
Charlie Company, 1st Battalion
7th Cavalry, 1st Air Cavalry Division (Airmobile)
U.S. Army

Clinton Poley

Clinton Poley and his platoon are aboard a flight of assault helicopters in pursuit of what everyone thinks are the retreating North Vietnamese troops. In a classical tactic, the choppers set down in Landing Zone X-Ray. To their surprise, Poley and his men land in the middle of the North Vietnamese regulars, who turn and fight their pursuers. The 7th Cavalry soldiers quickly discover they are in a dangerous and very hot landing zone. During the heavy fighting, Poley suffers serious wounds on 70 percent of his body.

We landed in grass about five feet tall. We didn't know where the rest of our guys were. They sent one guy over from our company to lead us to the rest of the company, and I remember he was complaining because he had a hole in the top of his canteen where a bullet had gone through and his water had all leaked away, and he was wearing the canteen on his hip when it happened. We had a guy that was only there six days, our first replacement. He was our ammo bearer for the machine gunner. He never made it to our position, and he got killed.

We hadn't a whole lot of combat so you were kind of lulled into thinking that maybe you'd get this tour in, nothing big would happen. There was a lot of ways to die. We had two guys got killed in a helicopter crash, and one drowned, and one of our guys got shot by one of our men out on the perimeter.

Members of 3rd Platoon, Company A, 3rd Battalion, 199th Light Infantry Brigade,
silhouetted against the sky as they patrol along the wire (the first line of defense against
the Communist attack), on the south bank of the canal at Y Bridge.

They showed us where the rest of the guys were from our platoon and spaced us out and had us start digging a foxhole, but you could hear the bullets cracking around you. The area that I was in, we never fired our rifles that afternoon, that is, me and the machine gunner.

The next morning when they really hit my company, it was just getting barely daylight. They sent a patrol of our guys to look for infiltrators or something. They were only out there for a few minutes, and one guy came running back and he said, "They're coming. They're coming." And somebody over a foxhole away said, "Who's coming?" You know, like who would you think? We couldn't even see the foxholes. We couldn't even see the rest of our guys. We all opened up firing, and the machine gunner was pretty much prone, and I was on my knees in a foxhole. I had hooked hundred-round belts of ammunition together for him, and he was firing them up pretty fast. So I really didn't get to use my rifle much. Well, in doing that, then that's when I first got wounded in the neck. All of a sudden something hit me in the back of the head and, real hard, knocked my head forward so that my steel helmet fell off in the foxhole, and I quick turned around because I thought there was a guy had snuck up behind me and hit me with the butt of his rifle. Wasn't nobody there.

So then I took my hand and felt, and my finger was all bloody, and it felt like it went in a round hole. I was still conscious so I took my bandage thing and put it over there and went back to help. We only had one grenade each going in there. And pretty soon I heard a North Vietnamese speaking or Vietnamese speaking, and I was going up on my knees to try and see above the grass, you know, real quick, and then down and off to our right a little bit was four NVA. I could see the pith helmets, and I don't think they seen me. The front guy was kind of turning around like, barking out instructions, and they were spread out about three yards apart.

On top of this ant hill that was supposed to be where the platoon leader and everybody was, there was this NVA looking right down on us. And I threw the only grenade that I had, and it went just where I wanted it to, right over his head. I don't know if it was the same guy or one that looked like him popped right back up after it went off. But he picked up one of his grenades and threw it right back at us. It was like these broomstick, Chinese grenades. It landed about eighteen inches from my shoulder. I could see the fuse smoking. And I thought, you know maybe the guy counted too fast, that he was nervous, and I could quick throw it away before it blew up in our faces, and I was going to reach for it and the machine gunner said, "Get down." And for some reason I did. When that thing went off, there's a lot of dust and smoke and neither one of us got any shrapnel.

The machine gun had also been jamming, giving problems, and the whole bottom of the foxhole was full of spent casings. And when that dust and smoke kicked up, neither one of us said anything. We just upped at once and got out of there, and I got a ways from the foxhole, and that's when I got hit in the chest. It felt like a cow kicked me. Just that little bullet. You can't believe

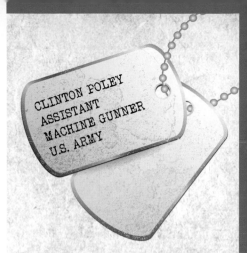

Clinton Poley

An assistant machine gunner with the 2nd Platoon, Charlie Company, 1st Battalion, 7th Cavalry, Poley suffered serious wounds during the heavy fighting at LZ X-Ray. After almost six months recuperating in Fitzsimmons Army Hospital in Denver, he returned to his family farm in Iowa following his discharge from the army in early 1966. Though he is 70 percent disabled, he still works his 120-acre farm, drives his tractor, and is proud of the role he played in the Vietnam War. Poley is a bachelor and lives outside Ackley, Iowa.

American artillery in Vietnam was highly effective, largely due to the skill of forward observers.
This Marine artillery observer was attached to the 2nd Battalion, 3rd Marines.

the impact of it. And it twisted me so sideways that I tripped up over my own legs and fell down. The trees were nothing you could hide behind. So I got back up and went a few more steps, and that's when I got hit in the hip. I came to part of a mortar platoon, and then the platoon leader had two guys take me to the battalion command post.

I was laying there not knowing what, what the wound to my leg here amounted to. I was already thinking, well, if they had to take that leg, could I still farm? And we have an old tractor that had a hand clutch, so I was thinking, that, possibly with a tractor like that I could get around okay and get the work done. So it was kind of funny. Kind of selfish thought, I guess, laying there, thinking that. The strange part that I don't understand is, you'd think a day like that would be the longest day in your life, and every time I think through, it's like I can't figure out how the day went that fast. It just seemed like you know, ten o'clock in the morning, we was going to leave for that place, and the next thing it was getting dark. After being wounded I was kind of numb or something and it wasn't terribly painful for me … probably mostly the one in the hip.

In the morning they just threw us in the helicopter. I carried my own IV bottle, while four guys carried me. They put me and the other guys on a stretcher. I remember one strange feeling was they just took an awfully sharp scissors or something and started right down there at the boot strings and cut everything all the way up. And they started giving me a transfusion. And it was already cool in the morning there, and I suppose the blood was cold and I was pretty much shivering on the trip.

In the hospital they was giving me shots, you know, for pain every four hours. After about three hours, they would come to take your temperature and wake you up, and then you had to wait another hour to get another pain shot. When they were going to operate on me, they took me right in. And then the electricity went off, and so they had to wait until they could get their generator started. I was so lucky. I was one of the last ones to go in there, and the next morning I was evacuated already. I didn't have to pick up body parts, you know.

When the one hit me in the head, I thought I'd seen a mental picture, when my head was down there, of me laying in the casket with the green uniform on, and the funny thing was I had the cap on in the casket, which you wouldn't have. I just knew that I was going home and I guess it's kind of like the two extremes. You're feeling as happy as you ever felt because you survived, but you're feeling as bad as you ever felt because you're never going to see these guys again. I didn't get to help to pick up any bodies. I didn't get to help anybody. I became somebody that had to be helped. When I was laying there at the ant hill waiting to be evacuated, that's when the napalm just missed it, and I felt a blast of heat from that, and a kid come running around there screaming. It had apparently hit him, and his whole face was just like an ugly Halloween mask.

I may hear a beautiful song or a bird, or see some beautiful scenery, and I think of all the guys who aren't here to enjoy such things. They never owned a microwave oven. Never owned a calculator, nor seen a man walk on the moon. It's not so much what we went through as it is knowing what the other guys went through. They died dirty. No bath or shower in two months. They died cold or hot. Hungry and exhausted. Some died trying to keep their intestines inside their bodies. They died thinking that their loved ones would never know how they died. They died among ants, scorpions, and snakes. They hadn't laid on a mattress or soft bed for two or three months. They died after two months of not hearing American music. They died without having anything cold to drink in over two months.

The whole two months I was there, I had one shower. When we really had it good in base camp, we got to sleep in our pup tents, which leaked, which had ants in them. One night I just about laid my head on a scorpion. So it was pretty primitive when we was there. No bunkers. No buildings. Couldn't have a light at night to write a letter, when we did have time.

Marine machine gunners in operation. The second man carries much of the ammunition around his neck, which was a common practice in Vietnam.

JACK SMITH

Private 1st Class
Charlie Company, 2nd Battalion
7th Cavalry, 1st Air Cavalry Division (Airmobile)
U.S. Army

Jack Smith

I flunked out of college and then I was thrown out of the house. I thought I needed a two-year vacation from the real world. My draft board told me that before I could work my way back to college, I would be drafted. So why not volunteer for the army? I thought that was a good i dea. I was a bit lost, like a lot of kids my age. I was nineteen years old. I wasn't ready for college life yet, and I needed a little adventure in my life. I needed to get away for a while and grow up. A lot of kids find themselves in that position. And in 1964, joining the army seemed like a pretty good idea. The war hadn't heated up yet. People didn't associate joining the army with going to Vietnam and fighting. There really wasn't much fighting in

Setting up base camp in the Vietnam jungle was the beginning of an experience as far away from home as many of these men had ever been.

Vietnam. It wasn't a hot issue. This was at a time when everybody, basically, joined the army. It was a common thing to do. People got drafted. It was a place where a lot of young men went to grow up before really going into life, going back to college and so forth.

I signed up for the Special Forces because I had a romantic notion about the army and war and that sort of thing. I wanted to have an adventure for a few years. Through various twists and turns, and the military bureaucracy, I ended up in the infantry. We spent most of our time cleaning our rifles, going on war maneuvers, war games, getting into trouble, very boring barracks duty. Then all of a sudden, one day we were told that all the short-timers were going to be let out of the army. People who had longer time to serve would be merged with an experimental unit called the 11th Air Assault. We knew that they were experimenting with helicopters. We were given M16s. We were given helicopter training. Then one day in July we listened to Lyndon Johnson give a speech when he announced that he was sending us, the 1st Cavalry Division over to Vietnam and that he was, in effect, declaring war on North Vietnam without really declaring war on North Vietnam. That's when it hit us that we were going into combat. You've got to understand, we were eighteen, nineteen, twenty years old. Very young. There hadn't been any Vietnam coverage on television. There hadn't been a war since Korea. None of us had a clue what war was about, even among the non-commissioned officers, the sergeants in my company. Only two or three of them had any

Soldiers cleaning their M16's. When first deployed, soldiers believed the M16s to be "self-cleaning," and subsequent fouling of the weapon led to extensive jamming in combat. Soldiers soon learned that cleaning their weapon after use was paramount to survival.

Jack Smith

A correspondent for ABC News since 1976, Jack Smith contributed to *World News Tonight with Peter Jennings*, *Nightline*, and other ABC News programs. He has won one Emmy and has been nominated for two others. For nearly a decade, he was the principal correspondent for *This Week with David Brinkley*. Before his Washington assignment he was ABC's Paris correspondent.

In 1993, for reports on *Nightline* and *Day One*, he returned to the Vietnam battlefield where he was almost killed as a soldier in 1965. He served in the U.S. Army from 1964 to 1967 and was decorated with the Purple Heart, the Commendation Medal, and the Bronze Star with V for valor. A graduate of Oxford University in England, he is a member of Phi Beta Kappa and the son of former CBS and ABC News commentator Howard K. Smith. He is a single parent and lives with his son Alexander outside Washington. Smith died in 2004.

This Marine, as part of a mine-sweep team, carefully probes for hidden Viet Cong mines along Route 9, on the way to Khe Sanh.

combat experience. None of the officers did. We were green, green, green—which is one of the reasons why we got into trouble.

We came over on a troop ship. The night before we hit land, we passed through the 7th Fleet at about four in the morning. We were all standing on deck with all our combat gear on ready for a combat assault on the beaches of Qui Nhon. We saw all around us the shapes of aircraft carriers, battleships, cruisers. And as the dawn broken, we saw wave after wave of aircraft taking off, going over our heads and going inland. In the darkness that still hovered over the hills that we could see in front of us, we saw bomb bursts. We heard the thud of bombs and artillery shells. Then we saw waves and waves of helicopters flying over our heads from the aircraft carriers, carrying more bombs and rockets. Then, in the dawn, we saw the beach in front of us and we said, "My God … this is war."

We landed on a beach, in full gear, into the surf, jumping off the ships. And we found a bunch of half-naked children, sucking their thumbs, dragging their dolls in the sand and looking at us. We were put on board helicopters or trucks and we were taken down Route 19 into the Central Highlands to An Khe, our base camp. We began with machetes and bayonets and pocket knives to carve out a base camp, chopping down all the shrubbery.

Once, just before Ia Drang, we went out on an operation. We were herded into two-and a half ton trucks. As we were driving along the road, here came a convoy of trucks going in the opposite direction. They were carrying boxes of body bags. Crates of body bags. I brought this to the attention of a couple of guys standing next to me and we stared at the trucks passing by. We were going out, and the body bags were coming in, and they were for us. Nobody said a word. We all just stood in the back of the truck, rattling down the road, staring at the body bags. That was a really chill feeling. That's what combat is all about.

We had been walking through the jungle, looking for VC who were never there. Not finding anything. For two months. A couple of operations where we turned up a couple of booby traps and a pig and a few things like that. That's all. No real fighting. We had fewer combat-seasoned NCOs. We had more goof-offs as privates. We weren't as well-trained—that we were sort of a parade ground outfit, a bit of a sham. That was the real feeling the men had of the battalion. I don't know how really justified it was, but that was the feeling we had. I think we were prepared as any unit's going to get prepared for combat. Nothing prepares you for combat. The best way to prepare a company for combat is to line the company up against a wall and fire a machine gun at them for about ten seconds. And tell the survivors, "You're now combat-trained." That's not pleasant, but that's what combat's like.

We walked in and we got into Landing Zone X-Ray on the third day of the battle there. It was just about over. We were goggle-eyed at what we saw. I had never seen men as filthy as that. They didn't seem to be wearing clothing. Their clothing was so covered with dirt, they looked like they were part of the dirt because they had been living in the dirt, living in foxholes for three days. They all had these thousand-eye stare that people talk about. The stare of someone who is nineteen years old but going on fifty, who has seen combat and been killing people and seen his friends killed under continuous bombardment, artillery, and napalm, day in, day out. Stacks of dead bodies, stacks of wounded, equipment around the v. And the one thing that sticks in my mind, there were bullets whizzing over the landing zone, humming like bees. The only person standing was this colonel. He was standing in the middle of the landing zone directing traffic like a cop. We were crouched down. It was Hal Moore. That was the first guy I saw in the landing zone. Made a very vivid impression on me.

I didn't know enough to be scared. The thing about a bullet is, you can't see them. All you can do is hear them. And until you connect the sound of a bullet with someone dying, you don't have enough sense to duck. That's actually what kills most people in the early stages of combat. They hear a shot, they stick their head up, and they get killed. Even though there were some minor attacks that day and probes, we really thought it was a bit of a game. Until you've actually shot somebody or been shot yourself, it doesn't really sink in. It was beginning to sink in. When I heard those bullets coming at me, I knew this was real combat. I knew those bullets could kill me. I kept my head down. I said, "Oh, my God. This is real." When the company commander said we were supposed to sit for the night, I dug a foxhole as deep as I could. The ground was as hard as gravel, so you could only dig it about six inches to a foot. Just kept my head down and hoped for the best.

The next day we walked to Landing Zone Albany for what we thought was extraction, being lifted out by helicopter. We were out for a Sunday stroll in the woods. We were strolling along, and we were a little apprehensive because we knew there had been this huge battle. We'd seen the bodies. Leaving the landing zone, you walk on bodies a hundred feet outside the dry creek bed and the foxholes. We knew there were a lot of enemy units around and some of us were a little apprehensive about walking in such a casual fashion. But we did, and a number of us remarked out it. "Shouldn't we have guards out?" And, "There are probably bad guys around here. I hope we don't get ambushed. I hope they (meaning our commanding officers) know what they are doing." In retrospect, knowing what I know now, our walk was a big mistake.

A couple of hours maybe to Landing Zone Albany, we were in an area where the brush was denser elephant grass, chest-high, waist high, razor grass. In scrub jungle, trees here and there, all around us. Not dense forest but very light forest. You could see the sky. The head of the column broke into the landing zone. A battalion of green troops stumbling around in the jungle the day after the biggest battle of the war against an entire North Vietnamese division, right next to the main infiltration route for them in their territory without any artillery or air cover, is just nuts. Without spraying the trees, recon by fire, without having guards out on the side. It's crazy. I

Soldier lights his cigarette with the famous Zippo® Lighter. Zippo® lighters were widely carried in Vietnam, often sporting unit insignia to identify the owner.

don't know why we were walking through the jungle. I don't know why we were walking that way. It was clearly a mistake. We were green. It wasn't just the privates who were green. Everybody was green. Our captains were green. Our lieutenants were green. Our battalion commanders were green. The whole division was green. And they showed it. We walked right into a big time ambush.

The troops arrived at Landing Zone Albany and waited while their officers interrogated two captured North Vietnamese soldiers.

We just dropped down on our packs on the ground and opened our shirts and lit cigarettes and drank water. And we waited. And we waited. We had no leaders. No more than fifty yards away from an entire North Vietnamese battalion were setting up their ambush quietly behind ant hills. They were tying themselves up in trees while we were sitting there smoking. Our company commanders were having a conference up at the front.

Suddenly the North Vietnamese ambush the unprotected, unsuspecting troops.

I was in a half crouch saying, "What is this firing that's going on all around me?" I turned to the lieutenant next to me—enlisted men always make fun of officers in the barracks but when it comes to combat you always look to the officer for guidance because enlisted men become paralyzed. They fire the guns but they have to be told what to do. The first two platoons of my company just fell down like you take a scythe and cut grass. No noise. Just the rattle of machine guns. These guys were twenty feet away, popping up behind ant hills, spraying us. Dozens and dozens of men with machine guns and submachine guns suddenly popped out of the ground and started spraying us. We were running toward them and I fell on the grass and began to bandage my friends up. The only time I fired my rifle, I was so confused. In combat, time stops. You have no idea what you're doing. I looked up in the grass and I saw right in front of my face and right above our heads the muzzle of a machine gun firing through the elephant grass. The firing was so loud I hadn't noticed it. I took my rifle, put it on full automatic, and stuck it through the elephant grass to where I thought the gunner's head would be, and squeezed the trigger and put a magazine into this guy's head and blew his head off. After the battle I was told that right by there was a guy with no head. Probably a nineteen-year-old draftee from the Hanoi Haiphong triangle. A city kid. Probably somebody just like me. I must have been about the only man in the first two platoons who wasn't dead or wounded in the first five minutes. It was the luck of the draw.

There was an older guy who had been in World War II, in Korea. He was dying from a chest wound, lying on his back and I was comforting him and bandaging him up. I heard North Vietnamese coming. I pretended to lie dead. They swept into our clearing on the crouch, a squad of them, maybe five or six guys. They had several light machine guns with them. They saw us. They jumped down right on top of us and used us as sandbags as they set up their machine guns and they started to fire their machine guns. I had a guy lying on top of me. We all played dead. I was covered with so much blood, my friend's blood, that I looked wounded or dead. I just lay still. And I willed myself to stop breathing and not to move. But I could not control myself from shaking. I was so frightened I couldn't stop it. The only thing that saved me was the fact that the guy lying on top of me was shaking even more than I was. Combat is terrifying so he didn't notice that I was shaking, too, and that I was alive. The hot shell casings were going down inside my shirt and burning me. My friends were firing grenades at these guys. I was on the verge of going insane from fear. I said to myself, if I stand up and say, "Guys, don't shoot," the North Vietnamese will kill me. If I lie here, my guys will hit me. No sooner had I thought that, than I felt these huge explosions all around me, and a barrage of rifle grenades landed right in our clearing. One killed the sergeant whose shoulder I was sitting on. And the other grenade landed on top of the guy on top of me and blew him to bits and wounded me on my left side. I was the only person left alive in that little clearing among the Vietnamese and Americans. I bandaged myself, crawled through the grass to where the mortar platoon had been. By then they were just a pile of very badly wounded men. That's where I stayed the rest of the afternoon and night.

Later they started to mortar us. A mortar went off behind me, almost between my legs and got me in the right leg. I actually severed a vein and I had to put a tourniquet on my right leg. It was dusk. I was in a haze of pain and shock but I was alive. I remember pinching myself and saying, "I am alive." The men around me were just groaning. Moaning, semi-conscious. I was sort of semi-conscious. I was saying to myself, "My God, I'm alive." To celebrate that, I wanted a cigarette. I pulled out a cigarette and both ends were bloody so I tore them off. I said, "You know, they'll see the smoke and kill me." I said, "I don't give a damn. I want a cigarette," so I lit the damn thing and I sat there and took two or three drags and it felt heavenly. I can't explain why one does crazy things. I was very lucky.

American machine gunners in heavy combat.

A Marine of the 2nd Battalion, 9th Marines, prior to jumping off on an operation

I heard the Skyraiders coming over the trees and I said, "Oh God, don't drop bombs or napalm on us, please. We're too mixed up, the North Vietnamese and Americans. You'll kill Americans." I saw stuff, big stuff coming down through the trees and I went, "Oh, no." Then in front of me there were a whole bunch of explosions and then there was a blast of heat like you open an oven door and the grass on top of me curled over from the heat. I heard people screaming and I heard them hollering in English, not just Vietnamese. Some of it got some Americans and it was right next to my position. That's really frightening. Napalm is really, really scary. It's a very effective weapon, though.

They were going through the elephant grass in the afternoon and at night killing the wounded. You would hear them walking through the grass talking Vietnamese. Then you would hear a lot of loud talking and then you would hear a GI's voice, "No, no. Don't shoot me." Then you would hear bang, bang, bang. They were going around killing the wounded systematically.

The wounded mortar platoon leader calls artillery in on their position, eventually causing the North Vietnamese troops to retreat.

That's what kept us all alive. Otherwise we all would have been killed. I think I passed out for a while. When I woke up it was getting to be daylight. The ground was littered with smashed equipment. Everything had been ripped and torn by bullets. The elephant grass was pressed down, squashed, cut down by bullets and fragments. The grass and ground were literally covered with blood. Everywhere you put your hand was sticky with blood and the place smelled of gunpowder, blood, and urine. There were North Vietnamese snipers hanging out of the trees, dead on ropes. They'd tied themselves up. In front of me was a dead man staring up at the sky. He had dirt on his eyeballs, and one of his legs was gone. There were body parts lying all around me. The dead were stacked on top of each other, sometimes with their hands around each other's throats. It looked like the devil's butcher shop. I've never seen anything like that in my life, and I hope I never, never ever do again.

When they came to get us out, our guys were walking toward us and I had a radio by then. I heard this burst of fire and I said, "Don't shoot, don't shoot." They said over the radio, "We're killing North Vietnamese wounded." And I said, "Don't kill the wounded, please. Don't kill the wounded." I didn't want any more killing. They said, "No, they did it to us. They hurt us. We're going to hurt them back." So the people who came to rescue me as they walked through the woods were killing the North Vietnamese wounded. That was in the heat of battle, I would maintain. I would maintain that what the North Vietnamese did to us was systematic. But at the time it didn't seem like much of a distinction.

U.S. Marines man an 81mm mortar.

I was angry at anybody who had anything to do with that battle. All my friends died there. I was even angry at the state of being human that the weakness of the flesh would succumb to shrapnel and bullets. I said, "How weak and flimsy we are that we all get killed like that." I became very cynical. Not only angry. But I became misanthropic. One day I woke up a few years later and I saw life as it really is. Life is pretty good. The world is a pretty good, warm place. People make mistakes. It happens in other wars. There's nothing I can do about it. Bearing grudges about it doesn't do anybody any good. It struck me that what was remarkable about that experience was not the feebleness of the human beings involved but the magnificent strength that in spite of bullets and shrapnel and things like that, human beings can endure and do endure.

No matter what people go into war thinking they're fighting for, ultimately when you get into combat you fight for completely different reasons. You fight in order to protect your buddies. That's why you form intense relationships in an atmosphere of death and self-preservation. When you're eighteen, nineteen, twenty years old, you've really emotionally separated yourself from your parents. You haven't yet acquired adult friends, an adult job, an adult milieu in which you move. You are betwixt and between. And so the friendships that you form, especially in combat, in the army, are very, very intense. That was the toughest thing I had to deal with after the war. These men, I really loved them, and they all got killed. Time heals. But I still remember them. I still go back to the Wall and I say a prayer for them every one in a while. I still mourn them.

We all found it very hard to accept the pain and suffering that we went through when we ended up losing the war. What, then, in God's name, was the point of what we'd been doing in that landing zone? What in God's name was the point of the suffering that we went through? It was for nothing. If we didn't win the war, and if maybe we shouldn't have been there, then how do you justify the suffering, the loss of friends. You can't. And that's what makes it tough for Vietnam veterans.

EARNIE SAVAGE

2nd Platoon, Bravo Company, 1st Battalion
7th Cavalry, 1st Air Cavalry Division (Airmobile)
U.S. Army

Earnie Savage was the fourth man to take command of his platoon in the Ia Drang Valley battle after he and his men landed at LZ X-Ray under heavy enemy fire. In the fierce combat, Savage and his platoon become separated from the main body of Bravo Company. They are the "Lost Platoon."

Earnie Savage

From the firepower coming down the hill, from the north, stuff that was going on, that was a good-sized unit we were in contact with. We knew that. There was a lot of things going all around us. There was the grenades going off. There was mortars going off. Dust everywhere. Hard to see or get any perception of what was going on around where we are, let alone thirty, forty meters out to the front. There's a lot of noise going on. It's not as if we're strolling down the street. There are people getting shot at all around you. So I took the third squad and flanked around to the right and hit the advancing enemy column. They're trying to maneuver on the squad. They didn't see my squad. They flanked around the bottom side of the hill, and it wasn't that easy to see. The brush was fairly high. And we hit them on the flank and started firing on them before they realized we were there, and we cut those guys down.

I looked around and moved a few guys to strengthen up what I thought was the weak points. I begin to fire just like everybody else did. What was going through my mind was probably kill as many of them as I could at the time. We were fighting for our lives. That's basically what was going through everybody's mind.

I know I don't think there was anyone up on that hill that can say they don't know they killed someone, because they were there. They were right in your face. The numbers don't matter, you know. But there were a lot of people dead … a lot of NVA soldiers died up there.

The next morning my soldiers look like a part of the ground, they've got so much dust and dirt thrown up around them. I look them in the eye, and they look sort of hollow-eyed, because that's the only thing you can see. The whole face is covered with dirt. So the eyes obviously stand out more than any other feature. Everybody's tired, thirsty. Waiting for what's coming next. We were afraid that they were going to overrun us. One thing I never said to anyone else was that I had thought once they started pushing from the LZ that they might just run right back over us. They were a very determined enemy. Very brave. Well-armed. They were brave. Didn't seem to have concern about dying. I think they were a little lacking in training, a little confused on what was really going on there, because they did a lot of things that cost a lot of their soldiers' lives that should never have been done. They would just walk across your front as if you weren't even there. You could fire on them. The next thing you know they'd be up, walking again. And when they were trying to flank us, they were just going around the flank, as if it was a training exercise. Until they suddenly realized that it was for real. So they made a lot of mistakes, and their mistakes is one reason that platoon survived.

I don't think anybody is willing to die for anyone. I think they're willing to take the risks that they may be killed, to save someone else. There's a difference.

Soldiers in combat.

Earnie Savage

Born in McCalla, Alabama, in 1943, Savage entered the army in 1960. In the heavy fighting at LZ X-Ray, he inherited com mand of his platoon in Bravo Company. He has a BS in Political Science from Columbus State University and a MA in Education Administration, also from Columbus State. After twenty years in the army, he retired in 1982 and works in Intelligence Research Analysis, Civil Service, Fort Banning, Georgia.

Before the battle, I always wondered what I would actually do under circumstances like that. Now I know, no different than anyone else. I would do what I was trained to do. Just as everyone else did. I think every soldier has the fear of not performing under fire. Once you've gone through that, then you know you've faced the test. You never voiced those things. No one ever does. But it's in the back of most people's minds. Would I go back and do it again? Voluntarily? Go into battle like that one? I'd be stupid to do that. You know? Do I hate that I was ever involved in it? No. Do I hate that there ever was a battle in Vietnam? Now, possibly. Do I regret it? No. Would I want to do it again? No.

The battle of Ia Drang is one of the first major battles over there where we were pitted against regular North Vietnamese army. And we did very well against them. We can't see what we gained out of the battle itself. And nobody's asking for anything from anybody, and thank you for fighting the battle because that time is passed. Just understand there were people there. The soldiers were people.

You either do it all as a group or you die separate, individually. That's just the way the concept is. When you're with a unit, bad decisions, good decisions are made. It affects the whole unit. If the platoon moved, the whole platoon moves, or the whole platoon dies. That's what it amounts to. I think your training always takes over when you get a level of fear. At that point, it just levels off, and you just do what you're trained to do.

ROBERT JEMISON JR.

Platoon Sergeant
Charlie Company, 1st Battalion
7th Cavalry, 1st Air Cavalry Division (Airmobile)
U.S. Army

No photo available

Robert Jemison, Jr., a career non-commissioned officer, is in the thick of the fighting at LZ X-Ray, where he suffers serious wounds. He will spend thirty-two months in the hospital recovering.

We went into the landing zone. Bullets are flying all over the place. Hell, we was under heavy fire. That's where it all started. Bullets, gunpowder and artillery rounds falling. You couldn't hear nothing but M16s talking and M40s. AK-47s firing back. It was just devastating. It was a little hard fighting in there. They really didn't want to give up. Like an old cat when you got him cornered, he put up a fight. When you're getting attacked from this side, from that side, and everybody got guns, it's got to be a lot of shooting going on. And you shoot back. And they're shooting back, There wasn't no water guns or nothing like that. We were shooting real bullets. So you get killed doing that. You get hurt.

While manning an outpost, Machine gunners turn their weapons on a potential target.

Soldiers carry wounded comrade to safety through a hazardous jungle stream.

ROBERT JEMISON JR
PLATOON SERGEANT
U.S. ARMY

Robert Jemison Jr

Jemison joined the army in 1951 and served in the Korean War as a squad leader and machine gun ner. Wounded in both knees and his shoulder in Korea, he received a Bronze Star. A rifle platoon sergeant in Vietnam during Ia Drang, he was again wounded se riously three times, in the stomach and the shoulder. He spent two years and eight months in hospi tal recovering from his wounds. Again he received a Bronze Star. He retired from the army in 1976 af ter twenty-four years' ser vice and currently works as a security guard. He has three children and is a grandfather.

The first time I got hit was right through the stomach. The bullet felt like somebody took a log and ran into you and knocked you down. That's how the force of the bullet was, and after I got hit, I just got up and went back to fight. That's all you could do. You either keep fighting and try to save yourself, or lay there and die and be killed. And I'm not never going to give up, so that's why I'm here today. The battle kept going on and on, and I was bleeding, bleeding, shooting. I got hit in this shoulder here. And the last time I got hit was through this arm. I got hit three times. One bullet tore the chin strap off the helmet up here and knocked that chin strap loose and knocked my helmet all the way off. And the last time, they tore my M16 up. They just ripped it up. I didn't have nothing but the plastic stock in my hand. One time I thought about, you know, I wouldn't give two cents for my life. Then you start thinking again, and you say, "Well, you know, I think I can make it," and that's what I did. You keep on doing what you know how to do.

I feel I lost something over there. I figured if I hadn't got shot over there, I'd been maybe a bit better, feel in better condition now. I suffer with arthritis and back pains where I got shot. And my shoulder—I have limited use of my arms, my shoulder, so I figure I lost something. But when you think about it, I'm lucky I got out of there, you know, alive.

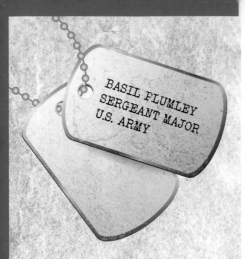

Basil Plumley

A "professional soldier," Plumley was the 1st Battalion, 7th Cavalry's sergeant major during Ia Drang. When he returned from Vietnam in 1966 he became command sergeant major for the 29th Infantry at Fort Benning, Georgia. In 1968 he was back in Vietnam for another tour, this time at Pleiku in the Central Highlands. He retired from the army in 1974 after more than thirty-two years of service and then worked in the civil service for fifteen years. Now fully retired, he is Honorary Command Sergeant Major for the 7th Cavalry Regiment. Much decorated, he has two Silver Stars, two Bronze Stars, and four Purple Hearts.

BASIL PLUMLEY

Sergeant Major
1st Battalion, 7th Cavalry
1st Air Cavalry Division
(Airmobile)
U.S. Army

Basil Plumley

We started to push out, and the North Vietnamese was counter-attacking at the time, coming at us, so we fell back into position. Called in air strikes on them. We were only going to push out five hundred meters. Police the battlefield, they call it. As quick as the air strikes were over, just ordered to fix bayonets and move out. Well, those kids didn't know what a bayonet was. They thought it was something you open the C-ration can with, for Christ's sake. They looked around! Anyway, they fixed bayonets. We moved out. Killed about twenty-seven or twenty-eight more, and that was it.

The noise and the racket is about like a Chinese fire drill. Firecrackers going off and all this stuff, but it's all artillery and mortars, machine guns, and all that noise going on. It's really deafening. You can't hear very much. They had to scream into the radios. It's not a real happy feeling, because you never know what's going to happen next, and we had dust and smoke and mortars, rockets coming in. The smell after a day or two is pretty bad. Dead bodies, what have you. There were a lot of dead American bodies. And of course, the North Vietnamese was dead. Some of them had broke the perimeter and were inside. The rest of them were around the perimeter, so their bodies were smelling too, see? It was a pretty nasty place to be.

We didn't have any body bags for a while, and we picked them up, rolled them on ponchos, loaded them on helicopters, whenever we could get helicopters in. We'd have to carry some of them a ways, and after a body gets stiff, the arms may be sticking straight out or something. Makes it awkward to carry, see, and people firing at you too—it was pretty nasty in there. We had wounded in there, too, that we were trying to get out. Some of them were screaming wounded. Not many screamed. Most of them were pretty calm.

Stolen Viet Cong knife

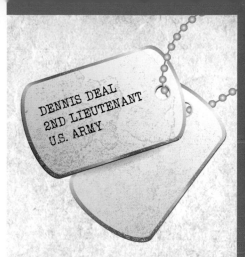

DENNIS DEAL

2nd Lieutenant
Platoon Leader, Bravo Company
7th Cavalry, 1st Air Cavalry Division
(Airmobile)
U.S. Army

Dennis Deal

My radio operator, right next to me, I was sitting and talking to him, and all of a sudden, his hip exploded. And I saw white bone. I guess his pelvic bone or something. It was a bad wound. I did what they taught us at OCS [Officer Candidate School]. When you have a casualty on the battlefield, the first thing you try to do is get them not to look at their wound. The second thing you do is to try to get them talking about anything but what just happened to them. So I'm doing all this stuff that I've been taught, the horrible wound, and he was looking at me like, come on, you know I'm hurt and I know it.

One of my troops got up to see where the fire was coming from, and he got shot. That's when I heard a bullet hitting human flesh. It was pretty incredible. I thought, "That sounds exactly like a canoe paddle when it's hitting mud." It was just this splat or this slap—bullet hitting flesh. It was another man down and every time a man went down in this situation, I knew how badly a casualty can affect the progress of a platoon in battle. One casualty that can't walk will wear a platoon out. We were taking casualties the whole time. I had to make a decision. I was figuring four men to carry each casualty that couldn't walk. And then I went down to three men. When I was starting to scale that down to two men per casualty I was being unrealistic. I had to make the decision to leave. And I did.

And we were a pretty pathetic little procession going through the jungle. There was one security guard for my platoon. That was me. Every other man had his rifle slung and was carrying a casualty. I don't know why the North Vietnamese didn't just take us right there and eat us up. I have to believe maybe they were suffering. I know we had dished out as good as we got, probably better. Or they were unaware of just how badly depleted we really were. But we were absolutely helpless. We were babes in the woods trying to make our way back through the encirclement to the landing zone. We were a sorry procession of American boys. If anybody could have seen us then, I bet it would have brought tears to their eyes.

It is a short time later.

I'm on the ground. I was pinned down by what I later discovered was a machine gun. Bullets are kicking up around me. Twigs and grass are hitting

Dennis Deal

Deal was born, raised, and educated in Pittsburgh, Pennsylvania, where he received his bachelor's and master's degrees. Commissioned a 2nd lieutenant in 1965, six months later to the day he flew into Landing Zone X-Ray in the Ia Drang Valley. After Ia Drang, he served as a reconnaissance platoon leader and was back home one year later. He stayed in the Army Reserves and National Guard and worked for the United States Postal Service and in marketing. Deal retired after twenty-four years of army service and ten years in the reserves. He currently lives in Oklahoma City.

me. And I'm rolling around trying to get away from this. I was terminal. I was gone. I was finished. I was dead. I was rolling around the ground. I was flopping around the ground like a fish on the deck of a boat. All of us are on our stomachs crawling on this assault line. You're not supposed to assault on your stomach. You're supposed to be walking. But they cut us all down. We were assaulting on a low crawl, which is an incredible thing.

I happened to look over to my left and that's when I saw an American run forward, throw a grenade behind this huge ant hill, and then he jumped around and shot into that ant hill. I knew I had seen something very, very special. I'd never seen anything like that since, and I'd certainly never seen anything like that before. That was an incredible feat of courage. It saved my life and it saved the lives of all the men that were left in my platoon, because Joe Marm was up, standing tall and running towards that machine-gun nest, charging it, assaulting it. I saw him fall to his knees, and I said, "Oh, God, oh, don't be hurt. Please, get up. Please, get up." But he never got up. He was shot in the jaw, in the mouth. Joe lived. Thank God, Joe lived. It ignited the men in that area. They all stood and charged forward. It really gave spirit to an entire assault line of about two hundred American boys.

General's Briefing - 4th Infantry Division - Vietnam 1966, by artist Private 1st Class Alexander A. Bogdanovich.

Love between a man and woman is not as strong as love between two men in combat. It is the strongest form of love that a person can develop. It is stronger than any other form of love. I dearly love my family. I dearly love my parents. Certainly have loved women in my life, but there's nothing like the love between two men who were in combat together.

I didn't think about dying. I didn't think, well, I might die here. I didn't have that thought. Later in the war, maybe a week later, I thought, boy, it doesn't always happen to the other guy. I shook later, but not when it was happening. You don't think about that when you're in an emergency situation. You think about overcoming the emergency. You don't think that you might get killed doing it. This particular event taught me a lot about myself. What I'm willing to do. What I'm capable of doing from a moral standpoint, from the standpoint of personal courage and overcoming fear and that sort of thing. It also has done something else that's very important to me. I'm no longer afraid to die. I haven't been afraid to die since then. Death holds no mystery for me.

I had tremendous respect for the abilities of the North Vietnamese soldiers. One American who was unhurt was very worried about a little red book on the ground. He didn't know what it was. He said, "Sir, there's

*Working as one
we weave our
way, a silent
armada the brass
thrown away,
something
so right our team
purpose sealed.*

*Wearing our
hope with just
grit for a shield.*

*Fifty men at my
hand, one cigarette
around, one hand
for another to
another no sound
a black man in
front and two
on the right.
Strangers at
peacetime now
soldiers alike.*

Zone D...65

War Zone still by James B. Channon

something over there. Would you check it out, please?" He was lying on the ground. None of these men were even sitting up. They were flat, prone to the ground. So I walked over and I picked up the object, and it was a diary. About three feet away from the diary was a dead North Vietnamese soldier who had been horribly maimed. But through his pain and through his agony that he suffered, he was so determined that we weren't going to get his weapon, that before he died, he took a hand grenade and he clasped it to the upper guard of his rifle, bent over double, and booby-trapped his own body before he died. This man was horribly, horribly wounded. They meant to win the war. These people were courageous. They were tenacious. They were tough. They didn't seem to know pain. From my little experience in seeing these soldiers who were trying to get us with their last living breath, I was almost in awe of their commitment.

GEORGE FORREST

Captain
Alpha Company, 1st Battalion
5th Cavalry, 1st Air Cavalry Division (Airmobile)
U.S. Army

George Forrest

From the standpoint of combat experience, no, they didn't have a whole lot of combat. They were well-trained air assault soldiers. Most of them had not seen anybody dead. We did see a lot of bodies and knew that something had gone on. We went out, did some recon forward of our positions, brought back some bodies, and really got to see the devastation that had gone on. Once you finish throwing up and once you get used to the smell, then you went and got organized. You spend a few minutes feeling sad and sorry for the guys, but then you go on about your job, and your job is to make sure that's not you out there. The night was the worst part, simply because there's some safety in darkness, but there also comes some danger in darkness and fear of the unknown. You don't know where the bad guys are. You don't know where your friendlies are.

We used to joke about the first six months in Vietnam you spent trying to learn how to survive. The last six months you spend surviving. It's based on a survival mentality. I don't think we ever thought we're killing these guys so that democracy can be advanced. No, killing these guys so they don't kill us. Unit pride and loyalty to your company, and loyalty to the guys in that hole next to you. There is a military term for operations called "search and destroy." We used to call them "search and avoid." If you don't see them, you can't find them. If they don't see you, they can't fight you. So they weren't itching to square off against anybody. And I think that's what a lot of guys soldiered hard for, so I can get out of here and go home in one piece.

They were young men who, because of the time that they were born, did what was expected to be done, and they did it to the best of their ability. You can't do it any better than to give your life. You can't do it any better than that. I still say it's a waste—giving your life or a limb. There can be no greater sacrifice than to lay down your life for your fellow man, not for a cause or a government, but for your fellow man, and that fellow man is the guy in the hole next to you or two holes down. I mean, most of the guys that I lost or who died would be in their early fifties. I mean, it could be much nicer for them to be somewhere doing whatever it is that fifty-year-old guys do, and not having gone and made that ultimate sacrifice.

George Forrest returns to the Ia Drang Valley one year after the major battle in which sixteen of his men died.

One of the things that you always fear is that you lose somebody or you forget somebody. And that happened. I received a letter from the young man's mother who said she had not heard from him since early November. She wanted us to check and see if we could locate him. Somebody in his unit said that they saw him being medevacked on the helicopter the next day after the battle. We checked all the hospitals but we could not find the kid. In March of the next year we went back there for a recon, and we found this kid's remains. Not really remains—just a boot, just this dog tag. We had a method in our unit where we carried one dog tag around the waist and around your neck, and the other one in the laces of your boots, which is probably different than other units. We got up there and at least found his remains. The hardest thing I've ever had to do was to write to his mother and tell her that we'd left that kid up there.

Soldiers on patrol often spent hours searching for hidden Viet Cong weapons, caches and booby traps.

GEORGE FORREST
CAPTAIN
U.S. ARMY

George G. Forrest

A graduate of Morgan State College, Forrest served as a combat infantry commander in Vietnam where he earned the Silver Star, the Legion of Merit, and two Bronze Stars. He served as commander of the Tomb of the Unknown Soldiers at Arlington National Cemetery and was professor of Military Science, St. Norbet's College. In 1980 he retired as a lieutenant colonel from the army after twenty-one years of service and became assistant head coach of football at Morgan State, coached high school basketball, and was an administrator for the St. Mary's County public schools in Maryland. He was a Torch bearer for Maryland in the 1966 Olympics.

There's a military term for getting holes punched in your ticket, so you can do that upward mobility that everybody wants. And being an infantry officer, the greatest thing that can happen is to command and to command in combat. The mission of the infantry is close with, kill, or capture the enemy, by whatever means, and after you hear that enough, you believe that's what you're supposed to do.

In retrospect, I wouldn't recommend it to any of my kids, and would probably think long and hard about doing it again. I think there are a lot of things in my life that I'd probably be willing to die for, but I'm not sure I'm willing to kill anybody else for anything. I wouldn't want my sons to have to go do that. For what?

LARRY GWIN

Lieutenant Executive Officer
Alpha Company, 2nd Battalion
7th Cavalry, 1st Air Cavalry Division (Airmobile)
U.S. Army

Larry Gwin

The battalion was sent out on the bush west of Plei Mei, looking for bad guys. We knew Plei Mei had been hit, and we had been briefed that there were North Vietnamese regulars in the area. The first place or two we went, we just circled the wagons, dug foxholes, and waited. The night of the fourteenth of November, when Hal Moore's guys ran into the enemy in force at X-Ray, we were notified to stand by because we were going to fly into X-Ray at dawn of the fifteenth. Then things got interesting.

I was in the third of three lifts. When the third lift touched down we were told there's been sniper fire on the landing zone, but flying into it, there was all kinds of heavy smoke and detonations and a lot of noise. Within seconds of hitting the tall grass and exiting the helicopter, one of my troops popped out of the grass, and his shoulder was opened up and he said, "I've been hit, sir." There was incoming rounds popping over our heads, so right away we knew we were in a hot landing zone. We patched up my guy, and my team of five packed up, and the captain on the radio told us to come forward. We're being held in reserve. And it was that hundred-and-fifty-yard bob-and-weave, pack-up and sprint, drop, pack-up and sprint, drop, run to what turned out to be Colonel Moore's battalion command post, where I got an understanding of what was going on. There was a lot of noise, a lot of incoming, a lot of dead under ponchos, cartons, and crates, ammunition scattered all over the place, and a lot of artillery and air on the left as I joined my company commander.

I could see a tall colonel. It was Hal Moore. I'd never seen him before, but I knew it was him. He had all his captains and colonels working madly on the radio. I'd never seen captains and colonels working so hard. It was a very scary situation because the rounds were coming in, and we really didn't know what was going on. I had the opportunity to sit back and relax for almost an hour and a half, watching the battle proceed around me. What I noticed was a lot of air attacks. A lot of bombing of the mountain that overlooked the landing zone, which was very threatening.

After three days of heavy fighting, the battle at X-Ray is over. American troops pull out, and Gwin and his men begin a long march through the jungle to Landing Zone Albany.

We'd been awake for two solid nights on 100 percent alert. Had not slept well the night of the fourteenth. All our troops were almost comatose. Captain told us to take a couple of APCs or Anacins with caffeine and to make sure we were alert for a walk. The troops were exhausted.

We knew what could go wrong if you fell asleep. We had to get out of there fast and walking over land didn't seem to be as bad, as we were infantry and it was nice to fly, but also walking in maybe gave us some opportunity to find something without making a lot of noise with helicopters. About four of the six miles were easily crossed. High grass, thickets—you could see fifty yards in front of you. Carrying sixty rounds of ammunition and combat gear and you've been up for three days, 102 degrees out there—it wasn't a walk in the sun. Four miles, a piece of cake. We had heat casualties, and some fellows who were carrying the mortar equipment needed help. We crossed a streambed and got into triple canopy jungle about a thousand meters

Helicopters were used in operations to ferry troops from one target to the next. Here a UH-1D helicopter takes off to pick up an injured member of the 101st Airborne Division, near the demilitarized zone.

Larry Gwin

An army lieutenant out of Yale University, Gwin served as an advisor to the South Vietnamese Army before joining the 1st Air Cavalry Division. Serving as executive officer with Alpha Company, 2nd Battalion, 7th Cavalry for almost nine months, he and his men made fought in six major engagements, usually against North Vietnamese regulars. Among his many awards are a Silver Star, Bronze Star, and Purple Heart. He returned to the United States in 1966 and completed his tour in 1968 with an honorable discharge. After completing law school, he married, raised two sons, and practiced law in Boston for fifteen years. He retired to write and teach. His memoir, *Baptism: A Vietnam Memoir,* will soon be published in paperback. Today he writes, arbitrates, and trains arbitrators for the National Association of Securities Dealers.

this side of Albany, and that's when the unit integrity and the formation that I think was effective began to close in. I could see maybe fifty yards max in front of me, and many times you have to keep your eyes open and see American troops. You didn't want to lose contact with your people.

A reconnaissance platoon captures two North Vietnamese soldiers. The force stops several hundred yards short of the landing zone so officers can interrogate the prisoners.

I don't know if they got anything special out of them. But during that time it gave the North Vietnamese that twenty, thirty minutes to get ready for us. We didn't connect the fact that they were two stragglers, maybe deserters, with the possibility that they were an outpost or a flag. In retrospect, I wonder how we could have been so stupid as to not immediately assure ourselves that there were bad guys immediately to our front.

The troops stop in place while their commanders discuss their next move. Then Gwin's team walks into LZ Albany.

I'd been in the grass less than a minute when firing started, and it was over where the first platoon had last gone around to the right. Two or three rounds and I thought, "Oh, we've run into the rest of the stragglers," and then, and then, whack! Everything opened up. Just incredible. There was firing all over the place. Instantaneously, it was chaos: rounds coming, bark falling off the trees, people screaming. Mortar rounds started coming in on our second platoon.

When you hear the whomp of incoming mortar rounds, it just scares the living bejesus out of you. The colonel's yelling, "Cease-fire!" because he thought there were friendlies shooting at each other. We had incoming radio reports from our first platoon that they were surrounded and being overrun by large groups of North Vietnamese. Our second platoon is getting mortared and calling in and saying, "We're taking terrible casualties, tell C Company to stop shooting at us." C Company was behind them. Again I heard the colonel say, "Cease-fire," and the word went out on the over the radio net.

I popped up and I could look across where we just exited the jungle, and there were twenty, thirty, forty North Vietnamese walking right across where I'd been fifteen minutes earlier. I thought, "Jesus, they're all over us." They had already run over the first platoon, wiped it out almost, except for three guys, and they were into the back of the second platoon. They'd cut off the head of our column from the rest of the unit, and everywhere you looked, you could see guys in mustard colored uniforms moving around the jungle. You knew right away that we had run into something incredibly heavy and incredibly big, and behind us the whole column was shooting. There was a raging battle in back of us where the North Vietnamese had wheeled and attacked the flank of our column, but we were very busy up front, too. It was nip and tuck for about thirty minutes.

1st Infantry Division soldier during intense combat.

You could see platoons of twenty or thirty maneuvering, kneeled down, and then they'd come across the field at you. It wasn't a human wave thing. They were very disciplined. They were superb jungle-fighters. They were up in the trees. I never saw any of them up in the trees, but there were rounds coming down at you, and they were using the ant hills to their best advantage. Their maneuver of the L-shaped, hasty ambush that we sort of blundered into was very effective, and my hat's off to those guys. They knew what they were doing.

I knew we were surrounded. Everybody was fighting like hell. Sure, I wanted to see a little bit of combat to see if I could measure up, but at Albany we got a full dose in a very short period of time, and I'm still getting over it.

It was a knock-down, sock-down, drag-out, close-run, hand-to-hand slugfest. You pop up, you'd see one, you'd blast him, you'd pop back down again. That's what we were into. We didn't have artillery support. We couldn't just sort of circle the wagons and protect ourselves. It was very, very gruesome, small unit, close, hand-to-hand. Kill as many of them as you can before they get you, that's all.

The first people I killed, I looked up and there was a platoon of North Vietnamese coming across the field about thirty yards away. I yelled and said they were coming and fired a bunch of rounds, and everybody fired and we stopped them cold, but they were thirty yards away from us. The first guy I shot I had to shoot twice because he kept crawling forward, and I was afraid he was going to throw a grenade at us. He was within grenade range of us, and we were lucky because

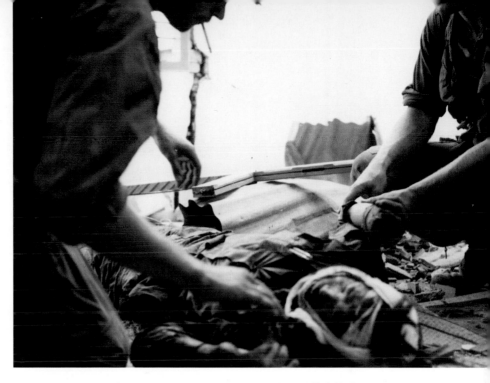

Members of Company "B," 2nd Battalion, 47th Infantry, 9th Infantry Div, treat a VC who was wounded during a house-to-house search.

we had a field of fire in front of us. The guys in back of us, coming out of the vegetation and the ground right next to them were the NVA, so they really didn't have much chance.

There's the combat shock and confusion, but everybody is fighting for their life. It's not a matter of "Oh, my gosh, we're all going to die." I never saw that attitude at all. I just saw people doing their jobs and just fighting like hell. I knew I was doing mine. But right off the bat, we knew we knew we lost our first and second platoons almost in total, and it was half our crew. We were the lucky ones.

The unlucky ones were in the middle of it. We were lucky because we were at the front of the column and had found that landing zone with clear fields of fire around us. And we happened to be with the battalion commander and his access to air support and artillery fire and his command crew, so what better place to be in a firefight than next to the boss? I'm sorry, it's not funny but there are ironies to it. I feel myself so lucky for having survived that, and anybody who was there with me knows that we are blessed, but C Company lost almost all their people in the battle, and that's a horrendous thing to accept as an American infantry captain. D Company lost two platoons, almost intact. We suffered almost 75 percent casualties in that afternoon. It was a devastatingly powerful bloodbath, and I don't think we came up second.

If you're an infantry lieutenant, you assume that your job will eventually throw you into a battle of some kind, and so you better be damn well ready psychologically to assume that stress. But nobody is ever ready for that kind of stuff. That's just absolute insanity. I mean, four hundred guys on our side and four, five hundred guys on their side, just charging each other and blasting each other for half an hour, or two or three hours in the afternoon. It is absolute insanity. But what kept me going was the responsibility to survive. Not personally, but to get as many guys as we could and win this goddamn battle, because we didn't go over there to die, you know. We went over there to kill more of them than they killed of us.

Early in the war (1966), Marines of 2nd Battalion, 5th Regiment boarding UH-34 Seahorse helicopter during Operation Colorado. These helicoptors were used early in the conflict, before the Hueys were adopted for widespread use.

Your mind is going so fast, being alert and tending to wounded and making sure ammunition resupply is available and looking for bad guys to shoot. You do your job fast. It keeps your mind off your trouble. Albany wasn't the last firefight I was in. I was in three or four good shoot-outs, but Albany was by far the worst. When you have a battalion of Americans almost overrun and chopped up like that, it's something I wish on nobody in this world. Either side. What saved us was the air strikes. A-l E Skyraiders had jogged over our positions while the fight's going on around us. We were told to throw smoke, and we circled our perimeter with smoke-grenade markers, colored yellow, purple, green, everything we could find. So the boys upstairs had a pretty good idea of at least where we were. They couldn't possibly know from that altitude where the rest of the battalion was. But I guess they were told to ring our position with napalm, because that's what they did. They came in ten, fifteen passes, dropping canisters of napalm into the jungle around our field. It was an incredible sight to see. Canisters of napalm hitting the treetops, and jellied gasoline trickling down like stalactites, and see fifteen or twenty North Vietnamese soldiers jump up from underneath it and try to escape. Jellied gas just dripped down on them and engulfed them all. I saw that several times, and it was just a hell of a scene, a hell of a picture. But the A-l Es saved us by ringing our position with napalm, and every time they dropped a canister, you could see bad guys jumping and trying to get away and not making it. So after our position was basically ringed, we knew that we were going to be okay. Nobody could come across that field without getting horribly burned.

When you call napalm on yourself, which is what we did, you're going to suffer casualties. I don't know if I could have called it in on myself. But somebody did, and they did save my life. I think we killed a lot of our own people. I don't know how many. Maybe five or ten, trying to save ourselves. That's got to be an issue for anybody who's been through that experience. It's an issue for me. I got some help from the VA [Veterans Administration] back in 1990 when I got some counseling for PTSD [Post-Traumatic Stress Disorder] or an evaluation, and then a wonderful doctor talked to me. She said, "Well, would you feel better if you had died?" So that put a nice period to the end of the issue. But it is an issue. And I think it would haunt all of us for having dropped napalm on our own people. But if we hadn't, we would've been dead and buried anyway. That's my guess.

Bravo Company was coming in to save us. We knew we were going to be reinforced. I knew we were going to make it. The perimeter was probably still smoking with napalm, and there were dead guys all over the place, but it was pretty quiet when they came in. They flew in a huge formation, maybe eighteen, twenty shifts, and

Huey helicopters withdrawing after discharging troopers of the 1st Air Cavalry, ready for an assault against the Viet Cong.

Marines boarding a CH-53 to be lifted back into An Hoa.

just as they came close, all of the jungle opened up and all the bad guys were just waiting for them. It was later afternoon, early evening. There was plenty of daylight. They all came in. They all shot left. They exited right, and they came into our perimeter and it was reunion week. The fact that they made it in told me that the North Vietnamese had pulled back, because even through there was firing, it hadn't been all afternoon. There was a guy waving an American flag. We were all hugging and shaking hands.

After B Company had come in and reinforced our perimeter, we did have some quietude to dig holes and lay fields of fire but we still couldn't make contact with the troops down the line. We'd been resupplied. We'd been reinforced. We had some helicopters come in and pull out some of our wounded, and it was dusk, getting dark. I dug a little three-inch hole in the ground—it was very hard to dig in that ground. I remember the ground was just filled with rocks. I laid out my magazines and grenades and my .45 and clips, so when they came that night, I'd know where they were and we could just fight. And I lay down in that hole as dusk hit us and fell asleep, and I slept for twelve hours. I don't remember anything about the night at Albany. I woke up the next morning. The gray fog of battle. It was quiet. I realized I was still alive. It was dawn or first light, and I could look around the perimeter and I could see American helmets facing out, waiting quietly for whatever is going to hit us. They had left the field. They never did hit us that night.

The morning was quiet. I guess we fired one mad minute. Everybody shooting in trees, making sure some bad snipers hadn't climbed up there at night. During the morning I stayed in the perimeter, basically in a state of shock and exhaustion and listened to the radio as B Company troops went out and policed up our dead and wounded. It was awful. It was awful. I went out in the afternoon, finally, to see where our people had been, and I saw them, and they were all dead, and they were spread out, and they were all fucked up. And I repressed that day for fifteen years. I thought after the battle at Albany, we flew into another LZ, and I've spent the night and then we went home. But I had repressed that day and a half of policing the battlefield of our dead and wounded. If you talk to anybody who did that, they'll all have similar reactions. We lost a lot of men fast. And they had been out there all night, and for a day they bloated in the sun. The place stunk. It was awful. It was terrible. Everybody was so depressed … dragging in bodies. It was a mess.

If anybody thinks it's good to go to war, they're crazy. And if anybody ever walked a battlefield with two, three hundred torn, bloating American and North Vietnamese bodies, then they shouldn't be qualified to talk about the glory of war because there is none. War sucks. And that has never left me. Jesus. A lot of good men died, fighting like hell. And one of the sad aspects of it to me is that, after Albany there was a stone wall about Albany. X-Ray had been a great victory, and that's wonderful. It was a victory. I mean, we'd beaten them good. But nobody wanted to hear about the 2nd and the 7th at Albany. We knew what we had been through and we knew what losses we'd incurred, and we also knew that we had stayed there and kept the field, and I know we hurt the North Vietnamese unit terribly. We had some esprit de corps and some sense of having accomplished our mission at the time and having sort of won on the field, so it was okay to us but we also knew we'd suffered 75 percent casualties.

The guys on the ground, the regular guys, they have nothing to be ashamed of, and all the things in the world to be proud of. How they served and how they didn't complain and how they kept getting back in those helicopters. After Albany we were out in the field again in December. I stayed with the division until July. Just to know that they'd keep getting on those ships and keep flying into hot landing zones and doing our job—it takes a toll. It's an extraordinary story of courage, and I just think those guys in the 1st Cav have a lot to be proud of.

I think anybody who went to Vietnam and served with the Vietnamese, or after two or three months and looked around, you knew there was something wrong with us being there. Something was wrong. It just wasn't a good place to be. It wasn't the right side to be fighting for. I can't put my finger on it, but it's too bad we got quagmired over there. Terrible, terrible. I think the sadness adds up and the depression adds up, and the fact that all my guys are dead and gone, that adds up. And then the rage begins to boil. And at some point it's got to blow. Mine luckily was vented in a healthful way, on the printed page with a bunch of angry words. But that helped me. I'm lucky.

I think it's important that the story get told and shared with the youth of America so that they can learn and benefit from it, and certainly the military can learn and benefit from the lessons. I think the Persian Gulf crisis was handled expeditiously because of the lessons learned from Vietnam. But America's got to learn from its mistakes as well as its moments of pride, and it has got to be very careful when it chooses to send American kids to fight a war, without really knowing if it's worth it.

RAMON "TONY" NADAL

Captain, Commander
Alpha Company, 1st Battalion,
7th Cavalry, 1st Air Cavalry Division (Airmobile)
U.S. Army

Ramon "Tony" Nadal

The enemy is coming down the hill in large numbers, and I think they are sort of using the creek bed as the avenue of approach and they are sort of guiding on the creek bed. The third platoon is engaged then. But sort of from there to the west there is large numbers coming down and they are running across the front of my third platoon, my first platoon, and into B Company. My second platoon, which is sort of acting as the link between my company and John's company at this stage of the game, is almost in a turkey shoot. There is North Vietnamese soldiers right across our guns, and B Company and my company are just basically mowing them down at that point of the game. It's like they weren't focusing on something to their front and they were running right across the front of our rifles.

There was a lot of enemy dead in that stage of the operation. It was at very close range. You know, this wasn't Desert Storm where you shoot at two to five thousand meters. This was about twenty, thirty, forty meters away. I mean, this is where you can see the guy you're going to shoot. The process going through my head was, you know, Gee, I have to get artillery here. I have got to maneuver here. I got to do various things that go into fighting right as a company commander. What it feels like is noise. It's adrenaline pumping through you. It's just, you know, talking to the radios all the time, talking to your platoon leaders, talking to the battalion command post. I don't recall being afraid. I don't recall being afraid. I subsequently recall being exhausted.

Belts of an M60 machine gun ammunition were always on the ready for quick use.

U.S. Marine scanning the hills around Khe Sanh Combat base for North Vietnamese Army activity.

Ramon "Tony" Nadal

During his first tour with the army in Vietnam, Nadal commanded a Special Forces camp south of the Ashau Valley before joining the First Cavalry in 1965. He was a captain at Ia Drang and a company commander during the battle at Landing Zone X-Ray. After Vietnam he received a graduate degree in psychology from Oklahoma State University. He spent three years teaching at West Point, then commanded an infantry battalion and taught at the Army War College. He retired a colonel in 1981 after twenty-one years in the military and worked in private business as a vice president of human resources.

My radio operator and I were joined almost like at the hip because for the whole time he carried my radio he was always either at my right side or at my left side because I had to be able to reach out and grab that hand-set. And you sleep together, side by side. You eat together. You do everything with your radio operators. We got word to launch an assault, and I was going to cover the flank, and they said there was a lull in the fighting. We were given a jump-off time. It was five o'clock. I got my company together in the creek bed, most of them, and I gave them a little pep talk, about, you know, it's been tough but we got a platoon out there of our buddies and we are going to go there and get 'em. And at five o'clock, I made a point. I was the first guy over the top, just like World War I, you know, follow me. And we launched it as an assault. Unbeknownst to us, during that lull, the North Vietnamese had been creeping up through this elephant grass. The Ia Drang is not jungle. It could easily be a state park somewhere. It's this grassy valley and small trees, sort of what we call scrub oak down South.

We hadn't gone fifty meters when all hell breaks loose. It's eyeball to eyeball. And it's very, very intense. Just chaotic noise and people shouting for medics and whatever. I'm standing in the grass, trying to see what's happening and get a sense of it. I'm talking to the forward observer, and I see the bullets striking him across the chest. He is carrying what we call an M-2 compass. It was a big compass the forward observers carry, and he's got a strap that's holding a map case, and as I'm talking to him, I see this thing explode. And then we tried to move forward. But we are not going anywhere because we are taking a lot of casualties. We are out there for maybe a half hour, forty-five minutes, and I start getting concerned over the fact that we have got a lot of casualties

and it's getting dark. I need to pull back, to get my wounded and get set for the night. I need to provide some means of allowing us to withdraw, so I called for artillery. I called for smoke.

The calculation I made is that we are intermeshed with the North Vietnamese and in order to get our troops back, I need to reduce the visibility, and you do that by firing smoke. Smoke rounds come out, it lands, doesn't explode. It just puts out this puff of white smoke. There is another round called white phosphorous, a terrible casualty producer. When it lands, it shoots up these little sparks of white phosphorous, a chemical that burns without needing oxygen. If it lands on you, it burns right through you until that white phosphorous burns up. But it also makes wonderful thick white smoke, better than the smoke rounds.

Soldiers and Marines in the field had to carry what they needed between resupply. Here, a Marine fills water containers.

I called this fire mission and I called it almost in the middle of us because that's where the North Vietnamese are. The artillery doesn't have smoke, so they fire the white phosphorous, and it lands and, you know, shocks the hell out of me. All of a sudden I see this big sort of really bright white and I know that's not smoke, and all these little flaming things coming out of it. And it lands all among us. I got on the radio and I shouted, "Cease-fire, cease-fire." And I surveyed what had happened and, you know, miraculously—I guess God plays his rounds where he wants them—because none of our guys get hit and it does make a big cloud of smoke. I said, "Let's do it again." They fired another battery of six rounds of the stuff, and once again it lands and it just covers the area but none of my guys is wounded by it. And it creates such a thick cloud of smoke that we get all our wounded back. We didn't get all our dead back until the following day. I stayed back and I covered the withdrawal of my company.

I was very, very thirsty. We all ran out of water. The first night they brought some water in and we could send a couple of guys back to the battalion command post to refill canteens. Just you know, emotionally and physically, just drained. I mean like the typical limp rag is what you feel after, what I felt like afterwards.

When you go through something like that, it sort of bores into you. Somehow I am different than people who haven't been through that. I am different in a variety of ways. I know I met the test of fire. I've been there, and I did the right things. I am different because there is a pain that doesn't go away.

Opposite: Soldiers advancing towards the enemy.

WALTER "JOE" MARM

Lieutenant, Rifle Platoon Leader
Alpha Company, 1st Battalion
7th Cavalry, 1st Air Cavalry Division (Airmobile)
U.S. Army

Most of the time when you think of Vietnam, you think of jungle, dense jungle. This was waist-high elephant grass, which was gray or khaki or tan in color, so it wasn't a thick, heavily vegetated jungle that we were used to. There was trees throughout the area, and it was fairly open country.

When we landed we couldn't see any fighting or anything that indicated any fighting. There wasn't a lot of battle noise at the time. It was fairly quiet.

In a lot of combat you really don't know the size of the enemy. You only see them in ones and twos in your own specific area. Because of the terrain, they were well camouflaged. We didn't see a lot of enemy moving around. I probably saw more there than I ever did before. They don't stand up for long. They're up and down. I didn't see masses of North Vietnamese. I was concerned, trying to distinguish North Vietnamese from our own troops, and that's always a problem. In any combat you make sure you're shooting the bad guys and not your friendly troops.

Control of your unit, in my case the platoon, is very, very tough when you have thirty some men spread out, moving forward. So I used my platoon sergeant, I used my chain of command, which are my squad leaders, to keep the men moving forward and going toward the objective. Battle noise is a problem. It's difficult to give commands by voice. I had radio communication, and I used my troops as runners from my sergeant to me. We didn't have direct communication to each other. It was by voice, or by arm and hand signals. But battle noise—that's the problem, particularly when you are shooting. It's very difficult to hear and to give commands.

Walter "Joe" Marm

Troops of "A" Company, 1st Battalion, 4th Marines, climb hills through elephant grass during an operation near landing zone Robin-Hill.

WALTER "JOE" MARM
LIEUTENANT
U.S. ARMY

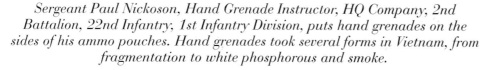

Sergeant Paul Nickoson, Hand Grenade Instructor, HQ Company, 2nd Battalion, 22nd Infantry, 1st Infantry Division, puts hand grenades on the sides of his ammo pouches. Hand grenades took several forms in Vietnam, from fragmentation to white phosphorous and smoke.

Walter "Joe" Marm

Marm was born in Washington, Pennsylvania, graduated from Duquesne University with a degree in business in 1964, and completed OCS at Fort Benning, Georgia, in 1965. After completing Ranger and Airborne courses, he became a rifle platoon leader in Vietnam in 1965. He saw heavy action and earned the Medal of Honor in the Ia Drang Valley in November 1965. Among his other decorations are the Bronze Star, the Purple Heart, and the Air Medal with two Oak Leaf Clusters. After thirty years on active duty he retired as a colonel, and now, after having restored his wife's family home, he works on his wife's family farm in Fremont, North Carolina. He helps raise hogs and ships them to Smithfield, Virginia, where they become, in Joe's words, "food for America."

We were taking heavy casualties and couldn't advance farther without taking more casualties. So we pulled back into the dried-up creek bed. My sergeant came back and very excitedly says, "Sir, we're surrounded." Someone said, "This is like Little Bighorn." We're in another fix, being surrounded. But no one had the sense we were surrounded because we were still able to get back to battalion headquarters whenever we would have wounded.

It seemed like every time we would move forward when the artillery would lift, we would get increasing fire from the North Vietnamese, so that we would

Even in the field in Vietnam, a wounded Marine enjoys one of the small comforts of home.

have to lay down some fire ourselves. There was one solidified ant hill, probably ten feet high by six feet wide. There were trees around that were deflecting grenades we were throwing to try to get the bad guys behind the ant hill. It seemed to me the best thing to do was to run up where the ant hill was and throw the grenade over the top. We moved forward to try to get up there, but the enemy fire started to pick up again after we moved. We got down again.

I told the men to hold their fire, so I wouldn't get shot by my own men. A lot of times it's difficult to point out the friendlies from the enemy, and I didn't want to be shot by my own troops. Then I ran forward. I felt, rather than waste any more time and try to get someone else to do it, I'd just do it myself. That's the principle we use in the infantry, "Lead by your own example." You wouldn't ask your men to do anything you wouldn't do yourself. I have four grenades, so I ran forward with my M16, pulled the pin of one, and lobbed the grenade and threw it over the ant hill. It's a five-second-delay fragmentation grenade. It takes five seconds for it to activate and explode. A very good weapon.

Once it went off, I used my rifle, and I went around to the left side of the ant hill, and I silenced the rest that were still up and moving and hadn't been hit by the grenade, I didn't fire that much. I didn't fire more than half a dozen times. It's kind of hazy. I didn't want anybody shooting at me. I wanted to make sure of that. You always try to get a wounded enemy because he's a good source of intelligence, but in the heat of battle I wasn't concerned with that. I didn't get shot going up there because I happened to be in the right place at the right time. In the heat of the battle you just don't know where the bullets are unless it hits you.

When the enemy was all silenced, I told my men to come on forward, "Let's go. Everything's okay." But there were other pockets of resistance so after I told them to come forward, I was wounded by an enemy soldier. It was probably a rifle. One of their AK-47s. It entered my jaw, shattered this jaw, then deflected downwards, and exited the right side of my mouth. One of my sergeants was the first to get to me and put a compress on me, and one other soldier helped me to the command post.

I was shot in the jaw so I was holding my jaw and walking back there with some help. A lot of pain, you know. I've never been wounded before. I always felt before that there wasn't a bullet meant for me, and that I had a kind of infallibility, but that really shattered that bubble very quickly. Once I got back, that was kind of it for me.

The battle of Ia Drang—there was only one Medal of Honor awarded in that battle, but there were plenty of various deeds, and the soldiers and their deeds go unsung. So I feel I'm the recipient of the medal for the many, many brave soldiers whose deeds go unsung. I'm the caretaker of that medal, so the medal is as much theirs as it is mine. It's always tough to get men to go into battle, but we were a tight unit, and there were Americans out there that we were trying to get to. We're all in it together, and we were fighting for each other and for our guys to make sure that we would get out and get home. When I said, "Saddle up, let's go," we're moving forward. The troops were fearless. They got up. We moved forward. What happened, happened. I had the best soldiers, the best NCOs in that particular time on that particular day that I could ever ask for. They would do whatever you would tell them to do. They were fearless, and they were just great Americans, and they're going to go down in history. So I'm just happy to be part of such a great outfit. It's the luck of the draw. I could have drawn another unit, but I drew the 7th Cavalry and the pride and the esprit was tremendous on that particular time and that particular day, so I'm just very, very happy to be a small part of the operation.

ROBERT JEANETTE

Lieutenant
Platoon Leader 1st Air Cavalry Division (Airmobile)
U.S. Army

Robert Jeanette

Within a short period of time, almost nobody could move because everyone had been hit. We were not ambulatory. So we were stuck. I was against an ant hill behind me, and I was sort of covering the front. And I was on the radio trying to get contact all the time. The first time I was hit when I was on the phone with my back against the ant hill, I unconsciously put my knee, my right leg up, like I was talking on the telephone, and that's when I got hit for the first time. It just knocked me over. Then I got hit several more times after that. There was no medic. I put a semi-tourniquet on it. I did the best I could. As long as I didn't move, I wasn't in any pain. I lost a lot of blood, and I know I passed out a few times but I kept doing what I could.

I got in contact with George Forrest, and I told him that we had a lot of heavy casualties and a lot of guys weren't going to make it unless they got some help. He said, "How are we going to know where you are?" I said, "Well, how about if I fire a .45 pistol when you tell me to." He said, "Fine." The patrol came out. "Fire one." And I would fire one. Then they'd say, "Fire!" and I'd fire. They came across a smaller group before they got to us, and they said, "We found them." And then I said, "No, you didn't." They said, "There's too many here. We didn't anticipate all of these. We can't take everybody back." I said, "Take whoever you can." "We can't take you." "I guess I stay." At first I wasn't happy, but you know I realized he couldn't transport everybody. And I just said, "You coming back?" He said, "We'll be right back." He left the medic, and that's the first time I got a shot of morphine or anything for the pain. A little bit later I radioed, "Don't come back," because the North Vietnamese were back in platoon force, walking through the area. I didn't want the patrol running into it, so I said don't send anybody. They said, "We won't," and we spent the night. We had to wait till the next morning.

I really had absolutely no idea what happened other than what happened in our own little area. Everything was so individualized. Everything was so vicious. Everything was happening around you, and you had no time to worry or interest in what was happening elsewhere. There was one point when one of the soldiers who was wounded next to me asked me to hold his hand because he thought he was going to die. I couldn't see no visible wound. I said, "You'll be okay." The next thing I knew he had died. I had no consciousness in between holding his hand. I woke up holding his hand, and he was dead. That shook me up a little bit. The other thing that shook me was the platoon kept saying, "Lieutenant, get your rear end out of there." Of course, they didn't say rear end. I said, "I'm not leaving the radio and I can't get the radio out of here." One of the soldiers got up out of his completely hidden, protected area. Came over to try to give me a hand, and he got one right through the heart. He died trying to help me. That I'll never forget.

A lot of dead bodies. A lot of hurt people. A very busy medic running around trying to help people. A lot of devastation. Trees cut. Foliage down. Then the sun came up and we heard over the radio, "Everyone stay down." They were going to have a "mad minute." What the heck is a "mad minute"? Then it dawned on me. They opened up, and those rounds were popping right where we were, and thank God nobody was hit in my area from the "mad minute." It was like being shot at all over again, so we were kind of grateful when that stopped.

Members of the 3rd Platoon, Alpha Company, 3rd Recon Battalion, aboard a helicopter during a reconnaissance patrol.

The pain was still there. I was on morphine, but the relief was it's over. They're coming to get us, and this terrible night is over. It wasn't joy. It was thank God, it's over with. I think I was probably half-hysterical because I think I was laughing when they came. I just lost it. They took me over and the doc went, "Leg wound, head wound, blah, blah, blah." I said, "No, no, don't forget the one back here." He said, "Oh, yeah." And I got put on a helicopter.

Robert J. Jeanette

Born and raised in the Classon Point section of the Bronx, Jeanette joined the army after getting a degree in chemistry from City College of New York in 1964. Commissioned a 2nd lieutenant, he arrived in South Vietnam in August 1965, where he served as a mortar platoon leader with 1st Air Cavalry Division (Airmobile). Because of his wounds at Ia Drang, he returned to the United States on Thanksgiving Day 1965 to begin his recovery at St. Albans Naval Hospital, Queens. Married with three children, he has been a teacher of chemistry and physics in the New York City school system. He has an MS degree and is currently a high school assistant principal in the Bronx.

JOHN HERREN

Captain, Bravo Company 1st Battalion
7th Cavalry 1st Air Cavalry Division (Airmobile)
U.S. Army

John Herren

I looked up, and there was the North Vietnamese about ten meters away with a burp gun—obviously the lead scout of a column of North Vietnamese. And so I fired at him. I got off a shot with my AR-15, which promptly fell apart, and I grabbed a grenade and threw it. I was a baseball player, so I was a pretty good pitcher and I could throw the ball. But in this case, it hit the tree right over this guy's head and bounced back right in front of us. So we all hit the ground, and this thing went off. Then I decided this guy was in the creek bed, and there have got to be people behind him, and if they're behind him, they're going to split my company right in two. I got out of the creek bed and went over—there was a machine gunner there—on the landing zone. I went over towards him to tell him that there were NVA in that ditch. About that time we started getting raked with fire, and I saw some other guys were on the ground, and we

Private 1st Class Terry M. Perrigo, a gun team leader yells out to position his men after receiving automatic AK-47 fire from a village 200 meters away.

During the fall of South Vietnam, two soldiers engage the enemy with an M79 grenade launcher. The M79 was a single shot weapon that fired a 40mm grenade out to 400 meters.

JOHN HERREN
CAPTAIN
U.S. ARMY

John Herren

Herren's father was regular army and Herren grew up on army posts in the South, Korea, and Japan. A 1958 West Point graduate, he served in Germany and then in Vietnam, where, during his first tour, he commanded Bravo Company of the 7th Cavalry. After the Battle of the Ia Drang Valley, he became battalion S-3. In his second tour in Vietnam he served on General Abram's operations staff in Saigon. After tours in Germany and the Pentagon, he retired from the army in 1985. He then became a foreign policy specialist for NATO and retired from that position in 1996 to enjoy time with his wife of thirty years and their three children.

dropped down beside them. You couldn't move. We're always taught don't ever let yourself get pinned down, but if we had kept going across that LZ, we would all have been killed, I'm sure. My radio operator turned to me and says, "I'm hit." And there was a bullet hole right through his helmet. Right through his head and he was dead.

On relieving his beleaguered men.

I was in shock, sort of. I was operating, gee, I don't know, hadn't had any sleep for two or three days now, pretty much. You could tell in the look of their faces. I'm sure I looked the same to them. Dark bags under their eyes. They were all covered with clay and red dust. They all just stayed where they were, lying down until we said, "Come on, guys." There were some hugs, and the main thing was to get them up and get all of the dead that we had out there and the wounded and get them, because we didn't know whether or not the North Vietnamese were there in force or not.

Then I moved on up and saw the platoon or the small group, and there were sort of three groups in different places. But the majority were in one area, and a North Vietnamese officer was propped against a tree with a grenade in his hand, and he was pretty dead or at least I thought he was dead. But he was sort of twitching, and the guys who were still there said, "Don't touch him. Don't touch him. He's got a grenade in his hand." And we just kicked him over, and he was dead. But they were so convinced, even with this whole company coming up now, that this one North Vietnamese propped up against the tree next to them—not very far away—they were afraid to shoot him because they were afraid that grenade was going to go off.

BILL BECK

Assistant Machine Gunner, Alpha Company
1st Battalion
7th Cavalry 1st Air, Cavalry Division (Airmobile)
U.S. Army

Bill Beck

The tough part is close-up. Seeing what a bullet can do to your friend. And that's the image I always have of war. And that battle—the fact that it's so ugly. And painful. Even though I knew we were there for a reason, war is very senseless. Changed a lot of people's lives. The ones that got killed, too—changed their loved ones, their daughters, their husbands, loved ones, sons. It's very painful for everybody. You do what you do to survive. It's unlike any movie anybody's ever seen. The real thing. It's very macabre and it's … I don't want to say it's in slow motion, but it's almost as if you're dreaming the whole sequence. And you really can't believe it happened until it's actually over. Sometimes you can't believe it till the day after, what went on the day before.

We fought for our lives. We all thought that we were going to die. We were surrounded, we were outnumbered, and we had to depend on each other. At a particular point, I thought I was the only guy alive. When I'm stuck by myself out in the jungle for a couple of hours, you hear other gunfire. I didn't see anybody else, any of my friends for a while. You think you're the only man alive, so you fight that way. You fight for survival. What you don't know, until after a battle is over, is they were doing the same thing. They were fighting for their lives. So everybody does that, we save each other. Or at least, what we could save.

We were outnumbered and we knew it, right off from the get-go. I had never seen anything like that in my life, initial onslaught like that, where everything is happening all around you. Just a million things going on at one time. Also the death. I had the misfortune of seeing my buddies get killed first, before I ever fired on a North Vietnamese myself. When you see something like that, it just destroys your thinking, and you turn into another person. You have to survive. And that's all that was on my mind is survival.

Lieutenant Taft was killed right in front of me. His radio operator was screaming for help. He said he was dying, and he's shot very seriously. And as he was giving first aid to him, he himself got shot in the back, in his radio, and I'd seen it explode. Right in front of me, another fellow got machine-gunned across his stomach. And he fell right in front of me, screaming. And I jumped beside a dead fellow, a friend of mine, and he was shot in the head. And then the fellow to the right of me he dropped dead. It might have been from the same machine gun. I'll never know.

I was twenty-two years old then. I reached Russell Adams halfway from the spot where we finally settled, closest to the mountain. He had the machine gun on his hip, on his side, firing from the hip. I remember seeing a North Vietnamese about thirty yards in front of him behind a V in a tree, and he was aiming at us with an AK47. But for some reason the blurred vision I had of this North Vietnamese I interpreted as being a GI, because he had a uniform on and he had a helmet. It was the first I had seen a North Vietnamese that close. I remember screaming at Russell Adams that it was one of ours, don't shoot. And at that time he left off a burst of M16 machine-gun fire, and pieces of tree went flying, and this North Vietnamese went down dead. When we got up to him it, indeed, was a North Vietnamese.

A machine gun team leader from Echo Co., 2nd Battalion, 7th Regiment finds the going wet and rugged while fording a rushing mountain stream southwest of Da Nang during Operation Pitt.

BILL BECK
ASSISTANT
MACHINE GUNNER
U.S. ARMY

Bill Beck

Beck graduated from art school in 1964 and went to work for a large corporation. The army drafted him six months later. He qualified on heavy weapons and became an expert with the M60 machine gun. During the battle in Ia Drang he was an assistant machine gunner. In 1966 he returned home to Pennsylvania to continue his career as an artist. Today he freelances, designs logos, and works in advertising. In 1996, after thirty-one years, the Army finally awarded him the Bronze Star with V for valor for his part in the battle at Ia Drang.

Just one minute in the Ia Drang Valley was like a lifetime. We spent three days doing that. Survival. Round the clock. No food. No water. Not knowing if we were next. When bullets crack over your head and snap the air and hit the ground beside you, and dust flies, and the bark on a tree shatters and breaks off, you know they're aiming at you. You know it's very close, and you know you're going to die the next second.

I came across an area behind a tree, which I remembered I was firing on the day before, and there were about eight North Vietnamese back there. They were all dead but one. Of course, we were told that any wounded North Vietnamese we carry to the LZ, and they would medevac them out to the medical stations. I came across one North Vietnamese who was seriously injured in the stomach. A friend of mine, who was killed later in a battle, and I carried him out. That North Vietnamese died on us. It's a human element. As long as they're at arm's length and you don't see them and have no personal contact with them, it's like target practice. But when it's up close, it's very painful. It never leaves you. The pain's always there. The memories—they never leave you.

WEAPONS OF WAR

The Vietnam War saw very few new developments in terms of weaponry. Significant changes to weapons would take place years later in Iraq and Afghanistan. In those wars, the computer, with its ever-expanding suite of software, changed how soldiers used their weapons. But in Vietnam, the weapons remained much as they had in Korea and the Second World War.

The M16, despite its many flaws, was the single most important advance in personal armament the American fighting man carried into combat in Vietnam. It replaced the older M14, soon discontinued by the Pentagon because it was a lesser weapon. Initially, the M16 frequently jammed and had other problems. These were fixed, often in the field, by the ingenious GI, which made it effective in combat.

Troops carried a variety of grenades into combat. These often gave the soldier or Marine an advantage over his enemy. Troopers carried white phosphorus and tear gas grenades that they used to clear tunnels that the Viet Cong often dug under huts in the villages they controlled. Deadly incendiary grenades burned and destroyed everything in their path. Soldiers used illumination grenades to light up an area of the jungle during combat. Smoke grenades helped screen troop movements, and sent signals to helicopters to help them find landing zones. It also helped fixed artillery positions and fixed-wing airplanes on bombing runs find targets,

A soldier manning a rifle in a bunker emplacement on the perimeter of Fire Base Center.

This man might be a long range reconnaissance patrol. LRRPs would insert into enemy territory for several days at a time in small teams of 4 to 6 men. They typically wore sterile uniforms (no insignia, nothing that shines) and had to carry everything they would need. This individual is carrying the M14 rifle.

While most LRRPs carried M16s or the carbine version, this M14 provided greater fire power, and as it fired the same ammunition as the M60 machine gun, it could be used to confuse an attacking force into thinking they were facing a larger force than simply four LRRPs.

Left: Corporal T. A. Fortney sights in on a target with his 106mm recoilless rifle

Right: Staff Sergeant Tommy Garland examines a captured 57mm recoilless rifle round

especially when men were in close combat. But most of the time, soldiers did not toss grenades by hand. That was the stuff of World War II movies. Instead, they employed the M79 single shot grenade launcher carried by one or two men in each squad. The awkward looking tube weighed 6 pounds and had a range of about 1,000 feet, much farther than a man could throw by hand. The M79's accuracy greatly depended on the aim of the man handling the weapon.

Originally, Marines used the 13-pound World War II bazooka, an effective, but old retread. They eventually replaced it with the M67 armor-piercing, recoilless rifle, an accurate and far more deadly weapon.

Mortars played an important role in combat. There were light and heavy mortars. The heavier 120mm and even the 300mm mortar were usually found at base camps in fire pits protected and surrounded by sand bags. These weapons were too big for men to carry into the field easily. Instead, they used the smaller, more portable 60mm M2 mortar and the somewhat bigger 81mm M2 mortar, both of which saw extensive action in the Korean War. Considered an area weapon rather than something employed for pinpoint accuracy, their success also depended on the skill of the crews as well as the clarity of forward observers, some of whom flew over combat zones in single engine planes called Bird Dogs.

There were 68 artillery battalions in South Vietnam. The most effective piece of artillery was the 105mm cannon that arrived in Vietnam in 1966 as the war was escalating. Weighing from 3000 to almost 5000 pounds, this cannon needed eight men to operate it. The gun fired from three to eight rounds a minute and had a range of up to 12,500 yards or about 7 miles. Trucks towed the weapon and its sister, the smaller M102, into action, or helicopters dropped the tubes and their operators into forward firebases.

Often, American firebases unloaded their armament on known enemy positions and where forward observers suspected there were enemy troop movements. Called H&I, for harassment and interdiction, firing into enemy zones lasted many hours, usually beginning at nightfall and ending at dawn. Despite the heavy bombardment, it was difficult to get a clear picture of the effectiveness of a tactic not known for accuracy. However, H&I continued without change through all the years of the war.

Left: ACAV, an armored personel carrier, and a M48 Tactical Tomahawk Convoy

Right: UH-1D Helicopter sprays a defoliant on jungle area in the Mekong Delta.

Tanks played a curious and not always satisfying role during the war. The most useful and popular tank was the Patton 48. Called the "jungle buster," there were 600 of these metal giants in use along the DMZ, in the Central Highlands and in the Mekong Delta. The Patton 48 was the only effective tank in a climate and terrain unusually hostile to armored vehicles. The tank had a 105mm cannon and some also had an M57 flamethrower attached to it. Called the "Zippo" after the popular metal cigarette lighter carried by many soldiers, it was very effective in combat. Some of the tanks even had a bulldozer in front, used for clearing the jungle ahead of advancing troops.

The jungle in Vietnam, exceptionally dense on the ground, was equally impossible to penetrate from the air. Designated as triple canopy, meaning there is a minimum of three layers before reaching the jungle floor, it is impossible to see anything beneath the top layer. Viet Cong and North Vietnam's regular forces moved with impunity using the jungle growth above to protect them from observation. To combat the movement of enemy troops, and to help United States forces, the Air Force started Operation Ranch Hand, first to burn off as much of the jungle as possible, and then to further destroy any remaining growth by using deadly herbicides such as Agent Orange. The huge attempt to defoliate over 4.5 million acres of jungle failed. The attempt to burn off the jungle did not work. The effect of Agent Orange has been disastrous for Vietnamese civilians who, into the 21st century, still suffer from birth defects and to the American troops who encountered the toxic chemical, which was often found stored in metal containers on the bases where they lived.

Smoke grenades came in different colors and were used both for concealment and to mark positions for artillery and close air support.

Boeing's B-52 F-70-BW
Stratofortress

120mm Towed Rifled
Mortar system

U.S. Army Flak jacket, 1971

B-52 bombers, flying from their base in Guam, tried desperately to end traffic on the Ho Chi Minh Trail, the many paths from North Vietnam through Laos and Cambodia into South Vietnam. Men and women on foot and bicycle made their way along the Trail, carrying as much as 150 pounds of supplies, equipment, and ammunition, on their backs. The B-52s bombed the Hoi Chi Minh Trail daily, leaving wreckage scattered on the jungle floor, but never stopping the flow of goods to the enemy's fighters. Some observers thought the intense bombing only served to increase the flow and movement of supplies from North Vietnam to its troops in the south.

There was one advance outside the world of destructive weapons that helped soldiers and Marines stay alive. That was the flak jacket, made to fit snuggly on the chest and back with the arms exposed. Originally made of steel plates and weighing 22 pounds, it was effective in protecting the men who wore it. Later in the war, the military developed a vest that weighed less than 8 pounds, and was made of several layers of ballistic nylon. Marines wore a slightly heavier jacket, also of ballistic nylon and fiberglass plates, that weighed about 10 pounds. Weight is important because in the hot weather and stultifying humidity, anything extra men had to wear caused great discomfort. Yet, despite the lighter weight, those in the Army and the Marines disliked wearing anything that impeded what little comfort they had. Surviving combat sometimes took a back seat when engaging the enemy. American troops, in order to endure the debilitating weather, did not always wear their flak jackets, sometimes to their own detriment.

Opposite Top: A soldier with a flamethrower in use.

Opposite Left: Private 1st Class Nayanes of Bravo Company, 1st Battalion, 26th Regiment 60mm prepares mortars for a fire mission.

Opposite Right: A 105mm howitzer provides fire support at Fire Support Base Alpine.

★ CHAPTER 2 ★

THE SIEGE OF KHE SANH

Khe Sanh is more than just a Marine combat base forever linked with the wearying and controversial seventy-seven-day siege in 1968. It became the symbol of America's will to stand fast against a presumed, but never-proven, major invasion of the North Vietnamese into the south.

In the northwest corner of South Vietnam, Khe Sanh was below the DMZ and astride the Ho Chi Minh Trail, which led in and out of nearby Laos. In 1967 General William Westmoreland upgraded the base in the belief the Marines at Khe Sanh would stop the flow of supplies and troops from the north. By early 1968 there were more than six thousand men on the base and in defensive outposts on the hills ringing Khe Sanh.

Covered by red dirt, the main combat base and its air strip were on volcanic rock. The camp was either dusty and dry, or muddy and wet, depending on the time of the year. Rain and fog seeped into and rotted everything during the siege, including clothing and the underground bunkers, reminiscent of World War I, where the Marines lived. An estimated twenty thousand or more North Vietnamese troops in the high hills above Khe Sanh soon encircled the base.

The siege started on January 21, 1968, when the North Vietnamese shelled the base with more than one thousand mortar rounds, rockets, and heavy artillery. There was no place to hide. The Marines started building underground bunkers, where they lived through the rumble of enemy artillery and the constant, merciless enemy shelling. Occasionally Marine patrols went in search of the enemy and engaged their foe. Mostly, though, they stayed in place. They did not understand what they were doing there, but being good Marines, they waited for orders to move out, wanting to do what Marines did best—attack—but the orders never came.

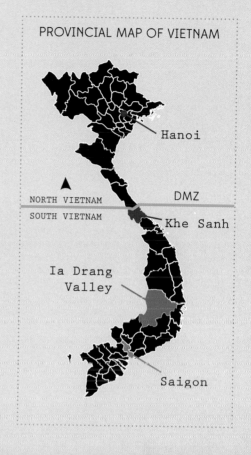

PROVINCIAL MAP OF VIETNAM

Hanoi

NORTH VIETNAM
DMZ

SOUTH VIETNAM
Khe Sanh

Ia Drang
Valley

Saigon

The shelling was ceaseless, making life miserable. The United States retaliated against the North's entrenched positions with massive B-52 tactical air strikes, and heavy artillery. Bombs sometimes landed as close as five hundred yards from the ring of barbed wire enclosing the base's perimeter. The rounds never stopped falling on the base. Ten days after the first shelling, the Tet Offensive started. With it, there was a growing belief that Khe Sanh was a diversion by the North, a way to keep six thousand highly trained Marines out of the fight. That is something we will never know.

The siege officially ended on April 7, 1968, with the arrival of the U.S. Army's 7th Cavalry. Two hundred five Marines died during the siege, and there were fewer than one thousand wounded. Some thought that was not a high price to pay, considering that estimates of enemy dead go as high as fifteen thousand because of the B-52 strikes and the heavy shelling of their mountain positions. U.S. troops departed from the base in mid-June 1968, but the base was reoccupied repeatedly by Americans until the end of the war. It was as if Khe Sanh had a mystical significance hidden somewhere beneath the dense mountain fog that covered the base from the beginning of time.

EARLE G. BREEDING

Captain, Echo Company 2nd Battalion
26th Marines
U.S. Marine Corps

Earle G. Breeding first arrives at the Khe Sanh Combat base in June 1967. In the spring there had been serious combat in the mountains and jungles surrounding the isolated base. Through the remainder of the summer, the fall, and into the early winter, there is only sporadic action in the area. All the Marine hill positions are important first lines of defense against possible ground attacks by the North Vietnamese. On January 26, 1968, he and his men climb Hill 861 Alpha outside the base. Breeding stays on Hill 861 A through the middle of April, when General William Westmoreland sends in the U.S. Army's 7th Cavalry, effectively ending the siege.

Earle G. Breeding

W e continued on and we got to the top of Hill 861 Alpha around midnight. The troops were just exhausted because we had to climb up a wash to get there. And I've looked at the map many times and I don't see the rough terrain that we went up, but we went up. Fortunately we encountered nothing on the way up or when we got up there. The weather, thank heavens, the weather was good, on one hand. See, we had no water. We went three days up there without food or water. And we were fogged in. The fog worked for us; it worked against us. At night you could gather a little bit of moisture on ponchos. I would really liked to have had a little rain up there, so we could have had water to drink. But if we had had very much rain, then we would have had an awful problem with what trenches we had dug and what have you. Probably at night, best of my recollection now, we were wearing, like, field jackets and what not. So it probably got down into the upper forties, lower fifties at night. Daytime, break in the clouds, it would warm up.

And it was on the 5th of February that they hit us bad.

We were mortared so much up there until we finally figured out how to live without taking casualties. At best, it's terrifying. You get used to it after a while, though. You really do. A case of survival of the fittest. You could pitch a pup tent in the middle of one of New York's busiest streets and after a while, you'd learn how to survive out there—given the opportunity. It got to the point when we were being mortared that we didn't ask did anybody get hit. It was, "who got hit?" And once you can get yourself dug in enough and get some cover, then we figured out how they were doing it and when they were doing it. You can beat the system. We beat the system well, once we became acclimated to what was going on.

They diverted B-52s, with some rather large bombs, flying up there at about fifty thousand feet. Not quite in on us. As I understand it, they ran closer than they had ever intentionally run in on friendly troops, and they're dropping these huge bombs with pinpoint accuracy. To go back a little, with all the firing that we were doing and all the support fires I had coming in, there's no way I could tell friendly fire from unfriendly fire. And then all of a sudden, this whole hill started shaking like an earthquake, and I thought, "Oh, my Lord, they've tunneled underneath us," which I was worried about and they were trying to set off charges to blow the whole

The B-52s, although designed for strategic nuclear bombing, were widely used in Vietnam, both for large scale conventional attacks in the North and for tactical strikes in support of American ground forces in the South.

EARLE G. BREEDING
CAPTAIN
U.S. MARINE CORPS

Earle G. Breeding

Breeding joined the Marine Corps in 1952. Discharged as sergeant in 1956 he re-entered the USMC as an infantry officer in 1960. During the siege of Khe Sanh he commanded the Marine rifle company on Hill 861. Among his deco rations are the Silver Star, the Purple Heart, and the Vietnamese Cross of Gal lantry with Silver Star. A major at the time of his discharge in 1971, he was Chief, Foreign Military Training Branch, Com mand and Staff College. From 1971 to 1991 he was a Special Agent, FBI. Today a private investiga tor from his home base in Roswell, New Mexico, he is also a special investiga tor for the United States Air Force, the Treasury Department, and the Na tional Center for Missing and Exploited Children.

hill up, which turned out later not to be the case. That was a B-52 strike. It just rattled that hill. It was unbelievable. As the planes are flying, you don't hear the planes. They're too high. Then all of a sudden, you see these bombs starting to explode, an effect like an arc as they go off in succession. It's an awesome thing to see them.

We were fogged in an awful lot. It's very difficult to bring a helicopter in, in dense fog. I brought one in myself one night to get a wounded man out. And in total darkness, absolute total darkness. And he had no lights. I did it by talking to him on the radio. I could hear him coming. Eventually I said, "You're right on top of me. Don't go forward and don't go sideways. Come on down." And I walked around with my hand in the air and I finally felt a tire. I talked to him. I said, "You're five feet off the ground, four, three, two. You're one foot off the ground." Then we got the wounded man on there, and I climbed upside the helicopter and talked to the pilot. I told him, I said,

"When you take off, make sure you go straight up and not forward 'cause you got a tree ten feet in front of you." But all he had to do was to rise up and break off to the left. At that time I thought that was just real simple. Since then I found out from helicopter pilots that when you don't have a horizon reference it's difficult to know whether you're moving forward a few feet or not. But he did. He got out of there.

There are an awful lot of parents out there of Vietnam veterans who have returned who entrusted the lives of their sons and husbands to the teenager, to the American teenager. When you take an eighteen, nineteen, twenty-year-old young lad and entrust him with lives of men, and I mean really entrust them with their lives, he has more responsibility than any bank president ever thought about having. Friendships formed the camaraderie. The faith you learn in your fellow man. When you stop to think that your sheer existence is in the hands of some teenagers that you hardly know, you develop one type of faith. Another type of faith is that the Marine Corps won't let you down. They were held together primarily by esprit de corps. They were given lectures before they went over there that they were going to stop the flow of communism, and God, mother, country, apple pie, Chevrolets, and all the rest of it. It doesn't take very long once you're over there to realize that that's a bunch of hogwash. What he gets is a strong feeling of ethnocentricity. The "we" feeling. "We" as a unit. "We" as a small unit. He starts fighting because of the guy next to him. We had very high morale. Oh, there was an awful lot of complaining about everything. But morale was good. Morale was very good.

Soldier directs a UH-1 helicopter to pick up injured soldiers after paradrop.

JOHN M. KAHENY

2nd Lieutenant
Platoon Commander
Alpha Company 3rd Battalion
9th Marines
U.S. Marine Corps

John M. Kaheny

U.S. Marine Corps John Kaheny arrives in Khe Sanh in May 1967, after the deadly hill battles in the late spring between the Marines and North Vietnamese troops near the combat base. He and his men are among the first reinforcements to relieve other Marines who suffered heavy casualties. During the siege, from January to April 1968, Kaheny is in the command bunker as communications officer.

We were down there in a place called Phu Bai doing another operation, and all of a sudden we got a message to saddle up and fly to a place called Khe Sanh, a place none of us ever heard of. When we arrived, it was a very eerie experience and a terrifying experience. As the ramp of the aircraft came down we looked out onto the airstrip. Winding down this long dirt road towards the mountains was all of the walking wounded from the hill fights. There were probably five to six hundred Marines standing in line, all bandaged one way or the other, covered with blood and mud. I had to take my platoon off the airplane and march them down this long road to an assembly point. Hardly anyone was saying a word. It was really terrifying. We set out to defend 881 South against a possible counterattack and that's when we found all the broken M16 rifles that hadn't worked, scores of helmets with the crown of the helmet shot out with AK-47 rounds, and literally scores of dead NVA bodies. It was a real graveyard.

We had been fighting the Viet Cong along the coastline. And we hadn't seen anything like that at all. It was a gorgeous place, absolutely beautiful at a distance. When we went on patrol from day to day we would just continue to find more and more dead NVA bodies. And, of course, the stench was ungodly. It was also difficult for the young Marines because when we found those broken M16 rifles, it kind of gave us a hint that the new M16s that we'd gotten weren't working all that well. And we found that to be true a couple of weeks later when my platoon and then all of Bravo Company got into it with the NVA west of 881 South. When my platoon got hit about 20 percent

John M. Kaheny

Born in the Bronx, Kaheny became a 2nd lieutenant in the Marines when he graduated from Mt. St. Mary's College in Mary land in 1966. He took part in the final days of the hill fights around Khe Sanh in the summer of 1967. Af ter being promoted to 1st lieutenant, he remained in Khe Sanh during the siege as a watch officer. For his service in Vietnam he re ceived the Bronze Star with V for valor. When he retired from the Marines he became a lawyer and joined the Marine Corps Reserve. In 1996 he be came City Attorney in Chula Vista, California. He was the national presi dent of the Marine Corps Reserve Association, and during the Gulf War he commanded the 3rd Civil Affairs Group.

of our rifles jammed after the first shot. Some of them were cleared, some of them were totally useless. We were very lucky. When Bravo Company went out about two weeks later, they got caught in a churning movement and got pretty badly chewed up. About 10 percent of their M16s went down. They replaced the M16s eventually with other models and that situation eventually resolved itself.

Prior to the siege, most of the junior officers in our battalion and the headquarters lived in a bunker we called the womb. We'd strung parachute lining over the ceiling just to make it look nicer. But the rats would walk across the lining at night, and one of the officers wrote home to get a BB pistol. We started shooting rats, and I think we probably shot twenty-five or thirty rats in that bunker alone. You didn't want to mess with them. They would bite you. The only thing you could do was not to keep any food around where you slept.

The siege of Khe Sanh started with a massive bombardment of the base on January 21, 1968. It would last seventy-seven days.

In the days before the siege, as things started to heat up a little, we started wearing our helmets and flak jackets all of the time and being on alert the maximum time available each day. On the morning hours of January 21, the NVA struck with rocket attacks. There was no doubt that we were in for it. They hit the ammo dump. It blew up in a huge explosion. I was in my position in the alternate command post. The sergeant major wanted somebody to check on the young Marine outside after a round came in that was fairly close. I got up, put my hand on the door to open it up, and the ammo dump went. And the explosion caused the whole door just to cave in and throw me against the wall. I was okay but some of them other people in the bunker were wounded. The door evidently shielded me from any kind of debris.

When I went on home leave, it was about half way through the siege. My orders came in and I either had to use my thirty-day leave or lose it. I went down to the

Deployment from helicopters during an operation was extremely rapid and often began before the helicopters even landed.

Recon team, "B" Company, 3d Recon, at logistics support area, Khe Sanh combat base.

airstrip, which was right next to Charlie Med, the medical facility. It soon became apparent that the only way was to act as a stretcher bearer. That morning our sergeant major had been severely wounded by a rocket. And I was a stretcher bearer for the sergeant major. That was a real eerie experience because he had come to Khe Sanh on his last tour. He had been a POW on Corrigidor during World War II. He was a fine gentleman. It was pretty apparent to me that it was going to be close if we could get him to Dong Ha in time. He had massive head wounds. But he died on the way to Dong Ha. When the sergeant major died, that still sticks with me. For many years, I didn't want to believe that he actually died in my arms.

Delta Med at Dong Ha was handling casualties from Hué City as a result of the Tet battle there. It was a horrific scene. They had stretchers and operating tables in this big room. To your eyes, it was something you would never want to have to see. It was very, very difficult. There were Marines suffering and dying all over the building. When I walked in with the stretcher, they handed me a squeegee broom and told me to go to work. And it didn't make any difference what rank you were. They just needed help.

We had B-52 support from the Air Force. As the siege got more and more intense, they got closer and closer with their drops. We had a little joke about how to make Khe Sanh coffee. You sit in your bunker. We knew when the air strikes were going to come. So you'd just sit in your bunker. You'd take your coffee out, and you'd put it next to your cup, and you'd put your sugar and your cream substitute next to it, and then you'd wait for the Air Force to show up to mix it for you.

During the day there wasn't an awful lot to do. So myself and one of the forward air controllers would go over to our secret cache of brandy and take a cup with us and share it with the radio operators and sing the Marine Corps hymn and have a toast of brandy.

I would call in either mortars or artillery to mark the targets. And Neil Galloway would call in one of the flights of Phantoms or A-4s to come in and bomb the target. We were sitting in the trench line, and a news team came up. I don't know from what network, but they had just obviously arrived at the base, and this was their first visit. This trench line just happened to be next to where the press had their bunker. They thought they had to see what was going on. They came over, and they stood up and started filming us. And we kept telling them they ought to get down because the NVA knew we're shooting at them. If they found out where we are it's going to get a lot worse. They started to film and said, "You've got to be kidding because we don't see any of them." I suppose they thought it was like a John Wayne movie where the Indians were to come over the hills riding their horses. Well, sure enough, we could hear the thumps of the mortars. They had us fixed. After a couple of splashes, that was the last we saw of that news crew. They were heading back to the airstrip. I guess they got all the coverage they needed.

When our battalion was finally leaving Khe Sanh after the siege on April 17, the Vietnamese were still shooting at us. They were still rocketing the base, so we had two separate landing zones picking up the battalion. Having spent eleven months at Khe Sanh, my battalion commander thought it would be a good idea for the young lieutenant to help coordinate the lift-off. I didn't appreciate that, having been there so long. I just wanted to get the hell out of there. So I went down to the airstrip, and the CH-46s would come down and pick up a load and take off right away because we were taking 122mm Russian rockets.

We finally got everyone loaded. I called divisional headquarters and told them everybody was gone except for the air liaison officer, myself, and my two radio operators. "Can we get the next bird?" Well, there were no more helicopters and they didn't have any room. And I talked to the liaison officer and I said, "I'm not going to spend another day in this place. It's been eleven months. That's enough." I don't know who he called, but he got one of the pilots to make a final run. But he had a problem. His tailgate on the helicopter was broken. He couldn't lower his gate. We were going to have to climb over the gate. And he wasn't going to stop on the runway, so we were going to have to get in there somehow as he was taxiing down the runway because he didn't want to lose any air speed.

We waited and, sure enough, here came the 46 down the airstrip. We ran out there, and we were running through craters and everything else and we threw the packs in. Then we threw the two radio operators in. Everybody was so anxious to go, somebody gave the crew chief the thumbs up sign and off took the helicopter with my cartridge belt caught on the rim of the aircraft. So as they pulled me in, my pants came off, and I went out of there with my butt flashing in the air and the other Marines in the other helicopters could see all of this. When we landed in Quang Tri, by the time I got to headquarters, everyone was talking about how I intentionally had mooned all of these North Vietnamese soldiers. It wasn't really the facts, but the legend lives on.

WILLIAM H. DABNEY

Captain, Commander
Combat Outpost, Hill 881 South, India Company
3rd Battalion 26th Marines
U.S. Marine Corps

William H Dabney

It was the highest hill in the immediate area, which made it a good observation post for the regiment. Khe Sanh was down in a valley and couldn't see anything. Up until the 20th of January it was relatively easy. There was virtually no enemy activity. The troops called it the Jolly Green Giant's golf course. It was gorgeous out there. Starting on the 20th of January when the North Vietnamese seriously invested it, it became, well, hell for a lot of them. I took 240 people up there. I brought back a whole seventy-seven days later nineteen of them. It was not a pleasant environment. In the vernacular of the Marine Corps at the time, one would have to say that there was generally a fairly high air/metal density index.

We were 50 by 150 yards. We had no timbers and no engineering capability. Anything big that hit went right through and exploded overhead. We were generally attacked with 120mm mortars. It's a Russian jungle mortar and an awesome one. In as much as we were in fixed positions and we controlled the area, they would set a mortar on the ground, fire registration rounds on whatever they wanted to attack, measure the angle, and then dig down twenty or thirty feet into the ground on that angle and bury the mortar at the bottom of the hole. Since they only needed a small hole, since the target wasn't going to move, they didn't need to range the mortar very much once they registered it. So they'd fire out of this twenty-

*Crouching under helicopter blades, fellow soldiers carry their wounded
colleague to the cargo bay of a CH-47 helicopter.*

90

foot-deep hole and it was be impossible to find them. They had bigger tubes and maybe more of them than we did in artillery. Their communications wasn't very good. Although they could pound the living hell out of fixed positions, they were not very good at adjusting the artillery to maneuvering troops in the field. Once you got moving, you felt relatively safe from their artillery, although they had lots of it.

We were so far out that reality started being a little different to us. I have a memory of standing in a trench line beside a young Marine who had a little pocket-sized transistor radio, and it happened to be tuned to Armed Forces Radio Network out of Saigon. It had been a rough day. We'd lost a bunch of people. We'd lost a helicopter. We were low on chow and low on water and all that sort of thing. They were giving some sort of summary of the evening news and at the end of it, they announced some local news. The lead item was the cancellation of a tennis tournament in Saigon. And we looked at each other and said, "You know, we're not in the same world. This is supposed to be our radio station, and they don't have any idea what's going on up here." Well, nobody did. We had no visitors. It wasn't exactly a tourist attraction.

The troops never saw the results of what they were doing. They were seeing their fellows going out in body bags and stretchers, day after day. They felt they had nothing to show for it. We needed something to jack up morale. Now technically we weren't supposed to, in those days, fly the American flag without flying the Vietnamese flag. When that was called to our attention, I remember somebody saying, "Well, the Vietnamese want to come up here and help us, they're welcome to put their own flag up." We never had any takers. So daily at eight o'clock, precisely at eight o'clock, and they targeted us, we would raise the flag. We had good, deep holes right beside the flagpole, and it took about twenty-five seconds because we knew the time of flight for the round was about twenty-five seconds. It was a very carefully timed flag-raising ceremony, and then we would jump in the hole and let the rounds hit and went out our business. We had a bugler, a lieutenant by the name of Matthews, who could do a fair rendition of the colors, albeit with speed. A little rushed from time to time. The bugle had a way of getting shrapnel in it. It didn't sound right but it didn't matter. But it was sort of giving the finger to the North Vietnamese. It was a gesture of defiance, and we really didn't have anything else to defy them with.

The only water we had was drinking water. We didn't shave, didn't bathe in any way. It didn't rain the whole time. We went seventy-seven days without rain, although it was very cloudy. We didn't get a drop of water. We used to put ponchos in the wind to blow the clouds against them and the dew would run down the poncho and fill the canteen. That sort of thing. In support of another hill when we had to fire almost a thousand round mission with two mortar tubes, the tubes were getting so hot, the rounds were going awry. We had to cool them. We used all the fruit juice we had, and we used all the water we had, except what was in each individual canteen. I wouldn't let them use that. Finally we literally got to the point where we lined the platoons up

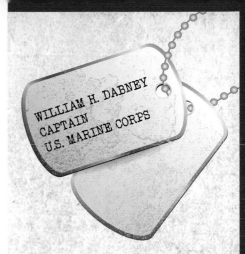

William H. Dabney

Born in St. John, New Brunswick, Canada, in 1934, Dabney was raised in Virginia and graduated from Virginia Military Institute. He served as a U.S. Marine for thirty-six years, from private to colonel. As a captain during the Vietnam War he commanded India Company, 3rd Battalion, 26 Marines Regiment ('67–'68) and the regimental combat outpost on Hill 881 South during the siege of Khe Sanh. Subsequently he returned to Khe Sanh as a major and senior advisor, 3rd Vietnamese Marine Battalion, during operations into Laos ('70–'71). Dabney commanded two battalions, a regiment, and two bases until retiring in 1990 as Commanding Officer of NROTC unit at VMI and Commandant of the VMI Corps of Cadets. Married to the former Virginia McCandlish Puller, they have three children and reside in Lexington, Virginia. Dabney died in 2012.

one at a time and urinated on the tubes to cool them down so we could continue the mission. Any port in the storm. You do what you have to do.

When I first got over there, troops were keeping ears. A rawhide thong with ears, hanging from their cartridge belt. In their view this was their way of meeting the high-level requirement that they confirm their kills. The first question I was asked when I took the company over was, "You want one ear or two." And I thought about it and decided that it was unlikely that a high-level staff officer was going to come down after a battle and go forward to the front lines to count for himself, so I just knocked off the whole requirement and told them to give me their best, honest guess.

The average age was nineteen. Just typical grunts. We'd have some awful days, and then things would look better for a while when we'd get some success. I remember a day we were loading out a half dozen seriously wounded on a CH-46 when a 120mm mortar round hit right between the rotor blades on the 46, and of course, now we've got twenty-five or thirty seriously wounded and a bunch killed. The inability to bring other helicopters in those circumstances and move landing zones and move all these screaming men, you know it wasn't a good day. Days like that, we'd all be pretty down, or days when we couldn't get our casualties out and they'd die in position because of the weather or the enemy.

A company gunnery sergeant and I were touring the trench line one morning, just kind of checking things out. The troops lived in the back of the trench. They dug what they called rabbit holes into the backs of the

View on top of hill, Khe Sanh Combat Base area. The bunker is covered with an unserviceable tent.

trenches because that was the only way to get decent overhead cover in case mortars came in. We saw this pair of feet sticking out and they looked grungy. They just looked grungy. We made troops take their boots off when they weren't doing anything because their feet got infected but these feet, just had all sorts of crud between toes. So the gunny woke this kid up and said, "Hey, son, have you got a kind of fungus infection or something?" He said, "No, no, gunny. That's peanut butter." And the gunny said, "Why the hell do you have peanut butter between your toes?" He said, "Well, I want a rat to come along and bite me so I'll get two weeks off the hill." Said in complete good humor. We made him clean up the best he could. We didn't have any water.

I never saw any of my superiors, only the troops. We'd go sometimes fifteen, twenty days without mail. It began wearing because every day we'd take casualties. Maybe just one. Maybe a sniper would wing somebody, and then next day an ammo party would get waxed. There was no dramatic day. It was just day after day. When there was any visibility at all, they zeroed us and there was nothing we could do to stop it. You just prayed the darn thing didn't land where you were. You would think that you would have people go off the edge under those circumstances, especially when their friends are dying around them. You'd think there'd be some fatalism. None of the above. That amazed me that these troops, fifty to sixty days into it, were just as alert as on watch. They were just as ready to do whatever it was you wanted them to do. The zones were always hot when we were medevacking because they always targeted them. I don't remember ever having to designate stretcher bearers. We always had more volunteers than we had a need for. It said a lot about the attitude of these young men. They were tough, tough young men. Now having said that, their belief in the war, I'm not sure they had one. They're

A Marine on patrol carries his M60 machine gun on his shoulder.

thinking down at the platoon- and company-level and not letting their buddy down and realizing that someday I might be on that stretcher, and somebody better grab me and put me on a helicopter. That's the level they were thinking and longing for word from home. They were every bit as good on the seventieth day as they were on the first, if not better.

We had two gunnery sergeants killed up there one day. They just jumped into a hole and the round followed them right in and there just wasn't anything to identify. We segregated the two as best we could, wrapped them a couple of ponchos and put them on the landing zone. These are what were called routine medevacs. They're dead. No doctor's going to help them now. That didn't justify calling a helicopter, and the tactical situation was such that we probably wouldn't have gotten away with it anyway. The next day it socked in and stayed socked in for two or three days. By the time three or four days are over, I've got the rats crawling in the ponchos. Of course in Vietnam's sun, it's getting pretty unpleasant up there. And the troops all know these are the two gunny sergeants. We finally get the bird in, and we must have had twenty men volunteer to go out there, grab those ponchos, and put them on the bird. That's heroism.

The dailies was where the heroism was. The kid who would shoulder his rifle and go out at night in front of the lines to the listening post and sit there alert until morning. The stretcher bearers—and there were a bunch of them—just volunteer, grab a stretcher and run out on that hot zone, hope they make it. The helicopter pilots—I never called a helicopter that didn't come. That weighed heavily because I had to be so careful when I called them because I knew they would come. And if I didn't need it, I didn't because the risk was substantial. Not only was the risk substantial, but if you lost a helicopter up there, you created at least the requirement for two more to get the casualties out. Everything was sort of melodramatic. There was nothing you could do that wasn't at the risk of life and limb. You stood in the trench and a round could go by, but you had to stand up in the trench and do your duty. So, the dailies, as I said.

There weren't a lot of us left of the original group. The battalion had changed command while I was up on the hill and toward the end of the siege, the new battalion commander came on the hill, took a look around, and it was a mess. C-ration cans lying all over the darn place and broken ammo boxes and C-ration boxes and discarded gear. He was appalled, and he immediately ordered a cleanup, a police call. And I told him, I said, "Colonel, yes, sir, but you need to understand that if you put men in the open up here in the daylight hours, then you're going to lose them. If you have no objection, I would prefer not to let the troops that are up here cleanup." And he said okay, and one of the other companies that came up started doing police call and didn't get thirty minutes into it before a couple of mortar rounds landed, and we had another hot-zone medevac on our hands and it wasn't worth it. We weren't on a parade ground. That's the sort of denouement that we had because they still had the big guns in Laos, way out west where we didn't ever find them even when the siege was ended.

The worst incident was riding down to Quang Tri, which was the secure rear-base on the coast. The division rear was there and the purpose of taking us back there was for what we called a dip-and-dunk. They were going to delouse us, give us all a shower, give us new uniforms, a big steak dinner and a couple of beers, that sort of thing. That's a big thing for troopers under those circumstances. We went through that and then we were assigned to billeting areas. The first thing some of my troops did was start to dig holes. That's sort of second nature to you. Home is where you dig it. Some colonel came along and said, "Hey, don't you dig any darn holes around here. Sleep in those tents. We set them up for you." All right. There's no problem. Well, about midnight, a 122mm rocket came in and hit the darn tent those troops were in and we lost six more after we left the hill. I just almost lost myself that time. I really almost lost it. I think in my Marine Corps career, that's the only time I came closest to losing self-control.

ERNIE HUSTED

Lance Corporal
Bravo Company 3rd Reconnaissance 3rd Marines
U.S. Marine Corps

Ernie Husted

We went up there during the dry part, October, late '67, I believe. Khe Sanh really has only two seasons, dusty and hot, and wet and muddy. We were there during the dusty part. The base had a lot of things above ground. They what we call the hooches, which were plywood, metal, and screening housing. We had tents that were probably used in Korea. We looked around and said, "Wow, here we are."

We started to run patrols the third day. Recons tended to be out like five to seven days and then we'd come in for a day or two, re-arm, and then we'd go back out. We knew it was a bad area because the main folk that were the enemy were North Vietnamese regulars. We noticed they were moving in like they were pre-digging positions, bunker complexes that would hold like a hundred or so folks. Road systems were starting to come in. We kept calling it back, and it's like they didn't want to believe us. We knew there was things starting to come in.

We were in our helmets and flak jackets. We didn't have very many bunkers because we didn't have time to dig them. That first morning when the rounds come in, we went out to a small trench that we had dug that had two layers of sandbags over it. The shelling started, and they were rockets because you could hear them scream all the way in and then hit. Shortly afterwards they hit the ammo dump and from then on, we couldn't tell what was incoming or our own stuff blowing off. There was CS tear gas going off, large amounts of artillery shells, plastic explosives, and so we were getting hit by our own ammo cooking off and producing shrapnel, plus everything that they were firing at us. It was still a little bit dark. The ground moved. It was just unbelievable. The sky started darkening because everything burned.

We had a base that was so secure, and everything changed. All the tents were burning, blown up. What few possessions we had was in rubble. The only ammunition on the base was what people were carrying. We went from what we considered home, and really home is wherever you're at, to everything changing, and it was a shock and a little apprehension—like, what next and what's going to happen?

We got busy starting to dig our bunkers and our protection. We went up and borrowed, which is a polite way of saying stole, some sandbags from another unit to fill, and if you had the incentive, you can work really hard. We were working. I remember stopping at lunch and I couldn't get the leather gloves off because of all the blisters and the blood. So you just poured water down into your gloves, so you could pull them off. You put some gauze on them and you put your gloves right back on and kept digging because everything above ground was going to be bad. If you had the incentive, you kept going deeper so our new goal was to get as much protection over as quickly as possible.

There were times the enemy was so close that they completely shot over from one side to the other and hit their own people, which we thought was wonderful. We would have a bunker that was maybe five or six foot wide, and six more feet of sandbags on each side of it, and six to ten feet of sandbags on top of that, and it wouldn't stop the rockets and the artillery. That's when I had both my eardrums broken twice. We were hit by

Bunkers in temporary defensive positions, like in forward operating bases, were key to survival. The VC would often drop mortar rounds into the bases.

Ernie Husted

A Midwesterner, Husted served one full tour and two voluntary extensions in Vietnam, from April 1967 to August 1969, as a recon Marine. He spent his nineteenth, twentieth, and twenty-first birthdays in the jungle. He participated in forty-one combat operations and over fifty long-range recon patrols, never once being wounded. After leaving the Marines he joined the Ohio Air National Guard, then the Army Reserve. His army unit served in the Gulf War during Desert Storm. Now a police officer, a firefighter, and a hazardous materials technician, he goes white-water rafting and hang-gliding. Recently married for the second time, he and his new wife look forward to their overdue honeymoon at Khe Sanh.

a rocket and the concussion was bad, and then a week later, we were hit by an artillery shell, and when the explosion went off, we were yelling to each other, "Are you okay?" And nobody could answer. We had blood coming out of our noses, and we couldn't focus, and blood coming out of our ears, and we were shaking each other. But we couldn't hear. We had some protection, but not for what they were throwing at us and the fact we were a bull's-eye. Airstrip matting was the greatest thing to use for roof support. The Seabees had this funny idea that air matting should be used on the airstrip, so we would trade with them and when that didn't work, we'd wait till there was shelling and then we would go up and steal the air matting they had and use it for our bunkers. We would cover it up with sandbags, and they would come looking for it and couldn't find it. The bunker was where two people could not lay side by side on their backs. You would have to have a person laying on their back and one person laying on their side. It was very close. Normally you couldn't stand up. The bunker would be any place from five to six feet high and dirt walls, unless you borrowed some plywood. The problem with that many people in such a small area, you really have to kind of get along because with all the shelling and the stress and the pressure and everything going on, it wouldn't take much for people to start fussing and picking at each other. Not because they didn't like each other, it was just the way it was.

A Marine of "D" Company, 1st Battalion, 9th Marines investigating an enemy's hiding spot during Operation Dewey Canyon. The VC and NVA soldiers spent a lot of time underground to both infiltrate South Vietnam and avoid American firepower.

The first day, every time we heard something close, we would dive to the ground and cover up just like we were supposed to. Then we realized we were spending most of our lives on the ground. So then you started playing a game. I need to get this work done. If they're kind of over there or they get closer, I'll drop to ground. This was a fair thing to do, except the mortars didn't give you a chance. You had to go on with your life. You had holes to dig. You had to try and find water. You had to try and get rations down. You had to be digging trenches. I pulled grave registration, which really isn't a great piece of duty. We would be up at the airstrip, helping them load casualties. Our commander was very quick to volunteer us.

There was one day we heard this really weird explosion in the air. We thought it was some new weapon. It turned out the enemy was dropping surrender leaflets on us. And it was so neat. You see all these people popping up out of their little holes, saying, "Surrender leaflets?" No kid on an Easter egg hunt ever aggressively went out more than we did. I brought one of them back and the enemy thought that this was going to be bad for our morale. It was wonderful. We were out there because we wanted souvenirs. They were saying things like, "If you surrender and come across Highway Nine, we'll give you a warm meal and a blanket." That wasn't much of a deal because most of us had two blankets and we had our warm meals, but that was one thing that we did because it helped break things up.

We were digging out on the airstrip, and we heard an explosion, what we thought was shrapnel coming through the air or because that ground is so hard, you could also get hurt by hard clumps of clay. Well, it was a combination of both. One of the people working next to us had ducked down but not enough and died. We looked over and it's like, oh wow. Again it was the suddenness of it. During the siege, a round hit close to a defense line and collapsed the roof of one of these on a several Marines. One or two died and one made it out but he had to be medevacked out because mentally he was no longer there. So much of it went on, I could accept death more by seeing it than someone just not being there. We would go out on work parties and come back and say, "Where is so and so?" "Don't know." There were people that disappeared that were wounded and medevacked out or were killed that we didn't know about right away, and it was very disorienting to have people in your team or platoon that just weren't there that night. I think that was the worst for me. Just who's not going to be there.

I stayed with recon the whole time I was there. We continued to run patrols up in that area because they wanted to know what the enemy was doing. I remember coming back from a patrol in which our recon team was surrounded by about seventy North Vietnamese before the siege broke. We got like twenty-nine confirmed kills before we were able to get out, and the NVA were rushing the chopper, so it was kind of a rough day at the office. I came in and I pulled my patrol book that was always over my pocket. I opened it up, there's a piece of shrapnel that went all the way through to the last page. And I'm thinking, "Oh gee." On a personal moment, that was one of the scarier ones—facing death. I still have that book.

We'd just been relieved, and then shortly afterwards I heard they were abandoning the base. And for me it was a terrible shock. It's like, "You're leaving? Why are you leaving? I mean, we really paid for this ground, and you're leaving." And they were giving some type of explanation about it was no longer tactically feasible to keep this ground. All the reasons I thought we were there still existed and they pulled back. I had some real funny feelings when that happened. I didn't feel comfortable with that at all.

During one period of my life when I joined the Marines I was going to be a minister. My religious beliefs were such that I didn't swear, I didn't drink. This was my personal belief. I didn't take my Bible out and thump it on people. It's just the way I felt. And the guys nicknamed me "Preacher" because they noticed right away that these were my beliefs and I wasn't pushing them on anybody. They would ask me, and I'd say, "Yeah, this is what I've chosen." And I seemed to have a charmed life, which, you know, probably did a lot for religion during that period because, "Boy, nothing bad ever happens to Preacher. Boy, this is something."

So in Vietnam everyone picked up nicknames, some good, some bad, whether you wanted them or not. Many times you never knew a person's real name. This was just the way it was. You could eat, sleep, drink with them, do whatever, but you may never know their real name because it wasn't used that much. So I picked up the nickname "Preacher." The longer it went on, the longer I stayed, the more and more people knew me. I had some trouble with religion during that period because, according to my beliefs, I was ready. If something happened I was going to heaven. This is cool. But people around me were dying. No matter what I did, they were still dying. So during that period of time this changed my religious beliefs. I no longer am interested in being a minister.

UH-1D Medevac takes off after picking up wounded soldiers.

RAY STUBBE
Lieutenant Chaplain
U.S. Navy

Ray Stubbe

I arrived there in mid-July of '67. At that time it was a nice place. It was actually very beautiful. It was detached from the rear. We didn't get generals too often or people poking around. It was cool, being high in the mountains. It was very colorful. It was full of activity. Most people regarded it as a good place to visit. Our experience of Khe Sanh is just something that, like one of our people says, "Then is always now," or "Now is always then." In July, August '67, life was a matter of digging bunkers, going on patrols. It may seem like really nothing was happening, and yet for those that were there, just the simple fact of going on patrol means going up and down very steep hills, being cut by elephant grass, and forming blisters that never really heal, broken bones, tripping over things, getting thoroughly exhausted. The humidity and the heat in the valleys being so intense, there were dehydration cases, cases of malaria. One fellow even dying from malaria was then taken naked up into a helicopter and coated with water and alcohol to try to cool him down, but he died anyway.

Those months were just heavy work in a beautiful setting. Then the rains came in September, October, November. Rains like you wouldn't believe. Ten, fifteen inches a day, day on, day off, where you would never get dry. Truthfully I can say I was never colder than I was at Khe Sanh because skin gets wrinkled and chapped and it's like being immersed in water all the time. It did get quite cool there during the monsoon season. At that time it was a matter of collapsed bunkers, the misery of never being dry, of mail not getting in, the necessity of air drops. The airstrip started to wash away which, necessitated tearing up the whole airstrip, putting down crushed rock from a nearby quarry, and then putting the airstrip back down again. So for a period of time in September through November, we were basically isolated. We didn't know quite what was happening. It was a time of uncertainty. It was a miserable time. The beauty vanished quickly.

All at once woof, woof, and bang, and the base was under attack. I was by myself in my bunker at the time and I guess it's human, I didn't want to be alone. But I knew and I had been told that you don't run during an attack because mortars explode upwards like a V, unlike a rocket which splatters or artillery. The supplies are all burning, and the oil, the gas, the drums of oil, they're all burning, big billows of smoke. The ammo dump started cooking off. Little flechette darts and CS gas powder covered the base, and the tears were coming down. Later on there was a lull and there were some casualties and a chopper came in, and one of the corpsmen came running back and said, "My casualty, who had a wounded leg, outran me to the chopper."

During the siege most of the time I was hopping around from bunker to bunker, trench to trench, and I did hold my church services, but they were only three minutes long. I gave out Communion. I had a one or two-sentence sermon. At the time, I think the text that I worked with was Jesus calming the waters. And a short prayer, and then I'd just sort of sit with the guys and see how things were. The men would joke with each other. They'd say, those bad shooters. That one was way off the mark. Or they would talk about their girlfriends or whatever. Then I'd move on to the next place. I did maybe fifteen or twenty of those a day during the siege. Some were underground. They told me never to gather any more than three or four people above ground because we had a ridge line to the north where they had spotters that could see us, and they'd call incoming on us. There were some that were out in the open. I would take off my helmet and have church.

*Seabees strain to build an extension of the airstrip at Khe Sanh. The "CBs"
or construction battalions, were U.S. Navy engineers who have supported the
Marines in battlefield since World War II.*

Ray Stubbe

Known as the Chaplain of Khe Sanh, as a navy lieutenant Stubbe conducted as many as twenty-five services a day for two to five men at a time in the trenches and bunkers on the besieged base. He received the Bronze Star with Combat V for valor and remained on active duty until he retired from the Navy Chaplain Corps in 1985. He is co-author of *Valley of Decision*, a history of Khe Sanh, and is the founder of a national organization of Khe Sanh veterans. Currently he does volunteer work at a downtown Milwaukee church and counsels various veterans groups.

There was a necessity for people to move casualties. Sometimes during the incoming, people would see somebody wounded out there or couldn't move and would dash out during the incoming to rescue them. This happened all the time. People would share their last drops of water with each other. We ran out of water quite a few times. Our water point would be hit. We would go for three or four days without water a lot of times on the base. Longer on the hills, maybe seven or eight days sometimes. We were down to one C-ration a day, and people would share that with each other.

I would say the men stayed pretty constant during the siege. They were still full of energy, ran faster, drove faster, never lost their humanity or concern for one another. Joking. Humor. They were in touch with fears, with laughs, with death, with life. The only people that cracked up, and there were a couple of them, were basically older people that probably had been through Korea or World War II. I have learned since that's probably accumulative, like radiation. You get so much, and that's it. These were people who would curl up in a corner of a bunker. There was one in the recon area who was a stickler for polished boots and close order drill before the siege, and when the rounds

Christmas service by Chaplain Ray Stubbe for the Marine guard detachment of 2nd Battalion, 1st Marines.

starting to come, he was curled up in the corner. His men actually dragged him out of the bunker and slapped him because they were desperate for a leader. So there were some very interesting everyday heroics.

I spent a night as a matter of fact in a bunker on the line near our position. I'm not sure why I did that. I just did. There was an intense nervousness, jitteriness, people moving in and out all the time. We would make a little stove by taking a C-ration opener on our can, putting a bit of C-4 or a heat tab in there and mixing a little envelope of coffee with a can of water. We were drinking that. There was a record player in there. Some men had radios, some had record players, and some had a little 45 record player. It was playing the Creedence Clearwater version of "I Heard It Through the Grapevine," which is a very jumpy version, "Do-do-do, I heard it through grapevine," kind of thing. The music sort of was the way they were. They were just jumpy. It was getting near the end of the day. One of the Marines in the trench was reading his prayer book. They were talking about what they wanted to do back home, what their plans were, what kind of car they were going to get, about their girlfriends. They'd joke about them and share their love letters with each other. About two weeks later that very bunker took a direct hit, and everyone was killed in there. I went down there with the Charlie Med people to help bring out the bodies. One fellow was missing his head. There was a neck with the strings of flesh. I carried him out. We were looking for his head. We couldn't find it anywhere. It evidently just exploded or something. They were very young. They were very, very young. These people were basically eighteen. They would do anything to save another person.

Khe Sanh sat on an extinct volcano. The place was born in violence and heat, and that's the legacy that remained. Like steel becomes coated with dust, everything became coated with that reddish-brown dust.

Medical evacuation of casualties from Operation Worth during the third day of the twelve-day operation, 15 miles southwest of Da Nang, Vietnam.

Almost impregnated with something you could not blow off. It became gritted, embedded in the paint and in the sandbags that were left, in anything that was standing. It got into our skin. When I left there, I would take a shower. It got into the skin so deeply that three months later you'd be rubbing taking a shower and you'd wipe yourself with a white towel and you get that brownish-red on the towel. It was almost as though the Khe Sanh soil penetrated our soul. It got inside us. It got into us.

They would make what they called roll-outs, which were little cavities in the bottom edge side of the trench that they could roll into and still be safe in case a round did land in the trench. Anyway, this clay when it got wet became as slippery as ice for vehicles or people. When it became saturated, it became pea soup, and anything below ground collapsed. We had built underground, and then the monsoons came and washed it all away. It was in many ways like World War I: gas trenches, fog, wires, same living conditions, dysentery. Just like World War I trench warfare. We would dig this long trench and it would collapse at times. Somebody would be in the roll-out and be buried under ten feet of dirt. Then the others would start clawing the dirt with their hands and their entrenching tools, until they found these men. There were two men who were encased, and they rescued them. They both lived with mouth-to-mouth resuscitation. A first few casualties are just very wrenching. Absolutely shocking, especially if you see a fellow missing his abdominal wall and you just see his intestines, or a man without an arm.

The fog would roll in in the morning. It was cool. It was mysterious. It was paradoxically a sense of relief and fear at the same time. It also gave us a time to relax. Everything is contrasts. We knew we weren't going to get any incoming. We could walk around. We could run around. We could resupply. We could get our C-rations.

Marines relax while waiting for their debriefing after a patrol.

We could do our repairs. We could build our bunkers. We could check in on our mail. See how people were. We could do anything. The fog would shroud any possibility of knowing what the enemy was doing as they crept closer. Were they massing? This is what the troops thought. We just knew that they were out there and, perhaps, probably creeping in. And then when the fog lifted, we might suddenly see in Cinemascope-fashion, a wall of people coming in on us. And so the fog created a kind of fear.

At night there's no lights. Before the siege there were no lights. Some people needed lights but for the trooper there were no lights. When the sun went down, that was it. Then if you had to walk around the base with all this internal concertina, with all these unexploded pieces of ordnance, trucks, jeeps, and wrecks of airplanes, walls of sandbags and old tent pegs that were still poking out, you were obviously going to trip somewhere. Then all of a sudden, there's a few rounds of incoming and you don't know where to run for cover. Probably just lay as flat as you can. At night most people were either on watch, on the lines, peering out into the unknown. It wasn't a sense of desperation. There was a sense of isolation. We were very vulnerable. There was that awareness.

I built my own bunker. I had wooden pallets on the deck and a parachute over the tops and the walls. I had a little three-by-three foot field desk. I happened to have a metal-framed rack, a bed. Casualties were in there, and they were sitting on my bed. Four or five of them. They were laying on these wooden pallets. During the night others came in. There were so many people in there, feet were dangling out. An Air Force officer was right next to me, sitting on the floor on the deck. And he was looking stunned. We looked at his back and there was a little piece of shrapnel right on the top of his flak jacket. Had it been one more inch higher, he would

An aerial view of Khe Sanh combat base. From lower left to upper right: regimental mess hall, LSU "C" Medical Company, graves registration, POL and 1st Battalion, 26th Marines supply areas. At the lower right is CBMU-301 area and Marine Aircraft group 36.

have gotten it in his spine. A round must have gone off right next to him, and he was in shock. A young fellow that I knew very well was dabbing his head with a roll of toilet paper that I had. It was filled with blood, and he kept crumpling these little pieces of toilet paper on the floor. Eventually, the floor was filled with reddish toilet paper. In the morning everyone left. I was walking around, and I found the fellow who had been dabbing his head. I said, "Well, they didn't evacuate you?" He said, "Oh, no. The blood on my head was the blood of all my buddies that were killed." It wasn't his own wound.

As any Marine who has been in combat will tell you, you don't want to leave your buddies. It's like being welded almost, in the heat of the battle. You develop such a closeness that is indescribably close. You don't want to abandon it. You feel alone. People are still sensitive. It's like one casualty after another. Numbness sets in. It's probably a survival technique. I have no doubt the feelings were still there. It's just we were not in touch with them. Perhaps since leaving, those feelings now emerge in dreams, with all the horror and fear. With veterans not just from Vietnam but from World War II and the Civil War, whatever. The people I don't think changed. They remained the same. They still rescued one another. They still did their job. They were unintimidated. They'd go for refuge during incoming but as soon as it would lift, they'd be right out. They weren't cowering in the trenches or bunkers. They were maybe the most marvelous people, as I group I've ever met, I've ever been with.

GLENN PRENTICE

Sergeant
Forward Observer, Radio Operator
India Company 3rd Battalion 26th Marines
U.S. Marine Corps

Glenn Prentice

In the beginning, just before the siege, we knew there was something happening. We had a lot of air strikes and artillery strikes really close to the base. We had to wear our flak jackets and helmets days before. I was walking to the mess hall real early in the morning of January 21, and I noticed some streaks of light coming in. They started impacting on the road. One hit the mess hall. Another rocket hit the ammunition dump. I can remember running from the ammunition dump and being knocked down by the concussion explosion. It was very intense. We had the ammunition dump blowing up and those incoming North Vietnamese rounds. We had a lot of incoming rounds. Some days, like thirteen hundred rounds impacting on the area, twelve hundred rounds, a thousand rounds hitting different areas of the base. It was mainly survival. The NVA gunners would pick certain areas of the base, and Charlie Company was hit quite frequently. It was an artillery battery firing against the NVA batteries and positions. When we were on Hill 881, I and the other Marines would sit outside of the area near the landing zone and watch the rounds coming in and actually be real close to the incoming rounds to warn the helicopter pilot and also warn the Marines that the next round would be impacting in their area. It was very interesting and intense. Very risky to do that.

They had different mortar rounds positioned on us. And rockets. Each of those have a distinct sound. Based on the sound, we had between fifteen seconds and twenty seconds to find cover. The other rounds we had was a recoilless rifle. We called those two seconds. And when we heard that sound, we knew we only had two seconds to hit the ground and we'd drop down immediately where we were. Some of the mortar rounds close to the battery area had a thumping sound, and we only had about another ten seconds before those rounds impacted. So depending on the sounds we heard, we looked around to see the best cover. Either the bunkers or the trench lines or just dropping down right where you were. And if you didn't develop that hearing, you didn't last very long.

The first part of the siege, the way we used to combat the rats was just leave the light on. That didn't work, so we left music on. That kind of scared away the rats. Then towards the end of the siege, the rats were so big and brazen, we'd actually have to have somebody standing watch on the rats with a big cane and hit the rats off your stomach or head where it landed so it wouldn't bite you in the nose or fingers. The rats were scary. We'd poison them. Take peanut butter and heat tablets, and we'd mix them together and then they'd eat and it would kill them. Sometimes it worked; sometimes it didn't. Sometimes it just made them mad.

A bunker was an engineering feat, I guess. With all the Marines, it was how do you build something to withstand a rocket round or an artillery round or a mortar round. And that was like building a fort when you were a little kid. So we stole matting from the runway and we stole different things from the Seabees and we'd kind of put it together. We used wooden ammunition carts for building blocks and filled them with dirt. We had a whole series of supports and sand bags and hollow areas to basically protect against the rocket rounds and artillery rounds and the mortar rounds. We had one experience where we didn't quite meet the specifications. The delayed round went through the bunker and it actually hit the floor inside but then failed to go off. Everybody was in the bunker. We had eight people in the bunker and it went through the roof and landed halfway through the door and floor and it didn't go off.

An ammunition dump at Dong Ha explodes after being hit by North Vietnamese Army artillery.

The Air Force would come in sometimes and land. And we would try to buy booze from them. Because there was no beer or whiskey or anything. We knew the ARVNs had rice brandy. They were at the battalion right in front of us. So we went out there to buy some rice brandy. We had to sneak through the lines and buy two bottles of rice brandy. We got into a firefight on the way in, and on the way back we ran into our battery commander and he chastised us for buying the rice brandy and poured it out in front of us. It was kind of funny, but it was risking your life to have some rice brandy. Kind of interesting.

Day to day, every day was different. It was basically survival. You had to listen to the incoming rounds. We had to repair phone lines. We had to stand radio watches. We had to be on working parties to repair the bunkers from incoming rounds. It was very dangerous. People were killed going to the head or to the outhouses. People were killed repairing sandbags. People were killed just getting water. You didn't know when the incoming rounds would come. During fire missions it was very intense. We had to go out and stand up. Normally when we had incoming rounds, the infantry could go into the bunkers and trench lines. In the batteries we had to fire the guns and stand up. We were in harm's way. It was very emotional just seeing the gunners firing back.

One of the scariest parts for me was when we had a big artillery hit. I'm deathly afraid of fire. I got caught in the open and I jumped under a supply rack. One of the rounds hit the fuel tank. There were fires in the battery area, and I was pretty afraid of getting caught on fire. I jumped back to the bunker full speed and dove into the bunker headfirst and really ripped off my clothes. It was kind of funny. They saw me all naked. I'd rather be naked than burned. And that was pretty intense for me that day.

Glenn Prentice

Prentice arrived in Viet nam on the Marine Corps birthday, November 10, 1967. A radio operator at Khe Sanh, he became an artillery forward observer and during the siege di vided his time between Hill 881 S and the com bat base. He is one of the nineteen survivors from Hill 881 S of the original 350 in Captain Bill Dab ney's India Company. After the siege he saw action in Hué, Da Nang An Hoa, and the DMZ, spending ninety straight days in the jun gle. He left Vietnam as a sergeant, married, earned three degrees, and worked for various city govern ments in California. Re cently he made three trips back to Vietnam to assist the government in rebuild ing the country. He has three grown children and works as Utilities Director for Corona, California. He relaxes by going surfing, scuba diving, sailing, and sky diving.

A Marine mortar crew fires on the Viet Cong's position, west of the Khe Sanh combat base.

Being radio operators, we were a prime target for the snipers and the NVA infantry. We had to kind of disguise ourselves, especially when we knew we were going into a hot area. They didn't teach us this in boot camp. It was passed down from radio operator to radio operator who'd been in major firefights. We had three-foot antennas above our head. We had handsets that looked like phones. So we had to disguise these. We cut holes in our sleeves and put the antenna down our sleeves. We put our handsets in our jackets and we put haversacks or coverings over our radios just so they couldn't tell who we were. We also never looked through the binoculars during the time because that denoted we were forward observer. We got rid of our .45s and took M16s so they couldn't tell we were radio operators. We did all that to survive. People who didn't do that tended to be killed or wounded a lot faster and more critically.

Being so close to death many times, death was measured in inches and moments. You help one another. When you got wounded you were there for your friend. Your friend saved your life. It happened countless times. A friend would walk up to you and say, "Let's get something to eat," and you'd go someplace else, and the next moment, the place you were standing in wouldn't exist anymore.

DAVID "DOC" JOHNSON

Corpsman
U.S. Navy

David "Doc" Johnson was a corpsman at the "Charlie Med" field hospital at Khe Sanh, in charge of medevac and graves registration for the combat base.

David Johnson

David "Doc" Johnson

Johnson entered the navy to avoid the draft, believing that he would not serve in Vietnam. The navy had other plans and made him a hospital corpsman, eventually sending him to Khe Sanh with the Marines as a medic. After returning from Vietnam, he was in and out of college. He drifted for many years and fought drugs, alcohol, and depression. As he says, he drove "a semi over the road for six years to escape society." In 1986 the VA awarded him a 30 per cent Post Traumatic Stress Disability. With their help, he returned to college and graduated with honors as a soil scientist. He currently works for USDA and lives in North Dakota.

You'd bring somebody into Charlie Med, and you'd fix them up the best you could. Often times you had a doctor there. You might give a person some minor kind of surgery, sew him back together again. Throw him on a stretcher, drag him up the ramp, and throw him on out the little area where we had sandbags, and you'd wait for the helicopter to come in. And when the helicopter would come in, you'd pull them on the helicopter and just hope he didn't get blown away by incoming artillery. Because about the time the chopper was down on the tarmac, you can figure that artillery would follow. They had been shooting at that place for five, six months. They had it exact. It was a barren place out there. There wasn't any place to hide. It was just a sheet of metal out there. You didn't have any holes to crawl in. You were just kind of at the mercy of whatever they threw at you. And if you were lucky, you got out there and got them on a chopper and got them out of there. I was lucky. I never got hit.

Someone would get blown up and rather than cry about it or something, you'd make some joke out of it. You know, try and add some humor to it somehow. You were trying to put a positive spin on everything. Sometimes it worked, sometimes it didn't.

We had a lot of people get bit by rats. They were just thick. The first night we were in the holes up there, I remember we were laying there and there was incoming artillery that was coming over the top of us so you didn't dare stand or anything. And you could hear them coming down the tracks. You know, just a little pitter-patter of feet. I bet there were seventy-five rats that just ran right across you. Just, zoom. You're thinking, God, I'm going to die. And then you're dealing with these rats. And I hated those things.

I had it pretty easy. I lived in a bunker. I had it pretty nice. I usually slept on a stretcher. Compared to the guys on the lines, I had it pretty cushy. At Con Thien, that was tough. There was mud all the time. Same clothes for two or three, four weeks at a time. Mud. Wet.

At Khe Sanh, where were you going to go? I mean, you were just there. I mean,

The Stokes Rigid Litter basket is lowered from a UH-1D helicopter by means of the internal hoist. The basket was used for evacuating seriously wounded soldiers and worked particularly well in jungle areas that were not large enough for a landing zone.

you couldn't leave. You basically had to put up with whatever was thrown at you. There was nowhere you could go. There was no one you could complain to. What good did it do? You were just there, you know. You couldn't walk out. It was worse outside than it was inside. So you were just there.

For most of it you were just bored to death. There was nothing to do. You'd make up chess games. I put tape around .50 caliber shells. That would be one side. And then the other side wouldn't have tape around it. The .50 caliber shell would be the king. And the .30 caliber shell would be the queen. And the shotgun shells would be the rooks and stuff. So we played chess like that.

We had one kid that was sixteen years old. Lied about his age to get there. We had a number of seventeen-year-olds, eighteen-year-olds. If you started getting up to the nineteen-year-olds, they were getting pretty old. They were getting to be seniors. We were just kids. I think about the kids today and to think, I've got a fourteen-year-old son, and I'm thinking in three years he could have been one of those guys. It just blows my mind. You seemed like you were so old at that time. You know, you knew everything and boy, you think back on it, it's a whole different thing.

On the constant shelling at Khe Sanh during the siege.

Some of them handled it quite well. Others didn't. We had plenty of guys that broke down. It was stressful to say the least. It was frustrating. What could you do, other than just hope the next one didn't hit you in the head. It wasn't like you were fighting somebody. You just sat there and they threw stuff at you. You just took whatever come. Sitting ducks, that's what we were. It wasn't exactly a picnic area. They had you right in their sights. You'd just walk on the tarmac, and you can figure that you were going to get shot at. Everywhere you went, you were always looking for some place to hide. You know, because at any time it could start coming in again. And they just played mind games with you. They were out there. We exchanged grenades back and forth on the lines and, you know, had firefights and had people killed outside the wire. It was not a nice place.

One of the most stressful things for me was you'd crawl out there, and you'd pick up some broken body, and often times it was your friend. You'd bring him back and do the best you could to save his life and throw him on this chopper, and he was gone. You didn't know if he lived or died, where he went. He was just gone, that was the last you ever heard of him. You never got a note on where he went or any damned thing. He was just gone. Flew off in this helicopter, and he was gone and that was it.

KEVIN MACAULEY

Corporal, Radio Operator
Bravo Company 3rd Reconnaissance Battalion
U.S. Marine Corps

Kevin Macauley

When Macauley went to Vietnam, like many kids from New York City, he had never before seen the jungle, let alone anything more wild than a cat, dog, or pigeon. Add to that the weight he carried, and he was suddenly in world he never imagined.

In addition to what was called a PRC 25 radio, which weighed about twenty-five, thirty pounds, I carried a spare battery. Then I carried food for the duration of the patrol, six to eight days. I would carry water in quart canteens. All our pack and our cartridge belt and all the armaments and ammo that we carried with us was about seventy to eighty pounds for the regular grunt soldiers and with the radio, mine was close to one hundred pounds. The area that we were in, Khe Sanh, was a very hilly, mountainous area. You went from triple canopy jungle to what they called elephant grass. The insects, the flora and fauna, was something that was totally alien to anything that I had experienced. The elephant grass has such sharp edges that you would be cut to shreds just walking through it. The animals out there were just absolutely amazing. One patrol, we were waiting for the helicopters to pick us up and an eight-and-half-foot-long Bengal tiger came out in front of us, not more than six feet away. I had a rifle ready to shoot it in case it jumped at us and I was aiming all over the sky, I was so nervous. Another occasion we had elephants in the area. We had apes.

Soldiers and Marines on foot patrol made sure to carry everything they needed, including ammunition for themselves and the machine gunners, Claymore mines, mortar rounds, and food and medical supplies for the platoon.

When monsoon season hit us, I don't think I've been colder in my entire life. Khe Sanh was socked in by clouds, and you'd have a mist, twenty-three out of twenty-four hours a day. I'm wrapped in a sleeping bag, wearing a field jacket because it was so cold. And the temperature dropped from daytime to nighttime, a good thirty to forty degrees. It really was cold up there at night. Out in the bush you were just totally exposed to the elements. We didn't carry ponchos because when the rain hit the ponchos, it made too much noise. So we just laid out there. If it rained, we got wet. It was hot, we baked. It was cold, we shivered.

There are stories of being separated from my team and running around like a chicken with my head cut off till one of the other guys found me and brought me back down to the landing zone. I thought they were going to leave me out there, but it was my own stupid fault for doing stuff like that. Watching a monkey jump out of a tree onto a patrol leader's face and having him smack at it, trying to get it off himself in the middle of the night, and we're all sitting there in total hostile territory laughing our heads off, watching this fool trying to protect himself from a monkey.

And turning around and looking at the faces of the guys who came in off a patrol where they had to stop at Graves Registration to drop off a friend's body. That will always be with me.

We took a lot of casualties in January and February. It seemed as though the guys who would kill were killed. We took nineteen guys killed during that period of time, and we just took wounded day after day after day. I sent people out on working parties, and they wouldn't come back. Some guy would go out and get something, and he wouldn't come back. And you never saw the wounded, so that added to a certain degree of demoralization.

The bunker that got hit was a bad experience. It's not nice ripping a bunker apart and finding only pieces left of people you had been talking to fifteen minutes earlier. As we got the top off, I found one guy who was just picked up by the blast and pushed up against the ceiling of the bunker, which was basically runway matting. And I never saw a person bleed as much as what this poor guy did. He survived but he was terribly wounded. And the four guys who were killed were horribly mangled. You're never really prepared for your first view of a dead person. And you got close with guys such that you would make plans for one another. And unfortunately, a lot of the plans were totally destroyed by what happened to us. So there are a number of experiences that I went through that still cause nightmares and still cause a lot of heartache.

Morale, at times, was very, very high, and morale, at times, was very, very low. We thought we were invincible. We didn't like the idea of being held on the base because everybody said that, you know, the Marines are hard chargers. We should be out there in the bush, going after the North Vietnamese. But on the other side of the coin, we would sit there and say, all right. Come on. Come on at us. Come at us. We'll take as many of you with us before we go than what

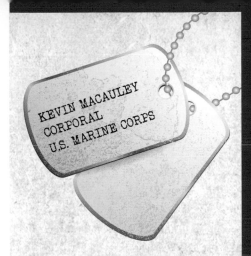

Kevin Macauley

In 1966, while a student at Niagara University and recuperating from a ruptured appendix, Macauley received his draft notice for the army. Not wanting to join the army, he enlisted in the Marine Corps for three years and arrived in Vietnam in the summer of 1967. His reconnaissance battalion at Khe Sanh went on patrols to collect information about North Vietnamese activity in the area. In charge of a radio relay station outside the base, he returned to Khe Sanh three days before the siege started. After his discharge in 1969, he worked for the New York City Board of Education where he is currently a school custodian. A member of the East Meadow, NY, fire department, he rose to chief and now serves as safety officer. Married for more than twenty-seven years, he has nine children and one grandchild and is active in the Khe Sanh Veterans Association.

they could afford. So our morale was high as far as that's concerned. But it never came about. There never was the actual big ground battle at Khe Sanh.

Basically it was hell. There was no place that was safe. One day we took over seventeen hundred rounds of mixed artillery and rocket fire. Another day we took in the neighborhood of six hundred rounds over the space of a four-hour period. And you're sitting in a bunker supposedly safe, ten feet below the ground. The safety just wasn't there. The 24th of January we had one of our bunkers hit. Had twenty-two guys in it. Eighteen were wounded and four were killed. And we thought we were safe inside and we weren't. Day after day we would constantly fill sandbags. You got so tired that you did sleep some. But the rats running around inside the bunker and on top in and around the sandbags, it really didn't make for much sleeping. You figure a room, not even a room, a space of about maybe ten feet wide by about six foot high by maybe thirty feet long and you'd have eighteen, nineteen, twenty guys inside that space. You'd be lying next to, on top of, underneath the guys in your platoon or squad, however many people could fit in the bunker. That's where we existed. It wasn't a pleasant situation, but it was the only situation that we had. It was the only way we could keep ourselves safe from the small pieces of shrapnel that were flying around, it seemed like all the time.

I went from November until probably the end of March without taking a shower. We had rain barrels that we used in the event there was a fire. And every once in a while you'd go down there and use the pretty much stagnant water to try and clean yourself up. Really never had the opportunity the better part of five months to wash your clothes. It would rot off on you, and you'd get a resupply. The water we did have was specifically for drinking. You really didn't use it for washing clothes or taking showers. There was a whole bunch of us who looked really strange with little tufts of hair growing out of our adolescent faces that we thought looked like the most macho beards and mustaches but we looked ridiculous, to say the least.

Well, we went through an awful lot of Tabasco sauce and ketchup and any other condiments we could get our hands on trying to make C-rations a little more palatable. Ham and eggs really wasn't one of our favorite foods, but the odds of the draw you would get ham and eggs. The worst thing that you'd get out of C-rations was what they called ham and lima beans and we had other terms—we called it ham and mothers. I'll use that half a word, anyway. They were the most God-awful tasting stuff in the world.

You know, this is something totally alien for an eighteen, nineteen year-old kid. I mean, when we were at home, we were either members of the 4-H Club or we were altar boys or we were captains of the football team. Now all of a sudden we were placed into a war. And I guess it was our baptism of fire, so to speak.

If you asked us in the beginning of January whether or not we were going to go home to Mom and Dad and see our girlfriends, a lot of us would have said might not be there, might not be there. I left Khe Sanh in April. I flew in there prior to the siege, right after the hill fights, and the countryside was absolutely gorgeous. We flew out in a CH-53 helicopter. As we lifted off the runway, we kind of corkscrewed up into the sky to avoid any of the machine guns and anti-aircraft guns that still might be in the area, and the thing that amazed me, the entire surrounding countryside was just totally denuded of trees. Everything was bomb craters. I turned and I looked at that, and I said, "God, look what we've done to this area. We've taken a beautiful, beautiful area and we've turned it into the moon." There was nothing but craters.

The bad times are still remembered, but you kind of look at the good times, and it brings a twinkle to your eye and a smile to your face when you think of things. We were always kibitzing and joking around. We were the greatest bunch of pranksters. Some of the pranks took a rather bizarre type of turn. One guy would unscrew the fuse of top of an M-26 hand grenade and he would break the fuse off and screw the top back on, pull the

Dehydration was a constant danger in Vietnam's extreme heat and humidity.

pin, let the spoon fly, and throw it at a bunch of guys. And everybody would jump and run away, and he'd stand there and laugh his fool head off. Well, it happened twice and then we beat the hell out of him, told him not to do stuff like that again. But we did anything to break the nervousness and even break the fear that we had.

Semper Fi meant "Always Faithful," but it was always faithful to the guy next to you. You would do anything for the guy next to you. You would lay down your life for the guy next to you. There were never any grandiose thoughts of, you know, we're over here fighting for the American way of life, for apple pie and mother. We were fighting basically for the guy next to us. You would fight because you were afraid of what the guy next to you might think if you didn't fight. I don't ever remember meeting a coward in Vietnam. A lot of guys dealt with things a different way, but you wanted to be part of a team. You wanted to part of a platoon, and the only way that you could do that was being faithful, Semper Fi, to the guy next to you. And that was the most important thing for us.

KREIG LOFTON

Corporal
Helicopter Crew Chief
U.S. Marine Corps

Kreig Lofton

I had been in Vietnam maybe eight months. I was pretty salty. We had arrived at Dong Ha to pick up fresh troops. These guys got on my helicopter, and they were in brand new uniforms. Brand-new greens. All their equipment was brand-new. And I remember being struck by their rosy cheeks. Just a look of how young these guys were, and I was twenty years old at the time. I suddenly realized right then that I was seeing them through the eyes of an old man. I had somehow become so callous and so uncaring about anybody but my flight crew that I realized that these reinforcements had no idea what they were in for, and it was a very tough moment.

We would launch very early in the morning, sometimes before dawn. As we approached the designated drop point, I was surprised at the small-arms fire that we had received, maybe just a few rounds, maybe some intense heavy weapons. We would insert these guys into a zone. They would start moving immediately and sometimes they would immediately get back on the radio and say, "Come and get us. We're in trouble." Invariably they wouldn't be in the same position. They'd been trying to run for it because we inserted them right in the neighborhood of the NVA battalion or company. So they're running for their lives. They were not able to make it to the top of the mountain. They'd be stuck. They couldn't go up. They couldn't go down. We'd have to hover on the side of the hill and pull them in one at a time. And they'd be carrying wounded with them, their equipment, and sometimes dead Marines. We would immediately start taking fire. I'd have to talk them into the zone and try to ensure that the helicopter blades didn't hit our guys or the side of a mountain or a tree. All the time under heavy fire.

We started receiving incoming rounds a little bit after 5:30 in the morning. The ammo dump was hit. Finally there was a massive explosion that leveled everything on the combat base. The concussion traveled through your body and almost knocked the air out of you. Word passed looking for the air crew. We were still receiving sporadic artillery and mortars. We assembled air crew and made a mad dash completely across the combat base which was probably three football fields wide, running from hole to hole, trying to dodge the incoming. We launched, and all the hills were calling for medevacs to come in. I remember looking at 861, seeing bodies in the wires, large numbers of NVA dead, Marines dead as well. The impact from the NVA artillery and rockets was so great on that one location that the top of the hill was completely obscured by dust and debris. Tracers going everywhere. We circled for what seemed like an eternity until finally it died down and we went in, picked up the wounded and whatever dead they could throw on, and we pulled out of there.

When we were inserting troops into the zones, we had to slow down. We had to fly very low, come in, set them down, and when you're doing that, you're a very big target. A helicopter is the thing that the NVA common soldier wants to shoot down. It's the ultimate trophy. It will get him leave-time with his family. It will give him extra pay. Grunts don't really enjoy that. I didn't enjoy coming out of a low and slow, but that's the frame of reference for a helicopter going into a LZ.

The Marines loading wounded men on to our helicopters were very motivated to make sure they made it happen very quickly because they were a target as well. If they weren't killed being loaded onto our helicopter, we would take them to Charlie Med, the primary hospital, where the NVA had the area completely zeroed in.

They were timing their incoming rounds to when the helicopters landed to drop off the wounded that the rounds would hit there at the same time. So a guy that was wounded on the hill had three, four chances actually of dying. The initial wounds, the wounds coming off the hill, the wounds dropping him off at Charlie Med, and if he had to be medevacked out again. After we supported the hills, the last thing we would do, we would go in and pick up the dead that were in body bags from Khe Sanh. And we would take many helicopters to

KREIG LOFTON
CORPORAL
U.S. MARINE CORPS

A UH-1D Helicopter lands ar FSB "Birmingham" on Hill 549, located approximately 15 kilometers southwest of Hué, with supplies for Company A, 2nd Batallion, 501st Infantry; D101st Airborn Division

do that on some days. It could be forty, fifty, sixty dead Marines in bags stacked up waiting for the helicopters. We would load them on and take them to Dong Ha. It was the last thing during the day.

There's typically ten guys in a hooch, and you're living with those ten twenty-four hours a day until the time they go home, you go home. You're flying with a lot of them, You know their families, though you never met them. You know their hopes, their dreams. So you bond tightly because combat has a tendency to remove a lot of the veneer at certain times. You're very vulnerable, more so than you thought you could be. So you share with each other your concerns and your fears, sometimes even though you're supposed to be big bad Marines, killing machines. That's not the case. You still are subject to the same emotions that all human beings are.

I left Khe Sanh looking down on it and headed east down the mountain. It was very difficult for me. I saw the suffering that the Marines went through. We had suffered through this. All the casualties that had mounted up in seventy-seven days. It was all for nothing. You know, we were totally abandoning it. I was having a hard time understanding that. And I still don't quite understand it.

A CH-47 helicopter of the 1st Squadron, 9th Cavalry, 1st Cavalry Division (Airmobile), dumps 55 gallon drums of CS (Riot-Control) gas into suspected VC emplacements.

KENNETH PIPES

Captain
Bravo Company 1st Battalion,
26th Marines
U.S. Marine Corps

Kenneth Pipes

I didn't know where Khe Sanh was or, you know, what a Khe Sanh was or anything. I requested to go there and got my stuff and got on a helicopter and landed. Bravo Company at that time was assigned a deep blocking position. So we landed into a designated landing zone, probably about ten miles outside Khe Sanh toward the Laotian border. The other remaining companies then started to sweep toward us early the last morning we were out in the field. Just before daylight we reported enemy movement in front of one of the platoons. The first platoon lieutenant, Don Jacques, swept through there and killed three NVA, which turned out to be a part of a NVA reconnaissance unit, and they were caught by surprise and, of course, scattered. They left some papers and packs that added a great deal of intelligence of what was going on at Khe Sanh. Almost immediately we were told to break off operations and get back to the base, which we did.

Then we went into the defensive perimeter there at Khe Sanh and began to dig deeper holes and put out more barbed wire. It was deep red dust and clay. When it was hot, it was very dusty. When it was raining, it became deep red clay, difficult to dig in. The men were working twenty-four hours a day, maybe getting two, three hours of sleep a night, if they were really lucky. In that time they were out on listening posts and on ambushes. So we may not have been dug in as well as we should have been. But we were dug in as well as we could, with the people we had. We kind of turned into gophers. The trenches were deepened in many places to something like World War I. Deep, well-dug trenches with firing steps and ammunition stored into the sides. Bunkers done as well as we could do them.

You know a lot of times some people have expressed disdain if you weren't in a front-line Marine Corps rifle battalion or Army rifle battalion. But the reality, and there were many realities for many of us there, but the reality at Khe Sanh was there wasn't any rear area. You could have been in Charlie Med as a corpsman, and you were just as subject to being grievously wounded or killed as a man from India Company on 881. You know, the risks were I guess equally shared by everyone.

We were sent there to do a job. It was on an individual basis to do your job and try to survive, to come back home if you could. I think for the commanders, fire team-leaders, squad leaders, sergeants, corporals, and the officers, it was not only trying to get home but the added, very deep responsibility to try accomplishing the mission that you had been given, to bring as many back with you as you could. I think the reality is probably much like the legionnaire and the legions of Rome. You were sent to the far-flung edges to serve, and that's what we did. You know, Johnson and McNamara were so far removed from us, I think, I hope, I speak for some if not all of the men in Bravo Company. We were sent there like the army was sent into the Ia Drang Valley—with a job to do, and to a man, they did it.

Private 1st Class Ruben D. William (left) and Larry L. Mock, members of the sniper team of 2nd Platoon, 3rd Battalion, 26th Marines getting ready for action in Elephant Valley, located 8 miles northwest of Da Nang.

My stepfather owned some liquor stores, so my mom would get Red Label Jack Daniel's. So she sneaked in a pint, a quart, you know. And so I would walk the lines and stick that in my back pocket, particularly at night. And talk with the men and pull that out and you know, give 'em a shot. You know, what the hell. One shot of whiskey isn't going to be too bad. That may be all they remember of me, is getting a shot of whiskey from somebody dark at night. I think all of us were not filled with very deep concern that they'd take the base. Concern was that the effort was going to come and that we could rise to the occasion. Now you look back and say, you know, "What, that piece of ground, then?"

KENNETH PIPES
CAPTAIN
U.S. MARINE CORPS

Kenneth Pipes

Pipes was commissioned a 2nd lieutenant in the Marines following his graduation from Fresno State College, California, in 1961. He graduated from the Marine Corps Amphibious Warfare School and from the Command and Staff College. He served as a captain for thirteen months in Vietnam. Among his awards are the Silver Star, the Bronze Star, and the Purple Heart for actions during Khe Sanh. He has a graduate degree in educational guidance and counseling from the University of Virginia. Retired from the Marine Corps as a lieutenant colonel after twenty-five years of active and reserve duty, he has two grown children and he lives in California with his wife. He is an avid supporter of the Khe Sanh Veterans Organization.

RALPH "DOC" DANIELLE

Corpsman
U.S. Navy

Ralph "Doc" Danielle

When you were in Vietnam, you didn't feel like you were on Earth or in this world. One of the most depressing feelings I had was "How will I ever get out of this place?" I mean, I'm so deep in the bowels of this country that I just don't know how I'm going to get out of here.

The memories are so jumbled. The first time we went out on patrol in Khe Sanh, we were dropped off on Hill 861. The night before two Marines and myself were pretty close, and we stayed up all night just talking. I remember Strong saying, "You know, Doc, I wonder how many guys are not going to come back from this." By morning we were running up the hill, and mortar rounds are going off all around us. And Rodriquez yelled, "Doc, Strong's hit bad." I remember running up to him. He was a little guy with blond hair and glasses. One of the lenses was popped out of his glasses. And one, one was cracked. I performed mouth-to-mouth resuscitation on him, and he just laid there dead. And, oh boy, that's probably my strongest emotional feeling. I remember going through firefights, getting hit, and taking care of wounded, and your hands are full of blood, and you wipe them off on your pants. After days and weeks of wearing the same clothes, your pants are still stiff from the blood. I remember always being hungry after something like that.

It was like hell. You felt you were so far into the bowels of the country that there was no way out. You just get used to artillery, noise going on all the time, artillery rounds, diving into holes and to walk around the trenches, the dirt and the filth. Everything, even little cuts would get infected. Diarrhea was an everyday occurrence. People would medevac out from dehydration and diarrhea. I was one of them at one time, too.

We lived in bunkers. Sandbag bunkers. Dirt. Dirt, sandbags, rats. I remember killing rats in the bunkers. I remember sleeping and waking up with a rat on my chest. The rats didn't seem to be that big a threat to us. It was one of the least of our worries. We'd become sadistic toward them. They were something to play with. I remember finding a rat in one of the trash cans. I'd squirt lighter fluid on it and

Outside view of a bunker at Khe Sanh combat base.

RALPH "DOC"
DANIELLE
CORPSMAN
U.S. NAVY

*Inside view of a bunker
at Khe Sanh combat base*

set it on fire. These are the things you did. Things that you'd never do if you were home. Your whole mental attitude changed.

There were times when we were just so bored. One of the things we did when we were so bored was shave our heads, just for something to do. Some of the times I laughed the hardest were in Vietnam. Just the silly things you'd do. I mean, we'd walk around with vanilla pudding up by our nose and walk around licking it and grossing people out, you know. I was twenty years old. But I knew a lot of twenty-year-olds who were a lot more mature than I was. I was pretty innocent to the world. I wasn't very political at all. I'm still not really. I grew up a lot there.

I never counted the rockets. It was just a constant barrage of artillery rounds coming in. After they stopped, if they stopped, we'd peek up and look at some of the explosions and then I remember going out and looking at the sandbags, and see hunks of jagged shrapnel that were huge. And, oh my God, I'd never look again.

I guess I always like to be self-sufficient. C-rations always had spoons in them, but oftentimes I'd get packages, and you could always tell they were my packages because I'm from an Italian family and the grease from pepperoni would just drip through the packages. And my folks would send me chocolate, vanilla pudding in a can. I didn't always have a spoon so I kept this spoon in my top pocket. I love to eat. The C-rations we had were left over from the Korean War. The peanut butter was really good, once you got the oil mixed back into it. Certain C-rations everybody would just kill for. Ham and mothers, that's ham and lima beans, were ones that you didn't want to get. They were just awful.

We were wet all the time in the monsoon season. It was just so annoying. Being out in the jungle you just shivered to the bone. The first time Dave Johnson asked me to sleep with him, I just kind of looked at him. And he said, "No, really," he says, "for warmth." He said we get under the poncho and sleep back to back. I remember me getting under there and putting our backs together and feeling, oh God, that's wonderful. It just feels so good.

MIKE HILL

Senior Corpsman
First Class
U.S. Navy

Mike Hill

Khe Sanh was different than some of the other areas we were in. Before we were getting a lot of land mines, stuff like that. But then we got a lot of rockets. We had took eighteen hundred one day. So we did get some rocket wounds. A lot of gunshot wounds because the ground people were really fighting, hand to hand some places. Scads of casualties all the time. Some days we had a few. Other days I'll get three, four, five and the next day we get ten or twenty. The most I saw was twenty KIAs in one day. Probably wounded, fifteen or twenty. One of the kids that came in that I saw that got wounded, was a kid I didn't know was even in the unit, was from my hometown. I recognized him right away. That was an experience.

The new Charlie Med was a huge bunker, a massive structure that could take a hit. You'd hear the rounds going off and sometimes you'd see dirt falling. But you didn't stop working. If we had casualties, we had to take care of them, and we had to make sure they didn't get hurt worse from the shelling. The bunkers at Khe Sanh were

The soil of Khe Sanh became a deep red dust that permeated everything when it was dry and when wet, became red clay which made it difficult to move through.

filth. We had sleep-in bunkers. We didn't have to lay on the ground, made beds for ourselves with stretchers. When it rained, the water just washed everything out all around. That's why we were lucky with the stretchers because it kept us off the ground and made it a nice place to sleep. You had rats coming in the bunkers. You had no electricity. If you were lucky, you had candles to put on at nighttime. It was a dismal place.

I was twenty-two, the old man of the group. You don't know names, have very few friends. I didn't get personal. I think that's the key that kept me ahead of a lot of guys, is I never got personal with anything. So if you came in, lost your leg, you weren't my friend. I cared about you and everything else. But I didn't try to get into it. I think that's what made it easier for me. I never made it a social camp, like a lot of guys became friends. I didn't because I always had to take care of the wounded. I had to tell you that you were going to die or lie to you. Most of the time, we lied. We'd say, you'd be okay. It's hard to live with. When we got dirty with blood, we didn't have a laundromat to take our clothes to. These pants would feel like cardboard. You'd have the blood smell. We ran out of solutions to clean instruments and stuff. So we were using Merthiolate. And you should see the doctor's hands. You know, everybody that was using it, his hands were getting red. We started running out of everything. The supply tent outside of Charlie Med where we had all the supplies got toasted, so we didn't have that much supplies. We couldn't get resupplied, and it was very hard getting it up there. And you learned to live with it. So it was better not to have friends, and I'm glad I didn't.

Sitting in a bunker. You'd go out on patrol, come back in, dodging rockets. It became a way of life. Marines would tell you that it was really tough for them. I used to talk with them and have them come in. We didn't lose a lot from mental stresses but you could tell it was taking the toll on them.

The first thing you did in the morning, you take a can and you make a cup out of it so that you can heat water. We usually used C-4 because it heated up water faster than heat tabs. You make yourself some instant coffee or hot chocolate, depending on what you had. Then I'd go down to the aid station and see what the plan was for the day. And then just wait. It was a waiting game most of the time. Just like in the emergency room, you wait for customers to come. That's the way it was. Sometimes it was real boring, sometimes it wasn't.

I left Khe Sanh for a week and went back because I couldn't take being down south. I liked being where the work was. I didn't like sitting in the rear with the gear. That's why I stayed up there until I got ready to leave the country. I like being a Navy corpsman. I like taking care of people. I liked being in hot situations where I could help somebody. That was the way I liked to live. If I had it to do over again, would I do it again? Yeah. I like the jazz. We do a good job. I don't kill a lot of people, but I save a lot of people.

MIKE HILL
SENIOR CORPSMAN
U.S. NAVY

Mike Hill

Hill served at Khe Sanh as a Senior Corpsman, 2nd Battalion, 1st Marines. He retired because of disabilities and attended St. Petersburg Jr. College and Eckerd College (also in St. Petersburg). In recent years he worked as a paramedic and physicians assistant and was a Health Advisor to the United Tribes of Kansas. After working with the wounded, "Most of the time our clothing was covered in blood. They would get hard like cardboard and the smell was gruesome. That's the most powerful reminder of Vietnam I have today." Married for thirty-two years, he has three sons and four grandchildren, and he and his wife Shirley recently completed a more than eleven thousand-mile trip around the United States, visiting the men he served with in Vietnam.

TOM CAMPBELL

Sergeant, Radio Operator
1st Marines
U.S. Marine Corps

Tom Campbell

I was a radio-wire man. Mainly we controlled the command center and all of the outposts and all of the communications to everything around the perimeter. Every time they'd get blown up, we'd have to get out there and start repairing them. Get out in the incoming. Intermittently you'd run to one area and try to find it, fix it. And as fast as you could, run to another trench or whatever. We would have to repair the lines in incoming. There's no feeling like it, after heavy artillery, the way it was coming in on us all the time. Scared to death. There was just no freedom of movement and, being confined most of the time to the bunker, you stayed around that area or wherever you worked you stayed in that area. It wasn't a place where you'd just go out and wander around. After being at Con Thien for a long time and getting a good pounding in artillery, I mean artillery is really a mind thing. We thought we were going to be going someplace nice rather than Khe Sanh after Con Thien. But no, we went right back into this artillery barrage thing. It really played on your mind. There were a lot of guys that actually had to be held down and sedated in one way or another. Mentally it just tore them up.

It seemed like the enemy was hidden all of the time. You'd get all this artillery and you'd never get to actually see the enemy too much. That really plays an effect on you. It was totally ridiculous. Any place you went, your ears were just listening for that background noise. Those little boop, boop, boops. All of a sudden, artillery comes screaming in. Normally you could tell that the volleys they had, about five round, six round volleys, where one would hit, where the next one would be. How close it would be. Well once the fourth round hit our door in our bunker, caved it in. We were on the ground with sandbags on our heads. We knew that next round was going to be ours. That was pretty strong. Pretty strong. They had to dig us out of there. We were lifted off the ground, concussion. But we didn't get any shrapnel or anything, the way the bunkers were built. If you could make it through that situation there, you're going to make it through life. We got so good at it, though, we could tell almost where it was going to go and go the other way. You were really locked in where you were. You didn't think of home. You thought of what was just going on at the time. Are you going to be the next one? Are you going to get hit? Every day was like that. You never had an eight-hour workday. Sixteen hours sometimes. You'd have a work party. You'd go down to Charlie Med and bear stretchers. Four hours was a good night's sleep, if you slept at all.

Being inside a bunker and living in California is about the same thing with earthquakes. But the B-52 air strikes. You'd be sitting there and the whole ground would just start rumbling and rumbling and rumbling. I mean really strong. And when you're underground with that effect, the whole ground is moving quite a bit. Everything falls. The dust, dirt and everything starts moving. Red dirt. Everybody's face was red. I don't think I had a shower for eighty-six days up there or any way to wash. Everybody was red. Their clothes was red. The trucks were red. Anything from the dust was red.

You were supporting the other guys out there. If one part of the job didn't work, then the whole thing was going to fall apart. We had to keep everything going. We weren't there for political reasons. We were there after a

Communist Chinese radio equipment and rocket propelled grenades are part of a huge arms cache uncovered during operations.

Tom Campbell

Campbell joined the Marines in October 1966 and trained at the radio and wireman school, Camp Pendleton, California. First an MP, he then volunteered for Vietnam. Arriving in late 1967 he soon found himself at Con Thien along the DMZ for eighty-six tough days of constant shelling. His next stop was Khe Sanh, then Hué, operating river boats on the Qua Viet River during the Tet Offensive. He put in three tours of duty in Vietnam, the last with Republic of Korea forces. He left Vietnam as a sergeant in 1970 and left active duty in the Marines five days later. Today he runs a business on Catalina Island, California.

while for one another. You know, to support each other. Just like a brother, a sister. Blood. It was that tight. I've seen guys do crazy things in certain places like that. Go out where you know they shouldn't be running out there and helping a friend that's down. They're just right out there. You know better but all of a sudden you don't think of that at the time. When you get done with doing something like that and sit there and ask yourself, what an idiot I was—I could have been killed. A lot of people were that way. But the Marine Corps is like that. We don't leave anybody. We took care of everybody. Adrenaline takes over. Some of the things you do, you have to do and you don't know why you've done it. It takes you a while after it's over and you start thinking about it. You're so pumped up and you're moving that you really don't think what you're doing. You just do it automatically because that's your job.

One thing about Khe Sanh. They thought the siege was over. They said the siege was over. But it wasn't over. We still got hit just as hard. And we still had the same casualties. You couldn't do anything. We ended up cutting out sandbags and blowing up the bunkers and the demolishing the place and getting out of there. Everything we could destroy or bury or blow up, we were doing it. And the bad part about it, we were blowing up our bunkers that we needed to be in. So we relied on trenches. It was a team effort. Everybody had to do everything as fast as possible before we could get out of there. We were tearing apart our hiding places, you know. To fight that hard for something and then just get up and pull out and leave was pretty heartbreaking. Then again, we wanted out of there. Man, it was time for us to get out of that kind of condition. I went out on the advance party in the helicopters. I remember leaving and looking down. What a waste.

But you know, we survived. That was the main thing.

A Marine walks away from the detonation of bunkers and tunnels.

Marine gets his wounds treated while Marine radio operator communicates with base.

Gas fire being put out by crash crew at Khe Sanh.

ROCKY DARGER

Captain
Helicopter Pilot
U.S. Marine Corps

Rocky Darger

The zones that we went into consistently—Hill 861, 881 North, 881 South—those were the three primary zones we seemed to work the most. The weather was an absolute nightmare. We would single-handedly go in there because all the LZs were so small, you couldn't get in with more than one aircraft. But after a while it seemed to be kind of a safer bet to go in with a lot of helicopters. Usually the number seemed to be eight and then we would coordinate our timing to be in the LZ maybe thirty seconds apart, so you get all eight helicopters in there and out of there maybe in four or five minutes at the very most. We'd carry external loads when were just doing resupply that would be hanging underneath the helicopter and we would actually go in, do a quick hover, release the load in the zone and then get out of there.

Occasionally, though, you'd be going in and you'd be dropping off troops or you might be picking troops up, and then you would have to land. And when you did, the co-pilot's responsibility when you touched down to the ground was to push the stopwatch on the panel and at twenty seconds he'd start lifting the power and we'd have to be out of there because within thirty seconds there'd be mortar rounds in the zone.

One day I remember sitting in the zone and looking down at a couple of Marines. They were in a trench right down below me as we were sitting in the LZ and they were sticking their M16s up over the edge of the trench and shooting over the top of their heads because they didn't want to get their heads over the trench in view because all eyes were on us when these helicopters were in those LZs.

The one grunt on the ground I would have really liked to have met was the radioman that directed us into the LZ on Hill 861. Sometimes when we'd be coming there, knowing we were going to start taking fire and stuff right away, he would be standing on top of the command bunker to get a better view to help get us into the LZ. He didn't use normal radio chatter. It was more a real down-to-earth way of talking and he was very comforting and very helpful. He actually got in trouble with some of the officers in his company because of the way he was talking to the pilots. We frankly got word out there and said, "Leave the guy alone. He's tremendous." I don't know his name. I'd sure love to find out.

When you're taking rounds you can hear the clicking when they're hitting the fuselage of the plane or you can see the instruments jump out in your lap because .30 caliber rounds come through the front of the helicopter. But you wouldn't hear anything other than when it finally hit the plane. You didn't know the mortar was there 'till it hit you. There really wasn't any warning on that at all. You might fly into 881 four days in a row and take no fire at all and the next day, just get the living hell shot out of you. So you never knew. It was a big surprise, the biggest surprise. I remember someone describing being a helicopter crewman as hours and hours of boredom punctuated by moments of stark terror, and I think that's a pretty apt description because you might fly for three or four weeks and nothing would happen and then in a period of one day, you'd be changing helicopters because the other ones were too shot up. And that's the way it went. Khe Sanh was like that.

Marine spotters directing artillery fire

ROCKY DARGER
CAPTAIN
U.S. MARINE CORPS

Rocky Darger

Darger was in Vietnam for 392 days between October 1967 and November 1968 as a Marine helicopter pilot based at Quang Tri. His primary mission was flying in and around the Khe Sanh combat base and the surrounding hills, bringing in supplies and troops and carrying out the wounded. He left the Marine Corps in 1970 after five years and has been with the Yamaha Motor Corporation ever since, now concentrating on government relations. He is married with three adult children, one who is flying Stealth F-117 fighters.

Early on it was pretty intense. It was a major changing point in my life, going up there. You have to keep doing what your job is and you just get along. I don't know how else to describe it. There was a period in the hooch that I was in, we had ten pilots in there, where we lost four or five pilots like in three days, not counting the crewmen that were on board, and you, you just go on.

The weather at Khe Sanh seemed to be a constant overcast. Sometimes to resupply the hills leading to Khe Sanh, we would actually slide over the side of the mountain and just start sliding up through the fog, trying to get up to the top of the mountain to the outposts to resupply them and then, in turn, pick up medevacs and slide back down the side of the mountain till we had visual flight again. That could get a little harrowing. The difficulty in dealing with grunts is they may be in dire need of ammunition or food, water, and because they were all socked in, they couldn't understand why we couldn't come in and just hover down through the clouds and land in their zone. Once you can't see outside, you don't know if you're flying backwards, forwards, sideways, or what. It was very frustrating sometimes when we wouldn't fly into their LZ that was completely zero-zero weather. That is to say, no visibility forward. You couldn't see anything. It was solid overcast. Solid fog.

I remember sitting in an LZ while we were trying to load on a forced recon team of about five or six Marines, three of which were trying to carry two dead fellow Marines and all their equipment. We are trying to get them on board the helicopter. And they were under heavy fire from a large number of NVA. We sat in the zone for over a minute and a half. I knew we weren't going to get out of there because we were taking all of this fire and we had no suppressing fire and I accepted the fact that we were going to die there.

The SEA stallion, known as the "Super Jolly Green Giant" in airforce service, was used by the U.S. military in service until 2012. Because of their power, distance, and range, they were often used to rescue downed pilots.

I looked at Captain Weigand and the only thing I could think to say was, "This is it," and he just nodded his head because we weren't going to leave until all those Marines were on board. At the same time, fifty to one hundred yards away, you could see these flashing lights all in the tree line shooting at us and lots of flashing lights. And it amazed me that anyone carrying a rifle could have just killed us because we were sitting there in this little glass cockpit and crewmen are in the back with little pieces of thin aluminum between them and death. We got everyone out of there and no one was injured. I still don't understand it to this day. I had accepted the inevitability that I was going to get killed. And once I did that, my sanity … I just didn't worry about it anymore, and that was real early on. And thereafter, I had a different attitude about what I was doing. I have a different attitude about death today because of that.

The camaraderie that you have with people in that type situation can't ever be duplicated. Things you do for the grunt on the ground you've never met, it's hard to imagine. You're willing to sacrifice your life, and if you're the decision-maker, the aircraft commander, you may sacrifice the lives of four other people on the aircraft for one person. The one thing, more than anything else I got out of the entire experience, was it seemed like everyone wouldn't trade places with the other guy. The grunts would always look at the helicopter crewmen and say, "God, I wouldn't do that for anything. At least I can hide in my hole." I think on the other hand, when we were able to fly out of an LZ and fly back to the security of a larger base, we wouldn't have crawled into that foxhole for anything.

BRUCE GEIGER

1st Lieutenant
Platoon Leader, B Battery, 1st Battalion
44th Artillery
U.S. Army

Geiger's platoon had four fixed gun positions on the northern perimeter of the Khe Sanh, facing the hills overlooking the base. He had a battery of quad-50 machine guns—four .50 caliber machine guns mounted on an electric turret on the base of a two-and-a-half ton truck. He also had two "Dusters," tank chassis with twin 40mm cannons on them. These were antiaircraft weapons during World War II and used to fight back human wave assaults in Korea.

W e were plainly visible. The mountains that rose above us were dominating mountains. I had a bunker with my platoon sergeant right behind one of the quad-50 positions. We were actually wired off from the runway. We were kind of a first line of defense. Behind us was the ammunition dump, which was directly across the runway. The 105mm howitzer battery was back there also. I suspect as far as primary targets were concerned, those were probably right behind us. The night of March 22, shortly after it got dark, we started getting hit pretty heavily with artillery, rockets, and mortars. It was the heaviest of all the time I was there. We lost land-line communications. I started making my way down the mile of trench line. I got no more than one hundred yards to the command post bunker. It had taken a direct hit. There were several Marines there. The bunker was on fire. It collapsed. They were dragging bodies out. I helped pull some people out, but there were no corpsmen nearby. So I got up out of the hole and took off through the barrage across the runway to Charlie Med to try to get a corpsman there. It was about five hundred yards and it was real frightening. There was incoming the whole time. I got a corpsman in there and got back. There was nothing else I could do there, so I made my way farther down the line to check my positions to make sure we had land-line communications, which we did.

The Marines lost five men that I knew very well. Five guys in one night in one bunker. It was a pretty horrible night. That was pretty much the scariest night that I remember there. We didn't live with fear every minute. We were afraid, but it wasn't something that ruled our lives there. It was bad in that the kinds of attacks that we had there, the barrages of incoming artillery and rocket fire and mortars when they came, they came in heavy bundles. There were snipers. So even when it was quiet, you couldn't just walk. You couldn't move around the lines. You had to move through the trench lines because snipers were out there all the time. In a lot of ways it was horrendous.

Bruce Geiger

After graduating from Rutgers University in 1966, Geiger received his commission as a 2nd lieutenant in the army. Ordered to Vietnam in July 1967, he was in heavy fighting at Con Thien, Cam Lo, and Dong Ha near the DMZ. In 1968 he flew to Khe Sanh where he replaced a wounded officer. There he commanded a battalion of M42 Dusters and Quad 50s for the next seven weeks in defensive positions at the besieged combat base where he earned the Bronze Star with a V. After twenty-five years in big business, in 1993 he became a grade school teacher in New York and currently teaches the fourth grade at an inner city school in the Bronx. Married for twenty-five years, he has two sons.

The VC and NVA feared the 105mm howitzer because of its precision and destructive force.

During the evening we'd fire into the hills. We would fire at suspected positions. We had by today's standards very antiquated night-seeing devices. Basically it was a single night scope that we used to lay on the barrels of the guns at night. We'd kind of slip it into the turret quietly so nobody would hear us, and we would line the guns up. If we saw one of the North Vietnamese lighting up a cigarette, it would shine like a bright light through this tube. We would line the tubes up with just Kentucky windage, and we'd blow them away. And we would know they were gone. They had tracers, so you really couldn't miss a target. You might miss with the first round, but you didn't miss with the second round.

On a clear night, although there weren't too many of them, if you looked up in the sky you'd see what looked like a star or a planet moving. What was happening was that the B-52s were flying toward the target and opening their bomb-bay doors. You'd see them turn around, and then five or ten seconds later, you'd hear the ordnance zipping overhead. An occasional one would get real close to the wire. They literally dropped them in a an area that moves like a strip of carpet—it lays down a carpet of explosives, probably anywhere from quarter of a mile wide to half a mile long, depending on how many bombs they were dropping.

There was a lot of tactical air any time the weather would get good. They did a lot of napalm strikes. We had them drop napalm on our wire because the North Vietnamese were digging tunnels and trenches up to the wire. From at least where my positions were, maybe one hundred yards, the heat was so intense that it would singe your eyebrows. First of all, it stole all the air. The oxygen was completely burnt off for hundreds of yards around. The heat that it gave off was incredible. It was like sticking your face in a hot oven. You know, it blasted right into your face. They had dug tunnels and trenches one night right up to the runway. They were wide enough for two or three Vietnamese soldiers to run side by side through. They dug with nobody hearing, nobody knowing. We suspected they were going to put satchel charges under the runway. We dropped quite a bit of ordnance to destroy that trench work.

During the daytime if we were to spot a sniper, or spot any activity, we would either call in or at times fire freely at those targets. The men were always heads up. They knew that those guns were going to be targets and if they didn't fire them instantly, we were all going to be killed. Heavy fog was a mixed bag. You couldn't see

Diesel fuel stores ignite after being hit by rocket fire.

them but they couldn't see you. Strangely enough, it kept them from moving because they weren't able to move in it. They couldn't find anything. It got so thick, you couldn't see your hand in front of your face. But it was frightening because for all we knew, in that kind of weather, they could have been right on the wire and we wouldn't have known they were there.

Water was in scarce supply. We had our own little shower at Khe Sanh. We had a little trench between one of my gun positions and my bunker. We had two trailers in there and we had put up a fifty-five- gallon drum. We used to draw straws to see who was going to be brave enough to bring a couple of five-gallon cans of water in it. We had a hole cut under the bottom of it and a piece of wood in there. We would catch rain water. But we would fill it up every so often, and we did get to stand under there and bathe in security because it was below ground level. Actually, I was probably cleaner there than in some places I'd been. Otherwise, it was pretty filthy there. It was muddy, dusty, and dirty.

I flew in by air, and I went out by road. When you went out, it was devastation. From the southern gates several miles down the road, there was nothing green, for the most part. The B-52 strikes and the artillery and air strikes had just devastated the entire area for miles around. It looked like a forest fire had gone through there.

JOSEPH BELARDO

Charlie Company
1st Battalion 44th Artillery
U.S. Army

Joseph Belardo

Before being assigned to Khe Sanh, in 1967 and into 1968, Belardo ran shotgun on convoys from Camp Carroll to Dong Ha or to Khe Sanh itself. Occasionally they drove what they called "the Road," dangerous Route 9, a treacherous, often muddy, rutted one-lane strip in the northeastern corner of South Vietnam. He returned in 1968 after the base had been relieved and the siege had been officially declared over. He was there when the base was torn apart and then abandoned.

It was strange place to go to because it took quite a long time to get there, to get across rivers and everything. The road was very, very dangerous. You always had sniper fire. You always had someone trying to stop you from getting there because that was the enemy's prime mission to stop you from getting there. We used to call it riding down the road to hell because the roads were brutal by then. Once you got there, you would enjoy it because it was a place that had a runway, planes coming in and out. It was a little different than being at one of the other local bases.

The base had been decimated by thousands upon thousands of incoming artillery shells from the North Vietnamese. When I got there, we started to clean up the area and police the area because of the large population of rats. So our first objective was to get rid of the rats out of our bunker, if possible. It would never happen. It was a nightly mission of chasing rats off you while you were sleeping.

And then it became our prime objective to dismantle the base. It became worse because you were now eliminating the bunkers that you hid in. You had fewer and fewer places to take shelter. The ones we could not take apart, a demo team came in and blew them up with C-4. Bulldozers would come and level them flat. More people were getting hurt then, than when we first got there. We would remove all the sandbags, remove all the metal debris just so the enemy couldn't get their hands on all this equipment to make other bunkers for themselves.

It just got worse and worse and worse as time went on. There would become fewer and fewer people to support the base. The runway was a mile or so long. With just a handful of us along the northern perimeter of Khe Sanh, it was our fear could we defend it if something happened? There was only nineteen army people and a small platoon of Marines. The more we got rid of the base, the more they would throw artillery at us. It just became a mental game with us. I wasn't used to that incoming. The cannon shells were playing havoc with me. I was starting to lose track of time. So was the rest of the people. The NVA would shoot in an arc. It would come across the runway and they would shoot straight down it, like a big windmill. After the first round landed, we would go out and take a look and see where it burst, and see where the next one burst. If you were in the arc, we would abandon our bunker and go to the next bunker. Every once in awhile, you'd get one really close to the bunker and the walls would buckle or you might be in the bunker and the walls came down

Members of "C" Battery, 1st Battalion, 13th Marines, fire their 105mm howitzer during forward observer practice at Khe Sanh

JOSEPH BELARDO
44TH ARTILLERY
U.S. ARMY

on it, and you would be inside of it and someone would dig you out, or you'd be digging out the next person or retrieving the wounded or the dead. When they would hit the trench area, the trench, even though it was like a little snake going around the perimeter of Khe Sanh, the ground was so hard there, like volcanic ash of some sort, it was like a pinball effect with shrapnel. It would bounce off things.

Our bunker must have been ten, twelve feet underground by the time we put all this roof on it. We ended up putting an ammo can and sandbag shield in front of the doors because the shrapnel would come through the doorway when it was ground burst and fly into the bunker and bounce around the bunker and wound and kill the people in there. I was wounded three times in Vietnam. At Khe Sanh I got hit with shrapnel. Nothing serious. I think most of the people around there were hit with shrapnel. It just seemed to be, who got hit the least.

We didn't have communication with anyone. Most of our orders were given by radio. You would go for days without having any communication with anyone from the base. We continued becoming a very tight group of people. And during this whole time we would be helping with the medevacs. They always needed support at Charlie Med to take care of the wounded and to make sure that our fallen and wounded comrades got back to safety. As we were getting rid of these bases on the hills, it was our impression that we were receiving more and more casualties.

Khe Sanh was mundane. It was the same thing every day at the base. You didn't have much change. Same sounds. Same music. Same incoming. Same dirt: the red clay of Khe Sanh.

Joseph Belardo

Belardo comes from a long line of veterans and he joined the army in 1966 hoping for an appointment to West Point. Instead, he was assigned to Vietnam and eventually promoted to squad leader on a Twin 40mm Duster. This is a track vehicle with "ack-ack" guns mounted on an open turret, an M60 machine gun, hand grenades, Claymore mines, Laws rockets, and personal weapons such as the M16 rifle. In Vietnam he saw action at Con Thien, the Rockpile, Calu, and Khe Sanh. Among his many awards are the Bronze Star with V for valor and the Purple Heart. Today he heads a metal fabricating company in New Jersey.

Convoy crossing bridge on Route 9, near Khe Sanh.

Some M-48 Third Marine tanks had gone out of the main gate of Khe Sanh. They were caught in an L-shaped ambush by an RPG team, and a very, very good friend of mine was killed. It seemed to bring us really, really down. We had seen many, many people die. And we had seen many, many people wounded. It was very difficult for us because we had been in many road ambushes on convoys with him, and we all survived. We considered him one of us, and we didn't consider him a Marine from another unit. All track people have this bond, and he was a track person. When he passed, I remember how mad we all became. How we wanted to go on what we called "The Hunt." Let's leave the base and go hunting. You knew it was a dream, a pipe dream, that it couldn't happen. When you used the 40mm gun you became very calloused. It was very noisy, very quick, very spontaneous. You became callous to the war and the situation around you. The loss of this man brought you back to reality. And it hurt. It really did.

A few bunkers were scheduled to be dismantled or blown the day we were leaving. We could never figure out how long we were going to be at Khe Sanh. They never told us when the last day was going to be. They never said this is the last day. It became a giant mind game for everyone who was left there. All of a sudden, one of the guys comes in and says, "Sarge," he goes, "there's no one here. Right?" They had already left. As far as I know, my track was the last track to leave Khe Sanh on the day they called the lights out. The first track was taken out. The second section started getting hit on the way out. The NVA were starting to mortar it, rocket

Marines wait in the field for orders to move.

it, artillery it. They were shooting snipers and small arms at it. Machine-gun fire. They were having a heck of a time getting down Route 9.

A marine gunny sergeant had come up to us and said, "Sarge, we need your help. We think we left people back there." I'm trying to figure out what he was even talking about. It turned out they didn't have enough backpack radios, and they were worried that in these foxholes that were still manned at the base, that they left some of their troops back there. So we took a ride around the whole base. It was the only time in the few months I was there that we ever rode the whole base. We never had reason to do before. There was no one there. And artillery's hitting the base. We're driving around looking in each hole. The guys are getting out, checking to make sure no one was in the foxholes. We had one or two stragglers we picked up that had missed the call. They jumped on the back of the track. We virtually, it seemed, not physically, fought our way out of the gates, but we were firing our guns when we finally left. We looked back, and we took some pictures as we left. We stopped the track. And everyone paused for a minute. And it seemed like the war had stopped. There was no sounds. There was no nothing. There was no birds flying or bugs flying. And it was very quiet for that one minute. And we left Khe Sanh.

VIETNAM WEATHER

Before the Vietnam War, most weather-related military actions of any duration occurred in winter. Those battles usually lasted months, not years. Think of Napoleon's disastrous retreat through Russia from Moscow in the dead of winter, 1812. Recall Valley Forge in the winter of 1777–78 with temperatures so cold that the weather alone nearly defeated George Washington's rag tag army. The Battle of the Bulge in World War II took place in the severe winter of December 1944 through January 1945 when the weather did as much damage to the Allied troops s the opposing German forces. American troops suffered greatly in Korea in the Battle for the Chosin Reservoir in the dead of late winter, 1950. In all those battles, American troops had an issue of inadequate clothing. Uniforms were too thin. Boots wore out quickly. Men were never warm. Those problems did not exist in Vietnam. In Vietnam, there was a weather-related problem of a different sort—the heat.

Army and Marine troops arrived in South Vietnam in Government Issue, starched, olive colored fatigues. Extreme weather plagued American troops every day of their tour of duty until they headed home approximately a year later, also in starched fatigues, when they were welcomed home to the far more livable climates of

Daily heat, rain and lightning storms made for constant uncomfortable conditions.

North America. The oppressive heat often stunned the arriving soldiers when they reached Vietnam. On landing in Vietnam, the temperature could be more than 100 degrees with a usual humidity of more than 100 percent. Excessive heat and humidity were the new realities for American troops. It stayed that way throughout their time in an inhospitable environment. Vietnam is best described as having a sub-tropical climate, where winter, as found in temperate climates, does not exist. Heat, and humidity were equal foes of the American forces, especially when soldiers went on patrol. Weather in Vietnam was better suited for shorts and T-shirts than for men in full battle gear.

South Vietnam, divided from North Vietnam by the DMZ at the 17th parallel, had a year roughly divided into two seasons. The seasons could simply be dubbed wet and dry. That border between the two nations was a jagged line through difficult terrain created by its former French occupiers. The dry season runs from November to April when it does not rain very heavily. The wet season, when it rains a great deal, lasts from May to early November. In the rainy season torrential downpours fall for an hour or more every day in late afternoon. But it could also rain at other times of the day as well. Oppressive heat and high humidity always followed the rain.

Average temperatures ranged from 77 degrees Fahrenheit to 95 degrees depending on the area of the country and the time of day. The average temperature in Saigon, now Ho Chi Minh City, was 85 degrees. There were many days when the temperatures soared well into the nineties. High humidity made it difficult to breathe. Deep in the Mekong Delta in the vast rice paddies south of Saigon it was even hotter. In the Central Highlands, the mountainous region of South Vietnam, the weather was cooler, but not by much, and it was equally wet. The jungles were always hot and wet.

April was the warmest month, with December somewhat cooler, but only by a few degrees. Between July and November, typhoons were common. They often came with a fury destroying nearly everything in their path, soaking American troops, the Viet Cong, villagers, and city dwellers alike.

Other than when American troops leaped from island to island in hot weather across the Pacific in World War II, they had never experienced anything like the weather they lived with in Vietnam and came to hate it. Hot weather played a role in the war that no one in the Pentagon anticipated. Troops could not ignore or escape the heat and humidity. Dehydration was a prime enemy of the American soldier. He never had enough water, and to survive the heat, he had to take careful sips from the many canteens he carried when on patrol. The more water a soldier or Marine carried, the less ammunition he had in his rucksack.

Private 1st Class, J.L. Laster carries canteens to fill for his squad.

Soldiers and Marines in Vietnam carried pills to protect against malaria and other water-born tropical deseases.

Streams rose and fell without warning, as monsoons and daily rain caused flooding that stalled operations and made for hazardous conditions.

Rain caused serious irritation to the skin as clothing became wet and usually stayed that way when on patrol. Socks remained wet. Boots were never dry. Extra care was necessary to keep equipment dry and mud free during monsoon season. Insects, leeches, snakes, rats, sporadic runaway water buffaloes, and the occasional sighting of a tiger made for uneasiness during patrols and firefights. In the wet season of the Mekong Delta below Saigon, called IV Corps, it was impossible for vehicles to move freely on washed out roads, of dubious quality to begin with, because "the area became a vast lake due to the heavy rain." Lightning in severe storms often knocked out all communications and left the men in the field struggling to find their way. Conversely, in dry weather, the tall elephant grass found in many parts of Vietnam, might suddenly burst into flames causing momentary and unexpected chaos for the soldiers.

The Huey helicopter had a tough time in wet weather. Pilots had to fly with reduced payloads because the heat and humidity "gummed up the engines and blades." Low cloud ceilings made it difficult for the choppers to find landing strips and locate new landing zones during combat. Because of low cloud ceilings that were often at zero, and heavy, wet fog, helicopters that ferried troops and supplies, and served to evacuate the wounded and dead had a hard time flying safely. The choppers rarely got off the ground until the weather lifted enough to allow them to again fly always-dangerous missions.

Troops on the ground sometimes could not find their way because accurate compass readings were impossible in hot and rainy, humid weather. When wet weather prevailed, men on patrol found it very difficult to find their way in jungle settings, especially in new territory, often the case during the war.

American Army and Marines did not always appreciate the uniforms they wore, but the right gear was necessary for survival. Sometimes Army grunts and Marines thought they wore too much clothing, especially on patrol and when engaged in actions with the Viet Cong and North Vietnamese regular troops. The troops may have complained but they understood the need for the kind of clothing they wore so the uniforms did not change.

In the Vietnam War, weather was a tenacious enemy sometimes harder for American troops than the battles they had with the Viet Cong or North Vietnamese regular army. Monsoon season did not favor either side in the war. Military operations were often limited during periods of bad weather but American troops sometimes had the feeling that their Vietnamese enemy might have fared better in bad weather than they did because the enemy was native to the country. We now know that life for the Viet Cong and North Vietnamese Army regulars was difficult in bad weather, too. Their supply lines broke down frequently, which made it difficult to get necessary food and ammunition to the troops. Even with a glitch in its supply chain, however, the communist soldiers did a better job of living off the land, either through intimidation or because of sympathetic cooperation from local Vietnamese villagers.

Despite seriously bad weather, battles continued. Fighting did not stop. Combat often slowed down enough for troops to catch their breath before their next assault and the next enemy attack.

Weather had an effect on every battle American troops ever fought in Vietnam. Different writers, journalists, and historians have a favorite few. In 1967, the seemingly never-ending hill battles around Dak To and Pleiku in the Central Highlands had more than a few rough patches of bad weather. Then in May 1969, infantry units led by the 101st Airborne battled hardened North Vietnamese Regulars in what became the infamous Battle of Hamburger Hill. Often hampered by bad weather, meaning fog and rain, the battle lasted ten days with the troops on both sides claiming and losing ground until the American forces prevailed. For me, the closest our troops came to trench warfare in Vietnam was along the DMZ and

Trying to stay clean and avoid trench foot.

26th Marines, resting in the rain with only a poncho to protect them.

a place called Con Thien, or Hill of Angeles, a Marine base. Rain and mud were more common than any other weather-related problem for the 9th Marines who battled the North Vietnamese off and on for more than a year from February 1967 to February 1968, until the start of the Tet Offensive. There are theorists who believe the North Vietnamese leadership in Hanoi decided to attack South Vietnam on the first day of Tet in 1968 because the weather favored its tactics. The surprise attack on Vietnam's holiest of days when there was usually no fighting, a sort of "holy truce" was a major factor in Hanoi's decision, but the weather was almost as important. The attacks came as the dry season was still in force and the North's troops could move more freely and easily than it could during monsoons season.

Still, though weather played a key, continuing, and often defining role every day of the war, no major victories or defeats can be attributed to it.

The aftermath of the monsoons left dampness and humidity. Medical problems, including trench foot, were rampant for American soldiers and Marines.

★ CHAPTER 3 ★
THE TET OFFENSIVE

Though the Battle of Tet officially started at 3:00 A.M., January 31, 1968, a telephone call from the American embassy in Saigon had awakened me shortly after midnight to let me know South Vietnam was under attack across the entire country in more than 168 locations. Vietnam was in shock. Most astonishing was the bold assault on the American embassy by as many as twenty North Vietnamese sappers, highly trained and daring communist commandos. The North Vietnamese and Viet Cong had simultaneously launched assaults against thirty-six of the forty-four South Vietnamese provincial capitals, five of six autonomous cities, twenty three allied airfields and bases, including Tan Son Nhut, Bien Hoa, and Long Binh on the outskirts of Saigon. In Saigon and at its two major airports, Tan Son Nhut and Bien Hoa, military police did the bulk of the fighting. Military police, whatever the service, normally guarded vital facilities. Though they had combat training, they rarely used those skills. During Tet they played a crucial role defending their positions when they battled at the American embassy in Saigon, inside the alleys, and on the streets of the cities. Equally important, the North Vietnamese succeeded in occupying Hué, the capital of the ancient kingdom and holding it for almost one month. There it would take tough, determined American Marines to destroy an implacable, deadly foe. All this happened during the planned and agreed-on cease-fire for Tet, the Vietnamese New Year. Traditionally it was the time opposing sides would lay down their arms for three days of respite from the war. It was a tradition from the Seven Years War but like that era, no one in Vietnam really trusted anyone, as the killing went on without end.

The psychological impact from the first wave of attacks was substantial. Though coverage during the war up to that moment had been extensive, something new was at work. Vietnam had become America's first television war. Network coverage dominated attention, with the ability to broadcast graphic and disturbing images directly into American living rooms and kitchens. The experience of the Tet Offensive was the turning point for American public opinion, after which discontent and opposition grew.

The great number of synchronized attacks by the North against the South demonstrated the ineffectiveness of Washington and Saigon in their pursuit of victory. Tet, as a military action, was a major defeat for the North Vietnamese and Viet Cong. The North gained no new territory. When the battle officially ended one month later, after American troops recaptured Hué, estimates of dead Communist troops numbered as high as forty-five thousand. This figure was many times greater than the American and South Vietnamese losses. Still, because of the power of television, Tet became a major psychological defeat for the United States and its ally, South Vietnam. The war was never again the same. It would take America five more years to get its troops out of Vietnam in 1973, before the war ended in 1975, with the collapse of the South Vietnamese government and the fall of Saigon.

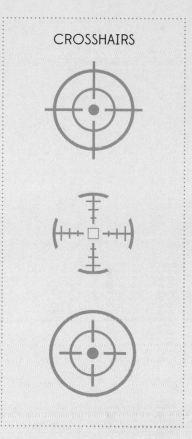

CROSSHAIRS

The Tet Offensive was the largest military campaign launched by the Viet Cong and North Vietnamese Army on January 30, 1968. It was a campaign of surprise attacks against military and civilian command and control centers throughout South Vietnam.

JIM McDANIEL

B Company 716th
Military Police Battalion
U.S. Army

Jim McDaniel

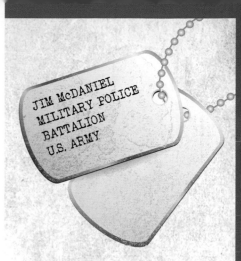

The day before the Tet Offensive we were put on full alert, and that meant that we were restricted to our company area. We had drawn all our gear. We had drawn our weapons, which were normally kept in the armory. We rolled up our mattresses and went to sleep on our bunks with full gear on so we wouldn't get boot polish on the end of our bunks. If we were called out in the middle of the night, we'd be ready to go. We'd never done that before.

We didn't get to sleep very early because the Vietnamese were celebrating Tet. They had these long strings of firecrackers hanging from the roof and they would stretch one hundred, one hundred fifty of them down to the ground. They would light them and all the firecrackers would go off and it sounded like war. So we had to wait till all that stuff was over before we could get any sleep. We didn't get to sleep until after midnight. About three in the morning, the alarm went off and we went downstairs to the trucks and waited for orders to move out. MPs were pinned down all over town. They were requesting assistance and teams responded. My team went to the American embassy. Twenty guys boarded a truck with canvas sides that we untied so we could see outside. There were people running everywhere. There were explosions everywhere. There was the smell of smoke and diesel fumes. There was just absolute chaos in the streets. We got up within a couple of blocks of the embassy, and we got out and pressed ourselves against a wall while receiving instructions. We moved parallel with the embassy and around the corner and as soon as we got within sight, we came under fire. It was difficult to tell who was shooting and what they were shooting at. There was tracer rounds flying everywhere. It was dark, and some of the tracer rounds were a real pale green so we knew those were AK-47s. Those were the enemy's. And there were red tracers, which we used.

As we got closer to the embassy, there were firefights that would go on for five or six minutes at a time and where tracers would fly everywhere. There'd be a lot of action, and then there would be like silence. Because we didn't have any communication with the Marines that were inside and the other MPs that were already there, we had to kind of communicate by yelling back and forth where

This dead Viet Cong infiltrator is dressed in civilian clothing and carried a captured American weapon. The VC guerillas often utilized what they could get, as opposed to the NVA who wore military uniforms and carried Soviet equipment.

Jim McDaniel

After taking a semester and half of college, and wanting to be on his own, McDaniel joined the army at age nineteen in 1966. He hoped to get experience in the military police prior to becoming a police officer in civilian life. From his first base in Germany, he volunteered for Vietnam. He became part of the 1st MP Company, First Division. Soon the army re-assigned him to the 716 MP Battalion in Saigon. His duties were not unusual for a military policeman until the Tet Offensive, when he was in the thick of the fighting. After leaving the army he married his longtime girlfriend Gayle, had three children and one grandchild, and, for the past twenty-nine years, has been a police officer, detective, and sergeant with the Santa Ana Police Department.

we wanted to go and what we were going to do next. We got into a building that was directly in front of the embassy, but across the street. We could get a clear field of fire. There were some bodies laying around big circular planters in front of the embassy. Now the MPs that were at the front gate were trying to get it open. They tried shooting the lock off and they weren't having any luck. They finally rammed the gate with a jeep and knocked it off its hinge. They were entering the compound, and we noticed there was some movement behind one of the concrete planters, so we started yelling to the MPs to be careful. The VC came into view and that's when we opened up on him so he wouldn't get a shot at the MPs coming through the gate.

I was most surprised by the fact that the Marine Corps security guards were able to keep the VC out of the embassy building itself because there were so many of them. The front of the embassy was shot up badly. The VC had fired rockets at the front of the compound, and a lot of machine-gun fire hit the embassy itself. There was lot of damage that the big boys thought was kind of needless. It was kind of a joke amongst us, that the next time that we went there we'd take some rubber bullets and not damage the place so badly.

Right away things started happening in the city because there was no trash pickup. The fire department wasn't able to work, so all the buildings were burning and within one week, the trash was out on the curb, high enough that you couldn't see the first floor of the buildings. It was that piled up. So there was a big problem with the possibility of disease. Everything normally controlled by the government stopped. Everybody threw their trash out on the street.

There were a lot of refugees that were sleeping on the sidewalk. They had straw mats, and especially in Cholon where I lived, it was a poor part of town, and there were a lot of refugees that just lived on the streets. When we put Saigon under curfew, they weren't allowed to get up and walk around. They had to remain exactly where they were all night. People that decided to move in the middle of the night would more than likely wind up getting shot. Everybody had to stay exactly where they were and nobody could move. The Vietnamese Army would string concertina wire across the street, and there would be a checkpoint almost in every block. You couldn't move on any street in Saigon without running into a checkpoint and you'd have to show your identification. If you were Vietnamese, you wouldn't be able to move anywhere. We were really cordial with the South Vietnamese. I remember going to dinner one night and it was really unusual for me because I'd never had chicken-foot soup before. It was something that I had to learn to enjoy.

The Viet Cong would launch these 122mm rockets in the town, and we would take bets on what time they would arrive because they would come almost nightly. Everybody would throw a dollar in the pot, and if you came closest to the time the rockets were out, you'd win the pot. One night we were on the perimeter of a bridge—it was a pretty small bridge—so I mean, somebody had to go out there and be sure that nobody crossed there in the middle of the night. We had to go through the rocket attack and while we were there laying on the ground, a bunch of Vietnamese ladies came out carrying candles or lanterns. And they were walking towards the hospital. They were all pregnant. Every time there was a rocket attack, they would come out. It would be their time to deliver. One of these ladies managed to walk up onto the bridge, and she got to the middle of the bridge and she lay down. That was as far as she could get. We didn't know if she was a sapper that was going to blow the bridge, or she actually was a pregnant lady about to deliver a baby. We had to crawl out there and see if she was the real thing, and then once we found out she was, we had to deliver the baby and wrap it in a T-shirt and drive her and the baby to the hospital. It was just a myriad of things that happened that aren't really connected to the defense of a military installation, but somebody has to do them. As MPs we just naturally inherited the job, and it was something for us to do.

JOE CENICEROS

1st Lieutenant
Platoon Leader
C Company 716th MP
U.S. Army

Joe Ceniceros

Ceniceros mostly conducted patrols at night throughout Saigon where there were seven precincts, a throwback to the old French system of dividing the city. He patrolled around Tan Son Nhut Airport, beyond the perimeter of the city and inside the city itself. Originally he had been attached to the Presidio District in San Francisco, so Saigon was a big change. Ceniceros says that his mission was a policeman's mission in a large city where they had murder, rape, drugs, bar fights—a typical big city atmosphere.

Drugs were pretty prevalent. Heroin, marijuana, not too much cocaine. It was very easy access for any GI to go down a little side street and purchase whatever he wanted. You had opium dens and I knew where they were situated. A lot of time, if we were looking for a GI or a deserter AWOL, that would be the prime place to look.

We are talking about 100 percent humidity and one-hundred-degree weather just about every day. Then you would have a very wet monsoon season, which was great for taking showers out in the open. Might cool off to like eighty-five, eighty degrees at night, and that's that kind of heat environment. We had just a little room with a little bunk and a closet and space for our weapons and uniforms, and that was about it. We had a little kitchen. I always liked to cook, and I did a lot of cooking for them. My brother Leon in Germany was able to send me cans of tortillas and chili, and so we had a nice Mexican meal that I cooked up for the guys. Men lived in villas but they were like barracks that housed the platoon. They had double bunks and air-conditioning. Always looking for air conditioners that might be handy to keep the place cool. That was a prime prerequisite, to stay cool. It was awfully hot. We had a barbecue area. One time I sent one of my men down to the port to see a fellow down there that owed me a favor. I said, "Go down there and see if you can get us some meats and steaks or something like that." Well, he came back with a big old box, and there were two long sirloin strips, and we put them on the barbecue. Then I saw the box and on the top of the box it said "General Westmoreland." So we enjoyed his New York steaks. That's pretty much how we lived.

Joe Ceniceros

Born in Los Angeles, Ceniceros first enlisted in the army in 1958 when he was only twenty years old. He completed his first tour in the military police, then re-enlisted, serving in Italy and going on to Officers Candidate School. He volunteered for Vietnam, became a member of the 716th MP Battalion in Saigon, and was promoted to 1st lieutenant. During the Tet Offensive he and his battalion saw heavy fighting in Saigon. He resigned from the army in 1972 and returned to private life where he entered the food service business. He is currently a chef and food service director at an Alzheimer facility in Sparks, Nevada. Married for thirty-five years, he has three daughters and six grandchildren.

Near Saigon, 1st Batallion, 18th Infantry, 1st Infantry Division, search a cemetery for Viet Cong snipers during the Tet Offensive.

The one thing I did notice about a month prior to Tet during the Christmas season, an awful lot of funerals. The Vietnamese in general make a big deal of it. They hire people to wail and cry, and they have long processions. They were able to bring in a lot of ammunition and a lot of whatever else they were planning, using the cemeteries as the caches. Because of the humidity and because of the ground, caskets are made of cement. They wouldn't disturb a casket that already had a body, but we found out later they were digging tunnels and storing their arms in cemeteries. This was a well-planned offensive.

They celebrate. It started in the morning. They just love their fireworks. Week before that we had been patrolling, and a truck came into town with a load of fireworks and it had blown up. This was not a pretty sight. As we were coming back, one of the monks decided to set himself on fire in one of the squares. And that wasn't a real good experience to watch. We didn't have any idea to the extent of what might happen, except just a lot of funerals. And there were cemeteries all over town and outside of town.

We got the word that Tan Son Nhut had been breached by the Viet Cong. By about one o'clock, that all started taking place. Then we got word that BOQ 3 was being attacked. Jerry got his men mounted up. Everybody

Private 1st Class Fred W. Grable, of Fountain City, Tenn., and Corporal. Anselmo Lopez, of San Antonio, Texas, signal for more ammunition during a battle with the North Vietnamese Army south of the demilitarized zone.

was assigned to either his reaction force or my reaction force. Men got on a truck, got their ammo, got ready to go. This was under blackout conditions now. There was nothing going on except the firing, and by that time there were a lot of bombs and grenades and mortars and just general chaos. The mortars were coming in from the back, and they were hitting the compound. Jerry took his troops and they had no idea … Jerry got through. His men got hit. The machine-gun jeep was able to get out. The men were all killed in the truck. One of our MPs was there, and he called for help.

That's when I load up my people. My orders were to go down and give him a hand. I took the same route. There was a little alley that was on an angle. And then there were other little side streets that went into the alley. There was a building on the corner, then the alley. Behind the building was a little cemetery. When I got to the other end of the alley, I dismounted the troops to see what was going on. I got the men out of the truck. On the other side were just shacks built on shacks. People lived upstairs and downstairs. The first thing I realized was there were no Vietnamese civilians around. None. It was pitch black. All the grenades going off. The machine-gun fire. The mortars and things like that. I couldn't see down at the end of the alley, so I positioned a squad of men around the other side, and they immediately started taking fire. The fire was

A wounded ARVN soldier lies at the feet of ARVN Air Force troops near the center of the Old French Cemetery during heavy fighting on the southeastern perimeter of the Tan Son Nhut Air Force Base.

coming from the cemetery. The Viet Cong had RPGs, which are rocket-propelled grenades. They had machine guns. They had their AK-47s. Hand grenades. On the other hand we just had our rifles, some hand grenades, a grenade launcher. My machine-gun jeep I held back. I didn't want to expose them.

By this time, I was in contact with Jerry in the alley—he had told me that he gotten hit and he didn't know how many men were. There was a lot of them that were wounded and screaming for help. So I was determined that I wasn't going to lose my platoon that way. So I had Sergeant Fish go up towards the cemetery. So he and another guy went up there, and boom, this blast goes off, and he comes running back and he looked just like Al Jolson, poor guy. His face was black, and he said we can't go any further. There wasn't much we could do at that point. Every time we'd poke around, or try to make a little move forward, they'd start opening up on us.

I put some men on the roof of this corner building. I gave them a box of grenades and told them to go up there and see if they can lob some. So they were throwing grenades. At one point I had gone up there and they were almost out of grenades and all of a sudden, shhhhhhhboooom! A grenade came back. That thing just bounced a couple of times. And one of my sergeants picked it up and I said, "Oh shit!" and he threw it back. It got to where it hit and pooooh, it went down, and we ducked, and I think it blew off part of his thumb. I sent him to the Third Field Hospital to get taken care of.

I had about four of my guys who had been hit by fire coming from the alleyway and the cemetery, and they couldn't get out. There was just a little firefight going on every time we'd try to get up and make a move to go down the alley. This went on for an hour and a half and it was just starting to get daylight. We were still pinned down. I had asked for more ammunition. We were out. The men that were military police had been doing police duties and they were instantly thrown into combat, and they were great, God bless them.

It was daylight, and we were able to see, but still couldn't see down to the end of the alley. I saw the truck. I saw bodies down there. There were two Vietnamese that we had shot that dropped right in the alley and they were still there. One of my men was over on the side of a building, and he had propped himself up. He had his flak jacket on but blood was just … he had been hit badly. Red-haired fellow, can't remember his name. He was quite a guy.

If we'd make a move, they would just open up, poom, open up. So the only thing I could think of was we had our deuce, two-and-half-ton truck, and I asked the driver, I said this is a voluntary thing. And he says, "Yeah, we'll do it." So we back the truck between the cemetery and the street and went for the wounded, where one of the guys were. I was able to take another fellow. We went in, and we were able to drag him out. He was really hit bad in the side. This firing went on until about nine o'clock. American tanks came down the street. I think there were ten or fifteen tanks. They were on their way through town, up toward the Saigon Highway, back toward Bien Hoa.

I remember flagging down the tank commander, and I said, "Can you just turn your tank in here and go down the alley, point your gun in there and just open up on the cemetery so we can make some advancement here." And he looked there, and he looked around, and he said, "Ahh shit, I don't have time." So he took off, and he got down the street about two hundred yards, and boom, the Viet Cong in the building down there just opened up with a blast with their rocket grenade, and just tore the tracks off this tank. And I just kind of went … a little irony there, you know. Later on, probably about one o'clock, we were still pinned down, couldn't go anywhere. All of a sudden, I hear this voice coming in on the tactical line. He was in an Apache helicopter, circling around. He could see down to where we were, so I asked him, "You think you could lay some rounds at this cemetery there, you know, get us going here." And he says, "I'll be happy to do it for you." So he was gone. But, oh, two or three minutes later, I hear this roar. And from behind the building, out comes the Apache helicopter. He says, "Are you ready to go?" I said, "Let me make sure my men are out of the way." He just kind of hovered there for about a minute. I said, "Yeah, we got everybody out of the way, behind the buildings." And he just opened up with everything he had and just leveled that thing. That was the end of the cemetery. We never did get any body counts. We didn't try to go in to look for anything, but we were able to advance up the alley, through the buildings, and finally got down the alley. An army personnel carrier had gotten all of the men that were killed and wounded out of the alley. So we just kind of mopped up. You know, the men were just fantastic. Not one man backed off. They did what they were told. They were just all so brave.

In between the racetrack and the city—the racetrack was a little bit south and west of the city—is where the Viet Cong had really infiltrated. They were coming in that way, and they were coming in in squad size. They would come up on our guard posts and they'd just open up, and start throwing their hand grenades and satchel charges and plastic. They'd booby-trap houses. I remember going into one house. One of my men had seen VC go in there. We went through the door. For some reason, I turned around and all around the door there were plastic charges that for some reason didn't go off. That's what they would do. A lot of sabotage. Until I

Members of Company B, 2nd Battalion, 47th Infantry, wait for word to continue their sweep during a lull in the house-to-house search of the area south of the Kinh Doi Canal and inside the cluster of villages south of the "Y" bridge during final mopping-up operations.

left there was dusk-to-dawn curfew. Nobody on the street—it was the MPs and whoever else. And you didn't know whoever else was. They could be Viet Cong dressed as civilian police or South Vietnamese Army. You just didn't know. As a consequence, it was shoot to kill. If somebody ran across the street, whooo, it was tracer city. Everybody would open up on everybody else. You did not know who was who under those conditions.

This went on for three days. None of us slept for the first three days. I think the first thing I remember eating was breakfast in the MACV compound. We came in just all filthy and dirty, and these generals and majors are looking at us, like where did these guys come from. We had eggs, and it tasted so good. I was there for another four weeks. I left at the end of February. In one day I packed everything up. They scooted us out to the airport, got us on the plane. As we were leaving as the end of the runway, we were getting fired up from the ground. I think the first thing I had on the airplane after we got up over the China Sea was an American hot dog. It tasted so good.

HANK LLEWELLYN

Specialist, Door Gunner
T-29th Aviation Assault
Helicopter Battalion, 1st Cavalry Division (Airmobile)
U.S. Army

Hank Llewellyn's job was taking care of the armament on his ship, a Huey, UH-1 helicopter, known as the Slick. He had to make sure it was always in working order. In flight, he was on the right side of the ship where he manned the M60 machine gun. During the fighting they would bring in and take out troops. His crew would deliver ammunition and food, remove the dead in body bags, and carry them to graves registration.

Hank Llewellyn

It was my first contact with Marines. They would come over and fill our sand bags for protection to put around our helicopters just so they could eat our chow, our hot chow, which we had quite often. I don't know what they were feeding them. We had a helicopter company and we had a little more flexibility in getting food and beer. More than one time, we would pool our money and send a ship—I don't know if we were allowed to—down country and come back with a pallet of beer and ice.

It was just routine flights until the end of January when the Tet Offensive started. At that time I had flown over Hué City going into our campsite. The city was intact. It was a beautiful city. When Tet started and the Marines and the fighting started, my next vision of the city was total chaos. A large portion of the city was in ruins already. The city was burning. It was in flames. You go back to an area that you had seen a couple of days before, and it wasn't there anymore. The buildings weren't there. There was a lot of smoke. There was a mass exodus of civilians from the city. I had no knowledge of an offensive buildup. We weren't privy to information. As a draftee, my primary mission was to survive twelve months and return home in one piece. When Tet broke the fighting was really intense. I got pretty nervous. A lot of concern about surviving.

Hank Llewellyn

A native of Norristown, Pennsylvania, Llewellyn was drafted into the army at age nineteen. He says it was "just weeks after signing up for the draft as a result of a traffic violation and the officer asking for my draft card, which I did not have." He reported to Vietnam in February 1967 and served as an operations specialist and door gunner with the 1st Air Cavalry Division (Airmobile) in the Central Highlands and the Bong Son plain. Then he moved north to Hue and saw action there with an assault helicopter battalion during the Tet Offensive. He left Vietnam in late February, the "oldest enlisted man in my platoon at the age of twenty-one." He is the service manager of a new car dealership. Married with two children, he maintains an interest in veterans' affairs.

Bunker emplacement on the perimeter of Camp Carroll in the 2nd Battalion 9th Marine Regiment area.

Most times when you go into an LZ, you wouldn't see the enemy. You could see the muzzle flashes. You'd see tracers coming at the ship but the enemy was very elusive. Actually they'd be hiding, running for cover, so you very seldom saw the enemy. At least from my perspective, landing and then leaving. In the Hué area, there was enemy actually running in the streets. You could actually see enemy at that point. That was one experience that I had not had before. To actually visualize shooting at somebody and to return the fire to somebody that you can actually visualize is a lot different than return firing to the brush. And I had to adjust to that. It's not easy. Everybody has a natural instinct to protect themselves, and when you're fired on, you're going to protect yourself and return fire. But it's a lot easier when you don't see who you are shooting at. There was a lot of civilians in the streets. With altitude it's tough to determine who's who. The men in uniform, our guys, are much easier to see. Sometimes you weren't always sure who you were returning fire on. At least I couldn't be sure.

M60 machine gun crew; the assistant is helping to feed the ammunition so that it does not jam.

Somebody would be in trouble, and you knew you were going probably to have to go in and help them out. Maybe you were going to get into some trouble that day. You didn't really know what your day was going to pan out to be. Each day was different. Some days were easy. Some days weren't. Transporting body bags—that was a little difficult to deal with. There was one particular time we were transporting body bags and the blood was leaking out of the bags. The blood built up on the aircraft floor. See, it's kind of tough to talk about …

Vietnam is beautiful. It had a wet season and a dry season. The time frame between the two was very short. Up north in the Hué area, it was cold and it was wet. It wasn't very pleasant We would burn anything we could to stay warm in the evening—trash, C-ration boxes. There was a large tent. We had a cot which was canvas with wooden legs. I picked the corner of the tent because we had sandbags all around and the corner had more protection from water. More than one time we had to change the tent because shrapnel pierced the tent and it was perforated. Wouldn't hold water anymore. I kept my stash of beer and ammunition underneath my cot and when I was down south I tried to fly night missions because it was cooler. I was always afraid of being caught with my pants down, so to speak, so I slept with my jungle fatigues on and I wore a

Private 1st Class Hundnall and Private 1st Class Smith from Delta Co., 1st Battalion, 26th Regiment fill sand bags.

T-shirt. It was one of the oddities I developed over there, but my boots were off. I didnt want to be caught in an attack and find myself running around in my underwear.

I didn't have much contact with civilians because I did not trust anybody. We kept to ourselves. That was instilled in us when we first go there. You learned you can't trust anybody. I wish I could have learned more about the culture. But I was drafted. My father was in World War II. My grandfather was in World War I. I had to go. I didn't want to go to Vietnam. I had to go. I got there. My primary concern was to survive and get home. Everything in between was whatever.

My time was up. It's really bizarre. I left the United States to go to Vietnam and I got on a commercial aircraft, just like I was going to Disney World, with stewardesses on the aircraft. And I returned the same way. I often thought about those people I left behind. You felt a rapport with those people unlike anything else. The camaraderie, the friendships you develop, and the situation that you're thrown into. Sometimes I felt guilty though, leaving. I wanted to go home and that was my goal but then you feel guilty about leaving those people there to carry on.

When I arrived back in the United States I still had that Vietnam smell on me. That was sort of hard to adjust to, to be plucked out of one situation that was sometimes total chaos, insanity, and then, boom, twenty-four hours later you're walking the streets of your home town. That was really tough. It took some adjustment for me. Not only the adjustment and the time zone and the temperature—it was February I got home—but the whole atmosphere. One day you can make a life-and-death decision, and it's routine. Then the next day you're arguing with a guy at Burger King. It was really bizarre. Really.

KENT MILLER

Lieutenant Colonel, Commander
Third Security Police Squadron
3rd Fighter Wing, Bien Hoa Air Base
U.S. Air Force

Kent Miller

Kent Miller and his 350 men had responsibility for an air base with a ten-mile perimeter, and several thousand Army, Navy, and Air Force personnel. Each day as many as 150 aircraft took off and landed. His security police were there to detect and stop sniper and sabotage teams. Flying crews always carried weapons, but most of the other military personnel on the base did not. At the time of the Tet Offensive, their assigned weapons were under lock and key.

The 7th Air Force placed us on maximum alert on the afternoon of January 30, the first time we'd been placed on maximum alert. Everything was quiet until about three o'clock in the morning of the 31st when an abundance of rockets and mortars came down on the base. We were used to being rocketed and mortared, but normally they were hit-and-run, maybe five or twenty rockets. This time it just kept coming and coming, and it was obvious that it was more than just a hit and-run operation. A couple of aircraft were burned, a lot of buildings were damaged, two or three were killed.

A lot of people were issued weapons when we were placed on maximum alert. We had .38 pistols, M16 rifles, M60 machine guns, a few grenade launchers we had traded for the army with. We had no flak jackets. We were supposed to be an internal security force, basically a police force and a guard force. The first instance we knew of a ground attack, we had about thirty sentry dogs and one of the sentry dog handlers radioed in that his dog had a very strong alert. He was told to pop a flare. We had hand flares. And when he popped a flare, he said something to the effect, "Oh, my God, they're everywhere," and the firing started. The main security control had been knocked out. The electricity had been knocked out. They'd breached the perimeter at three other areas. We had two chain-link fences. Between the fences was a minefield, but it was an old minefield. It was French, South Vietnamese, American. We didn't know where the mines were, but obviously the enemy did because they made their way through on to the base before we detected them.

The enemy made their way toward the aircraft and got as far as the aircraft engine buildup area, where the jet engines were repaired and restored. They were probably fifty yards from the aircraft. They were taken under fire by the security police, and after they got to the engine buildup area, one of the NCOs led a counterattack and started driving them back toward the perimeter. We were very fortunate in that we had on base the 145th Helicopter Battalion, Army. We couldn't get our aircraft off because the enemy was on the end of the runway, but of course the battalion helicopters took straight off and supported us with air. The Air Force was fighting on the ground and the army was up in the air, and if it hadn't been for them we would have taken a lot more casualties. Our troops were probably outnumbered four or five to one. We had to maintain security on the rest of the perimeter. They only hit us from one side but we didn't know if this was the only attack door.

Burned out hull of aircraft remains at Bien Hoa Air Base.

So our troops who were actually in contact with the enemy were probably outnumbered six or eight to one. We ended up with 135 enemy dead and twenty-five captured, and we lost two.

KENT MILLER
COMMANDER
U.S. AIR FORCE

Kent Miller

Born in Kansas, Miller spent his early years with his parents in the oil fields of Oklahoma, Texas, and Kansas. A graduate of Oklahoma State University with a Masters from the University of Arkansas, he earned his 2nd lieutenant's bars in the infantry in 1949 but transferred into the Air Force where he remained for the rest of his career in the security police with the Strategic Air Command and the Tactical Air Command. During Tet he commanded the security police at Bien Hoa Air Base outside Saigon, where he led his men in the first major battle of Air Force security police. After retiring, he became a high school football coach, teacher, and principal. He and his wife have three sons and one granddaughter.

JAMES F. McCOY

Private First Class
C Company
716th Military Police Battalion, Saigon
Military Police

James F. Mccoy

All day long the Vietnamese were firing off fireworks to celebrate Tet, celebrating with libations. During the day it wasn't too bad. But when it got dark, all these fireworks and small arms were going off, and the radio communications were going on. Everybody felt like we were going to get hit. It was kind of eerie. Like it was midnight. We were all out by the jeep. We were still awake. It was real hard to sleep because of this noise and racket. At midnight it's like somebody pulled the plug on the TV: pitch-black. All the fireworks stopped and everything went dead silent. I mean, if you dropped a pin you'd hear it in the mud, that's how quiet it got. And most everybody went to bed that night fully clothed, and our flak vests and helmets were right beside our beds. I don't think too many people slept too well that night. We kind of had a feeling we were going to be hit. Some of the guys asked for their weapons, and the captain didn't give them out. I'm sure it was because of a regulation, or they didn't want people on the base camp to have weapons.

It was two-thirty, three o'clock. Somewhere around there, all hell broke loose. They started dropping 122mm rockets and mortars into our base. There was small arms fire on the back of the compound. They were trying to get into the compound, which we abutted. There was quite a few VC out in the back

Roger Morris, a member of Headquarters & Service Company, 1st Battalion, 1st Marines, waits to leave Con Thien.

164

that were killed with small-arms fire from our camp. There was a lot of VC in the back of our base that were killed. I thought I've got to get my weapon. I mean, the noise was just unbelievable. The 122mm rocket just makes a hell of a noise, and they were shelling Tan Son Nhut real bad. I remember getting out of my bunk and running down about fifty yards to the armory, and I was yelling to the armory to give me my rifle and my .45. I wanted to go to the perimeter and see if I could help. Someone said, "Don't give out weapons." We had a little heated discussion and I ended up with my rifle and my .45, and I went down to where my tent was and we set up kind of a perimeter.

At the same time there was just total bedlam with communications. The radios were full of chatter. Guys were screaming for help. Everybody was being attacked at one time. We were getting calls from the embassy, from BOQ 3, from a lot of buildings we were guarding. They had to kind of tell everybody to stop the chatter and keep it to a minimum. It's pitch-black, you know. We're being fired on with small-arms fire and mortars and rockets. There was one alert force, the equivalent of a couple of squads, about twenty guys total. Lieutenant Ceniceros told me, "Mac, come with me." So I got out the deuce-and-a-half truck and went with him. This thing was three times as big as a coffin. It was supposed to have weapons and so forth in it, and now you've got guys on both sides of this box, completely enclosed with canvas, sitting on both sides on the seats in the back. Then behind that they had a machine-gun jeep with an M60 machine gun and a driver. We followed the alert force, the guys that went first to the aid of the people that were being attacked at BOQ 3. I was in the truck and Smith took my place when I went with Lieutenant Ceniceros. A kid named George Smith. You know, those guys, they all got killed. They all got killed.

We got to BOQ 3 and we were repulsed. We disembarked to try and come and help the other lieutenant. He was already hit. The deuce and-a-half was in the alleyway. The guys had been shot many times. They didn't have a chance. This alleyway had walls on both sides of it, and there was buildings behind the walls. The VC were at the mouth of the alleyway up on the roofs behind the walls, and when the deuce-and-a-half came down the alleyway, they let by the first jeep and then they either set off Claymores or rockets. They hit the truck. They blew the tires right off the truck, so the truck was stopped in the alleyway. Then the next thing that happened is they fired down on the truck and the guys in the back of the deuce-and-a-half were hit with automatic fire and then the VC were throwing hand grenades over the walls into the truck, on top of the truck, beside the truck. They basically didn't have a chance. The machine-gun jeep backed out of the alleyway. There was some guys that were still alive in the alley, and they were screaming for help, "Come down. Help us." And, you know, they just couldn't get at them. I mean it was total bedlam. People were shooting everywhere. We were firing. They were returning fire. And it was pitch-black, like four o'clock in the morning. It was utter chaos.

They organized an assault on the alleyway. We were trying to attack the two positions the VC were in on either side. We started going down the alleyway, and it wasn't constant fire but the minute we got to where the deuce-and-a-

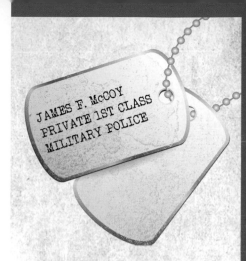

James F. McCoy

McCoy graduated from high school in Somerville, Massachusetts in 1963, and was inducted into the army in 1966. After basic training, he was sent to Vietnam in 1967 where he became part of C Company, 716th Military Police Battalion, based in Saigon. He worked twelve-hour shifts, seven days a week, with only one day off each month. He did guard duty and went on patrols until the Tet Offensive, when all the MPs went into combat to defend Saigon. Married thirty years with three children, today he is in the construction business in Massachusetts.

166

An area just off Plantation Road and outside the southwestern perimeter of Tan Son Nhut Air Base, devastated by air strikes and fires.

half was, we pulled out a guy that was still alive—shot six times. I don't know how he was alive after that period of time, but the minute they grabbed him, the VC opened up, started firing, everything. They were firing rockets. My rifle jammed a couple of times. Then a rocket came by my head and hit the tree behind me. And then the South Vietnamese panicked when they started firing rockets. They fired at an armored vehicle and just blew it up. They backed up and ran over a guy that was trying to pull some of the bodies out of the truck. I was yelling, "Stop, stop." They did and we grabbed this guy and pulled him out of the alleyway. At the same time there was a huge explosion a little further down the alley.

At that point we had probably a half-dozen guys stuck in a building down the alleyway. I went up to that roof with five, six guys. I had got an M79 grenade launcher, and I kept loading, pop it up, shooting rounds, down on the buildings on both sides of the alleyway. I got off the building. Lieutenant Ceniceros called in helicopters, and they were coming in firing rockets. I'm laying there and we're looking down the alleyway, and the rounds go right across this wide street, right down the alley. We're talking thousands of rounds going off and then you could hear the rockets go off. There was a black soldier that got hit just below the eye, and he was in shock. Then there was another man that came out, and his left arm was completely blown off. There was nothing left but a couple of bones sticking out. It still wasn't over. We were still getting fire. It was about five o'clock the next day when tanks came in and just leveled the houses. They just wiped them out and that was the end of that.

Patrolling the city after that was very hairy. Two nights afterwards we were driving down near the racetrack, and a Vietnamese woman come out waving her arms. It's pitch-black and this woman approached us and said, "My daughter's pregnant. She's going to have a baby." She didn't really say it like that. She showed her daughter, and we could see she was pregnant and she was in labor. So we threw her in the back seat of the jeep, and we started driving towards the Cho Ray Hospital. We got down one of the main boulevards, and we were fired on. I swear to God we both turned at the same time and bullets were flying through the jeep. We dropped the woman off about two, three blocks from the hospital because we were being fired on and we got out of there. It didn't make sense for her to get shot, and that's what was going to happen for sure. We just dropped her off and she went on her way.

We were up for three days, three straight days, around the clock. We just went from place to place, and it was very difficult to even take a catnap because you were always awake. I mean wide awake. I mean your eyes were like flying saucers. You were on edge all the time, and the adrenaline had to be keeping guys awake. I didn't see anybody dozing off, especially at night. At night, you'd be having sniper fire or there'd be flares going

Opposite: Black smoke covers areas of Saigon and fire trucks rush to the fires set during the fighting at Tet.

Destruction Cholon, Saigon, where ARVN bulldozers leveled buildings considered uninhabitable.

off. They leveled whole areas. City blocks. They were dropping 250-pound bombs on Cho Lon. If you went through Saigon, it looked like Berlin after the war. It was just a mess. One thing that amazed me about the Vietnamese is like right afterwards, within a week, they were picking through the rubble, trying to get material to build their houses again. Just amazing.

All the guys that were there, whether in firefights or not, just to be in Vietnam for a year, you know, a year's duty, I take my hat off to all of them. You have to be there, really. Get a flavor for this place. It's ninety-five degrees. I remember when we landed in country the first day. I step out of the plane at Bien Hoa Air Base and the heat from the concrete was coming up to the air-conditioned plane. When I got out of the plane, I thought I had landed in hell. I remember one thing from basic training. They said, "Watch out for the people with the black pajamas and the sampan hats." We got in this school bus that had grills on the windows, and we drive from the air base to the base camp. We're driving along and I'm looking and everybody has black pajamas and sampan hats. So I said, "Why do they have grills on the bus?"" He says, "That's to keep the hand grenades from being thrown into the bus." I said, "Wonderful. Wonderful." You would have to be there to appreciate the courage, the bravery, what these guys did under real bad circumstances. It was unbelievable. We were under the gun all the time. It was supposed to be a strike outfit. You'd have to have your uniform just right. All the time it's ninety-five degrees. You used take a shower, you'd towel off, and five minutes later, you'd be soaking wet again. You'd put on your uniform, and by the time you get out to your patrol, you'd be soaking wet. I weighed about 230 when I went in, and when I left there, I weighed 160 pounds or so. It wasn't a very nice place.

WILLIAM "BILL" PURCELL

Private 1st Class
1st Battalion 3rd Platoon
1st Marine Division
U.S. Marine Corps

William Purcell

Bill Purcell was among the first Marines to enter Hué City on February 1, 1968, when the Tet Offensive was one day old. He and his platoon did not know what they were getting into at the time. They did not know how deeply entrenched the North Vietnamese were. These Marines had spent most of their time in the bush, fighting in the jungle, slogging through rice paddies. Until then, fighting in Vietnam's cities was nonexistent. This was Purcell's first combat in a South Vietnamese city, and the one city that resembled northern Europe in World War II. His unit suffered massive casualties, and Purcell, seriously wounded during his third day of fighting, was medevacked to a hospital in Da Nang.

We were told we were going to the city of Hue to suppress a "massive student demonstration." We had basically our rifles and ammunition, and just outside the city we ran into our first incident where the fire commenced. Fighting our way through it we sustained maybe a half dozen casualties, at which point two Marine tanks came up the road from nowhere. We climbed on board the tanks and commenced the attack into the city, not knowing what we were getting into. When we went across a small canal, all hell broke loose for the first attack. It was going through a gauntlet. The first tanks received all the fire coming from the buildings and at ground level. The tank that got hit went out of control. Now, keep in mind there were Marines hanging on to the top of the tank, to the side of the tank. Anywhere we could ride free, we jumped on to a free ride. The second tank, that I was on, was next over the bridge, so we just knew we were going to get hammered. We got over the bridge and word finally came to disembark, and we got off.

There was a couple of towers that the South Vietnamese had. And we were getting fired from those towers, and they were firing down on us. We were returning fire to those towers with the machine guns and they told us to hold up, that they were friendlies. A couple of minutes later we realized that this was more than what they said. To see a tank twenty meters ahead of you cross a bridge and receive that kind of intense fire, you knew this wasn't a student uprising. This was a big problem, and all of a sudden you really stepped in it.

We got our wounded out of the street and from that point on we just started fighting our way up the street, one building at a time. There was fire coming from the buildings, and you had to imagine the scene now. It was like going through Queens or Brooklyn, New York, with all two and three-story buildings, paved streets, sidewalks, the whole developed side of things.

You have to understand the Marine Corps was trained to fight in jungles, was trained to make amphibious landings and they're shock troops. They come in, they get the job done, and they pull out and somebody else comes in a garrison mode and holds. The Marines had not fought in a city like that since Seoul in the Korean War. The people who took over were the inner city kids, the kids from New York, Chicago, Detroit, who were used to growing up in a city, knew what alleys were all about, knew what a roof was for other than the top of a building, and knew how to get in and out of things, and they just silently took over the role and got the squads in, got the fire teams in, and everyone just started working together and using the knowledge we had from growing up in the city. I grew up in the city of New York. I wouldn't call it a ghetto, but it was still the city of New York and we were able to understand the intricacies. The farm kids, the kids from the ranches, the kids from the outlying suburbs, really didn't have an idea of that and it kind of helped, it worked.

Purcell and his fellow Marines slowly make their way another half mile, moving ahead of a convoy carrying needed supplies. They reach a causeway a thousand meters long across two rice paddies that leads into another section of the dangerous city.

We started into the city—at which time again we came under massive fire. Everyone scattered to the ditch along the side of the road. Word came down that Alpha Six was down. Alpha Six was our company commander, and they wanted One One forward and all the One Ones started to get together. Our platoon sergeant, Sergeant Gonzalez, basically ran the platoon. We had a gunnery sergeant and that was it as far as leadership went. The balance was just the individual Marines, their squad leaders, their platoon, their NCOs. Sergeant Gonzalez formed One One on line, gave the order to fix bayonets. It's something we hadn't heard since movies that

Opposite: Marines of 3rd Platoon, "E" Company, 2nd Battalion, 3rd Regiment cross a muddy rice paddy during Operation No Name #97.

we'd seen with John Wayne in World War II. And on three we charged across the rice paddy. Luckily for us, only one was killed going across. He got killed just as we got to the other end. From that point we were able to crawl through a large sewer pipe, get into the first section of buildings where we were, and secure these buildings so the convoy could move forward and again proceed into the city. And we just kept fighting and pushing away, one building at a time.

The major objective was to secure the university. It was a mass of buildings that were surrounded by mansions. They were well-built, so they were difficult. All the Marines had were their rifles. Since someone thought it was a good idea to protect the city for historical reasons, there was no air support, no naval gunfire, something that the Marine Corps depends dramatically on, and no artillery. So when they said we couldn't destroy the city, the buildings were blown down one by one with hand grenades, satchel charges and tank fire, whatever tanks we had. And the tanks basically helped in the beginning but they ran out of fuel and arms, so at a point they were useless. It was done by hand and it was a big game of tag, and they were "it." And we were just trying to scatter and stay out of the bag, you might want to say. We lost a lot of people in the university. Each building was built in a square. In the center of the square was an open courtyard. So when you attacked one portion of the building, if you didn't have the left or the right side closed down, you'd be going around in a circle, chasing, firing, whatever.

Normally the front door is the easiest way into a building, but when you're getting fired at, any way in is the way you'll go. A window. A hole in the door. Since we didn't have any artillery support, we did have a bunch of 106 recoilless rifles. They're very heavy and awkward, and they fire about a four-foot rocket with a high explosive head. Normally they're attached to a jeep. When we came upon a position that we really couldn't get into, and it was just hotter than hell, somebody, an engineer or someone with a satchel charge, which is a bunch of blocks of plastic explosives, would get up to the side of the building and blow an enormous hole in the side of the building. It just became a little ingenious game

Opposite: Photograph taken through the barrel a recoilless rifle from front to rear, with the loader inserting a 106mm round.

as to how we were going to get in, and also at the same time, you're thinking, how am I going to get out. You had your way in and you really wanted to get your way out, especially if you were getting hit or you're getting your people wounded and you want to get them to the rear area.

We were able to see then actual enemy. We were in the DMZ a lot, and there were a lot of dead bodies laying around from the big air strikes that were coming in. What was left of them actually you could see in the distance walking around. So we had a glimpse of what we were up against. Now in Hué, the first day we were fighting just prior to the tanks coming into the city, we were fighting, trying to get across the street, and there they were, a half dozen of them, as big as I was, five-ten, six-foot, brand-new uniforms, big packs on the backs, so we knew we were in big trouble. These weren't the local guys that we'd been chasing around. These were the real army fellows, and I think the word got back that basically from what we understand now, I think they were raw troops. They were green troops from the North, which could have been a saving factor. Had they been experienced troops, it could have been a really bigger problem than we had on our hands. But still, when you're going up against forty to one, it doesn't, matter if they're raw, green, big or small—they've got you by sheer number.

You would like to think you had a full platoon, forty or fifty, sixty people. We didn't have anywhere that number, so there may have been six of us in a position, one or two on watch, the rest sleeping. It would rotate every hour or two hours, whatever it was. And the night before I got wounded seriously enough to be evacuated, I had a very bad toothache, and I couldn't sleep. I think I was up all night anyway with pain, so I might as well just stay on watch and let the other guy sleep.

We'd hold up in a building somewhere. Usually on the second floor of a building, and maintain radio contact. Hopefully whoever was controlling the battle knew where we were. And normally your biggest fear at night is having the rear not know where you are. At night we would settle in, since we didn't have any of our gear with us. At one of the universities, there was an elaborately decorated wing, and they had some windows that were ten, twelve feet high. And they had huge curtains on them, real thick draperies. I just cut a piece off, and that was my sleeping bag. And a bunch of other guys got the same idea, so we carved that stuff down and that was our sleeping bags. If you were on watch, somebody else who came off watch got that thing to roll up in as a sleeping bag, trying to stay warm and stay dry. If you got in trouble, just grab your socks and your wounded and get out of there, as best as you could, and try and make your way back to a position that was heavier defended than what you had. And that's how we spent our nights.

The first day we got most of the wounded out when we made the initial attack. A lot of them died waiting to get out. It took a long time, which was a first. Normally they'd get you out pretty quickly. But since there was no way in or out of the city at that point in time, the city was almost sealed off, we were at the mercy of the weather, which was turning bad. Helicopter support coming in finally got them out, and if you're really wounded very, very badly, and you couldn't get out that day, you probably weren't going to make it.

Luckily by the third or fourth day, the secure area that we created had grown large, and we were able to get the helicopters in. What they would do is they'd come up the coast, fly low, hit the river, and come right up the river and land on this big ball field or whatever it was on the river. And that's how they got the wounded out. It depended on the weather, how bad it was, how low the ceiling was. I think at one point there were nurses from the Air Force who flew in with the helicopters to get the wounded out, which was a no-no. You didn't bring women into the field like that, but there was no one else and they jumped on board.

We were getting ready to move up our street again. We were in a big courtyard just sitting around eating whatever we had. There was no food for the Marines for the first two or three days in the city. We were finally

Marines maintain radio contact as they move against the Viet Cong near Saigon during the Tet Offensive.

able to find a storehouse and get some supplies. There weren't that many of us left and we started moving up the street. We kept moving and with that, a barrage came in and hit the rooftops, and we all started running for cover and just starting to spread out. The artillery barrage worked itself right down the middle of the road, and that's when an awful lot of us got hit. Myself, my two gun team members, and probably five other fellows on the fire team. I was hit in such a fashion that I was conscious, unconscious, and going in and out. I don't remember, don't know how long a time span it was getting back, being put on another truck, waiting for the helicopters to come in and get the wounded out. That could have been two, three, four hours. I have no idea of time because I was just out of it most of the time. And that was the last time I saw anybody from the city.

You don't go out and say, "I'm going to be brave today, I'm going to become a hero." It doesn't work that way. I mean, first of all, you're scared to death. And you're so scared you can't even think straight. But the Marine Corps has trained you in such a way that you're not allowed to think. You just have to perform. You're to act. And you bypass just a normal reaction. It's like the bell rings, the dog runs. Theoretically when the fighting starts, the Marines are supposed to get in line and fight. And they know how to work. They just know how to coordinate with the team they're with, the fire team, the squad, the platoon. Whatever. It just goes on from there.

BOB RUTH

Staff Sergeant
E5 377th Security Police Squadron
Tan Son Nhut Air Base
U.S. Air Force

Bob Ruth

Bob Ruth was primarily an investigator with the Air Force. His concern was small crimes, theft, and drunkenness. Occasionally he investigated the rare murder committed by soldier against soldier or soldiers against civilians in Saigon. His biggest job was security at Tan Son Nhut Air Base. After he and his men responded to the initial firefights at the air base on January 31, 1968, he was on convoy duty in Saigon because he knew the city so well. He would be in charge of two jeeps and ten trucks, often driving through the thick of the action.

Members of Company B, 2nd Battalion, 47th Infantry, sweep through a ruined village, during a house-to-house search of the area south of the Kinh Doi Canal, inside the cluster of villages south of the "Y" Bridge.

We weren't really on alert because there was a truce, but we did know something was coming. The local commanders had taken certain precautions. There was more people armed and on duty than normal. At that particular time we did not carry firearms with us twenty-four hours a day. You went to work. When you got off work, you turned your weapon in at the armory. So we knew that when this attack comes, it's going to be hard to get your hands on a gun real fast because everybody's going to be swarming around the armory. So we went and checked out our rifles and took them over to the office and locked them into the office. As far as I knew, I was the first person that was off-duty to get his hands on a gun and I had to run about two blocks and I run fast.

Well, it was new to all of us. I don't think any of us had been in combat before, you know? So it was something new. It was unknown. But at the same time it was a challenge. It was a challenge to do your job, keep everybody alive, and get back safe. And we were very fortunate that the Lord watched over us.

Ruth sees limited action the first day of Tet. At Tan Son Nhut, he assists with wounded, stands guard, and responds to all calls for help. Despite the fighting, life is relatively normal.

On February 1st, they needed someone to take a convoy, to pick up a load of food down at the waterfront. I was the liaison between the 716th MP Battalion and the Air Force. I was one of only two or three people that had been downtown sufficient times that I knew the way around. We formed up a truck convoy to go into the waterfront to pick up a load of food. We went out through the main gate, and I was in the rear jeep. We made a right turn. I don't remember the street and went almost to the racetrack. The racetrack was VC headquarters at that time, and then we turned a left, which would put us into this center part of the city and unbeknownst to us that also put us to the first street to the rear of the presidential pal ace, which was under attack and you don't turn those big trucks around on those small streets. We come around a turn and here was the enemy on the right, the presidential palace and the palace guard and the South Vietnamese troops to the left. There was a tremendous firefight going on. There was nothing to do but gas it and go, and there was an A-1E came in a bombing run and dropped a bomb and both sides took cover. We went right between the two of them and never got a round fired at us. The bomb went off just as my jeep cleared. We did take a different route back.

We went to the waterfront. I got one box of lettuce on the truck before we got run out of the waterfront. Actually, I say run out—the MPs, more or less advised us that if we wanted to be around much longer, we should leave, so we decided that we would wait for another day to pick up food. Went back to the base and the mess sergeant wasn't too happy, but I let him know that if he wanted food, he was welcome to go get it. Then for the next three or four days, I run convoys in and out, mainly going in and getting people out of their quarters, the hotels and what have you and bringing them out. There was one time that we went in right in the center of Saigon. They had been requesting

Bob Ruth

Born in rural Southwest Arkansas, Robert joined the Air Force at age eigh teen in 1956 and became an Air Force security po liceman. In Vietnam he served at Tan Son Nhut Air Base as an investiga tor. During the Tet Offen sive, he was a squad leader protecting the main gate of the base and worked as an escort, mainly leading convoys of wounded to the 3rd Field Hospital. After almost twenty-four years in the military he retired, became a carpenter, and moved to Florida. Today he is back in law enforcement as a civilian employee of the Palm Bay Police De partment assigned to the evidence section.

Military Police Private 1st Class R.C. Nildebrand stands on guard duty in front of damaged civilian stores.

the evacuation for several hours, if not days. Just before we got there we had word that they were down to three guns and seven rounds of ammo and we pulled up. We had sent word ahead of time for them not to come out until we got security set up, a perimeter set up. We set up a perimeter and the first guy out hugged my neck. Big tears. He was happy. That's basically what I did for the rest of that week—run convoys in and out of Saigon.

Streets were empty. Very seldom did you see anyone because just about anything moved got shot. So the streets were pretty much empty. The only thing you saw moving was military. You'd see the national police. You'd see the American military and the South Vietnamese military. And that's about the only thing that you saw moving for several days around there. If you saw anything else moving wasn't readily identifiable as American or South Vietnamese, you shot it. As far as people, the first two days I don't remember seeing anyone other than friendly or enemy forces. I don't remember seeing any civilians. I will tell you about one civilian, though, about one of the barracks maids. Now the barracks maid's job was to shine our boots, press our clothes, wash our clothes, and make our beds. Now that's all these ladies knew. One lived in the area that was off the west perimeter, and they captured her family—tied them up and skinned them alive trying to make her talk, a little eighteen-year-old girl.

Actually, after it was over, it was a relief that no more people got killed and injured than did. Not after the Tet battle was over, but at the end of the war. It was very disappointing that all those people, the friendly as well as the enemy, had died for nothing.

CAREY J. SPEARMAN

Medic/X-Ray Technician
91st Evacuation Hospital
An Hoa
II Corps

Carey Spearman

Carey Spearman, in Vietnam from May 1967 to May 1968, was an X-Ray technician/medic with the 44th Med Group, stationed at the 91st Evacuation Hospital at An Hoa, near Hué. There during the Tet Offensive, he says at its start no one knew what was happening. Though his shift usually lasted only eight hours, he and the other medics would hang out in the clinic because there was nothing else to do. They always worked whenever wounded arrived from the field. Twenty-three years old during the Tet Offensive, he calls himself, "One of the old guys by the time I got there." To this day he wears a medicine bag around his neck given to him in Vietnam by a Native American. He says, "It takes away some of the pain."

One of my techs was working call that night, and he came and said, "We're getting casualties in. Do you want me to get the rest of the guys?" We handled casualties before. Maybe two or three of us. I said if something comes in, give me a holler. And … they just started coming, and they didn't stop coming. So the rest of the guys when they seen everything coming, they just automatically came back to the clinic. But it was like something that, you know, we'd never seen before. I mean, we've had casualties before, but this time, they just kept coming. You know, we had the helicopters coming. We had the ambulances coming in. We had some of the civilians walking in. They were just coming from everywhere. We just looked up there and the helicopters, the helicopters almost blocked out the sun, that's how many of them were coming in.

Whenever you could sleep or whatever food you could get, you got, but, you know, nobody really went a distance away. Change of clothes was out of the question. We caught food now and then, but we kept on the same clothes we wore bringing in wounded. We kept them on. Naps? As far as that went, you took a nap on the table with dried blood and stuff, and that's where you slept. Or you'd get a nap in a chair or something like that, but, you know, you didn't leave the clinic. We needed somebody, we knew where they were—because the easiest way to do that was everybody stayed in the clinic. From everywhere they were coming in. You know, soldiers, some Korean soldiers, civilians, and then we also had some enemies coming in that they brought in. Our job was taking care of people. We took care of people that were hurt. And I think that was probably the best thing. If we tried to differentiate before, then, you know, maybe I don't work on a guy because he got blond hair or

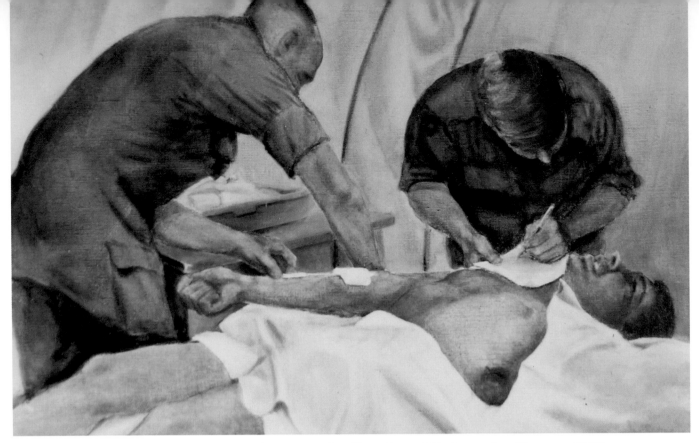

"Next of Kin?," a painting by Private 1st Class Samuel E. Alexander, Vietnam, 1967.

he's six foot, and this guy is fat, or something like that. I mean, we can all find all kinds of reasons not to like somebody. I'm not saying we liked everybody, but we had a job to do, and we did it the best that we could do it. So basically, we ran the whole gauntlet of everything. One guy that was out on the line, and he stopped, he stopped breathing, and I was giving him CPR, and he caught me off guard, and he spit vomit and blood in my mouth, and I swallowed it before I really knew what was going on. I don't know if he lived or not.

But the worst was the children. You know, everything else you could take into account. Okay. But children were not supposed to be there and die. They were supposed to be out playing someplace. I think that when that came in, that hurt a lot of people, to see kids coming in. But there was nothing you could do about it. I picked up a little girl from the line and I was carrying her to the O.R. and I could just feel the blood running down my hands. By the time I got her to the O.R., she was dead. The thing was how do you tell somebody that their daughter's dead, that you can't speak their language? That the Americans are supposed to fix everything? You can't fix that. How do you tell them that. They expect that once he turned her over to you, Americans are going to make good. Americans couldn't make good that time. Those times I can still taste the blood and vomit easy. And as far as like little girls, I just started hugging my niece recently because that was the whole thing with the little girl—carrying her.

The thing is that we never got to know the names of the patients. We knew them by wounds. Like you could say, "Well, hey, you know the guy with the sucking wound?" Then you remember him. Or the guy whose legs were blown off. You remember him, but names you never remembered. So they could tell you a wound, and you could remember who that person was. The problem was a lot of women and men, doctors and nurses, that had kids, they always went to the person that was screaming the loudest and that wouldn't be the one that would die. It's just that they're so used to, you know, going to the person that's lying there crying and screaming, because of kids. And the guy next to them could be quiet, and that's the one who's dying. And so lots of time we ended up picking up a litter, carry a litter in, and there's some guy holding on your leg. He wants to go in, and you've got to push him away because you've got to carry this guy in. And you come back and he's dead.

You can't let a patient see that you're scared. You can't let a patient see that the wound is worse in your eyes … because then you can lose him. What you basically have to do is just shut down. You don't feel anything. You can't show it. It takes a while to do it, but after a while you just shut down because you know, you're no use to a patient if you're crying and you can't stand to look at the blood, you can't stand to look at their wound. Because then you can lose them. The medics are almost like gods to them. So a lot of things that you said and a lot of things that they see in your eyes is what they believe. And so you've got to make sure that you couldn't show it. You just had to internalize it and turn it inside out and just leave it there. They could look in your eyes and tell. Sometimes they would ask you. The thing I have trouble with is sometimes you lie to them. Because you know they weren't going to make it, but once you told them they did, they were comfortable. And they could close their eyes and it was comfort to them but it wasn't a comfort to us.

One of the guys that come in, his partner had been hit, and I had been to the PX. I had bought this Seiko watch, that was the watch at the time, like the Cadillac. I had one that you could see in the dark. And he was admiring the watch that you could see in the dark, and he kept on admiring it, and so I told him, "Well, hey, you know, you want it?" So he said, "Yeah." So we traded watches. So he had a Seiko watch. But I couldn't figure out like, if you're in the field, why would you want a watch that glows in the dark? You know? But we traded watches. He went out and he left. I don't know if he ever made it because he didn't come back to us. And I've still got his watch. I'd sure like to meet him and have a couple of drinks and change watches again.

I've talked to some medics, and the thing is that, what's bothering a lot of them is if you feel bored and you want work, somebody has to die. Somebody has to get blown up. Somebody has to die. Somebody has to get shot, all because you're bored and you want some work to do. And then when it starts, you can't stop it. I think that's what a lot of guys carried around. They can say, "Oh yeah, I got nothing to do today. It's slow." All of a sudden it opens up. And now you've got kids coming, seventeen, eighteen-years-old, blown apart, mutilated, all because you got bored. I mean, it's not that, you know, you didn't do it, but you kind of feel if I didn't say I wanted something to do, maybe these kids wouldn't be coming in. And you can't say, "Stop," because they come in until it's over.

You can't compare to anything the friendships you made there. You will never be as close to anybody as you are to those guys. I mean, we did everything together. We seen death together. We seen bodies blown apart together. We got blood on us together. We cried together. We told each other everything about our personal lives—what we wanted to do, what we were going to do, and we went everywhere together. So particularly for me with my five guys that were with me, we knew everything. And for me to leave, it was like me leaving brothers, and wondering if they were going to make it back. It's a closeness that will never be again, unless you go through the circumstances like that, when you really hit rock bottom, and you've seen the worst that man can do to man and still hang in together. There'll never be a closeness like that.

I used to go down to the Wall in D.C., but I knew nobody on the Wall. I know wounds, you know? I know faces. But I didn't know any names on the Wall at all. I couldn't go mourn for anybody. One person that I found out that I could mourn for, I didn't want to because he shouldn't have been there. And that was another medic. I served stateside with him. And when I volunteered to go to Nam, he was still in Georgia. And the next time in Nam we hugged, we kissed, we drank vodka, and he never came back.

RICHARD LYONS

Chaplain,
1st Battalion
1st Marines
U.S. Navy

Richard Lyons arrived in Vietnam in August 1967. First stationed at Chu Lai, he was also with the First Hospital Company. He conducted services for the men and said Mass. He was at Con Thien along the DMZ during what many Marines consider the most intense shelling of the war. Before Tet, along with many other Americans, he was suspicious of the North Vietnamese and any unusual movements of young men. He received information from the French Jesuit missionaries at Hué University that many of their students who registered in September 1967 were from North Vietnam. The missionaries had very little hard intelligence and no way to act on what they did have. He had been at the Marine base in Phu Bai, north of Hué, when he went into action. Wounded in the fighting at Hué and hospitalized for more than two weeks, he returned to the field to be on the front lines.

Richard Lyons

Marines of 1st Battalion, 3rd Marine Regiment cross a rice paddy during Operation Ballistic Arch in Quang Tri Province.

A wrecked bridge with a pontoon bridge in the background.

Richard Lyons

Lyons became a Jesuit priest in 1964 and joined the navy in 1966, becoming a lieutenant JG in the Chaplain Corps. By March 1967 he was in Vietnam with the Marines. The first navy chaplain to enter Hué with the Marines during Tet, he helped evacuate many of the wounded and dead. In the midst of one heavy action, he suffered shrapnel wounds and spent several weeks in hospital. When healed, he returned to Hué until the battle ended. Lyons was the only Marine chaplain in the Vietnam War to receive the Silver Star for valor. After leaving the Marines in 1975, he left the priesthood and married. Today he works as a counselor.

I went north to join my battalion and when I landed, I was asked if I'd like to go into the city of Hué for an afternoon of street fighting. And since we hadn't been doing street fighting, it sounded interesting, and I said sure. We got across the bridge over the Perfume River, and the resistance was extremely heavy. The bridge had been partially blown, and there was a narrow street with two-story houses along the street. On both sides of the road were rice paddies. And you could see the cathedral far on the left. And then there were two or three houses together, and we were receiving real heavy fire from them. We went up a street until we got to a wide boulevard that was being covered from inside the citadel by the NVA. About a little past these houses, I crawled across the road to assist my friend, the company commander of Alpha Company. Crawling across the road there were two dead corpsmen who had tried to reach him. The third corpsman reached him. It was an indication of the heavy losses the men took in Vietnam. The captain, though wounded extremely gravely, I thought he would die—He had heavy machine-gun wounds in his right thigh and I didn't expect him to live—but they got a jeep and they took him for medical attention and he survived.

In the city again, we really didn't have any artillery or air support. You learn pretty quickly to go up the street by staying in the doorways, and going from doorway to doorway. We learned tricks of fighting in the city. If you have to go down a city block, and the bad guys are on the roof, or in the high upper

Religious services were held in the field, for all faiths.

stories, you go into the building, and you blow a hole in the wall and just keep going through from room to room, blowing holes in the wall. You ruin a lot of real estate, but you do get up the block. It's humorous now, but if you take a recoilless rifle up to the second floor and blow away a house across the street, you knock out the wall of the house you're in. And they learned not to use recoilless rifles indoors. We have to find humor where we can, and we did.

I never measured real estate when we were in the field. It was slow going through a rice paddy or the jungle mountains where you never move as fast as you want. We were heading east, and we were receiving heavy fire. Then we hit this one large boulevard that went from the river up to the Citadel. And it was a field of fire that we could not cross. And we tried it with trucks. We had Marines who were able to hot-wire some trucks, and we tried to get across but there was no way with the heavy fire we were receiving. There were extremely heavy casualties the first day. Alpha Company was decimated. Then the 5th Marines took extremely heavy casualties. We were able to get some of the wounded out that day and that night early, and then we went back to the MACV (Military Assistance Command Vietnam) compound and set up a defense. It was real quiet and nothing was happening and then about three o'clock in the morning, all hell broke loose. I thought it was an attack by the NVA but what we did was we had every gun that we had open fire into the darkness for about two or three minutes, and then it stopped again. It was just to see if there was anybody out there, and if they would respond. And they didn't. The rest of the night was absolute quiet, and it was real spooky being surrounded. But I knew that there was enough Marines that there was no fear that we'd be overrun.

The Marines have tremendous courage. I'm plagiarizing, but "uncommon valor" was a common virtue that day. And secondly, and probably more important, was their leadership abilities. When a company commander or captain was wounded, a lieutenant would take his place. And when the lieutenant had to either move up, or was wounded or killed, a sergeant would take his place. And then we'd have a corporal take the sergeant's place. I never figured out how they knew which corporal or which lieutenant would move up, but they did. They knew the basics and they all could do the job. We never lacked of leadership. We lacked the number of men we needed, but we never lacked of leadership or courage.

There were times when Chaplain Lyons picked up, carried, and used an M16 rifle during the fighting.

It was done the first day to cover the evacuation of our wounded because I would never kill anyone. But I could lay down fire. I have no problem with that, laying down fire. I don't kill birds. If I had my choice, I'd kill an NVA, but I know I didn't. I just laid down coverage. And I also didn't want to be taken prisoner. Without an M16, you look like an officer, and you don't want to be hit by a sniper, or taken prisoner. So I wanted to look like a snuffie. Just a little old grunt. I had a friend, a Jesuit who was an army chaplain with MACV, and he was in Saigon and he asked, "Where was the best fighting going on, where was the best battle?" And he was told Hué City. So he flew to Hué and went in with the 5th Marines and he was killed. There were no witnesses to his killing, but he was found inside the city with a bullet wound in his head. He was probably captured and executed right away.

After being wounded, Lyons finds himself in the field hospital in Phu Bai. While recovering, he helps tend the wounded.

They used to bring in every day a continual stream of dead and severely wounded Marines. And I became depressed because of the number. That's all I saw. I didn't how well we were doing against the North Vietnamese but I seriously considered resigning my commission. But then I realized that there would be no one to replace me, not necessarily. So I knew I had to stay. From my vantage point it looked like we were losing. We weren't losing but we were losing a lot of men and we were strained all across Vietnam from the south to the north. But I realized we were in a war, and we were going to lose people and we were going to have people wounded. I remember once they told me that this one Marine had a head wound and a sucking chest wound, and they said, "He's going to die," and they couldn't do anything for him. So they put me in a room with him, and I held his hand and talked to him until he expired. That was real depressing. But, you know, comforting, that I knew there was somebody that was talking to him. They just didn't put him in a room to die. They said, "Chaplain, you go in with him." I can remember a Marine was brought in one time, and he had both legs off at his calves, and he looked down, and the first thing he said was, "I'll never be able to drive a car again." You don't know what that does to you. It helps just to take care of those people because they were so good.

With the troops it was bonds that would exist until we die. Unashamedly I would say I love my Marines. And I know my Marines loved me. I would go to sleep at night when we were at an operation, and I never slept soundly because I knew the thousand Marines would give their life before they would let anyone get me. Out in the field when you go out on an operation, you carry half a poncho, or a poncho which is half a tent. And so you have to get together with someone to put up a tent. And when you sleep with a guy, you talk, and you talk about things which I don't know if they tell their wives. I know we talk about things which mean a lot to us. The friends I have made in the Corps during that year will be friends forever. And I know they feel the same way about me.

Two Viet Cong bodies on the grounds of the American Embassy in Saigon during the Tet Offensive, January 1968.

PAUL HEALEY

Private 1st Class
716th Military Police Battalion
U.S. Army

PAUL HEALEY
MILITARY POLICE
U.S. ARMY

After one year in South Vietnam with the 101st Airborne Division, Paul Healey decided to stay on for an additional six months as an MP in Saigon. January 31, 1968, was to be the day he rotated back to the United States. Healey had a four-hour shift January 30 as a courtesy to his last day on the job. A short shift usually meant a quiet shift. Everyone, including Healey, believed he was going home on schedule. Little did anyone know. Healey later said, "The first day of the Tet Offensive was my last day in country." His last shift began midnight on January 30. It was very quiet night. Healey went for a sandwich and brought one back for the MP working the desk.

Paul Healey

Paul Healey

His father a truck driver, his mother a housewife, the oldest of five children, Healey graduated from high school in 1965 and joined the army in January 1966. After serving a tour in the 101st Airborne, he extended his stay in Vietnam in the military police. Only hours before being sent home, the Tet Offensive started and he, along with other MPs in Saigon, saw heavy fighting. After the army he became the youngest person in history to join the Boston Police. He retired ten years later, received his U.S. Coast Guard captain's license, and formed a yacht charter company. Currently he is captain of a 110-foot motor yacht in South Florida.

And the calls started coming over the radio while I was standing there. There were four or five calls. People screaming. Gunfire. We responded. We got sent to the Philippine embassy and as we pulled up there the lights were off. There was one guy behind a tree. It was a Viet Cong. You could see it was. And I shot him and took the handgun he had stuck in his belt.

Then I got sent to the American embassy. We pulled up. There were already four military policemen killed. Two in the jeep out front and two were on the side of the building. Both guys were dead. The guy I worked with, guy I was on patrol the day before—they killed him outright. He just didn't have a chance. I was the first person there that was alive. I was probably the only guy in the unit that had any in-country training as far as weapons and had been in actual combat. We decided to wait until the sun come up because we couldn't see what was inside. We saw the hole that they had blown in. The reports we were getting were that there was a bunch of them inside. We had no idea how many.

The sun came up. We made a decision. We decided how to get in. Only way in was through the gate. The gate was locked. We tried cross-firing from both sides of the gate. I drove the jeep. Tried to jam the jeep but the gates opened out so we couldn't break the gates down. I went up with a .45. Six shots blew the lock off, took the thing off, and pulled the gate back. I stood on top of the jeep and I was firing. It was a ten foot wall. I was on my toes firing over the wall. There were people behind like flowerpots. I went to the first tree, to the second tree and then I ran for the front door, cherry-wood doors. And it wouldn't open. There was a Marine inside, and I'm yelling at him trying to find out what's going on, "Is there anybody inside?" And he was scared to death and he said, "They're not inside." He wouldn't open the door. At the same time I felt something against my leg and it was a grenade. It was a VC I thought I had killed about four times from outside. He was lying behind like a flowerpot and he had rolled over and tossed up a Chinese Communist grenade, the stick with the grenade on the end of it. Hit my leg and dropped. And I just somehow jumped behind him. I got a piece of shrapnel in my hand. He took the brunt of the explosion.

I didn't have any idea of the layout, so it was just one step at a time. There was three or four guys behind me, sergeant right beside me. We looked around. One guy came around the corner of the embassy after we entered the front door. I was working my way around the side and I had like three bullets left in my gun. And I'm yelling for ammunition. And I yell, "The next person that comes in without ammunition, I'm going to shoot him." There wasn't any. One of the guys brought in some more. A guy had walked around the corner and I was up on a three-foot platform, and he had come from below and it was a shock. Just me and him, face to face. And I just fired and I killed him. Then reloaded. The two VC had just come from around the corner. There's a good chance there's somebody else there, so I threw a grenade and the grenade exploded. There were three bodies there when we went around the corner. You know, I was very, very lucky. Things just went my way that day. I had a flak jacket on, and I had lost my helmet some place coming around the building. And I'm carrying an M16 and the .45 on and I had the .38 stuck in my belt. I looked like a cowboy, I think.

We have this one corner to check. There's a pair of bloody sandals. One pair of bloody sandals outside the back door in the bushes. American's don't wear sandals, so it was Vietnamese. We yelled, "Military police!" and there's a man upstairs on the second floor, George Jacobson. He's the mission coordinator, the third person in charge of the civilian part of the government. He yelled down that there's somebody downstairs. So we stepped back. The Viet Cong was in a pantry-type kitchen, and he just started firing. Put his gun out and started firing in our direction. We ducked and we didn't get hit. We had no way to get him out. We worked our way around the building to the opposite side to a set of doors. We popped the doors, and myself and a Marine went in side by side and I'm left-handed and he's right-handed, so I was on the left, he was on the right. We started in step so when my left foot went down, I'd fire up. When his right foot went down, he'd fire. We'd go in and just keep firing. But we get halfway into the room and the VC stuck his arm out, fired, caught the Marine in the groin. If I was on the right I would have got it. I grabbed him, and he kept firing and pulled him back out again. He was hurt pretty bad. Then called for tear gas. Tried to get some tear gas in. We started throwing grenades. We threw about four grenades in there. We rolled them down to the area he was in but we didn't get him.

I realized Jacobson didn't have anything. I went out and took my .45, and I threw it up to him. Took about ten throws to get it up to him, and then I threw two magazines of ammunition. And then I got a gas mask for him to tell him we're throwing gas. Then we broke the windows on three sides of the house and threw the gas in. And that forced the last guy, a big Vietnamese about six-foot tall, up the stairs. When he got to the top of the stairs, George Jacobson killed him. And he wouldn't give my gun back. He kept it. He said it saved his life.

Earlier at the embassy while we were trying to ascertain what's going on, a big black old thirties-type car, a big black limousine-ish car came speeding down the street with no headlights on. We yelled for it to stop. And it didn't stop. He drove through the checkpoint, and we just riddled the car with automatic weapons. It went off the side of the road. Then afterwards what they suspected was he was the driver of these nineteen because we had nineteen bodies. Nineteen were inside the embassy, and this guy was the driver, supposedly to pick them up, but he never picked them up.

This Marine is left-handed. Unlike many combat weapons, the M16 is ambidexterous.

Six and half hours later we've got the embassy back. Looking at it afterwards, the whole world was looking. My mother was watching TV, you know. They're watching Huntley-Brinkley and here I am on the TV and she's at home. She was pretty shook up about it. Right after the embassy they were doing pictures and stories and the public information officer was bringing me to *Time* and *Newsweek* and *Life*. I just wanted to go and go back and do some fighting. See, everything wasn't over. It was like you know this is secure. So let's go to another situation. You do what has to be done and then you figure it out afterwards. You always respond to the situation. Just go and you do it, and then you pay for it afterwards, if you're lucky enough to.

LEN WUNDERLICH

Major, Operations Officer
1st Battalion, 5th Marines
U.S. Marine Corps

Len Wunderlich and his battalion were based fifteen miles south of Phu Bai and were under constant attack before the Tet Offensive. Most of their work was along Route One, the major highway north and south, in South Vietnam. His unit came under constant mortar fire before January 31, 1968. Then he and his men had direct contact with the North Vietnamese at Hué.

Len Wunderlich

U.S. Marines on the move heading into combat.

Although the higher authorities indicated that they were aware that something was about to start, they certainly hadn't communicated that to us. And so it was a complete surprise to the units in the field. Just all of sudden, you know, regardless of where you were or what you were doing at that particular minute it was a lot of enemy incoming from unknown positions. Our reaction was to return fire on suspected mortar positions and other enemy locations. A lot of activity involved identifying casualties and getting them ready for evacuation. It was dark and scary and all of those other things.

There weren't any U.S. forces in the Citadel at that stage. We received our orders to go into the Citadel and consolidate the position in the vicinity of the 1st ARVN Division. We got there by landing craft utility vehicles up the Perfume River, off-loaded and then we marched in. We had some difficulty getting them to open the gates because they weren't really sure who we were. And apparently nobody communicated to them that we were coming.

It was a heavy urban area. The streets were narrow, but the buildings were all something new to those of us who had been out in the field. They were all concrete buildings and there were an awful lot of enemy located in those buildings, so they were difficult to get out. There was an awful lot of contact and there were an awful lot of casualties during that first initial confrontation. And that created some significant problems. Commanders were wounded or killed, and new people had to be assigned to take over. It was a very harrowing experience, although the issue was not in doubt at any time. We always knew that we were going to win that fight but we just didn't know when. We had a lot of casualties but you couldn't dwell on it. Some people just continued to fight for days on end, even though they had minor wounds.

The Marines in the front lines went house to house and it was very slow. Progress was really measured in feet on some days, and some days there wasn't any progress. We were talking about maybe moving eight hundred to a thousand yards. That's all we had to do to get to the wall position. But it was just foot by foot, yard by yard. We had a serious resupply problem because the only way into the Citadel was the way we had come in. The Citadel itself was surrounded by a wall that was concrete and filled with dirt and it was probably thirty or forty feet high and thirty feet wide. The NVA had dug back under that wall and had an awful lot of protection from our supporting arms. The weather was really bad, and so the helicopters were having difficulty flying although we were able to evacuate most of the wounded. We didn't get a lot of resupply. It took time to develop that.

Most of the time while we were in the Citadel we probably were no more than 50 percent combat strength. Because we had been in contact with the enemy for two or three weeks before that we had suffered casualties in those engagements, too. So the companies were small. They may have been sixty or seventy people in them, where normally we would have liked to have had around two hundred people.

Len Wunderlich

Wunderlich was born and raised in Idaho and gradu ated from the University of Idaho. He was commis sioned a 2nd lieutenant in the Marine Corps in the summer of 1958, and nine years later was in Vietnam as a major and operations officer during the Tet Of fensive in Hué. He later served in infantry com mand positions with the First and Second Marine Divisions, and commanded the Marine Barracks in Panama. After twenty-nine years in the service, he re tired as a colonel in 1987 and since then has owned and operated an insurance company in Southern Cali fornia.

1st Battalion, 5th Marines, making a sweep along Highway #1.

The thing that stands out in my mind, more than anything—there were many, many heroes. Some of them recognized. Some of them probably never received the appreciation or thanks they deserved for the job they did. You certainly have to admire the Marine Private 1st Class and the Lance Corporal who was there on the front lines under fire twenty-four hours a day. Everybody rose to the occasion because there wasn't any other alternative. It was not anything that anybody had experienced before, and Marines have a way of rising to those occasions when the going gets tough. They have for many years, and they will in the future, too. I think we're pretty good.

TOM MITCHELL

Corporal
Delta Company 1st Battalion
5th Marines
U.S. Marine Corps

By January 1968, Tom Mitchell had been in Vietnam for seven months. He had just returned from R&R in Australia. Stationed near Da Nang, his unit roamed a horseshoe-like area that ended just north of the Hai Van Pass. There to secure the rail link between Da Nang and Hué, they provided security for convoys that traveled along Highway One. Until the Tet Offensive, Mitchell saw mostly small unit action and light skirmishes.

Tom Mitchell

Tom Mitchell

Mitchell enlisted in the Marine Corps in 1966 and arrived in Vietnam as a corporal in 1967. Promoted to sergeant in 1968, he received a battlefield commission as 2nd lieutenant. He served as a machine gunner, platoon sergeant, and platoon leader. His major operations included the battle for Hué during the Tet Offensive. The Silver Star is among his many commendations. After more than twenty-three years, Mitchell retired from the Marine Corps as a major and went into private business.

As we started to move forward, we got hit heavily outside a church area, just at the main entrance to the split between old Hué and new Hué, and started clearing houses. And that's when we found out there was a lot more of them than there were of us. We knew we were in for it because it was a combination of NVA regulars along with Viet Cong. The fighting started, and we started losing a lot of casualties. Normally we were bush fighters. We never really saw the enemy. Very few times, unless we were being overrun or it was a major battle. And that's about the time that we found out that people that came from the cities, like Chicago and New York, knew how to fight in cities. They knew about alleys, and underground passages, and walls and how to get into houses, how to get out of them, especially on rooftops. Whereas a lot of people had not been used to it, it was a major change for us. Even though we'd had training in the Marine Corps about house-to-house fighting, it was nothing compared to what we were actually going into. As we started learning how to street fight, we would clear a series of streets, and the next thing we'd know the enemy would pop up behind us, and we just started losing a lot of people. I know in our company, in the first five or six days, we probably had about fifty killed and one hundred fifty wounded. The odds just aren't in your favor, and yet we constantly were able to pull through with good fire discipline, fire control, and controlling fear. A lot of us figured we were dead, anyway. When you get into that situation, you're not sure you're going to go home. In the bush, you know you had chances. Here, you're actually face to face with the enemy. I had experience in not only hand to hand, but facing the enemy very close. It was hard to ensure that your people had the confidence in themselves that they could take care of what they were doing and keep it up. It's an experience that's very hard to describe to people because you have to live it, to feel it.

Kit Carson Scout Pham-Duoc (left) tells Lance Coporal R.D. Kiluer (center) and Corporal P.F. Collins (right) the location of suspected enemy installations near Hill 65, some 20 miles south of Da Nang. Pham-Duoc, age 22, served with U.S. Marine Corps units for more than five months, providing intelligence information to operations and patrols.

As we got into Hué, we were finding out we were having difficulties figuring out where everything was because we had no really good maps. So we would actually go into Esso stations, gas stations, and steal their street maps so we could actually coordinate what we were doing. There were periods of time that you could close your eyes, pull a trigger and kill somebody. There were that many enemy. You could see them running around. Many times you could actually smell pot, marijuana, and things floating across when they were getting ready for their attacks just a street across from you. The difficulties that we really had in the house to house was sometimes you'd run into hand-to-hand combat. And when you're trying to wield weapons, especially the M16s, which we only had a few months, there was no punching power to get in. So a lot of us started stealing shotguns, especially from the army, and we'd use the shotguns because of the wider perimeter going in, so that we could assure that when we fired it into a building, that we could clear it out, keep the enemies' head pinned down until we got in. There was also a lot of conscripted people that had been chained to their machine-gun nests so they couldn't run. So they had to shoot. They were chained to the "spider nests" in the buildings. Was it just on purpose that they were chained by the higher command or some of them did it for themselves to fight through whatever was actually going to happen? And they were very difficult to take out. So that as one group would penetrate, someone who actually could, would swing behind you, and they would start shooting at you from the rear and you would be caught in a cross fire. And you'd have to fight your way back out.

As we got into the Citadel wall, we found out that not only was it twenty feet high, but they had these towers along the wall. They had machine-gun nests and recoilless rifles that were stitched inside. And you had to take the towers because the towers controlled everything up and down the actual area itself. And each of the towers had ramps and it was almost like watching the old Norse movies, or "55 Days at Peking," when they were running up and down the ramps, trying to take the towers.

Our biggest concern as we got in was trying to get the dead and wounded. It was a constant battle, and a lot of time our own mortar fire would hit the top of a building, just because the building was in the way, and would shower down on top of us. We had people that didn't even get hit with a bullet, but the bullets would chip into the buildings so bad they'd send the concrete from the buildings in and that's what would penetrate their bodies and cause wounds. We used to say every time you got in a combat scrape is, you know, a combat loss. That's how you got rid of all your supply problems. Everything they were looking for at the time, you'd write it off and say, "Well, we lost it at this time." In a way it was easy to write off a lot of combat loss about all the sins that you'd have for people just throwing packs away or forgetting them or not knowing where they're at. People were still carrying some things that they wound up losing. I'd lost a lot of pictures, a camera. My pack was sitting off to the side and got blown up when they hit us.

It's very difficult to ask somebody to go into harm's way, to be shot at. Yet I don't think there was a reluctance on anyone's part. There's a very unique tightness in the Marine Corps family, especially in the infantry for those that have been in battle. My biggest concern were new people. We didn't know them. We didn't know if we could trust them. Each of us that was still alive knew how to react to each other. We knew what we were supposed to do. You knew who you could count on and new people have a tendency to draw your attention away, trying to protect them, to make sure they're doing the right thing. And it's very hard to concentrate on what you're doing. Usually we place them in positions where they're under other people. You very rarely slept. Catnaps. We call them power naps. Thirty minutes here, twenty minutes here. Especially at night. You never knew who was crawling through, who was coming after you.

In my platoon, I had a total of eight that started at the very beginning of Hué, and we did get several back that were wounded, came back and joined us after Hue itself. We worry about post-effects because of the bad water. When you'd have deaths and blood and terrible weather, you worry about malaria, dysentery. You wonder what you're eating, and you just go hungry sometimes. We had a lot of bodies in the river. Wells were contaminated. One of the things that our corpsmen and doctors had passed on to us to watch out for dogs and animals, because of rabies, eating the dead. And we had to shoot several dogs that were foaming at the mouth. The one thing you never wanted to run out of is ammunition. We had plenty for our rifles. We started to run out of water. That was one of the key concerns that we had. Matter of fact, we actually cleared a lot of stores. Hands Across the Sea store, liquor store, buildings and different things. We started trading cases of beer and booze for water because we couldn't get enough water.

The NVA had a particular mission. They were very disciplined. I think they were like us. They were very tenacious. It was sort of a professional group. Once they were committed to a plan, they stuck to that plan. They didn't have the ability that we had in changing or adapting to the environment. When a skirmish would occur and it was not going the way that they had mapped out, they would be very confused. But they were strong. They weren't tiny, little people. They looked like they were well fed, very experienced. They were able to work in teams very well.

We had refugees streaming through and passing us the entire time we're fighting. It was very difficult. You were trying to screen them because you never knew who was going to be in what we called "no-fire" areas where you would get shot at and where you couldn't return fire. Most of them were coming in waves, streaming out, taking everything they could carry. We knew there was a lot of infiltration occurring at that time. Some of the NVA were probably late in getting to where they were supposed to get and used the refugees for cover. But how do you tell? I mean, it's not stamped on anyone's forehead. We just wanted them to stay away from us. In

A member of the 35th Ranger's scurries across a Cholon street exposed to Viet Cong fire.

the only other areas that we saw a lot of civilians is where we know they looked like they had been assassinated. I remember running across some graves where the North Vietnamese had killed a bunch of civilians, and they'd thrown lime and just dug up graves and shot people and threw them inside. People were lined up and they were just shot when the city was first taken over. The graves were very difficult to look at. We had come across several other civilians that had been killed where we lost ground, and some NVA and Viet Cong had cut off their genitals and had marked up their bodies. A lot of times we had our own people thinking about it, but we never really got to that position. I don't think we'd stoop to that level. We could also see where a lot of the North Vietnamese that had been killed were dragged back, and they were tossed into the large areas and lime was put over them and then hastily covered up. They usually tried to recover their dead as quickly as possible but as we moved forward, we started moving too fast, and they couldn't do it.

As we continued to fight we started to actually break them. Once we were actually starting to penetrate, we knew that they were starting to leave the area. You could start seeing signs. We fought all the way to the Citadel itself and actually broke across the tower. Heavy resistance as we were fighting in there. Then we had the Citadel itself and I went up to get the Citadel flag. The flag was actually flying off the top of the tower. It was an NVA flag. We were finally breaching it. Our platoon moved forward. I said I was going to get the flag. Resistance started backing off. They had a bunch of snipers in the area, but we could tell they had started to back out of the Citadel. So we just stormed up the top, yanked down the flag, and we threw up an American flag. I packed up the NVA flag and threw it in my pack and said it's staying with me. Too many people were killed trying to get that darn thing, because we could see it for several days just looking down the street when we could only move inches.

We were halfway through and almost had it cleared out and we were told to back off. The South Vietnamese were going to come in and sweep through our lines, and they were going to be the ones clearing the actual Citadel. So that occurred, and then we were pulled out, and we went on mop-up operations, sweeping out in certain areas to clear up or chase them. Twenty-eight continuous days of fighting was very unusual in Vietnam. When you take a look at the people that survived or actually came out of there, that was an insult.

DALE HATTEN

Gunnery Sergeant
81st Mortar Platoon
1st Battalion, 5th Marines
U.S. Marine Corps

No photo available

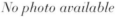

Dale Hatten had been a drill instructor in the Marine Corps for thirteen years before he arrived in Vietnam in April 1967. He commanded ninety men in an 81mm mortar platoon that increasingly found itself in heavy combat in I Corps. But he also recalls an incident that was as frightening as combat.

It was one of these political holidays. I had left Tam Ky and was going to be delivered out to this Hill 57, I believe it was, the 5th Marine Headquarters. The guy that was driving me missed the turn-off and we went down the road, and I about fell over because here was this checkpoint and here was two NVAs sitting there in their gray suits with their pith helmets on, you know. And we turned around and made a big U-turn, and they were just as shocked as we were. We turned around and drove back again. We could have very easily been POWs or been dead. It had not been one of these "supposed-don't-shoot-holiday" things that was on there. And, so when I got back, you know, I said, "For crying out loud, these guys are right down the road." That was a real close call for me. I had seen the NVA there up close and like this, but the majority of the time you saw them after the damage was done and the results of whatever you did.

When the Battle for Hué began, Hatten and his men provided weapons support for Marine infantry trying to reach the Citadel.

We entered the Citadel area. And we set the platoon up in an open area. The back wall of the Citadel was just right to the rear of where the platoon was, and we looked down through the city from that point. We immediately started taking sniper fire from the higher elevations of the city. The total distance, amazingly, was like no more than four, five thousand yards from one end of the Citadel to the other. The concern was how do we get these guys to realize that they've been out in the jungle, running Indian fashion one after the other. We had to tell them, "Hey, you have to cross these roads in squad rushes and little groups of people." But there wasn't enough time to sit down and really get this across to make them realize that this is going to a different game than what you had before. Almost immediately it was just a knock-down, drag-out. I can't describe the amazement at the amount of fire power and everything during the Vietnam War. We tried to fire out at least one hundred yards in front of the men. But they were engaged house-to-house. So we learned the hard way. So we put delay fuses on the first set of eight or twelve rounds, and these would go down to the first floor and make contact and detonate, which would loosen the roof up.

And during this time, there was always this fact that, Jimminy Christmas, we're firing this barrage of rounds and here we got our own people just close, you know. It was one of the most trying times of my Marine Corps career, because I knew that there had to be occasions when we're going to be so close that we could actually

An M48 tank in position at the 2nd Battalion, 4th Marines command post.

hurt our own folks. We had a lot of casualties. I do know when Delta Company came out, I think they had twenty-one left. I think he went in there with eighty or ninety and he came out with twenty-one guys. They were walking. I asked at the time, "I hope we didn't hurt anybody." And I think they told me, "Just a few." So I didn't get out of it clean. I'm sure that there was some that was hurt with our fire. We really had no choice.

We fired, Jimminy Christmas, thousands of rounds. I think like eleven thousand rounds during the course of that time out of this one little platoon. I'm not even sure that during World War II if there was ever a platoon that fired that kind of fire. By midway through, the platoon was as good as you'll ever get. I mean, they could put a hundred rounds airborne in no time at all. We didn't have time to sleep because they just went night and day. It was amazing at night because our forward observers would call in, and they'd be whispering over the radio and they were whispering because the NVA would be just yards away from them. And they'd call in a mortar barrage onto the street. And twice during the battle I know they interviewed NVA people that they had captured. Both times they came back and told us that mortars gave the biggest fear and the most trouble. Both times they said mortars. They said it just rained mortar shells.

These NVA guys were dedicated. They had their flag hanging over the Citadel and they weren't about to give it up. It was really as bad as World War II. You had to exterminate them step by step. Give them all the credit. They were a very professional fighting force and a lot of times I think we underestimated their ability to turn around and stand tough and engage you man to man, because they did. We knew that they were inside there. We never dreamed that they were in there in the magnitude that they were and that they weren't going to try to get out. They were going to stand and fight. When it got all through, we devastated the city itself and their historical sights.

While not appropriate for jungle warfare, M48 tanks were useful in the recapture of Hué City after the Tet Offensive. These tanks are in a ditch next to the University of Hué during Operation Hué City.

In Vietnam, there was more individual hand-to-hand and close combat. You had to let us get real close because if they fired too soon, we'd just back off and dump the world on them, and they'd be done for. The guys knew that they had to wait till the last minute to fire, and these young guys, they did participate, on a personal basis in Hué and they definitely was involved where they went and engaged the enemy at very, very close quarters and where they could actually see them eyeball to eyeball, so to speak.

I knew that in the end this was a battle that was going to be recorded in history, one of the biggest the Marine Corps had ever fought. The end result was that the resolve of a bunch of young kids and the professional leadership kind of made the difference. These are the guys that have to close with the enemy and actually take the ground and hold the ground and make life-and-death decisions every minute. I never realized what we really ask of kids seventeen, eighteen years old to go and do in combat. It's amazing what they did and how they did it and when they did it. We knew how to fire the blocking fire that allow them to move one house or two houses, and then very quickly let them go into that street and block off the other side where the enemy couldn't turn around and see them. The other side, they started to wilt once they started to take casualties and everything.

Finally, the big final firing when we had them backed into one corner and everybody just cut loose, 105s, and all of us, you know. We fired a tremendous mortar mission down on them there. So the end result of that was the city was finally was ours. Then we packed up that very next day and went out on a sweep to the north of the city out there and continued to move. And it was another time of your time that you had to spend in Nam.

JAMES GALLAGHER

Captain, Company Commander
Delta Company, 1st Battalion, 1st Marines
U.S. Marine Corps

James Gallagher

Jim Gallagher had been in Vietnam since June of 1966, a long-timer, someone who knew the country and the people better than most. Near Hué, immediately before the Tet Offensive kicked in, Gallagher had his suspicions that all was not well in his area of operations.

I remember distinctly the road as we went through this main part of town which linked up with Highway One, which would go ultimately to our destination, which was Phu Bai. There were a number of bazaars and open-air markets and all the people were out. It was a beautiful day. It had rained previously, and it was crisp and clear and the sun was shining. We went through there about three in the afternoon. I remember seeing a number of men that were in the crowd that as I looked them right in the eye, they would look me in the eye and I could see sort of a glint of hatred for me. I didn't see that among the civilians. Even if they disliked us for whatever reason, you didn't see that deep-seated hatred. There was a steel-like look from one after another as I went down the road looking at the people in the bazaar. While we were going into the truce period, still again, I was wary as I always was all through the time I was there. It was sort of a premonition, if you will. I had this feeling that, gosh, what's wrong with this picture? We went back to Phu Bai and went to bed. When I did hear about what happened during the night, about two in the morning, I was honestly not surprised because this was something I was sure was going to happen sooner or later.

When looking at Hué City, we were really looking at a city that had been spared the ravages of war, not only with the French but also through the period with the Americans over there. And that first night when I went through the city, I was taken with the beauty of the city. It was a magnificent place. It exuded culture. It had the French influence. There were a number of Catholic churches in Hué. I remember one of the buildings that we had to attack was the Joan of Arc School. It was a girls' school. I remember going through the school and seeing their desks and their papers and their work. Even though some of the walls were blown out, interestingly the school desks sat like ordered rows, as if somehow it was spared all the armaments that were used against the building walls, blowing out windows and the masonry around the windows where the enemy was shooting back at us. Nonetheless, the building itself survived and the desks were lined up like the students were going to come in that day.

It was sort of spooky, especially going through. I went through myself because being a Catholic, there was a certain mixed feeling of having to be the instrument to destroy this and seeing some of the very culture that I went through having gone to Catholic school. I recognized some of the implements of learning that these children had that I had. And it was with a certain amount of sadness that I had to do this. The Mother Superior was in the Hué University along with all the other refugees. And I made a trip to see her. They were carrying out about five to six, seven people a day with cholera and they were dying, of course. They were being carried out dead in the university area. And there was human feces all around the open area. It was really a scene of deprivation, not because the people were deprived, but because of the dire straits that everyone found themselves in because of the war. I went up to the Mother Superior and she was there in one of the rooms and I said how sad I was to have been a party to the destruction of this school. And I remember her saying that those things happen in life and she told me not to worry about it, that Hué would be rebuilt afterwards. And she was sitting there perfectly sublime, as if she was somewhat detached from all the horrors of war that were going on around her.

For some of us in some ways it was like being in combat while at the same time having nice accommodations because essentially you were indoors at night. You didn't have to live in the field in the same sense where it's pouring rain, as it was during almost that whole month of February. At least you had a roof over your head. There were fireplaces in some of the buildings to provide heat. There were heating devices and pots and stoves and so forth that provided heat.

What made it unnerving for me was the devastation of the buildings as we battled over the ground through the city. And also the sense of death that happened to the city. It was almost like there was no one out on the street. You would look out or walk out onto the street at different times. You had to be very careful because sometimes there would be a sniper in one of the buildings across the way or some distance away. So it was very easy to see anyone. You looked down the street and there was no one. Not a soul. You look around the city that I saw the day before the Tet Offensive, and I could also like flash

Aerial view of Market street and waterfront, Da Nang.

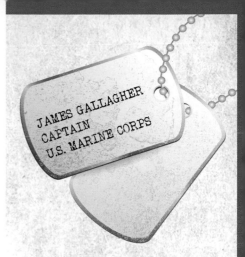

James Gallagher

Gallagher enlisted in the Marine Corps in June 1962. He was a company commander in Vietnam when wounded by shrapnel in his back in June 1967. He fought in Hué in 1968 during the Tet Offensive and he received the Legion of Merit with the Combat V and the Bronze Star, also with the Combat V. He retired as a lieutenant colonel in 1986. Married and the father of four children, today he teaches seventh and eighth grades.

back and forth between what I saw then and what I saw later. It was an interesting juxtaposition because you saw it was teeming with life. This pastel-colored city bathed in sunlight and then the rain, and then the destroyed buildings, and then no one seemingly alive in the city. The absolute quiet. Not a sound in the whole city. That part was unnerving. It's quite a bit different than when you're out in the field, and you're actually fighting among the vegetation. There's a sense of life still there in the trees and in the flowers and so forth. If you were in France in World War One, it would be different. But not in Vietnam.

In combat the enemy is somewhat of an abstraction because generally if you see the enemy up close, something has gone wrong. Either they have gotten too close to you and your means to defend yourself have somehow been breached. So it is something that while I was there, I always tried to make sure didn't happen by being vigilant, by using good tactics. In Hué I did see a squad of North Vietnamese Army personnel run across the street and actually saw them in plain view. That was the first and only time I had seen them. The NVA did have a supply route that came through their own territory, and they were masters not only of supplying themselves surreptitiously, but they were also masters of hoarding their supplies in places that couldn't be found or were difficult to find. And then going to those supplies at the time they needed them. They were also very good at hiding themselves because they realized that in a toe-to-toe battle with the United States, they would come out on the short end of it. They were hit and run, and when they hit and stayed, they took some very serious loses. I think that overall they found that that was not a winning combination.

There have been some questions as to whether we should have been there. But of the men and women who went to Vietnam, they went because they thought it was the right thing to do. I still do think it was the right thing to do—at the time to defeat the Communist's very concerted effort to conquer the world may seem strange today, thirty years later. Thirty years ago that was not a pie-in-the-sky notion. All of them and all of us came and served the best we thought how. And I think, all things considered, we can feel that we did honorable service—performed honorable service.

ARVN soldiers peering around a corner during house to house fighting.

FOOD IN VIETNAM

We know what American troops carried into to combat. We know the weapons with which they fought, and the clothing they wore in mostly inhospitable terrain and climate. Despite the heat, humidity, rain, mud, the strange flora and fauna they faced every day, the American soldier and Marine had to eat as best he could to stay as healthy as possible under terrible conditions. What they ate, how they ate, especially in the field either searching for the enemy or fighting, is an important part of the life they led in Vietnam.

In past wars, at least until World War I, combatants on all sides lived off the land. The Viet Cong and North Vietnamese regulars did the same. It was easier for them to do so than to depend on very long supply lines when they had a greater need for ammunition and military equipment. Food was always available to America's enemy in the villages they either controlled or terrorized. And in the current fight

Private 1st Class Bohringer, Bravo Battery, 1st Battalion, 13th Regiment sets up house with stove made of C-ration cans.

Adding coffee to the water.

Cpl L.F. George digs into an extra can of fruit cocktail.

Marine cooks for himself and members of his team.

against terrorist organizations in the 21st century, America's enemies still survive by taking what they can from the countryside and cities they control or want to control.

However, the Pentagon wanted its troops in the field to have meals that would satisfy, if nothing else, their hunger. Commanders in the Department of Defense wanted the fighting man to have the best possible nutrition to sustain him on his dangerous mission. But what the troops had to eat, though offering all the necessary vitamins, proteins, starch and minerals, did not always taste good. Less than perfect, it filled a need, but not much more than that. Sustenance was more important than satisfying the troop's taste buds. After a long day humping in the field any food was necessary, even it only adequate, when a soldier was tried and hungry. Troops wondered if anyone in the Pentagon ever had the pleasure of eating a week's worth of C-rations. Scratch a soldier from the Vietnam War and he will probably tell you the food was usually awful. In fast food restaurants, in drive-ins, diners, and roadside joints back home the grub was far better than what soldiers got to eat, most of the time, in South Vietnam.

Soldiers had to eat when in the field on a mission. But what they ate had to be simple, easy to access, and to prepare. Freeze dried, vacuum packed and dehydrated, the soldier ate most of his meals cold. Based on the C-ration concept from World War II, the original premise was to provide each soldier with one canned item, one precooked item, and one prepared wet ration. That custom continued into Vietnam. Forever called C-rations by the troops, but technically called Meals, Combat, Individual, or MCI, there were twelve different menus based on feeding a soldier three meals a day. Each meal had approximately 1200 calories with the daily ration of three meals working out to about 3600 calories for the day, considered enough nutrition to sustain a man in a combat zone. A package of meals weighed about 2.6 pounds. There were four can openers for each case of 12 meals. A man had one spoon for each meal kit.

Each menu had a canned meat item or combinations such as ham and eggs, BBQ beef, beans and Frankfurters in tomato sauce called "Beanie Weenies," ham and lima beans, beefsteak and potatoes, chicken or turkey loaf, chopped ham and eggs and spaghetti and meatballs. There were various cheeses including one with pimento and cheddar cheese as a separate offering. The meals also offered fruit salad, peaches, pears, pecan rolls, fruitcake, pound cake, various jellies and jam spreads, peanut butter, biscuits, and two pieces of chocolate. Only white bread was available throughout the duration of the war.

A kit contained an accessory packet with cigarettes, matches, chewing gum, toilet paper, coffee, cream, sugar, and salt. When helicopters or trucks could not bring in potable water, troops used iodine tablets to purify water collected from jungle rivers or mountain streams. Heating tablets in a canteen cup sometimes used as a portable stove warmed the food and allowed soldiers to create their own recipes even in the jungle, in a rice paddy, or the hills of the Central Highlands. Ever resourceful, Army and Marine soldiers learned to improvise with the food they had on hand. Grilled cheese and ham sandwiches were a seemingly universal favorite. Cooked in the always-useful canteen cup, they would mix a mess of cheese,

Marines enjoy some hot chow in the field.

Two hungry Leathernecks of the 1st Battalion, 9th Marines, exchange C-rations before digging in for the night, during their unit's sweep of a Mekong Delta area on Operation Deckhouse 5.

The tropical climate of Vietnam provided additional foods and drink for soldiers.

Crates of food, awaiting distribution.

the ham, and the white bread and get a fair approximation of an American favorite, the grilled cheese sandwich. It usually beat the monotony of eating ham and lima beans. (With thanks to the website, Charlie Company Vietnam, 1966-1972.)

If a squad had any luck, perseverance, or knew a quartermaster, it might find itself in possession of LRRP (Long Range Reconnaissance Patrol) rations, the high end of the U.S military's prepared food packages. These patrols were often secret and dangerous, sending the men on missions into North Vietnam, Cambodia and Laos. Better made, the soldier only had to add water and heat the packet for fairly satisfying meals, at least under dangerous conditions. Though the meals were better than C-rations, they too, were less than perfect.

Cooking in a mess hall behind the lines, not directly in a combat zone, or at a firebase close to the action usually provided better fare than the meal packages assigned to each soldier. Some mess halls were homey and, under the circumstances, comfortable. Others had a plain pipe rack look where the cooks made do as best as possible. Though C-rations might be on the menu for breakfast and lunch, the evening meal was usually hot and, considering the situation, not bad, at least in the eyes of many of the troops. Certainly those meals were better than the boxed meals the men had to eat when on patrol. If lucky, men might get a mess hall breakfast of eggs, sausage, pancakes, toast, juice, and coffee. For dinner, soldiers might get roast beef, mashed potatoes, thick gravy made with flour, and a vegetable, usually from a can. Sometime hamburgers and pork in some form or other might be on the menu. All told not a bad eating experience, especially when budding chefs dabbled in making pies, cakes and cookies, always welcomed by troops far from home.

The best mess halls were on the big Navy ships at sea, watching the coast for enemy movements and shelling targets when called on to do so. Served three hot meals a day, the men in the Navy ate better than their counterparts on land, though they, too, complained about the food, which was normal

and persistent for all troops. Air Force men based in Guam, and in Thailand at Udorn, Korat and Utapo, among others, also ate better than their fellows on the South Vietnam mainland. They had real food in real mess halls often making a big difference in lives lived on the edge.

Historically, even in a war zone, America makes sure that its troops get special attention on holidays such as Christmas and Thanksgiving. In the last century it happened in World War II, Korea, and of course, in the Vietnam War. On those special days in almost every situation, the troops had hot meals of turkey, baked ham, stuffing, sweet potatoes, mashed potatoes, hot apple pies, pecan and pumpkin pies and every other trimming imaginable. For a moment the men in the field could eat favorite foods and forget about the war they were fighting.

Marines of 2nd Battalion, 1st Marine Regiment receiving hot chow at Con Thien. The larger the base, the better the amenities.

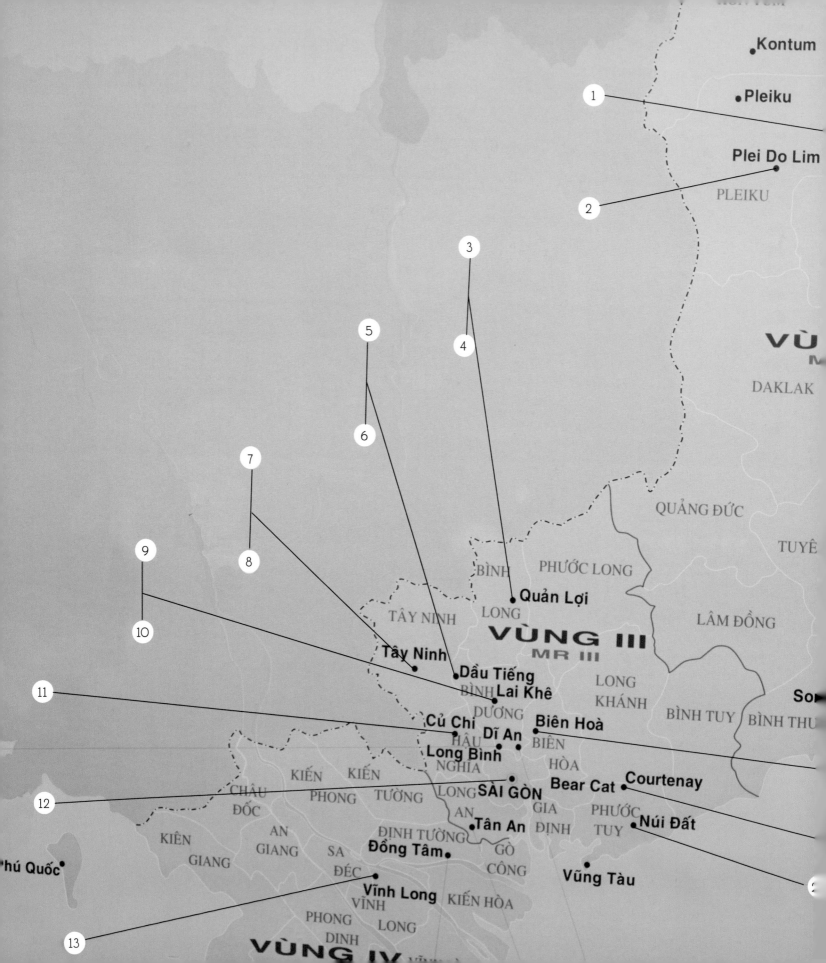

Kontum

Pleiku

1

Plei Do Lim

2

PLEIKU

3

VÙ

M

5

DAKLAK

4

6

QUẢNG ĐỨC

7

TUYÊ

9

BÌNH   PHƯỚC LONG

LÂM ĐỒNG

8

TÂY NINH   LONG   Quản Lợi

10

VÙNG III

So

MR III

LONG
KHÁNH   BÌNH TUY BÌNH THU

Tây Ninh   Dầu Tiếng

BÌNH Lai Khê

11

DƯƠNG   Biên Hoà

Củ Chi   Dĩ An

HẬU   BIÊN

Long Bình   HÒA

KIẾN   KIẾN

Bear Cat   Courtenay

CHÂU   PHONG   TƯỜNG   LONG SÀI GÒN

12

GIA   PHƯỚC

ĐỐC   AN   Tân An   ĐỊNH   TUY   Núi Đất

KIÊN   AN

GIANG   ĐỊNH TƯỜNG   GÒ

GIANG   SA   Đồng Tâm   CÔNG

'hú Quốc   ĐÉC   Vũng Tàu   E

Vĩnh Long   KIẾN HÒA

VĨNH

PHONG   LONG

13   ĐỊNH

VÙNG IV

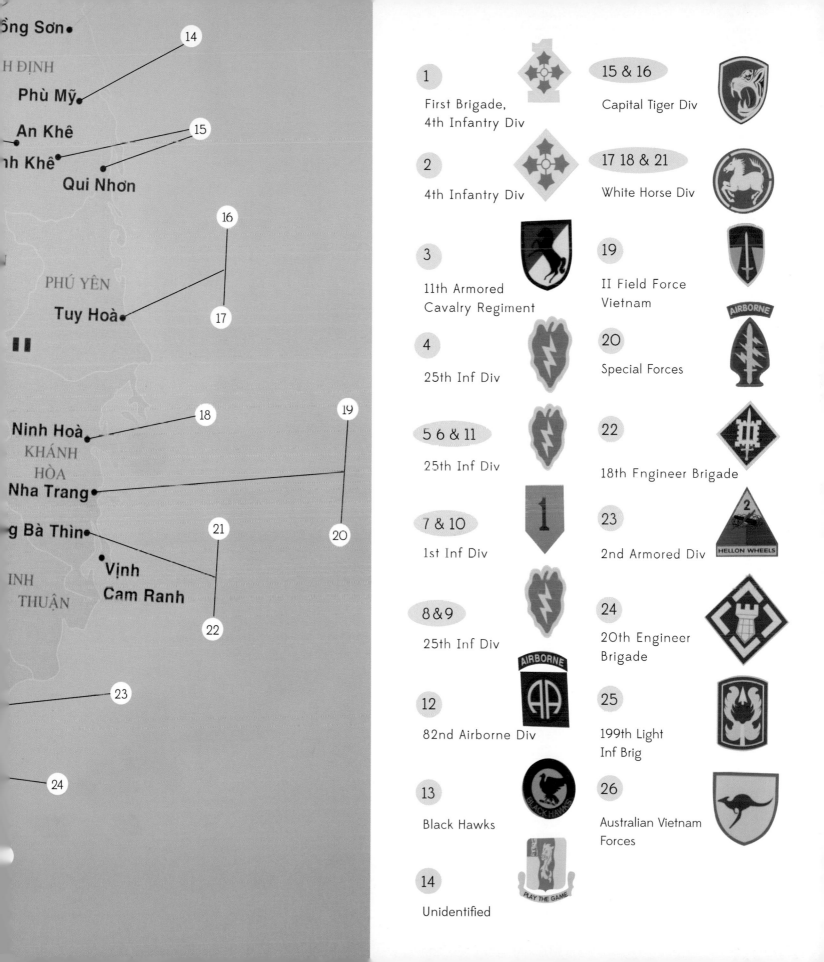

ồng Sơn

H ĐỊNH

Phù Mỹ

An Khê

h Khê

Qui Nhơn

PHÚ YÊN

Tuy Hoà

II

Ninh Hoà

KHÁNH
HÒA

Nha Trang

g Bà Thìn

**Vịnh
Cam Ranh**

INH
THUẬN

14

15

16

17

18

19

20

21

22

23

24

1 First Brigade,
4th Infantry Div

2 4th Infantry Div

3 11th Armored
Cavalry Regiment

4 25th Inf Div

5 6 & 11 25th Inf Div

7 & 10 1st Inf Div

8 & 9 25th Inf Div

12 82nd Airborne Div

13 Black Hawks

14 Unidentified

15 & 16 Capital Tiger Div

17 18 & 21 White Horse Div

19 II Field Force
Vietnam

20 Special Forces

22 18th Engineer Brigade

23 2nd Armored Div

24 20th Engineer
Brigade

25 199th Light
Inf Brig

26 Australian Vietnam
Forces

★ CHAPTER 4 ★

THE SECRET WAR

All were volunteers from Army Special Forces, Navy Seals, the Air Force Special Commando units, and sometimes average GIs who wanted something different from the war. All put their lives on the line in paramilitary, clandestine, covert operations, mostly behind the lines in Cambodia and Laos. We have to think what they accomplished, their dedication, their spirit, and how few there were who practiced their highly unusual, specialized trade. They were members of SOG, the Studies and Observation Group, a purposefully mundane, nondescript name that was almost meaningless, but a brilliant cover for the Vietnam War's contribution to unconventional warfare. They never numbered more than two thousand men.

Based in the Central Highlands, these units worked with Montagnard tribesmen and highly trained South Vietnamese special forces. Usually dressed as peasants, they carried no identifying papers or insignia, no dog tags, no pictures from home, wearing nothing that would identify them as having anything to do with the United States, whether South Vietnamese or Americans. Their equipment—radios, submachine guns, and their other weapons—was usually from foreign countries, and, if not, the men removed all identifying marks with acid or chisels. SOG members killed or wounded on their counterinsurgency missions were never officially "lost" on a mission behind the lines. When men died or sustained wounds during cross-border operations, to protect the secrecy of their mission no one ever learned this occurred outside South Vietnam.

The SOG units raided remote regions in Cambodia and Laos in these "black operations," attacking enemy installations, spotting enemy troop movements, and sabotaging the Ho Chi Minh Trail as best they could. Some units went on long-range patrols for weeks at a time. Others sat on top of mountains with sophisticated radar equipment inside Laos and Cambodia, coordinating artillery and air strikes. There were those who reported on North Vietnamese and Viet Cong troop movements and assessed bomb damage on the ground after tactical air strikes and B-52 raids. The most sought after prize was a captured enemy soldier. Nothing was better than information from a warm body. Many of their operations remain classified, known only by the men who were there and their former "masters" in Washington.

Operation Phoenix, though, was the most secret, the most controversial, and the most criticized in the annals of the Vietnam War. It eventually became known to the public as the American secret program of assassination and torture designed to eliminate anyone, weak friend or deadly foe, who stood in the way of allied success in South Vietnam.

Despite some success, Operation Phoenix had its share of failures and will forever be a program deeply shrouded in mystery. The CIA ran the program, working closely with their South Vietnamese partners. Together these counterterror operatives moved with stealth through the countryside. Here too, as with SOG, one of the aims was to capture and bring back enemy communist agents known as cadre. A live Viet Cong or North Vietnamese with fresh information was the best result of a shadow operation. Their mandate was to find and destroy the Viet Cong and North Vietnamese who had infiltrated the villages and who continuously intimidated the frightened peasants.

STAN SLIZ

Radar Operations Controller
Top Secret Lima Site 85
Northern Laos, 1967-68
S.O.G

Stan Sliz helped operate secret Lima Site 85 in northern Laos, where he guided F-4 and F-105 fighter bombers with ground-controlled radar bombing assistance on targets in North Vietnam. Lima Site 85 was overrun on March 11, 1968. Sliz was one of four survivors.

Stan Sliz

The site was chosen because we had all these forces out of Thailand that were going to bomb targets in the North when weather would move in. So here's this huge force of F-4s and F-105s streaming into North Vietnam, and the targets are obscured. These guys didn't have the capability to drop the bombs through the clouds. Consequently Phou Pha Thi mountain was selected as the location for a radar site to give our pilots an all-weather capability. Located only 150 miles from Hanoi, it was well within the range of the Skyspot radar system. The Army Corps of Engineers went in there, leveled the top of the mountain and brought in all of the equipment using choppers.

We were selected as members of the radar-bombing team. We had to go through a screening process. I imagine the "suits" who interviewed us were CIA. They made sure that we were patriotic and that we were the kind of people they wanted to do this kind of thing. We were moved out of the military ("sheep-dipped") so that we could be civilians. We all signed papers and were discharged legally from the Air Force, so that we could be hired as radar technicians by Lockheed Aircraft Corporation. That's how we got paid. We felt we were the elite, and I still do believe that everybody up there was a special individual. We thought we were going to shorten the war because we could bomb the North during the monsoon season.

I remember the first trip we made up there. Everybody was pretty jolly and joking until we crossed the river. Then we got very somber. It was like there was a curtain over Laos, and there wasn't any joking around anymore. Everybody got real serious. There were other Americans stationed at the helipad. I'm pretty sure they worked for the CIA and ran the "road watchers." They spoke the language pretty well and did keep track of what the enemy was doing.

All the missions out of Thailand came right over our site as they headed north. We usually saw them, and it was quite a sight to see them swoop down after they flew over the mountain. You could stand out there and look down at this whole force flying north. It was pretty awesome watching them swoop down through the valleys.

Laotian Hmong tribesmen and Thai mercenaries guarded the secret site from possible attack, but it was impossible to keep the location hidden for very long. Everything soon changed.

We knew that the enemy was coming. We could see them on the other mountains around us. You look out through binoculars, you could see them. They'd throw a finger at you. You'd throw a finger back at them. That kind of stuff.

On the 12th of January, I was showing a Thai NCO our newly constructed bunker next to our living quarters. As we were standing there, all of sudden all this commotion started down the side of the mountain near the helipad. I looked there and saw these biplanes circling around, dropping some kind of ordnance. I said, "My God, what is this? The Spanish Civil War?" I jumped into the equipment room and got on the radio to Udorn, and said, "Hey, they're bombing us up here!" Just to show you I didn't know what the heck was going on, when they asked me the size of the bombs, I answered, 250 pounders. (They were actually dropping grenades.) I looked out the door just in time to see one of these biplanes hovering over the helipad and aiming right at me. He nosed up and fired a salvo of rockets right over the top of the equipment room I was standing in. I found out later that a Thai captain was standing in the middle of the helipad with his AK-47, which he emptied into the belly of this aircraft as it flew overhead. His action saved us because he must have hit the pilot and caused the guy to flutter and lose his aim. This aircraft staggered off and crashed. Another biplane was shot down by an Air America chopper who flew alongside it, so the crew chief could shoot it down.

As a result of this action we were armed with M16s and grenades. The most significant thing that happened was that they gave us a couple of survival vests—or I wouldn't be here today. These vests are the kind that the pilots wear when they fly, so that if they bail out, there's a little radio in there, as well as flares and other survival equipment. If it wasn't for that radio when we got overrun, I wouldn't have been able to talk to the guys that were flying overhead and direct them in making strafing runs in our support.

The day that we got overrun, my crew was on the day shift. We worked from six in the morning to six at night. Afterwards both crews sat in a meeting about the situation getting grave, and did we want to get evacked out tonight or the next morning. We decided to spend the night. We had targets for the night, so let's run them, and we'll get out first thing in the morning. Just as we were getting ready to break off, this loud explosion occurred outside the door. We found that when we ran into the bunker for protection, a rocket had made a direct hit on the corner of the bunker. Because of the condition of the bunker, we decided to hide on the reverse slope of the mountain, below the equipment. I went to get some cigarettes out of the carton that I had on my bed in our living quarters, and found that a piece of shrapnel had torn through the whole carton. I didn't have a salvageable cigarette in the whole bunch. We all grabbed whatever we could; I grabbed the survival vest off the corner of my bed and put it on. We all stayed on the side of the mountain until the barrage ended, for about three hours. Deciding to see if the radar was still in operation, Bill Blanton's crew found that the equipment was okay, and started making bomb runs. The rest of us decided to spend the night on the mountain side in case of another attack.

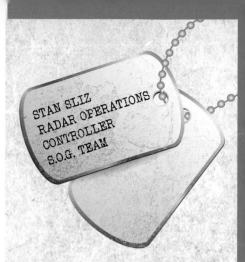

STAN SLIZ
RADAR OPERATIONS
CONTROLLER
S.O.G. TEAM

Stan Sliz

Before his tour in North ern Laos, Sliz assisted in the development of the Skyspot ground-directed radar bombing system. From June to December of 1966 he served as a Skyspot controller at Bien Hoa Air Base. By Septem ber 1967 he was part of the secret SOG project in Northern Laos. After being wounded at Lima Site 85, he spent several months in hospitals and underwent numerous operations be fore returning to active duty as a major in July 1968. He was awarded a Purple Heart and recom mended for the Silver Star as a result of the action at Lima Site 85. He retired af ter twenty years of service in 1972 and today works part time as a consultant and sales representative of electronic equipment in Colorado.

Lima Site 85 image with locations identified

PATH DOWN TO LZ — TACAN — GENERATORS — OPERATIONS — MAINT & COMM — LATRINE — LIVING TRAILER

Etch, Hank, and I set up a portable HF radio with a battery pack and contacted our HQ at Udorn with a report of what was going on. Then we fell asleep.

We were awakened by the sound of automatic-weapons fire from the vicinity of the outposts on our inner perimeter. Hearing footsteps and voices above us, we sneaked down the mountain about twenty feet to a cave where Danny and Monk were sleeping. There were five of us in that little hole, with just barely enough room for two guys. It really wasn't the greatest spot, but it worked well for most of us.

We heard all this commotion going on above us, guns firing, grenades popping. Soon everything became still. Etch was watching the trail above and whispered, "Stan, there's people coming!" I said, "When they get close enough, shoot." So he did. Almost immediately all hell broke loose. They opened up on us from all over, throwing grenades and firing their AK-47s. The first burst killed Hank and that's when I got wounded in my thighs. John also got wounded on that first attack. The pain was unbearable, but we just managed to fight them off. I don't recall ever looking at my watch or wondering what the hell time it was. We were more interested in trying to stay alive, using our weapons and firing back. Grenades kept coming in; bullets fragmenting all around. I soon reached the threshold of pain where I just didn't feel anything anymore. I felt my body vibrating from the hits. It became just like the nuisance of standing in a heavy rainstorm. Another grenade came in but I couldn't reach it. I thought about jumping onto it. John said, "Here grab, Hank, he's dead." So I took Hank and went on top of the grenade. It blew us back, the concussion knocking me out. When I came to, pieces of Hank were all over me. But the rest of us weren't killed. I got a real big piece of it in my thigh, and saw that my hands appeared mangled, but seemed useable. But we didn't get killed from the grenade. I thought I was close to death and the thought flashed through my mind, "So this is what it's like to die. I wonder what the final feeling's like?"

I know at one time someone, I don't know who, brought up the idea that maybe we should surrender. I said I thought that was BS, because I was pretty sure that they weren't taking any prisoners. I remember turning to John and saying, "They couldn't take us anyway, you're shot in the legs and so am I. There's was no way we could walk out of here."

During lulls in the fighting, using my little survival radio I contacted a C-130 flare ship circling overhead, dropping parachute flares. He encouraged us to "Hang on, help's on the way." Sure enough, a pair of A-Is from NKP arrived overhead at daybreak. Contacting them, I found they were armed with 20mm cannons and CBUs. I oriented them to make strafing runs from the Tacan building toward the radar equipment where I figured the enemy troops were. Each aircraft made two passes, with little effect on the enemy fire. So I asked them to drop the CBUs along the same axis of attack, saying, "You might as well. We're goners anyhow, so

A UH-1B helicopter with a Red Cross on the front, indicating medical evacuation landing on a rice paddy to pick up a wounded soldier.

you might as well do it." So they made their passes and dropped the bombs. It was like setting off a string of firecrackers, only a thousand times magnified. It was just horrendous noise. After a while everything was deathly still. I thought I'd gone deaf.

After the A-1s dropped their bombs, I couldn't hear a thing. Just ringing in my ears. Then I heard this chopper, an Air America Huey. I got on the radio and talked to these guys, telling them where we were. The pilot asked if we had any smoke down there? I pulled it out of my vest and said, "Yeah, it's purple." I handed the flare to Etch because my hands were too bloody to pop it, and he set it off. The whole cave filled with smoke and we sat there gagging. The pilot said, "I gotcha," and lowered a jungle penetrator to us. Etch needed help opening the leaves before we put Danny on it. After reeling him up, they dropped it down so I could be pulled up.

As they lifted me up, I swung sharply away from the mountain and the back swing crashed me back against the mountain. I was stunned as they continued to pull me up, but I remember looking down and seeing one of our guys, Willie Husband, coming around the side and waving at me—like don't forget me. I remember laying on the floor, staring at the tiny particles of metal as they were getting everybody else up into the chopper. That's when they opened fire on us. I saw this little hole in the floor beside my face and thought, "Hey, that hole wasn't there a second ago. And what's that red spot? My God! It's blood. I've been hit again." Then I looked up at Etch as he was falling out of the canvas seat above me. The bullet had gone right up through him and got him internally. He was killed instantly. The pilot, realizing he was taking fire, went into evasive action by slipping down to the right, away from the mountain.

I kept passing out from loss of blood, but each time I awoke, I got a cigarette from the crew chief. And when I passed out again, he took it from me. That's all I remember until I woke up in Udorn.

JACK STARLING

Radar Maintenance Technician
Lima Site 85, Northern Laos, 1968
S.O.G.

Jack Starling

They came in and said they had a volunteer program for this mission but they didn't tell us where it was until we were ready to go over there. I have no idea why I volunteered. I wouldn't do it again. I wasn't scared. I wasn't excited either. You know, it was just part of my job.

It was kind of awesome. It was so high on one side, they had hardly no runway. They had a landing spot for helicopters. And it's five thousand feet coming in from the other side. So when you fly into the mountain, they come up the side. It's foggy up there. You can't see nothing. Usually they'd just have to climb until they hit the plateau there so they could land. Once you get there, it's just kind of jungle. A lot of trees and everything. It was about two hundred yards I guess from the runway up to the radar site, the radar site being the highest point on the mountain.

It didn't bother me too much at this point because you know, they had told us how secure this thing was. Then after you get up there and look out, you could think how easy it could be secured. Which it wasn't. I don't know that I was happy. One side, it barely had one corner that was unsafe. But that was supposed to be land-mined. I mean, it was approachable by foot. And down on the other side, they had the Laotian army and some Thai army down there. I knew the North had army within five miles just about all the time. But we felt secure on our own where we were. Observers came by the day it happened and said it looked like there might be an attack or something like that. We were called to a meeting up in radar about five or six in the afternoon. We were in the process of grilling steaks outside the radar unit. While we were in there having that meeting, the first round came in and just blew the living quarters away. That kind of broke up the meeting. There was no more discussion about who was going to leave and so forth. We all kind of took cover on the opposite side of the mountain from where the rounds were coming. Most of them went over us. They were lobbing those things in from about twenty miles away. We were pretty secure with all the rounds that were going over us. They couldn't actually get to us the way they were firing. We figured this would happen in the future, but we didn't figure there would be a land assault that same night.

About four or five in the morning the rockets stopped for what seemed like an hour. They hadn't fired anything. Then all of a sudden, we started hearing machine-gun fire and hollering from the Vietnamese. It looked to me like there was probably a couple of hundred of them out there, and no Thai army, no nothing. Now I'm scared. I got to the point where the closer they got, I just knew I was going to be dead. And it didn't bother me anymore. By this time the Air Force had F-4s and those helicopters with mini-guns. They were strafing the ground troops, trying to get them to abandon the site. There were nine or ten people down around the same area we were. You come off this cliff and you go down around it into a little plateau that's on the mountain, and it's about a twenty-foot wall of rock there. And all the way around on this side of it here was five thousand feet straight down. Me and one other guy was laying beside a rock about six-foot tall, right in the path. They started lobbing hand grenades in there, and Fred reached out there with his foot and kind of kicked them off of the side.

Then behind us, these Vietnamese came in there with machine guns and started shooting everybody. One of the first guys that got shot was on the wall, next to the wall over there. He got hit with a hand grenade in his right arm. It was completely off. He brought me his M16 because mine was still down in the shelter. Evidently

Lance Corporal Harry J. Howell and Private 1st Class Pete G. Heckwine, 'Lima' Company, 3rd Battalion, 7th Marines, with an M60 machine gun crew at the ready, receiving firing instructions.

JACK STARLING
RADAR
MAINTENANCE
TECHNICIAN
S.O.G. TEAM

Jack Starling

Starling enlisted in the navy in July 1952 and served three years before he joined the Air Force and became a communications technician specializing in radar and a survival training instructor. Wounded twice in 1965, in the foot and leg, he received the Purple Heart. In 1968, as a member of SOG, he was a volunteer in Northern Laos on Lima Site 85 as a radar technician. He served twenty-two and a half years in the military, retiring in 1974. Married and the father of seven children, he retired in 1998 from his job as a hospital engineer.

it wouldn't fire because shrapnel hit it and it had a shell in it couldn't get out. About this time the Air Force came in and started strafing. Me and him was laying there, and these two Vietnamese came down to where we were and they jumped over him and landed on my ankle. I'd already been hit in the leg with a round they'd snipered earlier. When they jumped over him, they turned around and they just opened up on him. How they kept from hitting me, I'll never know. On the other side of the rock about three feet away, a guy was calling for help. Because of his arm he was bleeding to death. They heard him and they went over and just opened up on him. I didn't see it. I could hear it. The guy laying next to me had his leg over mine to kind of keep from falling off this cliff. They got him pretty good and at that point I just figured I was dead. What I was afraid of started—coming around looting, taking watches, stuff like that, money. When the aircraft passed over, the Vietnamese came over this way and then they saw a chance to escape so they got out of there. When they were doing all the strafing, these two Vietnamese are down there, running back and forth trying to keep from being shot. Helicopters came in and picked up guys. I said, because I couldn't walk, "I'm over here." They started shooting at the helicopter, and he had to take off.

The U.S. facility atop of Phou Pha Thi, known as Lima Site 85, was the site of a major battle on 10 March 1968.

I was by myself. It seemed like about twenty hours but it was only probably five or six hours. I just stayed there and kept still because I didn't have anything to protect myself with or anything. And then when the aircraft came in all I had there was a flashlight that you know they got the lenses on the bottom of it. And so I held a red lens over it and was pointing towards this chopper so the chopper would come in and pick me up. And he couldn't land. They had to take me up by a wire rope. I was too close to the edge of the mountain. They were strafing the two Vietnamese running around. I was kind of glad of the strafing, even though I was worried about getting shot or hit. But I think if they hadn't of done that, then with too much idle time these Vietnamese would start collecting weapons and little gold watches or whatever the case may be. I sort of pictured them doing what the Germans used to do to the Americans. If they came for me, I was going to try to kick them over the side of the mountain. At least I would try to do that because I didn't have a gun to shoot them with or anything. I knew I was the last one. When my generator guy came by, I was the only one in that immediate area that was alive. When they had taken all the other people there was only two places where people were. They were going to come over and get me until the aircraft started drawing fire. Then they had to leave. It kind of scared me a little bit but I was already scared as hell, you know. But I felt good when they came back.

I felt I was lucky to get out. But then it turned out it wasn't so secure. When I got out they took me back to the hospital and I was there two or three days. And somebody showed up and asked me how long I was going to be in there, and I said, "Why?" And they said, "We got another unit, another site down over here." I said, "You send somebody else over there because I want my airplane ticket out of here when I leave." And so I did. I left from the hospital.

Prior to the day that that happened, I got the feeling that it was supposed to be a secret but then I found out that everybody in the world knew about it. Except I didn't know about it, until after I got back. I'm sure the North knew about it, and the powers that be knew about it. And a lot of people that wasn't supposed to know about it knew about it. I got a Purple Heart but through the mail. It was kind of weird, but I didn't care. I was glad to get out of there.

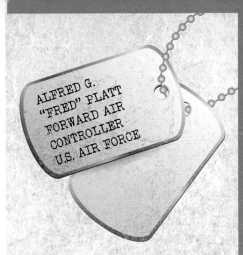

ALFRED G. "FRED" PLATT

Forward Air Controller
Laos
U.S. Air Force

Alfred G. "Fred" Platt

During the Vietnam War, Fred Platt was one of the early Ravens, a member of an elite team of forward air controllers (FAC) in the secret war in Laos. Though in the U.S. Air Force, he operated under CIA control.

Alfred G. "Fred" Platt

Sector Forward Air Controller in the Central Highlands of Vietnam, Platt flew under the call sign of Walt 43. A Special Forces volunteer, he flew as a Raven FAC, operating out of several different sites in Laos. Shot down in Laos in 1970, and rescued by Air America, he sustained serious injuries to his back resulting in his third Purple Heart to go with his forty other combat decorations. He retired on disability from the USAF, works continuously to rehabilitate himself, and sits on the board of several veterans' and charitable organizations.

You know, you become a living legend, which is funny to be. The day a new Raven arrived, you would process through the American Embassy to get your Laotian drivers license, to get your embassy ID card. Especially in the early days when I was there, I was completely "sheep-dipped." I had resigned from the United States Air Force, and I was technically an employee of the Department of State. The end of the tour we would go back into the regular Air Force and it was like we never left. If you were shot down, they would say you had been shot down in Vietnam. But they wouldn't say Laos.

We were kind of larger-than-life figures. When you walked into a bar anywhere else, you had a natural arrogance. As Dizzy Dean so famously said, "It ain't bragging, if you can do it." And the guys that were there, they could do it. You were out there getting shot at every day, and except for one strict Mormon who didn't drink, they did have a lot of good times. You were out there getting shot at almost every day, all day long, and when you blew off steam, they knew you were in town. So everybody eventually knew who you were.

We lived up country. We ate the food. They didn't teach me the language but I knew the people. I ate with them. I drank with them, and you learn to be a hunter and tracker to find the targets and go out there and take the war to the enemy and take the enemy out of the war. We didn't come out from an air-conditioned base somewhere at six hundred miles an hour. I was generally flying sixty, seventy miles an hour, low and slow or sometimes high. It depended. Sometimes you needed to be down in the weeds. Sometimes you were at the tree tops and sometimes you needed to be about twenty-five hundred, three thousand feet in the air. Depending on what the threat was from the air, you could read bent grass, you could identify footprints or types of footprints. You learned to be an expert.

We would go out and do reconnaissance and get intelligence from other sources, locate targets, then bring in air power or whatever. Sometimes it would be artillery if it was close and we could discover something. But usually it was air power. It doesn't matter if you were a lieutenant and this flight you're directing of 105s or F-4s or Navy A-7s has a navy captain or an Air Force colonel leading the flight. You are the battle-scene commander. He doesn't strike until you tell him that he can. You clear him in. You clear him off. You tell him where to put his bombs. You run the operation, so in a sense you're like the Valkyries. You pick who gets to be a hero, and who gets to die and go to Valhalla today. It was an interesting mind game. Of course, the best part was the flying and the guys. Because the guys were doing the thing that they wanted to do. If they didn't fit in, usually they didn't handle it and we got rid of them.

I flew over 780 combat missions that the Air Force recognizes. I flew well over 1,500 missions in the O-l. I flew over 800 missions in the U-17. And I got a patch that claims some phenomenal hundreds of missions in the T-28. What I logged officially and put down in the book was different, because you get into flying so many that to tell your war story, every one was a war story.

I had one mechanical crash with an engine that blew up. And I crashed-landed that T-28 down in Thailand. I was picked up behind the lines by Air America three times with O-1 crashes and I had seven other incidents where I put it down on a friendly strip. One that I don't count as a crash was in a U-17. I had a round come up, and it blew off the left gear. I set it down, and they welded new parts on it and it was flying the next day. That wasn't a crash to me. I don't count that. I had another U-17 that the guy flying with me was shot through the leg. We lost a large part of the tail, and we lost all the flight controls except the aileron and the throttle. That one I crashed, and it was a ball of scrap metal. We both got out alive. I patched up his bullet hole. I say I was shot down ten times and had eleven crashes. The things to me were the courage of the troops on the ground and being able to help them out.

Opposite: A pilot from the 147th Aviation Company, marks radio frequencies in grease pencil on the windshield of his CH-47 "Chinook" helicopter.

HARLAN "RIP" VAN WINKLE

SOG Team
Relief of Hill 471
U.S. Army

Harlan "RIP" Van Winkle

SOG was top secret in Vietnam. Officially its full name was MACV-SOG, which stood for United States Military Assistance Command Vietnam—Studies and Observation Group. A joint volunteer service made up of Army, Navy, Air Force, and Marines, SOG was not a special studies group. The men participated in many cross-border operations, going from Vietnam into Laos, and Vietnam into Cambodia. They conducted reconnaissance missions, sometimes known as a "hatchet force," designed primarily to hit enemy targets, to help get other recon teams out of trouble, and to secure downed aircraft. Much of what SOG did and saw remains classified, and supposedly the force never exceeded two thousand men.

Huey helicopters on a mission flying over South Vietnam.

Well, the morning of the 29th of January, a recon team, one of our local recon teams, left probably somewhere around 8:30 or so and somewhere around 10 or 10:30 they were ambushed near Hill 471. Bill Wood was able to get out with one other American and when they brought him in the helicopter, he said that Gary was up there dead and Mahoney was missing and that several of the Yards [Montagnards] that were with him were either dead or missing. At that point the FOB (Forward Operations Base) commander said, "Well, we're going to send someone up to get them." And that fell on the "hatchet force," which is what we were involved with. We took four helicopters. You could see everything from there. There were six people on each helicopter. We had been told that the bodies were in the saddle between 471 and a small peak off to one side just to the southeast of it there. Hill 471 was surrounded by higher ground but at the same time, it was a very strategic hill. You could see everything from 471. You could see the FOB. You could see the village of Khe Sanh and you could see Lang Vie from there. I'm told, not too long ago, that the Marines had a recon patrol up there the night of the 20th and got ambushed. Of course, you look back on it now, and I say, I wish I would have known that then.

We landed unopposed and actually set up a perimeter, a hasty perimeter, still unopposed. Chuck Trednik and John Frescura moved across. We didn't find any bodies but at that point we knew that there were enemy troops around. There were a bunch of enemy troops trying to flank us between 471 and the village of Khe Sanh.

We were discussing at that point what we needed to do. There was a bush, the hill top was basically covered with three-foot-tall elephant grass, you know very short height. There were a few scraggly bushes, nor many. But there was a bush immediately in front of us and he was standing over my left shoulder, when all of a sudden a bunch of rounds come flying out of that bush. He looked at me, and I looked at him and I said, "What was that?" And he said, "I don't know." And at that point we started receiving fire that I recognized.

It was pretty close then for a while. We didn't see a whole lot of people. There were some. I dropped a grenade into the hole that the soldier popped out of. I remember some of the grenades. I don't remember the sky turning black with them. I'm told by some of the others that it did. I recall as Jim Taylor says, he gave me a friendly shove. And one went off between my legs and I recall at that point a lot of grenades that I was hearing, they were almost duds. They didn't explode with the bang you associate with a U.S. grenade for sure. At that point the lieutenant was wounded and we went to see about him. He had been shot in the throat, and I took one look at him and decided there's no point in me being over here. We were already taking heavy fire. I was trying to get some air support started, trying to get some artillery started, and I heard a round hit somebody behind me. And I turned around, and Trednik was on the ground.

And kind of for me, at that point, things went a little south. Now here's a member of my detachment, you know, and he's down and hurt. Well, I got to him just about the same time and we're working on him. He's shot In the chest, low down on the left side. And he looked at me and said, "It hurts real bad, sir." What we didn't see was the exit wound in the backside until later. We were getting word from the FOB to stay and explore the situation, and I said, "Hell, you know, I can't hold what I got and you want me to explore something!"

At that point everything changed. I knew we had to get off that hill and get a medevac. We're going down the north side of the hill trying to find a place to carry the wounded and call in the medevac. When we started to pull off the hill we were stumbling all over the area where we thought the bodies were. And we never saw any. The bodies were recovered in April. They never did locate Mahoney. At one point, probably the only Americans left on the hill were John Frescura and Craig Lansing and myself and a few Bru [tribesmen]. Just the Bru that were with me.

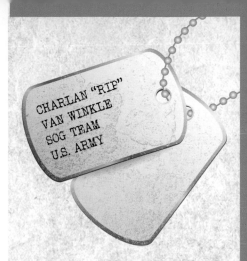

Harlan "Rip" Van Winkle

Raised on a small ranch in central Texas, Van Winkle joined the army in 1960 following a year and a half in college and volunteered for airborne training. After Special Forces training and a year in language school, in 1967 he was in Vietnam assigned to SOG outside Khe Sanh. He finished his tour and then, after attending the U.S. Army Ranger School, he was back in South Vietnam in Bu Dop and then Song Be, north of Saigon. He attended the Infantry Officers Advanced Course and has a BA from the University of Nebraska. After serving twenty years in the army around the world, he retired in 1980. Since 1983 he has been in business working with the same company. He is married with a married daughter and a son, a veteran of the Gulf War, in the army.

JOHN FRESCURA

SOG Team
Relief of Hill 471
Special Forces

John Frescura

After finishing my training at Fort Bragg, I was assigned to the 7th Special Forces. I was there about three months and I got levied for Okinawa, which is the First Special Forces. I was chosen as a junior demolitionist to go on one of the SOG teams. I had heard about it. I figured it was top secret because there wasn't a lot of rumors going on about it. You hear stories. It was kind of a challenge. You say, "Well, if they can do it, why can't I?" It's just a personal challenge. You see other people doing things. It's the old story of why would you want to jump out of a normally functioning airplane? Because it's a challenge to be in the Airborne. And it was a challenge to go in Special Forces. More challenging than being a line soldier, you know, and police up the area. A lot of training, but a challenge.

Our job was camp defense and training the Montagnards in booby traps, weapons defense, and tactics. They had mostly pungee stakes. We had mostly anti-personnel mines, toe-poppers. They knew how to build their own stuff. We trained them in American equipment because they weren't that familiar with it.

I was assigned to our A team. I was a combat engineer. I blew things up. I broke things. We carried seven hundred, eight hundred rounds of ammunition, ten, twelve, your choice how many grenades you wanted. Smoke grenades, survival radio, strobe light, a knife. I carried a knife. Some guys, I had heard, carried hatchets. They were more comfortable with hatchets. What you would carry would depend on the duration of the mission. If you were going in just then and coming right out, you might have a meal with you. A lot of us carried a bag of rice with us, and all you had to do was add water to it. It was just something to munch on.

We were the combat backup unit, I guess you would say. If the recon team got in trouble and needed help, our unit, as a larger force, would go in and try to help them out.

Outside Khe Sanh from our FOB (Forward Operations Base), I was on the third lift, the third chopper into 471. Two choppers were already in. The third chopper came in. There was me, another guy and four Bru. And when we hit, we went in on the left flank of the hill. The fourth chopper came in. They unloaded. It seemed like nothing was going on. Why did they let the choppers come in, off-load, and let the choppers leave? What was the reasoning? Because they liked to break our equipment? And why they never shot at it later on in the mission, I've never been able to figure out.

Once on the hill we started getting a lot of incoming fire. Then we figured there's a lot of people that are trying to kill us. We couldn't attack. There wasn't enough of us, in my opinion. My M60 machine gunner couldn't fire. He had taken a round in the receiver, so it was inoperative. I told him to hang onto the gun. You can always use the spare parts. But keep the gun and stay with me because I would be his gun now. I would shoot for him. I remember laying on the hill and I'm watching puffs of dirt and I'm thinking to myself, "What the heck is that?" You know, just a dirt shoot. And then it dawned on me—these bullets are doing this. Because you don't really comprehend what's going on. Your minds not blank, but on a different plane, maybe would be the word. You're not conscious of a lot of things going on or the time frame that it happens. We were pulling back and

Machine gunner Corporal Fred G. Angehra of "L" Co. 3rd Battalion 7th Marine Regiment in action during Operation Zippo.

JOHN FRESCURA
SOG TEAM
SPECIAL FORCES

John Frescura

In 1967 Frescura was as signed to Special Forces A Team and stationed at Khe Sanh. He was a com bat engineer and demoli tion expert who trained the Bru Montagnards in the use of anti-personnel mines, trip flares, Clay more mines, M79 grenade launchers, hand grenades, and other weapons. Along with building defenses and trenches, he frequently went on patrols. After being discharged in 1968, he went to work for the Ford Motor Company. Mar ried since 1971, he has a daughter and son and regularly attends reunions of his unit.

trying to get away from contact. The only place was behind us to go down the hill and get out toward the FOB. On that mission we had one KIA American, one wounded American, two Bru dead or wounded. So four out of twenty four people wounded. That's, you know, 15 percent.

It all alike to me: Vietnam, Laos, cross-border or what. On the relief of 471, I don't remember what chopper I came in on but one chopper had already been hit. The skid blew out. We tried to get the destroyed chopper. Captain Van Winkle was injured. A couple of Bru were hurt. We tried to get a big enough chopper in to haul that one out. They never could get one, and we ended up destroying it. So we took all the radio equipment, first aid, all the ammo, everything we could use, and we ended up pouring oil over the chopper and burning it up. So there's a half million dollars, whatever these things cost, sitting over across the river. They probably got it scrapped by now.

It's nice to get back with the guys that we were there with and talk about the stories. I think we tell more comical stories than we do anything else. We just talk about the goofy stuff we were doing, you know, not the combat side of it.

CRAIG LANSING

Relief of Hill 471
SOG Team
U.S. Army

Craig Lansing

I worked with Montagnards. They were by and large inexperienced people, very primitive. You know, loin cloths, crossbows, live-off-the-land kind of people. They didn't understand airplanes, fire alarms, and so we had to train them from the ground up to teach them twentieth-century weaponry and how things worked.

First of all, most soldiers that you see in movies of Vietnam or in pictures wore steel pots, flak jackets, that sort of thing. We never wore those. We didn't wear steel pots and flak jackets. For whatever reason, we just didn't do it. And our web gear, our load bearing equipment that we carried our combat gear on, was different. Most soldiers, all soldiers in Vietnam, carried ammo pouches. We carried canteen covers. An ammo pouch will hold three or four magazines, where as a canteen cover will carry seven. And most of us carried five of those canteen covers on our pistol belts, which gives us a lot more capacity for ammunition. Instead of having two ammo pouches with four or five magazines, we've got five canteen covers with seven per. Normally, typically we'd have anywhere from ten to fifteen hand grenades on our web gear. We carried a knife, we carried pin lights, a device we used for shooting star clusters in the air for signaling, that sort of thing. We carried two canteens of water. So you're talking nine pounds, or so I suppose, of web gear you're carrying when you're going out in operations. If you don't include anything else, your weapon. And if you're going out for any extended period of time like we did if we went over the border, we had to carry rations for a certain amount of time or we're not going to survive. So you're carrying quite a bit of weight. We wore black uniforms, and when we went across the border we never wore any kind of identification dog tags, ID cards, rank or anything. So they had no way of knowing who we were.

Lansing talks about the same ambush on Hill 471 previously described by Harlan Van Winkle and John Frescura.

When we got on the ground, it seemed to me like we were surrounded. The whole mountain erupted on us. I can recall hand grenades flying in from all kinds of directions. There were B-40 rockets coming on us as well as small-arms fire. Fortunately none of the people were hit with that. The kind of hand grenades that the North Vietnamese used were Chinese Communist, Chi-Com grenades and they were a kind of potato-masher thing. They had a wood handle on them, and they had a cast iron front end on then and they weren't that effective, not nearly as effective as ours. If it had been our kind of grenade, it would have pretty much destroyed all of us.

Captain Van Winkle sent me off to secure a draw that the NVA could run up, get in position on top of the ridge, and then roll us up from a flank. I went with four or five or six Montagnards to secure the draw. And as I got over there and began to set my people up, they were scared to death, because they apparently could see what I couldn't see. They knew there was camouflaged NVA around and they were unmanageable for me to position. I had to manhandle them in the positions and secure the draw. The NVA as well as the VC were absolutely just masters of camouflage. You couldn't see any of them. They were right next to us and you couldn't tell it, you didn't know it, you didn't see them. Van Winkle tried to call in close air support. The first ones were helicopters. We didn't have what we called fast movers, or jets, available yet from Da Nang. So we were trying to hold the bad guys back until we could get our fast movers in with the big stuff, with our own helicopter gunships. And they were coming in so close and so low to me they were literally strafing me. I can recall our gunshots and automatic 40mm grenade launchers. The choppers had 2.75 rockets and they also had 3.75 machine guns on board. And they were just raking my position and I thought because I was separated from the main body that our gunships thought I was part of the NVA because we were all wearing black. The VC and the NVA did that. So I raced back to Captain Van Winkle to advise our gunships that the group over there was me. We were the good guys. Quit shooting at us. And the response from Captain Van Winkle was that he knew that we were the good guys but we were surrounded by the NVA and he was just trying to keep them away from us. The pilots in the air could see movement on the ground that you can't see when you're on the ground. I was surrounded and, gee whiz, I didn't know that.

An ammunition supply point at Thien Ngon for the 2nd Brigade, operating in Cambodia.

When I got back to my position, all my Montagnards were gone. I'm wondering where the hell they went. I hollered to Captain Van Winkle, "My people have run off the hill." And he said, "Well, go get them and get them back into position." I look down on the north side, and my guys are running down there. So I go down to the bottom of the hill and I stopped them. I got a hold of my one machine gunner and this fellow's name was Pa Lang. He was the biggest Montagnard we had pretty near, and he had a goiter problem, a big lump on his neck. So I grabbed Pa Lang by the web gear, and I picked him up in my right hand and I'm marching back up the hill with him. I've got my Carbine 15 in my left hand. I always keep my weapon on safe until I need it. It's real easy to accidentally discharge, and you don't want to do that because you can kill your own people. So I'm headed up to the top of the hill and just as I get to where I need to position Pa Lang, there was a hole in the ground that I didn't see and, hell, if I had stepped in it, I guess I would have fallen in on this guy. But the guy came out of the rat hole and emptied his AK-47 at Pa Lang and I. Pa Lang went down, and I emptied my Carbine 15 into the hole, and I grabbed Pa Lang and down the hill I went.

I was given instructions to meet down at the bottom of the hill at the bombed trail. I went back to where my Yards were and they were scared to death. They were huddled in a little draw and I got a hold of them. Down we went. Bomb craters are everywhere. Now I'm scared because I don't know where my main bodies are. I'm over here away from the main body wearing a black uniform, there's NVA all over mountain, and we've got close air support coming in now. So I just grab my people and I headed across the rice paddy because there was a little bit of ridge across the other side and I said let's go. And away we went. I just about got to the ridge and I heard Frescura and Van Winkle hollering at me. I turned around. I was pretty happy to know that those guys weren't that far away from me, maybe one hundred meters. I didn't know where they were for sure, so I settled down behind that little ridge and waited for them to come back across. But that whole period from the time he sent me over to that little drop to secure it until the time that I got back across that rice paddy, I don't know if I did anything successful. I got a guy killed over it and I don't know if I secured that draw or not. I probably didn't.

Members of the 327th Infantry, 101st Air Cavalry Division, move toward the airstrip at Fire Support Base "Birmingham." They will be airlifted by UH-1D helicopters to Landing Zone Tabat in the A Shau Valley.

BOB DONOGHUE

SOG Team
Khe Sanh
U.S. Army

Bob Donoghue

I wanted to go back to Vietnam again, and if SOG was the only way to go back, then so be it. Basically we had spike teams, called STs, which were reconnaissance teams. We had HFs, which stood for hatchet force. Hatchet force was approximately twenty to forty people that would go out looking for trouble, and the spike team, or the recon team, would just go out and try to avoid contact. As a spike team basically we were just running local patrols out of Khe Sanh at the time because the siege had started and we a hard time getting helicopters to take us over the fence. We were just trying to stay alive at Khe Sanh which meant a lot of local patrolling. Every night we had to have listening posts outside to give warning in case of a large attack. The enemy was using tanks in the area. A special forces camp got run over by tanks. So we tried to have small two-man teams forward out on the avenues that the tanks would take to hit the camp. They would have to lay out there all night and just listen to see if they could hear any activity.

Well, it was scary because the camp itself was surrounded by anywhere from twenty to forty thousand North Vietnamese soldiers. You go out either yourself or with one Bru tribesman, or two Americans or two Bru

tribesmen. You'd have to wait until it got dark. Then you'd have to go through the wire, go out through the mines, which we knew where our minefield was, so that was no problem. Then we'd move anywhere from a couple hundred to a thousand meters away from camp and just sit alongside one of the access roads and lay there all night with a starlight scope or a metascope, which was red, and just observe the roads for activity. During the siege we were losing a couple of Americans almost on a daily basis from rockets, artillery rounds, and pulling missions. I don't know anybody that came back from SOG that wasn't wounded. I mean it's just kind of understood that everybody has a Purple Heart that was there.

I was on one operation once where there was an enemy squad coming down a trail and we thought that's all there was. It's night time and it's dark. It's hard to see how many enemy troops there are. So we open fire on them and killed and wounded most of the people in the first squad but what we didn't realize was that there

Jungle Trail, *Sketch by Samuel E. Alexander. Oil crayon on paper.*

was probably anywhere from thirty to sixty more troops coming down behind them. The second enemy squad turned to run back up the trail and the third squad coming down opened up on their own second squad. So we stopped firing and for several hours afterwards we just listened to them shoot at each other. We thought that was kind of neat because they never knew where we were. We just fell into the thicket and just lay there for the rest of the night and didn't have to do anything. They just shot at each other.

We had wire-tap missions where we would go out usually with an interpreter and a tape recorder. There was communications wire all over the roads and stuff in Laos. We'd just go up and find a place and tap into the line using an induction coil. We'd have to cut the wire. You'd just wrap the induction coil around the communications wire and then run your own wire into the bush. Then sit there with your interpreter with a set of headphones and a tape recorder and tape record the message traffic that was coming along the wire. You try to find a good spot to watch the major trails, the major roads, but where you're not going to be observed from their side. You just sit there and watch and observe, and then try to report everything that you see. Our job wasn't to interpret the information. Our job was to just report the information. So every truck or troop formation or anything else we saw or heard, we'd report back.

We would conduct ambushes. We would see, you know, the enemy six or seven feet in front of us, walk into our ambush and we'd initiate the ambush usually with Claymore mines or hand grenades. And then depending on how many troops we were engaged with, we would fight from anywhere to a couple of minutes to a half hour. Then at which time we would usually try to withdraw out of the area because one of the things we couldn't do obviously was we couldn't reinforce. So once the enemy knew where we were, it was important for us to try to break contact and leave the area so they couldn't fix on our location and then bring in a superior force against us.

We had the Bru tribe, a Montagnard tribe, that has villages in South Vietnam, North Vietnam, and into Laos. When I got there, there was already Bru assigned to my team. You develop a pretty strong bond with the people because you're going out on operations, you're eating and sleeping together, fighting together, dying together. And the Bru were great people. They were very loyal. There were times that we were on missions where they couldn't get enough helicopters to pull us out on the first flight, so the helicopter would come in and say there was twelve of us and you could only put six people on the helicopter. The Bru would be telling me to get out and I'd be yelling at them, no, I'm the last one going out, for them to get on the helicopter. And we'd actually have a shouting match going on while the helicopter was coming in to see who was going to get on it. They were afraid the helicopter wouldn't be able to come back and they wanted to make sure that I got out. Of course I was trying to take care of them and make sure they got out. They were paid approximately twenty to forty dollars a month. The squad leaders, interpreters and machine gunners were paid forty dollars a month. Basic rifleman was

Bob Donoghue

Donoghue joined the army in 1964 after graduating high school. His first tour in Vietnam was for one year in the Central Highlands in Pleiku. After undergoing more training in the United States in the Special Forces, he returned to Vietnam. Based at Khe Sanh, he worked with Bru Montagnard tribesmen in Vietnam and Laos. He conducted cross border reconnaissance missions, bomb damage assessment, and ambushes. He completed his tour in 1968 and left the army. He is a reserve master sergeant in the Special Forces and a police officer in Springfield, Massachusetts. In 1992 he returned to Khe Sanh to locate and help the Bru tribe he worked with during the war. He has since journeyed back to Khe Sanh six more times and formed the non-profit Cedar Point Foundation to assist those whom he says, "gave so much in support of our missions."

twenty dollars a month. We provided them with food, clothing, and medical assistance to their families when possible. That was kind of hard to do at Khe Sanh because their families were living outside the wire.

There was concern by the Marine commanders at Khe Sanh that the North Vietnamese were going to take Bru families and put them in front of their troops and attack forward positions with the purpose being that our Bru wouldn't fire upon their families. That never happened and I guess we'd never know what would have happened. I do know from my Bru—I would let them sneak out every once in a while to check on their families—and they would come back and say that their mother and father had been killed. And I'd ask them were they killed by the North Vietnamese and they'd say, no, they were killed by the B-52s. And I'd say, well you must be very upset with the Americans for killing your family. And they'd say, if the North Vietnamese hadn't come, the B-52s wouldn't have come. And I always thought that if the situation was reversed, I don't think I could have looked at them so objectively. The Bru basically loved us. We cared about them and I think it was the first time in history that somebody outside of their tribe actually took a deep concern for them and cared about their well-being and made sure that they had medical attention if they were sick, took care of their families, and made sure they had enough food to eat.

Most of your conventional American units were wary of any people that weren't Americans and did not want them inside their compounds. The Marines at Khe Sanh wouldn't let Bru into their compounds. When we abandoned Khe Sanh we stopped at Camp Carroll, which was the artillery base that supported Khe Sanh during the siege. We stopped there over night and they wouldn't let us inside the compound. Bru and the other Americans with their Bru teams had to sleep outside the wire in front of their Claymores, in front of their machine guns, in front of their bunker system all night because they wouldn't allow us inside. I guess they were afraid that out Bru might be enemy and wouldn't let them in.

The other Americans I worked with and the Bru I worked with, I wouldn't want to be in any other type organization. Everybody was out 100 percent to help their teammates. We had the best equipment that the government could give us at that time and we had all top-notch people. The Bru were just unbelievable. You couldn't ask for a better combination. Things that affect us now, how we relate to people, little idiosyncrasies that we have, a lot of it has to go back to what happened in 1968, and it's hard to explain to people what we went through. I was twenty-one years old at that time, and I was at an impressionable age. Of course we all thought we were infallible but at the same token everyday somebody that we knew would either get killed or wounded and they'd put them on an evacuation helicopter never to be seen again. So it kind of took that feeling that my time is going to be soon. It could be tomorrow, could be next week, could be next month. So I might as well do the best job I can now because who knows what's going to happen a month from now.

In 1992, after trying for probably four years through official channels to find out what ever happened to the Bru, I went back with another Special Forces soldier to the Khe Sanh area and located the Bru I worked with. I found the interpreter who was on my team but his family was sick. It was the end of the dry season and the whole village were getting water from a muddy little stream. A mile away there was resettled Vietnamese that had one water well for every two families. And I said, how come you don't have a water well. They said they can't afford it. I asked how much for the water well. And they said fifty dollars for a small one or one hundred dollars for a big one. So we paid and had a water well put in. I've been back to Vietnam six times. We've put in four water wells. We bought seven cows. We've been constructing fish ponds and everything else we can to try to help. One village, for ten babies being born in a year, seven would die in the first year. So we'd been bringing in hundreds of prenatal vitamins. Now this past year, the village has not lost a single baby that was born. I think they had eight babies born, and not one of them died.

Marines and South Vietnamese Popular Forces of Combined Action Group 4 open fire on a sniper while on a patrol south of Quang Tri City. The patrol was searching the area for Viet Cong suspects when they received sniper fire from across the river.

JON R. CAVAIANI

Sergeant, Special Forces
SOG Team, Hickory Hill Radio Station
U.S. Army

I was closer to my Montagnards than I was with my own family. I had one of them that I started to put my hand down on a trip wire, and he saw it and I didn't. He dove over my shoulder and took the full blast. There aren't a lot of people like that. They stand up and get shot. They know I never left a man on the ground. Those were the rules we lived by. First man on the ground, last man off the ground. There was a certain amount of esprit de corps between all these individuals. Guys that weren't necessarily the best garrison soldiers but were excellent guys on the ground. After putting teams on out, I found it was more miserable being in there waiting to hear if a team really got hit bad, to a team that didn't come back. I mean the blood, the sweat, the tears that you have.

When I first got up to Hickory, it was in pretty shabby condition. I got up there and most of the concertina wire was hanging on the berm or right on the sandbags and out around the edge. So, first thing I did was brought in a Navy Seabee and brought in a

Jon R. Caviani

little tank, blew up a bunch of old French mines and a bunch of old American mines. Cleared this area. We put in new tanglefoot and concertina and everything, and built up the camp. I had approximately sixty-seven indigenous personnel, primarily Montagnards, and then I had twenty-seven Americans.

After Sergeant Cavaiani sets his defenses, Hickory Hill soon comes under attack.

During the night Charlie went in and put a bunch of Claymores. Because they lay this on the ground, here were these Claymores all pointed toward our camp. So I grabbed an M60 machine gun and went around and laid down and peeked over and jumped up, shooting the stands off of them. Got all the way around to the last one and then somebody got wise to it. I peeked up over and as soon as I put the machine gun over, they set the Claymore off and it wounded one of my Montagnards. I did a quick evaluation of the situation. We knew we were going to get hit, but when? I was so sure we going to get hit I wrote my father the night before and sent it out on helicopter, telling him that this would probably be the last letter he would get from me.

About that time we realized they had dug in, Charlie holes or Charlie positions. They had machine guns. They had several snipers. Plus they had this whole hill that went up front. I started engaging this first machine-gun crew with a .50 caliber and I took out that crew. They jump up with rockets and shoot rockets at you. All of a sudden this guy Walter comes crawling up alongside me and he goes, "Hey, Sergeant Cavaiani, well, I kind of thought I might take over the .50 caliber machine gun." There's a lot of people back there don't know what they're doing. I looked at him and said, "What do you know about .50 caliber?" And he said, "I don't know

Marines of Whiskey Battery, 3rd Battalion, 11th Marine Regiment, preparing for action. This is an 81mm mortar. Unlike the lighter 60mm used by platoons in the field, the 81mm was a crew-served heavy weapon.

Jon R. Cavaiani

Born in Royston, England, Cavaiani came to the United States as a child in 1943. In 1968 he became a naturalized citizen. He joined the army in 1969 and volunteered for Special Forces. In June 1971, Cavaiani was awarded the Congressional Medal of Honor while serving with SOG as a platoon leader on an isolated radio site deep in enemy territory. For eleven days after the action, although wounded, he evaded the enemy, but was then captured and spent the next twenty-three months as a prisoner of war in North Vietnam. After his release he continued in the army and retired as a sergeant major. He currently farms in California, and has three grandsons and two granddaughters.

anything." And I said, "Get the hell out of here." And he said, "Well, I thought you were Special Forces. Train me in three minutes." So I put him on the .50 caliber and I told him keep it pointed down range. "If you see anybody, fire. Engage him." I put one of my Montagnards there to keep the gun firing down range. I said, "Okay, you're right. Bye. You got it?" He said, "Yep, I got it." So I start moving around the camp, getting everybody set in their defensive positions.

So I move around and I hear a big boom up at the other end of the camp. I get around the corner and here is Walter. He's standing and trying to pull the .50 caliber back into the camp. I race up and dive and knock him on the ground, and I roll him over. What had happened was the rocket hit the top of the sandbags. The sandbags were like concrete. The rocket just literally sandblasted him. I mean his face looked like hamburger, and his glasses were completely frosted over. I said, "Can you see?" And he goes, "I think I'm blind." I go, "Does this help any?" And he goes, "I can see a little bit." I pick him up, throw him on my shoulders, and run across the helipad, zigzagging. I drop him off.

Charlie was probably the best mortar men there is. They dropped over a hundred fifty rounds and not one round went outside my walls. And we counterbatteried. I had about a fifteen-foot pole and I would run out, stick this

Members of the 5th Battalion, 2nd Arty, II Field Force, fire their quad .50 machine guns to check their operation at Fire Support Base "Nancy" or "French Fort." The quad .50 was originally designed as an anti-aircraft weapon during World War II but proved so effective against ground forces that it was often used to great success in the Vietnam War.

pole out, count how many rounds, 'cause you could hear thump, thump, thump, thump, thump, and say okay, I've got five rounds in the air. You wait for five explosions. Fifth one hit, jump up and run out there and you feel in the crater and find out where that fuse went, slide the pole in it, get an azimuth off it or direction, and then look at the angle and set your gun up just like you'd start, boom, boom, boom, and try to walk mortar round right them for counterbattery.

I had a couple of more guys get wounded. I get ships start coming in. I'm loading people and getting them out, and we have to wait and listen for mortar rounds and then as soon as the mortar rounds hit, in would come the ship. Then you'd throw everybody on it real quick. In ten seconds I'd have them all back out there.

It's about four o'clock in the afternoon. They call in and say, "John, this is the last helicopter." I got twenty-six little people. I got four Americans. I got a combo man who was really good. I realized our chances of getting away weren't real good, so I didn't want him here. He knew everything about the equipment, the systems, the codes, everything. So he was on the helicopter. Another combo man on the helicopter. That left Jones, myself, and seventeen little people when the ship lifted off. I would have had twenty, but two grabbed hold of the skid of the last helicopter. I said, if you can pull them in, pull them in. If you can't pull them in or the ship's going down, I said shoot them all. I'd rather do that than have them falling. One guy had fallen off and on the other side, pulled the guy in. I put Walter on that helicopter but he already slid out of three helicopters. I told one of my Montagnards if he starts to get out, you shoot him through the leg. I told Walter the same and I got him out of there.

We knew we couldn't defend the whole camp, so Jones and I decided we were going to defend half of it. I don't know why, but we were standing up on top of a damn bunker, kind of looking out and I mean people could have been shot. We're looking around and all of a sudden, the mortar round came right in between us and it was a delay fuse. It went all the way through the bunker and blew up inside. It took me and threw me about twenty yards out of the camp. Outside of my concertina and tanglefoot that I knew nobody could get through. It didn't take me more than ten seconds to get back in that camp. Oh, fear will do a lot for you. It didn't hurt either one of us. We decided what we could defend. Pulled one hundred buckets out from beneath the outhouse and I put one of my Yards that I called Moat, which was number one. Then I had another one set up a machine gun in a bunker. Then I took a machine gun and got up on top of the ammo bunker. We had blown up one portion of the wall so I took a 106 round. Took out the fuse and pack it with C-4 and then put a detonator into it with a pressure plate. I put it in a hole right there and I lowered the sand bag into it. So this looks like another blown sandbag. And I had this real flimsy stick and I lower this thing to the plunger. And then I haul it back. My Yard is sitting there with his eyes just getting bigger and bigger.

Charlie decides to attack. But he's not attacking with a big force. He's attacking probably with about fifteen to twenty guys. And the first thing they do is run through that breach. It blows. Needless to say, there wasn't any more attack. So we wait. It's starting to get a little bit darker. I put trip-wires and grenades into the bunkers that I left there at the base. We booby-trapped them. In come fifteen guys. And we'd hear booby traps going off. They finally got to the edge. Now you got to keep in mind, this whole camp is sixty-eight meters long and it's only twenty-four meters wide. So it's not a real big place. They continued to attack us and they would try to attack across the helipad. They never could locate us because with three machine guns in cross fire, nobody lived to say where we were firing from. We kept this up till almost two in the morning. Nobody had attacked for almost a half hour. Then they changed their attack plan.

Charlie started a major push with everybody. He was just going to overrun us. So I stayed up on the bunker, and I yelled to Moat and High and some of the other Yards to start pulling back. About that time I got a dumb attack and decided to stand up and start shooting. And I did. Then I got a sane attack and said, "What the hell am I doing here." I started to turn around to get down off the bunker, and I got hit in the back and it went

Carrying a 90mm recoilless rifle, a soldier of the 9th Infantry Division passes a burning Vietnam Cong base.

all the way up to my neck and threw me off the bunker. Moat and High came running back. They were going to police me up and carry me off. I told them, "No, you get the hell out of here." I didn't know how serious I was hit. I had already been hit through the face here so I told them get out of here. "You guys can make it back." Both of them did. Both got the Bronze Star with a V. Most of the guys went over the hill. Six or seven of them got captured. I went back. My partner was on the radio and I told him, "Come on, let's go." He said, "Just a minute." Next thing I know, Charlie rushed across the hill, and we were trapped.

I told my partner to get off the top of his bed and get down underneath so now if anybody comes in I'll kill them. "Don't shoot because they don't know we are here." As luck would have it, the first two guys through the door, one of them has no weapon, the other one's got an AK. The one in front got a flashlight shining in that far. So I let him go because he doesn't have a weapon, and my threat is the second guy. I stabbed and killed the second guy. Turned around and grabbed the first guy and my partner let loose with a thirty-round magazine. So they knew where we were.

I didn't realize it but there was a big air hole in the back of this bunker. It was one sand bag big. A hand comes through it and drops a grenade. They drop it right between Jones' legs and it goes off. He says, "I got to surrender." I said, "I'm dead. Just keep that in mind, I'm dead." And so he ran out and unfortunately when you're surrendering, it's not a good idea to call them motherfucker, which he did. And they shot and killed him dead on the spot. Blew him back into the bunker. I played dead. Then I got on a radio. I'm on the radio talking and the next thing a grenade rolls in the bunker only this time it's one of ours. I saw it coming and I realized what it was, and all I did was yell "Grenade," and then I went into a fetal position, opened my mouth so I wouldn't start hemorrhaging my lungs. It went off and I was cross-eyed with it. It really messed up my legs. So I get up and I'm sitting back, got a machine gun across my lap and I said, "Well, the next guy that comes in has one of the bayonets out then, I'm just going to shoot him. I'll take my chances." As he comes in, he doesn't have his bayonet out and he pokes me in the chest. He pokes me three times in the chest. The third time I just let my hand fall and I had blood all over it because I still was hemorrhaging.

He thought I was dead and he walks out the door. He realizes the bunker is lined in tar paper. So he takes out his trusty little lighter and lights the bunker on fire, and they all stood outside to watch the weenie roast. Unfortunately I was in there a lot longer than I wanted to be, and I had tar all down my face and my hands and pants caught on fire. I'm trying to lay there, patting my pants, trying to get the fire out. They're staring at me and finally they walk off. I had already broken off my belt because it was so hot, ammo was going off on my belt. I threw the belt down in the corner where it would be the coolest. As I started to make for the door, my own machine gun cooked off and hit me in the steel pot. Knocked me out cold. There I am, with my feet about this far from the entrance of the bunker and it burned all night. Needless to say, it also burned the soles of my boots.

The sun isn't up and I'm getting a lot of ambient light. I decided to start ahead and I managed to get in another bunker. One of the North Vietnamese is still up on the hill. I'm sitting there and I've already taken out everything except a picture of my daughter, my Geneva Convention card, and my ID. Everything else I've already shredded and kind of cast around the room. The rest I stick that back in my wallet. Well, I've got meat hanging off my hands from being burned, and I'm kind of holding them up because there's a fog that's coming through and it feels pretty good on my hands. Because the bunker is half underground, half above ground, all of a sudden there's a pair of legs. This guy decides to come in and loot and as he does, I reach up and grab a piece of cardboard and I get behind it. I got it with my fingernails and I pulled out my knife. The poor guy just comes up, bring the cardboard down and I stabbed him and killed him. And all of a sudden my entire body said it's time to go to sleep. I crawled under the bed in the bunker and went to sleep. My body says that's it, I quit. I woke up and a guy had a hold of my foot and he was turning it around trying to see if the boots were too big. They finally got up and left. I crawled over the wall and then started escaping and evading for the next eleven days.

I finally got captured by a little old guy about seventy-eight years old with an old gun. Just as scared as I was. I had no weapons. They hauled me up North and I spent a couple of years in prison in North Vietnam and I got released in 1973 and was presented the Medal of Honor for actions up on Hickory in December 12, 1974.

I wasn't born in this country. I got my citizenship in 1968. I had lived in the States since 1947, and to me it was kind of like an obligation that I had to my country. I was a farm boy. Anti-war didn't mean much one way or the another. I never questioned the validity of the war because I believed that much in my country. The individuals I served with were just a general cross section of America: black, white, Asian, Hispanic. We were brought together, and they were all really professional. They knew what they did, and they did it because they wanted to and not because anybody ordered them to. They volunteered to get in Special Forces. They volunteered for Airborne. They volunteered for SOG. You had to volunteer for the missions they took. You ever look at that long wall in Washington, D.C., there's a whole lot of guys on it. They did it because of what we thought we could do, which is save American lives. And we hung our butts up to do that.

WARREN MILBURG

Operation Phoenix
CIA
U.S. Army

Warren Milburg

When I left Vietnam in 1966, I was contacted by the agency some months later to ask me if I wanted to go back to Vietnam to work in a program they were developing at that time. It wasn't called the Phoenix program at that time. It was basically the pacification program. What the agency was looking for were a number of people who had been in Vietnam before, and by 1966 there were not a lot of people who had prior experience in Vietnam, that knew something about the history, the culture, the language of the country, and had had some combat experience. I was one of the people who met that criteria. So I volunteered to go into training in the agency and to return to Vietnam in early 1967 as a pacification officer for the agency in Quang Tri.

I arrived in Quang Tri in the middle part of 1967, landing in a small single-engine plane on a dirt runway. When I got out of the plane there were a number of Vietnamese around and the guy who I was replacing met me there. He drove me in a jeep to where they were living, which was a little rented house on the outskirts of Quang Tri City, and the city itself was nothing more than a crossroads in the northernmost province where two dirt streets came together with a variety of shops, food stands, and things like that along the periphery where about twelve thousand people lived. So there was not a whole lot of anonymity in Quang Tri, but within Quang Tri there were other U.S. civilian and military organizations. On the other end of this provincial capital was a MACV compound that had a small number of U.S. military advisors to the ARVN, the Republic of Vietnam's army. They worked with the army trying to get them to improve their performance in the field. There were also elements of the State Department and U.S. AID as well. They worked with their counterparts in the provincial government to help them do whatever it was that they were going to do in terms of trying to improve the democratization of the country, agriculture in the country, food, health, education, and so forth.

My responsibilities essentially involved developing rapport with all of the Vietnamese officials who were somehow involved with intelligence collection and/or the using of intelligence to further the cause of countering the war effort on the part of the North Vietnamese and the Viet Cong. I was involved with developing relationships with the national police special branch, which was the internal Vietnamese intelligence collection structure under the interior department and the national police unit in Saigon, with the Central Intelligence Organization, which was their external intelligence collection arm, and a variety of other smaller activities, also involved with intelligence collection. What we did basically on a daily basis was to review various sources of information, which were being developed bilaterally or unilaterally by either my counterpart or myself, and to make a decision about which operations and which people we might want to fund, to work with those sources on what kind of information we wanted from them, to basically provide some trade-craft training to the sources and to our counterparts.

For example, if we collected information about a Viet Cong military unit that was moving from one place to another, then the decision had to be made was who was in the best position to take action, to intercept that unit and do whatever might be necessary to counteract it. In some cases if the intelligence indicated a major military unit was moving from one place to another, for example, a North Vietnamese army unit that was a fairly large unit, then we would probably provide that information to the Marines, which were located within the province.

Our job within the Phoenix program when it evolved into the Phoenix program was to identify who these individual cadres were, what they were doing, what the directions were, and basically try to develop programs which would otherwise neutralize the ability of the provincial committees to carry out the tasks that were assigned to them by the North Vietnamese.

If information indicated that a person had been identified by name and location as a member of the Viet Cong infrastructure we would attempt to determine how accurate the information was. We had a name, we had a place, and was this person really a Viet Cong or was this person's name on this list for the wrong reasons. The wrong reasons could have been anything you could guess at, from somebody reporting somebody because they didn't like them, because they stole their pig, or they were growing rice in a place they shouldn't be growing rice, or they really were in a Viet Cong infrastructure, a member. We would attempt through various means to cross-check this person's name to see if it was showing up on other lists that had been collected from other sources or to otherwise verify that this was a valid person to target. In the context of the Phoenix program, "to target" meant to me that we would then attempt to capture that person, we would try to find out where that person was and when he or she was most vulnerable and to intercept that person by whatever means possible. By whatever means possible either meant a U.S. military unit would be assigned the task, or that a South Vietnamese police or military unit would be assigned that task or in some cases members of the provincial reconnaissance units, which were mercenaries hired by me and paid for by the CIA, would be used depending on who was available and what made the most sense. Once that person was identified and captured, and I emphasize that the goal was to capture that person, then what would typically happen was he would be moved to a South Vietnamese police facility, sometimes a province interrogation center where that person would be interrogated for applicable information that he or she might be able to provide us leading to the identification and capture of yet other people who were of military operations that the Viet Cong or the army were planning. And sometimes these people would be cooperative. And there was a program called the Chu Hoi program which was a program designed by the U.S. and

The evacuation of Army, Air Force, and civilian personnel from Da Nang, Vietnam, was carried out by Marine Corps helicopters. Evacuation security was provided by men from K Company, 3rd Battalion, and B Company, 2nd Battalion, 9th Marine Regiment. Security actions included road blocks and searching of the Vietnamese passing through the area.

The Montagnard tribes were an indigenous people who suffered greatly under the communists in Vietnam. They were widely respected by American Special Forces who worked with them to fight against the North Vietnamese Army.

South Vietnamese to basically get North Vietnamese or Viet Cong people to rally over to the side of the South Vietnamese where they would be given food, shelter, housing, and education and even perhaps a job. And it was a moderately successful program. As you can imagine, life as a Viet Cong in the field was not a life of luxury, it was a life of privation, of danger and death. There weren't a whole lot of Viet Cong that went on to be national leaders. In any event, we would capture these people or try to capture them, move them into interrogation system, try to exploit the information that we developed from them as quickly as possible. And then those people were passed on to the judicial system within South Vietnam where they were tried.

The people who were leaders of the Viet Cong clearly did not want to be captured and they often moved with armed groups of Viet Cong for protection. And whenever that happened typically what might ensue would be a firefight of some sort between their forces and ours. And this I think is where most of the stories of abuses within the Phoenix program stem. When those firefight ended, people were frequently wounded or dead, and it clearly was not the intent to kill people when we went out to capture them. But yet this was a war zone, people knew that if they were captured they would probably were going to have a difficult life afterward and did not want to be captured. So there were any number of incidents where the result of the operation were dead people.

War is an awful thing no matter how you slice and dice it, wherever and whenever it takes place, it's an awful thing. It's something that you almost have to experience to get the visual sense of what is actually occurring. Vietnam in the years that I was there was a very disorganized and confused place. If you read anything of

An aerial view of Quang Tri, in northern South Vietnam, a prime target of the Communists during the Tet Offensive.

Clauswitz you quickly come to understand what he meant when he wrote somewhere in the 1830s about the fog of war. Everything was foggy in Vietnam: policies were foggy, operations were foggy, nothing was really clear. You didn't really clearly know who the enemy was. It was not uncommon, and did in fact happen on a couple of occasions that we, in our little compound in Quang Tri, were attacked by women and children. We had a little guy who used to deliver bread, French bread, little baguettes of bread in a bag every day, and one day instead of delivering baguettes of bread he delivered hand grenades that he threw over the wall. Children had somehow been perverted into a combat role. We had women who were members of the Viet Cong and carried rifles and went into combat like their male counterparts did.

The fog of war was everywhere. It was really different in terms of trying to figure out who was on your side and who was not. I still recall an instance when one of my PRU guards—the PRUs guarded our compound as well as our operations—brought a fellow into the compound by the scruff of his neck, who was kicking and screaming. On his person we took a notepad and when we translated the notepad it turned out that it was a list of all my comings and goings from the compound we lived in. The conclusion we came to was that this was an assassination diary. That what this fellow was doing was collecting information on my patterns, and I,

A soldier talks to a Vietnamese woman whose home was destroyed in the Cholon area of Saigon during the Tet Offensive.

as an intelligence professional, would like to think I didn't set daily patterns, but of course I had. He had the time and date when I ever left the compound, and where I went and when I came back and so forth. And this guy lived right across the street from where we were. We saw him frequently, and it was only once the guards got suspicious of what he was doing with some binoculars and went over and chatted with him, saw his notes, and took him over to us, and turned him over to the police. And the only reason I share that story is that you never knew where the threat was, you never knew in what form it was going to come at you. In the course of having to live like that, abuses occurred. People did things that they probably shouldn't have done, but it was all justified under the overall rubric of war. And war is awful and ugly and hardly ever solves whatever the political problem was that you started out to support.

Here I was, a relatively young CIA officer on the ground in Vietnam, and my job ostensibly was to basically train a Vietnamese counterpart in his intelligence organization, to be as professional as I was. And I had the resources, the background, and the training to do that. Well, here I had arrived in this little crossroads in the northern part of what was South Vietnam only to meet a counterpart who was about twenty years older than I was, had worked in intelligence all of his professional life, had been part of the intelligence resistance to the Viet Minh years before. And I quickly found that I was learning more about intelligence collection and operation in an insurgency warfare then he was learning form me. My other colleagues in the program and other provinces, when I got together with them and we talked about this, made it clear that I was extremely lucky. Many of the colleagues and counterparts that they had in their provinces were not nearly as professional or as competent as I was. Many were corrupt, many were inept, many were cowards. And as a result, the people in other provinces who had the same job and responsibilities that I had had miserable times when they were there trying to accomplish anything. And many of them went home bitter and disillusioned. The same thing did not happen to me. And again I think it was primarily because of the sincerity and ability of the Vietnamese that I was working for and within that province.

When I volunteered I was in my early twenties, and I was probably one of those kind of people at that time who believed that life was a series of exciting adventures—that once you pursue that the only way that you were going to die was somebody was either going to drive a wooden stake through your heart or shoot you with a silver bullet. You believed in your own immortality. I also wasn't quite aware then as I am now about how the political operations of this country work. After I came back from Vietnam, I got to work pretty close to the White House and with many of the people that were making policies and continued to make policies. I got to understand the basis on which a lot of decisions were made that resulted in the death of a lot of people, lists, citizens and others. So would I do this again? I clearly would not do this again at this point in my life. If I knew then what I know now, I probably would not have volunteered. Such is the process of learning and growing.

We saw all kinds of atrocities that occurred at the hands of the North Vietnamese and the Viet Cong as a way of that country's implementation of its own policies. They basically terrorized the people in the hamlets and the countryside. We saved a lot of people from that fate. And so I feel like that was a major accomplishment. In some cases we were able to arm and train villages to defend themselves from intimidation and coercion or death at the hands of the Vietnamese, of Viet Cong who would impress them into the military, would steal their rice, who would rape and loot villages for a variety of reasons. To continue their own cause. We were able I think on a personal level to save a lot of people from that fate. Of course, I have to say that within the context of what happened in the post-1975 period, when a very brutal Communist regime swept into Saigon and caused millions of people to flee the countryside, to be in re-education camps for years and basically to vote with their feet or their very shaky boats when they put out to sea and risked their lives and their families' lives to escape.

JOHN COOK

Captain
Operation Phoenix
U.S. Army

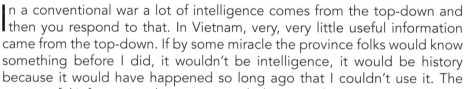

John Cook was an Army intelligence officer with Operation Phoenix in the late 1960s assigned to the Xi An district in Bien Hoa province, near Saigon.

John Cook

In a conventional war a lot of intelligence comes from the top-down and then you respond to that. In Vietnam, very, very little useful information came from the top-down. If by some miracle the province folks would know something before I did, it wouldn't be intelligence, it would be history because it would have happened so long ago that I couldn't use it. The most useful information that we responded to was what we generated ourselves. And so what you would do is you would gather your own intelligence, you would refine it, and you would act on it. In one maybe successful operation you would make a capture or you'd capture documents, and they would lead you somewhere else. So you would go wherever the evidence would take you and slowly a picture would emerge of the Viet Cong structure in your own district. And so you'd start to fill in the blanks and once you had the Viet Cong district chief, then you would try to put in the Viet Cong village chiefs and the hamlet chiefs. Then once you had their starting line-up in place, so to speak, then you would start going after them. And you would do whatever you had to do to get those guys. The idea was to take out that leadership because the most hardcore of the Viet Cong by definition would be those in the leadership positions. So those were the ones you wanted to go after. They were the most zealous of all. Now if you eliminated a guy, he would be replaced. But you were banking on the fact that his replacement would not be as idealistic as the guy you had eliminated. And so through attrition you would get them to a point where they would basically become ineffective. And that's precisely what happened. Over a period of a little over two years, we totally eliminated the Viet Cong infrastructure in Xi An district. By totally eliminating the Viet Cong infrastructure, you by definition eliminated the Viet Cong influence.

The name of the game is you want to take that guy out of play. Clearly your most attractive option is to capture him, because if you capture him he can talk. If you kill him, that's not bad. I mean that's your next option, down the line. But clearly the number one option is let's capture this guy. Let's capture him, let's get all the information we can out of him, and then we'll use that information to get more. But if you couldn't capture him, then you had to eliminate him. Most of the operations were clearly geared to capture—a raid, a snatch operation, ambush. And if that didn't succeed, then you would try something else. But the name of the game was to take him out, and the first choice would be capture, the second choice would be kill him.

Chin Hien was a Viet Cong village chief. He was a fairly bad guy. He had been responsible for the death of several of the villagers. We planned an operation, several operations, to get him as a matter of fact. One day we got good information that led us to a tunnel in the process and rarely would they come out of the tunnel. We would always, you know, ask them to come out, Chu Hoi, which was the open-arms South Vietnamese program to get them to surrender. If they are very, very hardcore Viet Cong, which was by definition what it took to be a senior member of the Viet Cong infrastructure, they wouldn't do that. And so what would happen is you would usually get some exchange, they may even try to throw a grenade out of a tunnel, which is a very, very poor position to take. We would wind up throwing grenades in the tunnel. This happened over and over again. In the case of Chin Hien we pulled him out of the tunnel. He was obviously in very bad shape. He was mortally wounded but he was conscious. And I think he knew he wasn't going to make it.

My counterpart was with me, and we would talk about everything that went on with the operation. So Chin Hien was trying to talk and we all moved down very close to see what it was he was saying. Was he making some last death-bed confession, so to speak, or rice paddy confession? What he was actually asking was, how bad am I? And the reality was he was very bad, he was going to die. He asked my counterpart if he would do him the honor of killing him. And he took out his .45 and shot him in the head. That incident at the time did not seem all that far-fetched because I think all there had hoped that in that same situation our enemy would have probably granted us the same courtesy and the same dignity. Even though Chin Hien and my counterpart were diametrically opposed on the political spectrum, there was still a certain element of strange respect that they had for each other. I think that was a very profound scene that I witnessed. You know you could argue that technically was that a war crime, probably was, but I don't think any of us at the time thought so.

Once the Viet Cong influence had been eliminated, then the government programs key to pacification could go forward. For example, you could go out there and you could raise rice again, you could build schools again, you could build roads again. And the economy would thrive again. So as soon as we eliminated the Viet Cong at any particular hamlet or village, we would have to have a program to put right back in there. One of the most successful programs we had was a pig raising project, where we would give the villagers piglets, and then they would grow them to market size and they'd sell them in Saigon. You would replace communism with good old-fashion capitalism. And they liked it, they liked the idea of making a profit. And it was their profit.

As far as the South Vietnamese and the Americans were concerned, the emphasis was to attack the enemy and the goal was to save the people. With the Viet Cong and the North Vietnamese, attacking the population wasn't a mistake or an accident. It was a matter of course. It was part of the doctrine to sacrifice a certain part of the population to send a message to the other part. And their principal weapon of choice was terror. That they would go in a hamlet or village and tell the people, we don't want you cooperating with the government—if you do, we're going to come back and we will kill your children. This wasn't an idle threat. So the burden on the government was to protect the people at the same time they were attacking the Viet Cong and the North Vietnamese. The North Vietnamese and Viet Cong had no obligation to protect the people. Their principal purpose in life was to attack the government and the Americans and to show the people that the

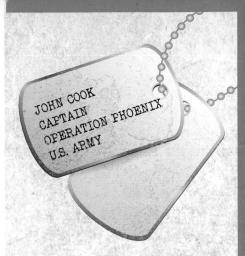

John Cook

Born and brought up in the coal fields of West Virginia, Cook attended the University of Delaware and Boston University before going off to Vietnam in 1968 as a 2nd lieutenant in the army. He served as the Phoenix advisor to the Xi An District and then as senior district advisor, the only captain to have a district. He left Vietnam after twenty-five months. Cook retired a lieutenant colonel from the army in 1988 after twenty-one years of service. He works as a consultant to the army, teaches, and is the author of *The Advisor: The Phoenix Program* in Vietnam. He lives in Maryland with his wife and two children, where he continues to pursue his writing career.

government couldn't defend them. So in a lot of ways the advantage, all the breakpoints went to the enemy and very few of the breakpoints went to us. We would be as careful as we possibly could in taking out only the Viet Cong and the Viet Cong leadership and leaving the people intact. Otherwise there was no point in being there.

Because they all looked the same, the Viet Cong during the day may very well be a member of the hamlet or the village, he may actually have a job in the major population center. He may actually be working for one of the American units on the base camp, he may be working in the kitchen, he may be processing some of their travel orders. It was unbelievably difficult, it's like taking the chocolate out of chocolate milk. So therefore you become totally dependent on having very, very good information. And not just some guy coming in saying, you know, he thinks that Nguyen Van Tu is a VC and he's saying that because he's upset with Nguyen Van Tu because Tu took his girlfriend. I mean you would have to do two or three checks on that until you were confident that this information was good. But then on the other hand if it was good information, you had to react quickly because it was very perishable. Just because the guys going to be there tonight doesn't mean he's going to be there tomorrow night.

Our chief interrogator was a South Vietnamese army sergeant. We called him Sad Eyes because he always had the saddest look. It was never much happiness with him. But he was a very, very effective interrogator, not in the sense that he would take them in the back room and slap them around a little bit or hook them up to generators or anything. But Sad Eyes was a master of psychology. He knew where their weak points were. And if you captured a guy, you had some advantages in the district before he got in to the system. Sad Eyes would explain the government program to these guys in no uncertain terms. He'd say look, you know how would you like to be rated? Would you like to be rated as a captured Viet Cong enemy soldier or would you like to have your status upgraded to one of defector, rallier, a guy who surrendered. If the guy was wavering a little bit anyway and had a lot of doubts about the Viet Cong, this was a very, very effective tool. Sad Eyes had a very effective way about empathizing with the guys. He would often tell them that he used to be a VC but that wasn't true. It was: I know what it's like to live in the tunnels, I know what it's like to live in the rice paddies and all that. In some cases he would have the guy going, if we captured him in the morning, he would take us back to where the other VC were by that afternoon. So he was absolutely a master.

Probably the most notorious group in the district when it came to assassination was a group we called the Chau Thoi Gang. They operated out of the highest point in the district, the Chau Thoi mountain. These were the folks who would go out and in essence assassinate hamleters and villagers if the leadership said that's what needed to happen. So they were one of the highest priorities we had, eliminating them. We had some good information. We launched an operation. We did not realize just how strong this group was. We thought it was probably four, five or six, it turned out to be twelve or fifteen of these guys. And they were in a very heavily wooded ravine. We actually had to call in gunships to blow them out. And when it was all over and we had eliminated them, killed them, we found lots of documents. And one of the most satisfying things about the Chau Thoi operation was that we actually had lists for the first time of who their potential victims would be. So we had names of rice farmers and the satisfaction of knowing that that rice farmer would not die because we had actually eliminated these guys. All day we spent on this operation and at that end of the day we piled them all up and took all the documents back. And it was a wonderful feeling to know that we had actually prevented those guys from killing more of our people.

Each operation in essence was tailor-made for what you expected to find. Now this is not an exact science because if you think you're going to go out and get three guys, you had better be prepared to handle eight or nine because you know you can be off that much. But if you're fully expecting a lot of action, then you take a large force. A typical force would be a province reconnaissance unit, a platoon of popular force, maybe a platoon of regional force. And if there was a U.S. unit in the area, let's say an infantry battalion, we'd get a company of those guys. That would be a very, very effective force, because now no matter what you run into, you can call in tactical air, you could call in artillery, you could call in medical evacuation. So each operation depended on what you expected to find and you could mix and match. The district chief had total control over all the district forces. And in Xi An district alone, if we mobilized every popular force or platoon, every regional force unit, the PRU, we had a force of some six hundred or seven hundred soldiers. We could never put those together at any one time but that would be our total operational forces.

The entrance to a Vietnamese tunnel complex. The Communists used extensive underground tunnel systems for command and control centers, ammunition storage, and medical facilities.

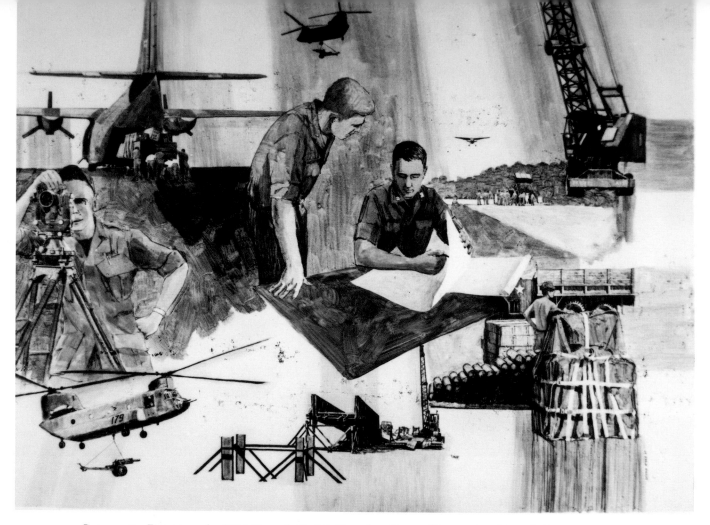

Composite Painting, *by SP4 Dennis D. McGee. Acrylic on illustration board, Vietnam, 1967.*

A Viet Cong tunnel was not a very elaborate affair. I, an American, really couldn't fit in one. You would have to crawl around. There were living areas, there were sleeping areas, there were eating areas. A typical tunnel, not there was such a thing as a typical tunnel, may have five or six different entrances. They were sectionalized, some of them actually had different stories. You could go down two stories in a tunnel. The amazing thing about the tunnel system was that you could walk over an area any number of times deliberately looking for a tunnel entrance, you'd never find it. Because they were masters at disguising it. They would build the tunnel opening into the grass, into the surrounding terrain. The only way we ever found the entrance to a tunnel was someone pointed it out to us. I remember walking over the same area several times, probably walked over the tunnel entrance and then when we would find a defector and he would point it out to us, it really makes the hair stand up on the back of your neck because you had been there, you had probably walked over that tunnel. And he goes over and he reaches for what you can't see, usually a wire handle buried in the grass, gives a yank and out comes a wooden opening that's perfectly set to go into the sides of the tunnel frame. I was constantly amazed at the workmanship that went into the tunnel and the mastery they had of disguising it. You will never find one by mistake, or stumble on it.

I can't think of a case, a single case where anyone in a tunnel actually surrendered but you would go through the ritual of telling them to surrender. Sometimes they would actually toss a grenade out, or actually try to come out and fire at you. If you're outside a tunnel, you have all the advantages over someone inside the tunnel. And the easiest solution at that point was to just roll a grenade in, and usually because of the blast of the grenade in a confined space that usually takes care of everyone in the tunnel, at least in that portion of the tunnel. And that's usually how a tunnel operation would end in my district, was a grenade would go in the tunnel and that would be the end of it.

In one case I remember clearly a beautiful young woman had become a tax collector in Dong Hoa village, and we had gathered a lot of information about her. We tried to get her to defect and none of that worked. Rarely did that work unless you could capture someone who knew them directly and then you could go right up to do the capture. She was one of the victims of a tunnel-bombing. She was in there with some members of the Viet Cong, wouldn't come out, and she was killed. And very beautiful, beautiful young woman, only nineteen years old. I think one of the saddest days I had personally was pulling her out of the tunnel, because it just seemed so wrong to have a woman killed in combat. I realized that was simply an emotional opinion on my part. But that story was very poignant when we pulled her out, beautiful girl.

That wasn't a weakness in the system or fault in the Phoenix program, but she was a casualty of the war. In her own way she was probably as effective as a lot of the other members of the Viet Cong infrastructure. It was simply my emotional reaction to all the twisted broken bodies we had hauled out of tunnels. The first time you haul a beautiful young woman out had an impact, it really did. And I think part of it was that she only had a couple of small wounds, but one of them was a fragment of a grenade went through her skull. She almost looked asleep when we pulled her out, but she was dead.

In context, you're in combat, you're in a war, there are people out there doing very, very bad things to your people. One of the things that happens to you is you start thinking of it as your district, these are your people. Some forty thousand people living in Xi An district, trying to make a living and all they want to do is be left alone. They don't want anyone harassing them. They certainly don't want anyone killing them. They don't want to give half of their income to the Viet Cong. So day after day when you would see the results of the Viet Cong, the atrocities, there was a certain kind of very, very real red-hot hatred that you would feel for them. We would set up till late into the night to plot attacks against them. Even though as a professional intelligence officer I realized that my first objective was to try to capture them alive, it really didn't matter to me at certain points whether we captured them alive or whether we killed them. The name of the game was to get rid of them because this was truly the enemy. The striking back was very rewarding. I did not work the Phoenix daily but became the district senior advisor. I got involved with more of the pacification programs which was very important, very helpful, very beneficial to the district. And by the time I left in July of 1970 all thirty-six of our hamlets had received the highest rating that they could under a program called the hamlet evaluation system. Which meant that you could drive anywhere in Xi An district in July of 1970 alone. And the biggest danger you would have is some guy running you off the road with a Lambretta. So to me that was success. We had eliminated the enemy in Xi An district, and that was as good as we could get.

MOVING TROOPS AND SUPPLIES

The men who served in the infantry in Vietnam, America's front line troops, spent most of their time walking. Once on the ground, they walked into battle. That was their job. When they walked, they slogged through miles of rice paddies. They plowed their way through jungles and endless plantations of rubber trees, originally planted by the French colonizers of Vietnam. They trudged up and down the seemingly worthless rocky hills and scrub bushes found on the mountains in the Central Highlands. They walked what felt like forever until they engaged their enemy in battle.

When a soldier or Marine received some respite from walking he experienced a degree of happiness. He was able to relieve his aching legs, his battered feet, and his sore back, if only for a moment.

The majority of action seen by men on patrol was usually in small units, the squad, the platoon, and the company. When troops had long distances to travel, they might arrive at a staging area far from the combat zone on a C-47 Skytrain, the 123 Provider, the C-130 Hercules, or the C-141 Starlifter, among others. As their names imply, those big aircraft ferried men and supplies throughout South Vietnam where there were landing strips long enough to allow them to land safely. Before he walked into combat, the trooper arrived at the proper location by truck, by Chinook 47 Helicopter, or by the smaller all-purpose Huey. He might arrive also at a jumping off point on the odd looking Army C-7 Caribou that traveled throughout Vietnam, carrying both soldiers and equipment. Once in the combat zone, other means of transportation took over.

Getting men in place is only part of the story. Every general in history from Hannibal and Napoleon to General Erwin Rommel and General Dwight D. Eisenhower knew the importance of supplying troops with what they require in the field. War and the needs of warriors remain unchanged through time. In order to function the best they can, Army troops and Marines need food, water, shelter, medicine, and ammunition. Equipment and supplies from the United States arrived by air and boat at heavily guarded supply depots in Saigon, Qui Nhon, Phan Rang, Nha Trang, Cam Ranh Bay, the military section of Tan Son Nhut Airport outside Saigon, and other locations in South Vietnam.

The United States Army Transportation Command was in charge of moving supplies and men around the country. Once in place, the supplies moved by

This is an M113, an armored personnel carrier with a .50 cal machine gun in support of Marines. The M113 could carry up to 11 passengers and could be modified for many uses, including medevac and command & control. Because they had relatively thin armor, the sandbags on the front were probably added to increase protection against rocket propelled grenades and heavy caliber machine gun fire.

Military Police (MPs) closing up a truck as they prepare to patrol.

A 2½ ton truck fords a river, moving 1st Cavalry division to camp.

An M113 moves past the result of combat detritis. Originally designed in 1921, the M113 is carrying an M2 .50 caliber machine gun, which is a devastating weapon originally designed to shoot down airplanes.

single truck or more usually in convoys, mostly by the famed deuce and a half, the two and half-ton truck used for everything in the country. The M520 Goer, an Army heavy duty, amphibious and articulated monster of a truck had the ability to move easily over rocky terrain despite its 8-ton size, through streams and small waterways and to go where few other trucks could. The transportation command also moved supplies on rivers and inland waterways by boats attached to the specialized Riverine Force.

Convoys often had as many as two hundred trucks of all sizes on the road at the same time. Many convoys moved along Highway 1, one of the better roads that bisected South Vietnam and ran from the coast to the Central Highlands carrying supplies to cities such as Pleiku, Kontum, and An Khe. Because of the long trip, the mostly slow-moving fleet always seemed to come under enemy fire. Enemy ambushes were regular occurrences. Ambushes caused pain, injuries, damage, and delays in getting supplies to their destination. But the convoys kept traveling, despite what some drivers called annoyances. The drivers had a job to do—men needed supplies and ammunition.

After too many defenseless ambushes in places they called "Ambush Alley" and along the "Devil's Hairpin," American ingenuity took over. Drivers decided they would try to defend themselves if attacked, which they knew would surely happen. Some clever soldiers loaded a

A Special Forces team is lifted out of the jungle with the use of a McGuire Rig. The McGuire Rig allowed for rapid extraction in an emergency without the helicopter having to land.

A CH-47 Chinook on the ground.

few two and half-ton cargo trucks with two M60 machine guns surrounded and protected by sandbags. In some cases, they even added other weapons, such as .50 caliber machine guns. Over time, the sandbags proved to be too bulky and soon steel plates replaced them to help protect the men operating the weapons who were defending the convoy. The newly designed weapons trucks took on names such as "Iron Butterfly" and "Deuce is Wild."

These gun trucks neither deterred nor ended the enemy attacks. The Viet Cong and North Vietnamese soldiers continued to ambush the trucks as they moved everywhere on good and bad roads in South Vietnam. But having armed trucks in the fleet gave other drivers a bit of security that they did not have before those trucks could provide a limited defense against a well-hidden enemy.

★ CHAPTER 5 ★
THE AIR WAR

Unlike anything else in the Vietnam War, the war in the air is at once the most exciting, the most dangerous, and the most difficult to gauge and appreciate.

When measured in numbers, air power was particularly deadly and effective. The Air Force had frequent flights from Udorn and Korat, Thailand, from Tan Son Nhut, Bien Hoa, and Da Nang. Fighter and fighter-bombers attacked enemy troops on the ground and gave close support to troops during combat. They pounded the Ho Chi Minh Trail whenever possible. Navy aircraft flying off carriers in the South China Sea regularly hit enemy traffic in ever-changing shipping lanes. Marine aircraft flew from Da Nang and Chu Lai to protect and aid the grunts on the ground in I Corps, northern South Vietnam. Silent and deadly flights of B-52s from Guam dropped huge amounts of bombs on unsuspecting enemy below. F-105 Thunderchiefs and F-4 Phantoms roared out of the sky to attack the enemy on the ground and get into dogfights over North Vietnam with Russian and Chinese MiGs, piloted by the North Vietnamese. Soon we had American "aces," a special breed of jet jockey's who had destroyed more than six enemy planes in the air during high speed, hi-tech dogfights. Even now, the names roll off our tongues. The F-100. The A-7. The A-4 Skyhawk and the A-6 Intruder. Search-and-rescue operations. Jolly Green Giant helicopters on search and-rescue operations for downed pilots, who were often knocked from the sky by heavy enemy flak.

Helicopters were the workhorse of Vietnam in their role as troop transports and close fire power in support of ground troops. The UH-1 or Huey was an unforgettable symbol of the war. The Air Force created Forward Air Controllers (FACs) to guide and control air strikes on enemy positions in the jungles of Vietnam. Flying in their light propeller-driven aircraft—O-1 Bird Dogs, OV-2 Skymasters, or twin-engine Broncos—FACs were daring young men in their flying machines.

In some ways, the pilots in Vietnam, as in all modern war, were carbon copies of pilots from World War I. In 1917 those bold young pilots often cruised so low to the ground they could clearly see the face of their enemy as they imprecisely tossed bombs and grenades by hand from their tissue-thin airplanes. In the Vietnam war, most of the pilots were just as young and vigorous, and just as daring. Every one of them was brave. They loved flying. Some dreamed of being in the air from the time they were children. Danger and frequent flights into the unknown became a thrilling way for them to live. Yet, as they maneuvered through the air in their massive, powerful, multimillion dollar machines, they depended on each other the same as men did on the ground in hand-to-hand combat. We saw this in those pilots shot down over North Vietnam who did everything they could to evade capture. Other fighter planes and helicopter pilots would search the jungle, find, and rescue the downed pilots when they could. They were a close-knit fraternity. Some pilots and crew unfortunately not rescued became prisoners of war. More than five hundred of them spent the remainder of the war behind bars under subhuman conditions in Hanoi. No matter how much torture they suffered and how much indignity they experienced, they pulled together and they endured, again a testament to the human spirit and the powerful will to survive.

BOB "FRENCHY" GIBEAULT

E4, Helicopter Gunner
UH-1C Huey Gun Platoon
U.S. Army

Bob "Frenchy" Gibeault

The longer I was in country, the more that I had this feeling like I wasn't doing enough. I used to see these choppers flying and I heard about they were looking for gunners. The catch was you had to extend your tour for six months. I had been in country for about four months and I said, well, that's what I want to do.

I got up there and there was nothing. It was just a bunch of tents and a lot of mud and revetments and helicopters and guys building latrines and filling sandbags and laying out barbed wire. I didn't start flying right away because they test you to see if you had the stuff that it took to be on a crew. The right stuff would be the ability to face your fears and suck it down and carry out the mission. That in a nutshell was what they were looking for. After a month I was picked to start off flying in Slicks, which is UH-1D helicopters as a gunner. My first helicopter ride I said, "I don't think I'm going to like this. These things are kind of squirrely."

I'm sitting in a well facing directly outside of the helicopter perpendicular to the pilot. I've got an M60 machine gun linked to a grenade box that probably has about four thousand rounds of ammunition in it. There's a pole in front of me. It's got an assortment of grenades, everything from tear gas to CS, to Willie Peters [white phosphorous], to red smoke, blue smoke, purple smoke, you name it. Part of our job was when you received fire would be to grab a red smoke, pull the pin, and drop the grenade. Where it landed was a marker to where the fire was received, so you could come back and call the gunships on the location. I'm on an open door. We did have what we called chicken plates, ceramic plates that we wore as a vest. It had Velcro that went around your chest. They were relatively small, but supposedly would protect your vitals from a small-caliber round.

On a mission a few of us started to flare approaching the LZ. It was like a ballet. Everything was coordinated. The gunships would be flying right alongside the Slicks, leading them a little bit. All of a sudden we flew into a very deliberate set-up—a professional killing zone, where they triangulated with .51 caliber machine guns and were dug into heavy bunkers there in force. When they started firing, I didn't think, I acted. I fired and I kept firing and kept firing. Everybody was going down and we were hearing Mayday's all over the place. And so we just sort of went around and tried to pick up any wounded and downed crews and get them back to a safe spot and go back and do the same thing over again. There were only three ships left out of the eight ships that went into the LZ. The grunts were in a very bad situation. They were surrounded, and the enemy was using downed helicopters as bait to suck us in. So they would hold their fire until somebody tried to pick up the crew or a wounded guy. Then they'd open up with a .51 and it would do quite a bit of damage.

The pilot would be sitting in the seat, and he would be directing fire with his mini-guns and rockets through a range finder. The grunts would tell us where the fire was coming from and where to lay down the fire. Our job in the "free guns," of course, was to sweep the LZ, see where the fire was coming from and direct our fire into it where the pilots maybe couldn't see. It was like a battle. Everything was coordinated. It would start off with an artillery preparation of the LZ. The artillery would be called into the LZ and would be pounding it for quite a while. You wouldn't do that in a populated area, but you'd do it if you were by the Cambodian

This gunner is in a gunship version of the venerable Huey helicopter. The machine guns mounted outside of the door are aligned to fire forward for close air support of ground troops.

BOB "FRENCHY"
GIBEAULT
E4, HELICOPTER
GUNNER
U.S ARMY

Bob "Frenchy" Gibeault

In 1965, three months after graduating from high school, Gibeault enlisted in the army and was in Vietnam in December 1966 as an MP with the 199th Light Infantry Brigade. After four months he extended his tour and volunteered to be a helicopter door gunner. He flew with the 187th Assault Helicopter Company, "The Blackhawks." He carried troops and handled resupply and medevac missions. Later he flew Huey gunships, giving fire support for assault troops and the infantry. Awarded the Distinguished Flying Cross and a Purple Heart, he completed his tour in the summer of 1968. Married with two children, he recently retired from the Metro Boston Fire Department with the rank of captain.

border. So the gunships would be flying right alongside the Slicks, leading them a little bit. Our job as the Slicks were being inserted into the landing zone was to lay down a tremendous volume of fire to keep the heads of the enemy down. Sometimes that was successful and sometimes it wasn't. The enemy had become very sophisticated in his antiaircraft techniques, and large caliber weapons were being employed by him at the time in the area around Cambodia.

You were over the LZ all day. You flew all day. You tried to help the guys that were in the LZ or trying to escape an ambush, or to overcome some enemy. The Slicks were there doing their thing or they may set down at a base or they may be called in to medevac. Then we would support them in their medevac. But we usually hung around and followed them in their lead. We were so close with the infantry troops who we fought with and lived with and medevacked and died with. In my mind there was no distinction. But we were air crews and we knew they were grunts. And we had a mutual admiration society, and we still do to this day.

JOHN FLANAGAN

1st Lieutenant
Forward Air Controller (FAC)
U.S. Air Force

John Flanagan

I volunteered for either the Sky Raider fighter bomber or O-1E, forward air controller, because I wanted to be in the middle of combat. Here we were in Vietnam in a guerrilla warfare back to what we know in the United States as our early revolutionary war. Guerrilla warfare, small patrols, small squads working stealthily through the jungles and trees. So here we are with the technology of supersonic fighter bombers that were unable to accomplish the mission. They were impotent in that environment. Now the Air Force didn't have any forward-air-controller airplane. They took Cessna L-19s. It's all metal, two people, one engine, top speed of one hundred miles an hour if you point it straight to the ground. They borrowed them from the army, painted over the olive drab, put an Air Force serial number on it and said, "Okay, that's it." That's what we flew. We had no flight manuals. This is an airplane. Here's how you fly it. Push the stick forward, pull the stick back. Quite different from Air Force training.

The forward air controller was really a hybrid. We were as much army infantry as we were fighter pilots or jet pilots. We had to think from the perspective of some poor GI on the ground who was getting shot at, who was frightened, who was scared, maybe bleeding, ambushed, panic setting in, and we were right in the middle of it. We were that reassuring voice. We were his window to the outside world. He wasn't abandoned. They just loved the forward air controller. FAC, help me, please, FAC. Then you get them calmed down and then you start to order. We were as much counselor and psychologist as we were warrior.

Now the fighter-bomber pilots were highly experienced jet pilots, but separated from the war. They lived in a hooch or a permanent building. They had clean sheets. They had housemaids. They ate American food. They had mess tables. They had bars. They could be flying out of Thailand where they had entertainment. We were living in the jungle, in tents, and flying out of dirt strips and always afraid that we were going to be mortared or overrun or attacked at night. They all wore flight suits and oxygen masks, parachutes, ejection seats. We didn't even bother wearing a parachute because the altitudes we were at, we would never have a chance to use it anyway. I used to put mine over the back of the seat to stop the bullets from coming up behind me and shooting me in the back. The fighter bombers usually had armor plating in the seat. We didn't. They gave us infantry flak jackets. I put mine under the seat to sit on. We flew with the windows open so we could hear the ground fire coming up. You could hear the snap of the bullets or of heavy weapons. I remember I was up near Khe Sanh flying over a ridge line. I had to get to a target and I took a short cut through a saddle and so I was pretty close to the ground, much closer than I should have been. And they had big guns up there, and they loved to shoot at FACs. I went through there and before I even heard bullets coming by, I heard the bang, bang, bang of the machine gun coming at me. I said, "Oh God, I'm in trouble now." And I saw the tracers come whipping up so I just dove over the tops of the trees and got out of there, but frequently that's what you relied on.

We flew at whatever altitude that was required to get the mission done. The Air Force had a regulation that you shouldn't fly below fifteen hundred feet because this is the effective range for small arms. You could see from fifteen hundred feet. You could observe and you were pretty impervious to ground fire. When the weather went bad or you had to really search for something or an American patrol or a Vietnamese patrol

The M60 door gunner on a helicopter, at the ready.

JOHN FLANAGAN
1ST LIEUTENANT
U.S. AIR FORCE

John Flanagan

In 1966, as an Air Force lieutenant, Flanagan volunteered for combat as a Forward Air Controller flying the O-1E Bird Dog. Flying reconnaissance missions, he directed air strikes and artillery support for allied ground troops. He served with the Republic of Korea Tiger Division, the 101st Airborne, and the elite Project Delta of the Green Berets and flew three hundred combat missions over South Vietnam, North Vietnam, and Laos. Since Vietnam he has had a wide-ranging career, including working for the White House, being a Department Chairman at St. Francis College (NY), and serving as an international consultant and lecturer at the Air Force Academy. He is the author of a combat memoir and a brigadier general in the Air Force Reserve. Married with three children, he lives in Connecticut.

was ambushed, you would be right on the tops of the trees. Now your roll was CAS, or close-in air support, supporting friendly troops on the ground. You were talking to them on the radios. FACs were the go between for the fighter bombers and the army on the ground. We would describe where the target was or we would frequently find it because as soon as the enemy saw us they would start shooting. They'd hide until they found us and all hell would break loose. They knew there was a rule in Vietnam that no air strike could be conducted without the control of a forward air controller. That's why we put in so many air strikes without hitting any friendly troops or any friendly villages because the forward air controller was intimately aware of the area.

I was assigned to Project Delta, the counterterrorist force. The mission was to go into the border areas in War Zone C and along the Cambodia border. I spent eight months with them as a forward air controller. We dropped a team off the night before by helicopter. Two Americans, four Vietnamese. Then they'd creep through the jungle getting in observation positions. I took off; the sun wasn't even up yet. I went out to make contact with the team. You always wanted to check on their security and help them and see if they had any targets. Frequently they would have to move during the night to avoid capture if they were being pursued. If they lost their bearings they always wanted to know where their location was, so they didn't get trapped against a river or something like that. I made radio contact with this team and they said we think we have a target for you. I stayed off to the side three miles, not to compromise the mission. One of the Vietnamese sergeants crept down to the

Smoke rockets were often used by light aircraft flown by forward air controllers who spotted targets for strike aircraft and helicopter gun ships.

riverside and peered through the jungle. Not twenty to thirty meters away on the other side of this small river was a Viet Cong company of about 120 men doing calisthenics in PT formation. The American got on the radio and he said we got a group of Viet Cong doing PT. We want an air strike on them. I said okay.

I radioed back to the base camp, and I said I need an immediate strike. Scramble fighters now. He radioed back to Direct Support Center, Bien Hoa, very close to Saigon. They were on five-minute alert. The pilots were basically sitting in the cockpit all strapped in. Ammunition armed hot. We scrambled the fighters and out they came, headed towards me, and as soon as the fighters got close enough, they called me on another high frequency radio. So the forward air controller is right at the center of the communications network. Talking to the ground troops, talking to your Air Force ground controller, great young men, just gutsy people. Finally there was the UHF radio to talk to the fighter bombers. So you're pretty busy in the cockpit switching back and forth from one radio to another. You can listen to all three at once but you could only talk to one of them at a time.

We knew precisely where the enemy was underneath the jungle, totally camouflaged. I had the fighters holding about four to five miles away, out of sight. Two F-100s loaded with cluster-bomb units. Cluster-bomb units were about the size of a softball, loaded with thousands of little pellets inside of each one. They also had napalm, jellied gasoline. A little over one hundred yards east of the target I dropped a smoke grenade. I just flew straight and level and just dropped a red smoke grenade out the window and it fell straight down. It didn't detonate. Nobody could see it until it hit the ground. Then I flew on for another two hundred, two hundred fifty meters and dropped a yellow smoke. Wings level, right over the top of the Viet Cong. They kept on doing their PT. The guys on the ground say, "Hey FAC, they hadn't paid any attention to you."

In the meantime I had given the heading to the fighter bombers and they were streaking in at 420 knots probably at about 150 feet over the tops of the trees. I said just take that heading and when you see the red smoke, start dropping your ordnance. These cluster-bomb units came out like a waterfall. They came out in a stream, in a sequence. I said, "Start and when you hit the yellow smoke, release the trigger and pull off." They said, "Rog, we got you." I cleared them in hot and I just took a slow, gentle circle, turned around to the south to come back over the target. And they came. I'm watching these fighter bombers and I'm saying, oh God, please let them stay on their heading because if they were as much as two or three degrees off their heading, or twenty or thirty meters off the target line, they would hit my buddies on the ground, the friendlies.

I told them on the ground, I said, "Get your heads down. Here they come." They said, "Right." And the cluster-bomb units went right through the middle of the Viet Cong unit, and they never knew what hit them. The lead airplane came off. Then the number two came right through on the same pattern. Then I pulled them up. I fired a smoke rocket in the middle because now the element of surprise was gone. They put napalm into the center of the jungle where they were located. I called the ground troops, these Special Forces Delta guys, and I said, "How we doing?" They said, "You're right on." I said, "What's happening?" He says, "Well, the PT formation is over. They just started first-aid class and they're looking for blood donors." I said, "Thanks a bunch you guys." A sense of humor. They were right in the middle of the Viet Cong camp, and they were making jokes over the radio. And so they just crept off through the jungle. I gave the fighter bombers their bomb damage assessment and they went back. I went over the top of that camp. There was nothing but devastation. They had wreaked havoc. There were dead and wounded lying all over the place. You could see them under the jungle and I could see the people scurrying around or running around on the ground in the places where we had put napalm and burned away the jungle canopy. And that was an absolutely pure, classic military strike.

FRANK TULLO

Captain
F-105 Pilot
U.S. Air Force

Frank Tullo arrived in Da Nang, Vietnam, early in 1965, shortly after the New Year. He flew missions into Laos and over South Vietnam. In Da Nang he lived in a tent with wooden floors. He recalls seeing C-130s pulling up and Marines deplaning, thinking, "I thought they said we should never get involved in a ground war in Asia, and here there are Marines landing." Because the airfield was under constant attack every night and the Viet Cong were shooting holes in the planes, he and his flight crew were soon flying out of Korat, Thailand. There he remained for the rest of his tour.

Frank Tullo

I don't know where the name of the airplane came from but it was Thunderchief, and we always called it the 5 or the 105. But everybody started calling it the Thud, and it sounded like a good name; I guess somebody had heard it hit the ground once and that's the noise it made. I don't know. A lot of them hit the ground. We lost a lot of airplanes there. It wasn't built for what we were doing. It was built for one time nuclear strikes, supersonic attacks, slip in and deliver a weapon, and you can go home. It was a good airplane. We liked it. It was a very responsive airplane, especially at low altitudes. It was in its element below three thousand feet because it went faster at three thousand feet with a load of bombs and with full military. That means without afterburner. The North Vietnamese MiGs could go at top speed at that altitude. So here we are loaded with bombs, it took us a while to realize that at first. When we would see a MiG, we would drop our weapons and engage. We found out that we could just keep on going. They couldn't catch us. And if we were low, their radar couldn't see us so they couldn't intercept, and they couldn't get an intercept angle. So we could just power our way downtown, or wherever we were going. A lot of weapons. That was the thing the 105 could carry, a lot of weapons, mid-air refuel, go a long way.

The F-105 had an emergency procedure book and the immediate action for a fire light was, if on fire, eject. That was the only immediate action we had in the airplane. We were doing that in war time. When we got a fire light, we were just bailing out. And of course, you went down right at the target, which was a big mistake. By the time I got shot down, we had learned a number of lessons and one of the lessons was fly that airplane as long as you possibly can. As long as it's responding and it can get you further away from the target, the better you are.

The idea of Rolling Thunder was to start real close to the DMZ and just work our way north. That is exactly what we did. Initially every mission was a big gaggle, forty to forty-eight airplanes, twenty-four airplanes, thirty-two airplanes. Always a lot of airplanes. Somewhere in the first quarter of 1965 we realized that we could do a little better job if we just sent flights of four against individual targets. Slip in, slip out. As we worked our way north, we came to a couple of places we learned to hate. Thanh Hoa Bridge was one of them. Later it was called the Dragon's Tooth. They had missiles there and they had guns there. I went there two times. In most cases somebody was shot down. It was either navy or Air Force who lost an airplane. I never went to the target without losing an airplane. The North Vietnamese had massed a lot of antiaircraft guns and they knew how to fire them. They were very, very good. And even though we jammed them and we suppressed them, we would assign the flight to certain antiaircraft sites that we saw. You'd be diving on them. You're going to drop eight

Infantry shown in a circle pattern providing security at a helicopter landing zone (LZ).

FRANK TULLO
CAPTAIN
U.S. AIR FORCE

Frank Tullo

Ironically, Tullo was pro
moted to captain in the
Air Force on the day in
1965 that North Vietnam
ese gunners shot his and
five other F-105s out of
the sky over Hanoi. He was
the only pilot rescued that
day by a Jolly Green Gi
ant helicopter (based in
northern Laos and flown
by George Martin). After
leaving the Air Force in
1966, he became a pilot
with Continental Airlines,
for whom he currently
flies DC-10s internation
ally and is a Human Fac
tors Instructor.

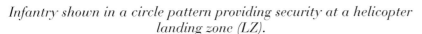

or ten 750-pound bombs, and they're shooting at you. They never stopped shooting. They didn't stop shooting until the bombs went off. They were very tenacious, very gallant fighters. Originally we didn't realize that, thinking they were just backward people. We found out they were very brave and loyal, I guess to their cause.

One day we went to what looked like a nothing target. As a matter of fact the target was so insignificant that they actually gave us two targets. They were small bridges and we were going to take the flight of four in there and split it up. Me and Donny were going to dive on the first bridge and the other bridge was a mile or so down the stream. Three and Four were going to dive. That's exactly what we did. We went ahead and dived on it. I went ahead and dropped my bombs and coming off, Three said, "You're on fire." I didn't know who they were talking to but when I looked back at Donny I could see Donny was on fire. And he never said a word. He just climbed ahead and he kept climbing until he got real slow. Then I saw his canopy come off and a ton of smoke came out of the canopy. I mean it's just pouring out of that canopy.

Once the canopy left off the cockpit, I wasn't close enough to see him but I could see his helmet. Then he ejected. I made a couple of turns watching him in the air. When I flew by him I could tell it was Donny but I couldn't tell whether he had his hands up on his visor or was looking at me. I just couldn't get that close to him. Three and Four went high to arrange for a rescue, and I just stayed with Don and he hit the ground. There was three or four little villages around there. He hit the ground and his chute spilled out. I timed my turns so that I would come right by him as he was touching the ground. I saw him as I went by very fast but I couldn't tell whether he was okay. I just couldn't tell. And about that time I accidentally flew right over the target again. And they were shooting at me now and of course there has been shooting at me before. But I was staying clear.

What I saw when I made a low pass going very fast probably somewhere between twenty-five and fifty feet, what surprised me was I saw somebody in what looked like a flight suit, but he was brown-skinned and he was waving, standing out in the middle of the field waving. I could see behind these stacks of hay in the field there were soldiers hiding. It's hay drying. They look like a mushroom, almost. And it was very obvious that this was a trap. They were not shooting at me. They were smart enough not to shoot. They wanted the chopper. Although I didn't want to say, "You know we can't come in," I did say, "I see a lot of people, I see a lot of people down there right where he was." And the chopper said, "We're leaving, we're getting out of here." The end result was that Donny was MIA for years. He was not a prisoner, although I told his wife I thought he was. If he ejected, I thought that he was alive and probably captured. He never did talk to us. I don't know whether it was a problem with his radio or that it was a problem with him or he was wounded. We found out in late '79 that he was killed. They had some photos from a North Vietnamese newspaper in that province. On that day that newspaper had a picture of a couple of soldiers standing around an American airman who was half-in, half-out of the rice paddy. In 1989, his wife, who I keep in touch with, called me and told me that they had recovered some of Donny's body parts, some bones and a tooth that were absolutely his. So they had some of his remains and they were sent to Oakland. She asked me if I would accompany them from Oakland to Louisville, Kentucky, where they lived. I stayed there the next day for the memorial service. They made a flyby and everything. Nicely handled.

We were losing airplanes at a pretty regular rate. Every couple of days, we'd lose an airplane and the sad part was the further north we went, the fewer rescues. We would launch these gigantic rescue efforts and we'd come up empty so often. I mean there was some rescues. The chopper pilots did outstanding work. However, the further north we went the less our chances came of recovery, so we had a lot of airplanes shot down but very few people coming back.

There was a thirty-mile ring around Hanoi which we could not fly in there under any circumstances. That allowed them to build up these tremendous antiaircraft and missile sites. A missile was fired at a flight of four F-4s leaving a target north of Hanoi, flying around that circle. And they were in weather and they couldn't see the missiles being fired at them. It went off right under them. I believe two airplanes were shot down and the other two barely made it to fields in Thailand. Two days later to nobody's surprise, we were going to get those missile sites. But they were in Hanoi and in some cases, right inside the city. Of course we were very nervous about that because we knew there were a lot of missiles and we'd have to get low. And when you're low, that's when you're vulnerable to flak. Even to a rifle or a pistol. But the decision was made to go in there on July 27, the very first time the U.S. Air Force or the Navy had ever gone up against missile sites. I know we hit a couple of targets besides the missiles in and around Hanoi, but most everything was right inside the circle.

When I took off that day I was number two with Bill as my lead. It didn't matter where we were going, again, I felt bulletproof. I was number two in the flight of eight because Bill was actually in command of two flights

Opposite: Door gunner in a helicopter keeping his eyes open for the enemy.

F-105 Thunderchiefs being refueled in midair. The Thunderchief, originally designed as a nuclear strike fighter, was the mainstay in the air war against North Vietnam. F-105 pilots had only a 75% chance of completing 100 missions.

of four. Charlie was leading the second flight. Our job was to check all the missile sites and to make sure they were all marked. If they weren't, we were to attack them. We had pods of rockets, and we had a 20mm cannon, the Vulcan. We flew in there, hit the tanker for refueling, let down and came at Hanoi, almost directly from the south over the hills. And as we come up over that last ridge, I'll never forget this as long as I live. We looked over the valley of Hanoi and there was literally a haze layer of smoke, a haze layer of flak smoke was what it was. They had their fuses cut to burst at one thousand feet or even below because that's where most of the airplanes were. We used to turn off our air-conditioning as we switched to combat frequency when we got into the dangerous area so that if our airplane came on fire, we didn't get smoke in the cockpit. I could smell the gunpowder. It was a real shocker to me.

Bill was leading the flight, and he was making general turns and he saw the site we were going after. We were very low and very fast. I would say we were somewhere close to six hundred knots and we were probably two hundred feet or lower. We wanted to pass over the target and if there was anything left, we were going to pop up, come back and try it with rockets. And just as we got to the target, just as it was right in front of us, it just exploded in smoke. Bill said later he thought he could see they were fake missiles and this was a flak trap.

They had put up wooden missiles and we attacking them. It was really just a bunch of guns. He broke hard left and of course I broke left with him. As I was looking at him to make sure I didn't run into him, and just as we rolled wings over, I realized I had a fire light. Big, big giant fire light, it seemed about that big that day. I said, "Lead, this is two, I'm on fire. I got a fire light." And he said, "Yes, you're on fire, clean your airplane." I blew off all my stores. We had a panic button to blow off all your stores. And I was a clean airplane. The front light was on and I had complete control of the airplane. Everything was fine.

I just headed west, which was something we talked about. We figured our chances were better straight west because that's where the real rugged country was. We'd try to go to a mountaintop if at all possible, so it'd take the North Vietnamese a long time to find us. One of the guys in the flight of eight said, "I can see your engines really burning. You ought to get out of it." A couple of times they said get out of it but I kept saying, "Everything is fine. I'm able to fly the airplane. I'm able to control the airplane, so I'm just going to stay here until it quits flying." We were going very fast but my instruments started to fail which meant my electricity was starting to go out. All I had was just little standby instruments but it was a beautiful clear day, and Bill was with me so I felt there was no doubt in my mind I would survive. As a matter of fact, I expected to fly all the way home.

The nose went down a little bit and we were low already. I tried to pull up and I brought the stick all the way back and couldn't get the nose up. And that's when I decided to go, so I told Bill, "Everything's just turned to shit and I'm going to get out." I looked in front of me and I wasn't to a mountain yet. I was still over the city but there was a big green patch in front of me and it was, I guess it was the Red River and the Black River come together, and beyond that was real thick forest or grass. That's what it looked like at the time. I ejected and the first process of ejecting is to pull up the handles, which locks your arms in, and the canopy blows off. Well, I wasn't prepared for what happened when the canopy blew off because I don't know how, but my instruments only read up to four hundred knots and they were pegged up. I was going very, very fast. When the canopy came off, the roar of the outside world just stunned me for a couple of seconds. Bill said, "Boy, you were really cool because you blew the canopy and then you waited three or four seconds so you could get over that green patch." Truth of the matter is I was shocked. I was stunned. I couldn't believe what was going on. It seemed like every piece of dirt that was in the cockpit was now in my face. Then I ejected. And it was a very violent ejection. I know that because my mind refused to register. I remember squeezing the handles and the next thing I know I was in the chute. When I was in the chute floating down, the one thing that kept going through my mind for the first minutes was that this can't be happening to me. This is something that happens to someone else, not me. I remember it took me the longest time to get over that. But I kept thinking it's a dream, something is wrong. I don't remember anything else. I had my helmet on and I had my chin strap on. I always had my chin strap on and an oxygen mask. At that speed it blew my helmet off anyway. There was a hard plastic cone around the oxygen mask and as the helmet was pulled off, this mask was dragged across my face and it cut my eye pretty bad. A little flap of skin fell down over my eye and my eye filled with blood. When the chute opened and I looked up to see if it was a good chute, I could only see out of my right eye. It didn't mean anything to me. It was insignificant. It didn't matter because I was alive. The only thing that mattered was I was alive. I wasn't hurt in any other way.

I was really in shock. I felt I was looking out of two holes, like gun-barrel vision. I can see Hanoi in the background. I can see the city. I can see a little farmhouse to the west of me that was not too far away, a mile or two. I realized I was going to land and I could see the place I was going to land and I landed. I started putting everything away and of course I got my radio on. I was trying to hide the chute. I was trying to be quiet, extremely quiet. I was trying not to breathe. I reached over and not thinking, I pulled the lanyard and the next thing I know this yellow dinghy is exploding and it's going, hishhhh. It's filling up and getting bigger and bigger and I was shocked. I couldn't believe it. We carried a survival knife in our boot so I reached down and pulled out my knife and I jumped on this half inflated dinghy and started to pound on it with my knife. It was tough. The first couple of times I hit it, I did not penetrate it. Finally about the third blow I put everything I had, it might have been with two hands, and finally poked a hole in it and deflated it. I thought then what this would look like to some North Vietnamese soldier to come up and see this crazy American killing his dinghy. As I was hiding the chute, Bill's flight came back over and the minute they came over me, I started hearing firing from the east. It was from a flak site that was not too far away. It was loud and I could hear the shrapnel hitting the grass and trees around me. I was in unbelievably thick elephant grass. You can hardly go over it and you try to tunnel but you keep running into these dead ends. You can't even tunnel. Without a machete, it's very hard to penetrate. Bill and I talked. I told him I had lost my cigarettes. I used to smoke at the time. There was no reason not to smoke. I said, "Bill, can you believe I don't have a cigarette to smoke, but I'm in a good place for pickup," obviously trying to get him involved in the pickup. He says, "Yeah, we're going to get you a chopper but we've been recalled. We have to leave."

I don't believe they made more than one pass over me. This is what I remember he said thirty-something years ago. Bill tells me, "Frank, it looks like it might be an all-nighter," because we we're so far up and it was late in the day, three-ish or so. But I didn't hear that. I don't know whether my mind refused to hear it or whether I truly didn't hear it. But they left. I was kind of glad because I felt when they were over me the Vietnamese would know where I was. I sat there and your training is to get ready for a pickup and that's what I did. I started getting all my survival gear out. I had flares and I had tracers for my .38. One of the first things I did was take out the regular bullets and put tracers in there because to be perfectly honest, I was interested in the one-man truce with North Vietnam. I was not going to do battle with 17 million people. The only time I was going to fire that gun was if somebody was putting me on a chopper. I was not going to try to hold up a North Vietnamese Army. Then I waited. I remember I tried not to breathe. I tried to breathe as shallow as I could. Every little noise, a bird or a rabbit or some kind of little rodent made a noise, of course I thought it was a North Vietnamese soldier.

Within fifteen minutes of hitting the ground another flight of F-105s came by. I got on my radio and talked to them and they made one pass over me. Once again the gun battery fired. They said they could see soldiers on the river obviously searching for me. Then they left. I was nervous about the fact that they didn't know exactly where I was. Nobody did. But I was preparing for a pickup. I was getting everything in order. I was going to put on a one-man fire power demonstration, fire as much of my rescue equipment as I possibly could, when the chopper came to get me. Then I hear a propeller engine, which was unusual for me. I had never heard that out there before.

And here comes these A-Is and I got out my radio, and we started talking. They came over my position real low but the gun was shooting at them also. I said, "I'm waiting hopefully for a chopper but I don't think anyone knows exactly where I am." This wonderful calm voice that really put me at ease said, "Don't worry about it, that's why we're here. We're here to rescue you and I'm going to find out exactly where you are now." He made some turns and I could see him coming. I told him turn left, turn right, and when he got right over me, I said, "I'm looking right up your wing tip at you." Then he said something that really meant a lot to me. He doesn't even remember saying it. But he said, "I got you. I know exactly where you are." Almost thirty years later he told me, "I really didn't have you. I just figured well he's in this area somewhere." Then he said, "We're going to have to leave. We're going to try and get you a chopper." And they left.

That's when I started hearing the North Vietnamese. I could hear them doing something that I had never heard before and that was shooting. For the longest time I just heard voices, real far away and thrashing. Then I would hear a shot accompanied by three hundred, four hundred gunshots. I didn't understand what they were doing except that they were shooting. I learned later that was a tactic of the North Vietnamese to try and get

Airborne assaults were extremely rare in Vietnam. This is probably the 173 Airborne Brigade, during Operation Junction City, in February 1967.

the pilot to flush and move so they could find him. I didn't budge. They kept getting closer and closer and again I had my doubts I would be rescued. I figured if I had to spend the night, I would spend the night. I would start walking west and eventually start walking south and I was going to do whatever it took to get back.

I was very, very hopeful. I was sure that somebody was going to come and get me. My first concern was that nobody knew exactly where I was, and having been involved in these rescues before, I knew it was every important to know exactly where that man is because a chopper won't come. You can't blame him. He's not going to come in and just stumble around, especially thirty miles or so from Hanoi.

I hear the A-1s again. I look up and turn on my radio. He said, "Dogwood Two, we got a chopper for you." Dogwood Two was my call. I said, "You do good work." And right after that I saw this huge helicopter coming in. I mean, I've never seen anything like it before. I wasn't sure that we had anything that could come that far north because we had trouble getting pilots out that far north. This was further north than anybody had ever been rescued. Especially that close to Hanoi. But in comes this chopper and I started. I popped a couple of smoke flares and I fired a couple of pen flares. I was talking to George at the time. George Martin was commander of the chopper. Greatest man I know. He kept asking me for directions and I kept giving him giving him directions and I was firing those flares. I said, "Do you see them?" and he said, "No." Then I popped two smoke flares and I was weaving them and he still said no. Then I pulled out my gun and I fired six tracers straight up and he said, "I see that." And he came right into me with a horse collar. To see this helicopter was so heartwarming, to realize that I had been there a long time alone but there were a lot of people who were doing everything in their power to get me out of there. That really meant a lot to me. I realized that it wasn't just the Air Force. It was the Navy and probably a bunch of other services, all involved in rescuing an American. It was the one time that it made sense to be brave. If you are going to be brave, be brave when you're trying to save an American. We can always go back to those targets.

George pulled up right over me. The sling came into view. I could see one his crew members hanging off the door and this horse collar came down. The horse collar was nothing but a loop and I had used it before in practice. What you do is climb into it so that

U.S. Marines relied heavily on radio communication throughout the war.

it's under your arms. I did all this and gave the thumbs up. They started picking me up off the ground and I got about five feet off the ground just high enough to get above the elephant grass and be totally exposed and it stopped. I kept giving him the thumbs up and he kept doing something and it became obvious after a while that the hoist had broken. They couldn't get me any higher so I just kind of dangled there. I don't know how long. While I was hanging there I could see the air was filled with fighters. A-1s in the lead. There were F-100s. There were F-105s. I believe I saw a B-57. I saw this myriad of airplanes up there, circling west of my position but I could see them. That gun site was shooting.

After a while, George realized he couldn't just stay there like that, so he got a little higher and he took off. And he just circled up there while they lowered me a rope, and I was able to tie the rope around the horse collar. It was really painful. Hanging in that horse collar is not pleasant. It was extremely painful, and it cut off the circulation to my hands. I'm trying to tie a knot and my hands felt like I had boxing gloves on. Eventually they were able to pull me up enough so that the original cable made a loop in front of me and I was able to put my feet in that and get some strain off my arms. While this was happening I would look down every now and then. Every time I looked down I'd see these little puffs of white smoke in the grass everywhere. I didn't like that because it was people shooting at us, so I stopped looking down. I just kept waiting for them to hoist me all the way up. Then it became obvious because the loop didn't get any bigger, they weren't trying to pull me up either. Then I felt the chopper really moving. He wasn't just going in circles. He was moving. Then I realized he was going at the farmhouse that I had seen when I was in the chute. I really was afraid. He was going to have to land and let me get in the chopper that way.

He landed. As I jumped in to the chopper, I looked forward and I could see the two pilots were crouched down hiding. And it dawned on me they were hiding because somebody was shooting at us from that farm house. Then they took off. One of the first things I did was go forward and I would have hugged them and kissed them if I could. I had to shake their hands and tell them how grateful I was. There were many reasons for George Martin not to bring that chopper into that area. I found out later there were nine Americans on the ground that day. Six 105 pilots were shot down and three Americans on a B-66 were shot down. He had an overheat light on. There were guns shooting at us and they had no reason to come there and pick me up. I will be eternally grateful to these gentlemen. These true, brave warriors that came in and got me that day and gave me a life.

The workhorse Huey in flight on a mission.

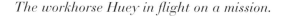

GEORGE MARTIN
Captain
Helicopter Rescue Pilot
U.S. Air Force

George Martin

They called us and said there's a big shebang going on up north near Hanoi. People were getting shot down. I started asking them where are the people because there's a lot of territory out there. They said over near Hanoi. Well, we had never progressed anywhere near Hanoi up until that time. We kept getting messages and they said, yes there was a definite shoot down, it was on the ground, they had his position and I was looking to get there. I tried to pin them down exactly where he is, so I could do some flight planning. How far do I have to go? How much fuel do I have to carry? I had in my mind at that moment I've got to review the map. I had no idea where I would be flying. The copilot got up and he went outside, started supervising the refueling and I grabbed the map, opened it up and started to look at it. It had big red stamps on it, unreliable for this reason, unreliable here, unreliable there. Nothing but a bunch of unreliable, which is no help at all. You get that old funny feeling something is wrong, something is wrong.

I put the map down and I looked and the engine temperature was way up. I was his only possibility. I didn't ground it because it was conditional in my mind. I was thinking about was I going to try and start, if it will start, then see if it will develop power, if it will develop the kind of power it has to develop. When I had the engine problems, then I really figured our chances were very, very low. I still figured, well, if you have a flyable aircraft, you're going to have to go. I'll be honest, I didn't want to go at all. And the other guys didn't want to go, and I don't blame them a bit. Then comes the moment of truth, after you decide do we go or don't we go. Of course I can't do it by myself. I've got a three-man crew behind me, so I had to more or less clear it with them. I can't command them to go. It sort of comes to that but not exactly. So the bottom line of the whole thing was if you do it and get away with it, yeah, for him, see and I did it and the engines failed and I hit the mountain on the way, then they would all say, dumb-ass, we never should have gone. He had a grounding situation. Why did he go?

So I called them over and I said, "Well, here's what we're going to do. We're going to crank it up. If it starts we'll take off to a hover. If it will hover, we'll make a couple of other little power checks and if everything looks within a normal range," I said, "I'm going. Who is going with me?" I didn't get any quick answers. Very reluctantly, this, well, I guess if you're going we'll go along. We get on board. We cranked it up and sat there and believe it or not, just like John Wayne, I said, "Well, you can't live forever," and I shoved the stick forward and we went.

I had never picked up a guy before off the ground. Even in practice I had never done it. I'd been on the airplane when other pilots had done it and watched them but I had never done it.

Flying over finally I did see some red smoke and what appeared to be red smoke to me. My thought process filtered up through the trees, it was. By the time it got all the way up through the trees, it was the very thing. And it was only pink smoke when it finally got to the tops of those trees. But it was just enough in a vast sea of green. Just the tiniest little hint of red would stand out and that's what I saw.

Crewman comes up and says, "Did I turn the hoist off?" I said, "No. I didn't turn the hoist off." I had the control right here under the grip and it's just conceivable in the excitement of the moment that you could flip the switch. I knew I hadn't bumped it. I said, "What's the matter." And he says, "Well, the hoist broke," and I say, "What?" I jumped out of the seat. I said, "We'll check everything and see. Check mine. Check everything." He's got a box back there by the door with all the controls on it. He checks everything. He comes back and he said, "I can't get it to run." I said, "Throw him a rope." They quick get the rope and throw that out. A couple of minutes later we still can't get him up. If you can't get him, you can't get him up. So my copilot, and I'll give him the credit—he's a great big football-type kid see, just in his twenties—he said, "You think I can go back and help them?" I figured three of them can get him up, you know. I didn't really want him to go because he's got a job watching all the instruments. If something's getting out of limit he calls me and says, "Hey, watch your so-and-so and here, quick, make adjustments," or whatever you have to do to keep flying the aircraft.

The kid went back and I said, "Now we've got it. The three of them will pull him up." They couldn't pull him up. And a red light comes on the sick engine. Not the good engine. The sick engine. I said, "There it goes. We're all going to be going down there any minute now. There's nothing I can do." Because you're hovering at full power and both engines are screaming, screaming wide open and the fire warning light comes on. I haven't a copilot to help me. They're all back there, hauling on the rope like a maniac. I'd been hovering there for about twenty-five minutes and that's almost unheard of. You just don't do that. It's very difficult, not to mention the stress on top of it. The red light came on three different times. I said, "We've got to get out of here."

I asked how far off the ground is he. I had a horror of dragging him through trees because you don't know exactly what the terrain is and what the trees are and everything else. Or what kind of shape he's in. He might be ready to fall off the rope and then one more little twitch and he's gone. He says he's clear of the trees. Are you sure? Yes, he's cleared the trees. All right, we're gone. I get up to thirty knots. I get a quick glimpse of him. I said, "Find me a place to land. I've got to land this thing." They didn't ask any questions. They started looking around. I was looking too. I made sure I stayed plenty high enough and we'd given up on the hoist. Not too far away there was this open spot. You have to assess, is this big enough to get the thing in there and to make an approach. Then what goes in must come out you know, or vice versa, I decided I could squeeze it in. Then you're thinking you've got to let him down gently so you don't dash him into the ground. You have to wait until he gets out of the way or you'll put twenty-two thousand pounds right on top of him and he wouldn't care for that either.

I put him on the ground and he ran off to one side. He ran maybe straight out from me or slightly to the rear and that makes it difficult to see. You don't get a chance to brief them to run to the front where the pilot can see. Then I would have known. I sat there and I made a fifty-foot hover which is high but not too high for this aircraft. Nobody says anything. I am sure he was on the ground,

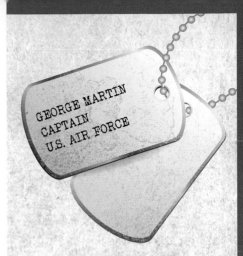

George Martin

Born in Illinois, Martin en listed in the United States Army Air Force in 1943 and earned his wings in April 1945. The war in Europe had ended so he saw no action. He stayed in the active reserve and continued flying. Recalled during the Korean War, he flew one hundred missions and received the Distin guished Flying Cross. He qualified to fly helicopters and headed to Vietnam, where he was in charge of two CH-3C rescue heli copter teams, dubbed by Martin "the Jolly Green Gi ants." He and his men res cued many downed pilots, among them Frank Tullo. After working as a civil ian flight instructor for the army, Martin finally retired, and now spends his time woodworking and traveling the country with his wife. He has ten chil dren, three of whom are in the military.

nobody tells me and I can't see for myself. I move the helicopter and it's pretty risky to try and hold it in a very steady hover and screw your head way around like that and try to look underneath this eleven-foot-tall monster. The copilot is still in the back. The seat is empty. So I'm stuck calling, what's going on back there? Is he on the ground? What's happening? He could have collapsed and somebody could have jumped out and dragged him out of the way or any number of possibilities. You can land on top of him and crush him to death. Nobody talks to me.

I'm screaming and I'm cursing. I'm doing everything and I'm totally helpless. I can't do anything but sit there and hold the airplane. Finally the crew chief in a very upset tone says, "Why don't you land." "Why don't you talk to me?" I said, and he said, "I came unplugged." He pulled the cord out of his helmet. He's talking to me all the time and I can't hear him. So I slap the thing on the ground and here comes Frank, do di do di, over the whole thing. And he just dove right through the door. Then everybody's hollering, "Let's go, let's go, get off the ground." They're pulling ropes and cables and Frank is in the door, and OK, one big jump and off we went. That's when we smiled.

All the windows were open because it was pretty hot and we swing around to the south, somebody let go with an automatic weapon on the left side, and man, it was loud. The good old copilot was coming back and putting his butt down in the seat when the guy hits the trigger and scared the life out of him. He comes back out of the seat and I'm hollering at him that he didn't have his helmet on yet. I heard him yelling he wasn't plugged in or anything. "They're shooting at us," he hollered. "Yeah, something's shooting." We got around, we got hit but we didn't know it at the time. We didn't find out until later.

Early in the war, before the large scale U.S. involvement. The machine gun in the door was a .30 caliber Browning of World War II vintage.

JOHN MCCAIN

Lieutenant Commander
Pilot, POW
U.S. Navy

John McCain

I was first in Vietnam on the USS Forestall. We had a horrible fire that began when a rocket was fired from an aircraft by mistake from across the flight deck and punched through the fuel tank in my A-4 aircraft. Huge fire ensued. Bombs went off and we lost 135 brave young American sailors who fought that fire as would be fought in hand-to-hand combat. These young people literally saved the Forestall. Following that, the ship went back to the Philippines, then had to return to the United States. I made one of the several tactical blunders that I made in my life, and that was when the recruiters came over from the USS Ariscany and said they were looking for volunteers because they'd lost a number of pilots. And for reasons I still can't explain, my arm shot up and I found myself on the USS Ariscany in a very famous squadron, VA-163. The air wing on the Ariscany, I'm told, had the highest losses of any air wing in the war. Part of that was because the Ariscany was in the middle of the escalation that took place in summer and fall of 1967.

On October 26, I'd only been on the ship for a couple of months. We went on a strike in the center of Hanoi for the first time. A thermal power plant. As is well known, Hanoi was at that time the most heavily defended place in the history of air warfare. It was about twenty-four planes in the flight. We lost three planes. One was me. When I rolled in over the target there were lots of surface-to-air missiles in the air. I released my bombs and just as I released the bombs, a surface-to-air missile hit and took off the right wing of my aircraft. I automatically ejected because that's what we're trained for. According to some observers, my feet barely hit the water. My chute opened because I was going straight down. I broke my arms and hit my knees very badly when I ejected. I sunk to the bottom of the lake. Couldn't get to the top once. Couldn't get to the top again. Finally got my teeth around the inflator of my life vest and floated to the top. A group of Vietnamese as I remember it, and I've seen a picture since then, pulled me into shore. The crowd was very hostile. They began kicking and beating me. I was bayoneted in the foot and in the groin. Another bayonet smashed my shoulder with a rifle butt. It was pretty tense and the army people came up, put me into a truck, took me to the Hanoi Hilton. I was in very bad shape so it didn't take a lot of interrogating. They would slap me a few times and I would go in and out of consciousness. But it was clear to me that they didn't provide medical treatment unless we gave military information.

I was on the floor of the cell for about four or five days with a blanket over me. One day the guard came in with one of his friends, pulled the blanket up. My knee was the size and shape and color of a football. I told him, I said, "Get the interrogator." The interrogator came in and I said, "Look, take me to the hospital, give me some treatment and then maybe we can talk about military information." He called in the camp doctor. He took my pulse, said something in Vietnamese to the interrogator, and the interrogator said, "It's too late." I said, "Look, take me to the hospital and I can get well." He said, "No, it's too late," and he left. Naturally I was a little depressed about that. Some hours later because I had been going back into unconsciousness, the door opened and the interrogator said, "Your father is a big admiral and we're going to take you to the hospital." So the fact that my father was an admiral in the navy saved my life. It had other repercussions later on, but at that time it was clear that he was an admiral made them do for me what they didn't do for others.

I was put in a small cell. It had a lot of water on the floor. I was taken out after I had been there for about a day. Put a cast on when they put me in a nice room. French TV crew came and filmed me and they put me back into this rather cramped, damp room. The guard who was assigned to me obviously wasn't well fed because he used to eat all of my food. So my condition gradually worsened. They gave me an operation, and the doctors cut the ligaments and cartilage in my knee. Then my condition seemed to worsen. The doctor came. The interrogator came in one day and said, "The doctor says you're not getting any better. What would make you better?" I said, "Well, I would be better, get better if I was put in with some Americans who would take care of me." That night they came and put me into a truck and took me on a stretcher into a room with two individuals. One, Major "Bud" Day, one of the most marvelous men, one of the heroes of our POW experience, received a Congressional Medal of Honor later. He had a broken arm and a bullet wound in his leg from an escape attempt that he had made. And Major Norris Overly took care of me and literally saved my life in my view.

For the most of the next three and a half years I was in solitary confinement, but almost always in constant communication with other POWs. The fact that I lived alone really didn't mean that much, except for a few occasions where I was physically separated from everybody else. I was always in communications with my fellow POWs.

In June of 1968 I was in a camp called the Plantation. One day they took me up to a room that was not a normal interrogation. It was a large room. Had some of those Vietnamese elephants. The regular interrogator, a guy we called The Bug was there. There was also another individual, one whom he identified as his senior officer or senior official. The guy talked to me for maybe a couple of hours, small talk, just routine things. Very pleasant. I was extremely puzzled as to what it was all about. At the very end of our conversation he said, "Would you like to go home. The doctor says your condition is still very poor. Would you like to go home?" I said, "Well, I'd have to think about that." I went back to my cell. At that time I was in communication with Major Bob Craner, one of the finest men I've ever known in my life. We talked about it. He recommended that I accept, and then we'd talk some more. I explained to him that the question was how bad is my condition. Was my condition such that I could live and I wasn't going to die. So I went to another meeting two days later. He said, "Did you think about our offer?" I said, "Yes, I can't accept that offer." He said, "Why?" I said, "Our code of conduct says you go home by order of those who have been shot down first, then the sick and injured." He said, "But you were injured." I said, "Yeah, but I'm going to survive." I was keenly aware of what made me different from anybody else was the fact that my father was commander-in-chief of U.S. forces in the Pacific. If I had accepted early release, they would have used that for propaganda purposes against other prisoners. So I said no.

The meeting ended. I went back to my cell. On the morning of July 4, 1968, I was this time taken up into interrogation. Same two people. Only I remember vividly the senior officer had an ink pen in his hand, and he had a copy of the

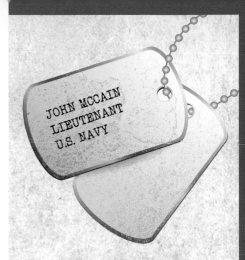

John McCain

Born into a Navy family in the Panama Canal Zone, the son and grandson of admirals, McCain graduated from the Naval Academy in 1958 and became a naval aviator. Shot down over Hanoi in 1967, he was a prisoner of war for five and half years. He retired a captain in 1981 after a twenty-two-year career. Among his awards are the Silver Star, Bronze Star, Purple Heart, and Distinguished Flying Cross. After retiring from the navy, he served two terms in the House of Representatives (1982-86). Elected the Republican Senator from Arizona in 1986, he was re-elected in 1992 for his second term. He lives in Phoenix with his wife Cindy and their four children.

After release from being a prisoner of war, John McCain had a lot to say.

New York Herald Tribune. And The Bug said, "Our senior officer wants to know your final answer." The guy had been talking, The Bug interpreting all this time. I said, "My final answer is no." He broke his ink pen and ink splattered. In pretty good English he said, "They taught you too well." He stood up and kicked over the chair, walked out, and slammed the door of the interrogation room, leaving me and The Bug in there in somewhat of an awkward silence. The Bug said, "Well, you better go back to your cell. Things will be very bad for you now."

When I was in high school I was defiant. When I was at the Naval Academy I was very defiant and broke all the rules. Didn't get caught at all of them, but did at many of them. And when I was in prison, I was defiant. We made fun of the Vietnamese. We would laugh at them. You had to do that, otherwise they became larger than you. They became significant in you mentally. I didn't like them. I didn't like the guards. I was hit by them quite frequently, obviously, but that didn't matter to me.

Christmas of 1969 I was still at the Plantation, and they came in the morning and said, "We're going to take you to a Christmas service." I said, "That's very nice, that's very nice." They're allowing us to have a Christmas service. I thought, gee, maybe something happened here. They took me over to this large room. As soon as I walked in I became enraged because it was all a setup with television cameras. There must have been five or six television cameras. This altar sort of thing and little creche and things around these pew-like seats. POWs sitting a far distance from each other, not allowed to speak to each other. Well, as soon as I walked in, I said, "What the hell is this?" Then I began yelling obscenities and said to the guy next to me, "Hi, my name's John McCain, what's yours?" And the camp commander was telling me to be quiet, be quiet, but they didn't want to come to me because then they'd get it on the camera. So then they'd get in the film, you know. So I gave them as much as possible of the Hawaiian peace symbol and used the F word with amazing frequency and basically disrupted their little show. Part of it was not that I calculated obviously because I thought we were going in there, we'd have a Christmas service, but I was just so mad that they would even debase our Christmas service for propaganda purposes. That was the fun part. They let me enjoy the rest of Christmas Day but the next few weeks were pretty rough. That was sort of the way I acted towards them. You had to stand up because they wanted to take your dignity and if they got your dignity and your pride then they could make you do what they wanted.

Later in late 1970 there was a change in our treatment. Ho Chi Minh died. We were put into large cells of two or three together in each cell. I was put in a cell with Admiral Stockdale, Robinson Risner, the other famous ones. But it didn't last very long because we had a riot over having church services. The Vietnamese wouldn't let us have a church service. The Vietnamese came and selected thirty-six of us, and we were taken out to a punishment camp called Skid Row. That was in December. They took twelve back some months later, and twelve more, and then finally the last twelve of us the following November. I was put in a cell with the senior-ranking officer Major "Bud" Day, tough, mean tunnel vision, great resister. American hero. Believe it or not, we had a wonderful time in that cell. We played cards. We had church services. I told one hundred movies. I taught a history course. We had a choir. Our choir director was a guy named Quincy Collins who had been the choir director at the Air Force Academy Glee Club. We had guys with wonderful voices. When people say how terrible it was in prison, this was wonderful, especially after what we had just gone through.

I said we came back in November, early December of 1971, from the punishment camp. We had already established because of the riot that we were allowed to have church services. We wanted to have a Christmas service and we needed a Bible. We asked the Vietnamese for a Bible. They said there were none. Thousands and thousands were sent to Vietnam. They just never reached us. One day the guard came in and told Bud Day that they had a Bible and one of us could go out and copy from the Bible. I was the room chaplain, not because of any excessive virtue but because I had gone to a boys' boarding school where we went to chapel every morning, church on Sunday, and chapel at night. At the Naval Academy we went to church every Sunday. So I knew a lot of the procedures of a church service. I went out, took the Bible, and studied. Our church service the following Christmas Day was that the choir would sing a hymn, and then I would read from that part of the story of the actual birth of Christ. The choir sang "Silent Night." I looked around that room and there these guys with tears in their eyes. In some cases streaming down their cheeks. The tears were not of sorrow and homesickness. They were tears of joy that for the first time, in the case of some who had had already been there seven years, we were able to celebrate Christmas together. It was one of the most, if not the most, remarkable experience of the time that I was in prison. It epitomized the kind of love and close relationship that makes me feel that the people I really knew best and loved most are those who I was in prison with. We did have arguments, sure. We did fight during a bridge game and, you know, afterward did not speak to each other. I got so mad at my dearest friend Orson Swindle during a bridge game, I wouldn't speak to him for a month. And then he was about to leave, and I felt terrible. But the fun we had and the joy we shared in that cell was really one of the most enriching times of my life.

PAUL GALANTI

Lieutenant
Pilot, POW
U.S. Navy

Paul Galanti

I was flying off the USS Hancock, doing everything I wanted to do from the time I was in the fourth grade when I saw Chuck Yeager fly at my father's graduation from an army school out in Kansas.

The primary missions were bombing targets that would come from Washington. They would announce it to the North Vietnamese. The North Vietnamese would move all their antiaircraft so they could defend those targets, and they'd send us in. Every time it changed, they put something a little bit higher on the category. Most of us wanted to go after the big targets right away. Just knock them out and get the war over with. The policy of escalation gave the North Vietnamese the ability to adjust to each of their incremental loses.

Nobody really relished flying the night missions over there. You couldn't see anything. There were a lot of mountains. We actually lost a couple of airplanes that were just unexplained. Nobody saw any flak. Figured they just flew into the mountains. You certainly couldn't see the targets very well during the daytime and the night missions were sort of a joke, particularly when you had to fly three hundred or four hundred miles to Laos to go looking for North Vietnamese trucks and the Ho Chi Minh Trail.

I went and got a little breakfast and was briefed for the next mission, and there were four of us. The target was one of these barracks areas that had already been bombed about three or four times. So we weren't really crazy about going. My skipper came in and said you're not going to that target. Something better. He said there were a whole bunch of boxcars about one hundred miles south of Hanoi. He said you're going to hit those boxcars instead.

I was flying back, just like the Blue Angels, tucked in real tight. I got hit in the engine, a generator exploded, lost all instruments. Then it snapped hard to the right, the fire warning light, and black smoke coming in the air-conditioning vents. I figured it's about time to go. So I pulled the face curtain and ejected right out of the airplane upside down. Ironically the airplane landed in the water. We were bombing from landward towards seaward, only about a quarter of a mile in. In the parachute I saw my airplane splash in the water. For the first bombing mission I ever had in North Vietnam they had a sea breeze instead of a land breeze, and it blew my parachute back in over the beach. Just before I hit the ground I looked toward the ocean and saw the helicopter already lifting off from the destroyer and I radioed my section lead and told him to send the chopper back. There is just no way they could come in and get me without being shot down. I said, "See you after the war." I figured I'd be about six more months. I came down right in the middle of them, a whole slew of armed peasants who were really not crazy that I had just arrived in their country.

There was one clump of bushes, and I just jumped in it right away. That didn't fool all these guards coming, and they had dogs with them. They looked like guards to me. It turned out they were militia, peasants with brown shirts on. They came up and they were scared to death. I didn't like seeing them all shaking with their fingers on the triggers. So I put my hands up and stepped out of the bush, and they captured me almost immediately and tied me to a tree and lined up like a firing squad. I'm sure they were getting ready to shoot

Remains of a building where Viet Cong troops held ARVN (Army of South Vietnam) soldiers during the Tet Offensive.

PAUL GALANTI
LIEUTENANT
U.S. NAVY

Paul Galanti

Galanti was raised in a mil itary family in the United States, France, Germany, and Japan. He graduated from the Naval Academy in 1962 and started navy jet flight training. After arriving in South East Asia aboard the carrier USS Hancock in November 1965, he flew ninety-sev en combat missions in his A-4 Skyhawk and was shot down on June 17, 1966. He remained a prisoner of war in North Vietnam for nearly seven years and was released on February 12, 1973. He then held a variety of navy commands before retiring and enter ing the world of business. Among his many decora tions are the Silver Star, two Legions of Merit for combat, nine Air Medals, and two Purple Hearts. He is a motivational speaker and technology consultant and is the Webmaster of the Vietnam POWs' site on the World Wide Web.

when what looked like a regular army guy all in brown came up and made them stop. It was a very interesting experience going through that because I don't remember being afraid at any time. Like I was a spectator watching this happen to this poor guy. When I was tied to the tree looking down all those rifle barrels I was just wondering if I'd be able to see the bullets before they hit. They started marching me north. They marched me through that village which was on the outskirts of where I saw the flak trap, saw the bamboo. They were box-car wheels, but on top they built this bamboo, and the thing had a million bullet holes in it because it had been bombed so many times. And the flak was just set up so they knew what line the airplanes would come to bomb that thing and the flak was just set to shoot at them. They took me to that village and paraded me in front of it in my underwear. Kids were out there throwing stones and rocks and stuff. Then they brought me some beetles to eat.

The commissar would come up and yell and scream and get the villagers all fired up. Then typically the guards would get us out of there just before they set the villagers on us to tear us apart. This happened probably twenty times in twelve days. If we arrived in the middle of the night in a little village they'd wake the whole village and get them all stirred up. And the same thing would start. The sticks, the stones would start flying. Occasionally little kids would come up, and you'd get hit in the leg because we were these vicious Yankee pirates that were destroying their country.

I was thrown into what we called Heartbreak Hotel. It was part of the huge Hanoi Hilton complex. It was the initial interrogation wing. They forgot about me for three days. I just sat in that room, no water, no food or anything. I'm convinced in retrospect, with all the confusion and bombing, they just forgot about me. Finally I yelled for the guard, and they took me to interrogation. It lasted several hours with The Bug, the most sadistic individual I ran into in North Vietnam. There are four things you are allowed to give them under the code of conduct: name, rank, serial number, date of birth. Nothing else. The Air Force taught us to start evading and lying and giving unreliable answers and don't take torture to the point of permanent physical disability. So they know that can't trust anything you say. They can't tell what's true and what's not. I was bound and determined they weren't going to get anything out of me. It got me wrapped up in the ropes. It seemed like forever but it was more like forty-five minutes or an hour. Blood circulation gets cut off. Your hands turn black, and it was described by one of the POWs as a pain that's so terribly intense if you had your baby there, you'd throw the baby in the fire to get them to take off the ropes. It's a terribly painful experience.

The Bug was sitting on a stool in front of a little bare wooden table with a blue tablecloth on it. There was an older-looking individual with gray hair who probably spoke English, but pretended he didn't, and The Bug would be his interpreter. In reality The Bug was the camp commander but he acted like he was just doing what this camp commander wants. There would be two or three enlisted sergeants behind them. Every time you did something that The Bug didn't like, he'd look up and nod to the guards and you'd get a whack on the head or knocked off the stool or wrapped up in the ropes. Being basically an optimist, I figured, well, if they're bombing inside Hanoi now, it's not going to last very long. I'll probably be out of here next week or the next ten days or so. I think probably in retrospect that optimism which all of us had is probably what got us through the situation.

I was raised all over the world. My father was an army colonel. I went to twenty-three different schools before I finished college. And I forced myself to go back and relearn everything I'd learned in all those schools. Whether it was navy flight training or at the Naval Academy or University of Maryland or in high school and Valley Forge Military Academy. All the way back through those times and tried to reconstruct classes in my mind and forced myself to just draw out all the stuff that I'd been cramming into my brain for the first twenty-six years of my life. How quickly it all came back. It was so clear that my mind could see inside these classrooms and the classrooms kept getting bigger. I realized that it was because I was looking at it from the eyes of an eight-year-old, a seven-year-old, and six-year-old. In my mind the teachers were all giants back then. But I could remember sitting around all the rest of the kids in the room. They were kids but they looked sort of like they were my age, but they looked like little kids. It was an incredible experience. The biggest lesson I learned is human beings can endure anything and come out of it in remarkably good shape. I watched hideous injuries heal themselves. It's painful and it takes a little time, but they heal themselves. I watched people suffer terrible psychological blows. The only mail the North Vietnamese would let us get would be some horrible news from home, like your wife can't take it anymore, I'm divorcing you. One fellow got a picture of his wife getting remarried with his kids in the background. Anyway people can come through that and they're really doing pretty dog-gone well since then. Our group as a whole is probably doing better than any group its size in the history of our country. And they really shouldn't. The psychiatrist said we were all supposed to be basket cases. That's what they told our families.

Opposite: Troops fording a stream on patrol.

FRED CHERRY

Major, Pilot F-105
POW
U.S. Air Force

Fred Cherry

I got involved in the bombing of North Vietnam in May of '65. I was flying the F-105 Thunderchief. It was just a magnificent aircraft. I loved it. I get tingles in my back every time I go to Bolling Air Force Base and see the one on the pedestal there.

When we went to Korat Air Base in Thailand there was absolutely nothing. It was just bare ground. We started to build hooches, as we called them. They were just pretty much open, built out of all wood up off the ground and they had bamboo windows to keep the rain out if it rained. And just bunks, and most of them were just rubber mattresses on a folding cot. There wasn't too much built but it was satisfactory.

Targets were radar sites and the Ho Chi Minh Trail. Shortly after we were bombing in the North. The Thanh Hoa Bridge became a very important target. We knew it was really heavily defended and you went in with the best tactics for everyone's safety. It was a hot target. But back then early in the war, we didn't care about what it was: just go get them. We had that attitude. We knew it was heavily defended but we didn't have anyone dropping out. "I don't want to go because it's too heavy." None of that. Everybody was hot to go.

About 11:45 in the morning of October 22, 1965, I was shot down. The ceiling was very low. Because everything else was canceled, I was the only flight over the whole of North Vietnam. If a recky found a SAM site we would retaliate immediately, and that's what happened. I had put the weapons on the target. After that we normally accelerate. I still had to stay low but when I realized I had been hit I got up just a little higher. I accelerated up to something like seven hundred miles an hour and that should be fatal in itself to eject at that speed, but it wasn't in my case. When I had to eject I noticed there was smoke in front of the instrument panel in front of me. I reached over to turn off some of the electrical switches, which I felt would solve the problem. As my hand got to the switches, the aircraft exploded right under me. At this point I was approximately four hundred feet. When the aircraft exploded, I ejected

View of the cockpit of an U.S. Air Force Republic F-105D Thunderchief.

immediately. I didn't look because the cockpit was instantly full of smoke. I couldn't see out of it so I ejected, and I didn't know but the aircraft had flipped on its side upside down.

The automatic release belt for the lap belt did not operate. If it had, at that speed I would have ripped the panels out of my parachute with the wind. I would have hit the ground much too hard to survive. I had to manually pull my rip cord and open the parachute. I looked up and saw the canopy open. I looked horizontal and saw my wing man and I looked down and I hit the ground, just like that. And I had a broken ankle, broken wrist, and my left shoulder was just smashed up.

I fell right in the midst of quite a few Vietnamese, some militia and some working in the fields. All ages carried rifles. I learned that everyone was shooting at us when we were down low. And we weren't aware of it. For the next seven-and-a-half years I was a guest of the Vietnamese. I was never really afraid when I ejected. The first thing that went through my mind, I'll be here a long time but I'm thinking a month or two, not years. They took my anti-G suit and almost stabbed me doing that because they were trying to cut it off. They wanted my boots and that's when I resisted. That was standard procedure for them but after I was so belligerent, they just let me keep my boots, which did help because my ankle was broken and to have the boot laced around my ankle was better for walking because I had to walk a couple of miles.

There wasn't much pain walking. After I sat a while the adrenaline stopped pumping, and I started serious pain in the shoulder and ankle. They were the injuries that I felt the most. I didn't feel a thing in the wrist. After I had begun to hurt I did have to walk three or four miles to a jeep they were going to take me in to Hanoi. And that was through rice paddies. There were followers. They were gong-ringing and everything up ahead and they were signaling through the gong communications that I was coming. I got to the first village, which appeared to be a middle or high school, after getting on the jeep. It was dark now and there was eight hundred people in the courtyard where they took me. The Vietnamese were telling me they were going to kill me unless I told them this or that because they were going to have trouble saving me. I didn't pay any attention to it, I had been through serious training on this kind of thing so I was pretty well prepared. I just did was I was supposed to as a military person, name, rank, serial number, date of birth. That's all we talked about initially. They weren't trying to kill me. They were just stooged. They didn't seem to be angry because I hadn't bombed anything near where I was.

They took me into Hanoi into the Hanoi Hilton. The first place they put me was not really a cell. It was just a room. Over the years the rats had gnawed the wooden doors. They needed to get through the building. I guess they figured they didn't have a way around so they just gnawed through the bottom of each door. While I was in there, the rats were running just day and night over me. Initially I didn't have a mosquito net and I still had my flight suit on for about a week. They hadn't given me anything, and there was some driblets of

Fred Cherry

Born in 1928, Cherry is a career Air Force pilot who flew fifty-one missions in the F-84 during the Korean War. Based at Yakota Air Force base in Japan, he flew missions over Vietnam in August 1964 after the Gulf of Tonkin incident. From Korat, Thailand, he flew fifty-two missions, including bombing North Vietnam. In October 1965 during a bombing raid he was shot down over North Vietnam. A prisoner of war until his release in October 1973, he retired from the Air Force as a colonel and was one of the men behind the building of the Korean War Veterans Memorial in Washington, D.C. He resides in Maryland with his wife.

Republic F-105D-30-RE Thunderchief in flight with a full bomb load of M117 750 lb bombs.

water I could sort of sponge off outside the back small courtyard. But not very much because I only had one hand and didn't even have a cloth at the time initially. Then they put me in the Heartbreak part of it. They were beating on me and banging my head on things, and my shoulder and ankle pained awful during that period. They didn't do anything medical for me for about two or three months.

As the war went on, more and more foot soldiers in South Vietnam were black and young. So by now they had figured out I was the only black they had in North Vietnam, and I was the first one. If they could get the first and senior black to denounce the war and they can pump this into the loudspeakers or however they do it down South to the young troops—"The senior Air Force black American is denouncing the war and what are you fighting for?" and that kind of thing. They were always telling me the same thing—why are you fighting this? They did have some knowledgeable Vietnamese interrogators who had read a lot of books about slavery and what's still happening at that time. The back of the bus and the restaurants and the whole bit. They used as much as they could. I knew exactly what they were trying to do to me, and I was just determined that they were not going to do it to me. I was successful and I didn't make a tape and I didn't write anything denouncing our involvement in the war or anything about the U.S.

I was tortured and punished for ninety-three days. Over that period I spent 792 days in isolation, solitary confinement, and fifty-three weeks of that straight without seeing or talking to anyone except by tapping through the wall to any other American.

When I arrived, the tap system was in place. You took the alphabet and put it in a five by five grid, leave out the letter K because if you really need K, you used C. So we just tapped the grid. And after a while you do it as fast as when you were typing. It was very, very effective. You could do it by audio. You could do it by visual.

Exterior of the POW camp in Hanoi where American airmen were held, called the "Hanoi Hilton" by the prisoners.

You could do it with your fingers. You could tap through walls. Just use your hand or do the same thing as if you were hearing it. It was a very versatile way of communicating. Along any wall you can tap from one end of the building to another and be heard rather clearly. Just put your ear there or we used a cup sometimes. We learned we could talk through a wall that is nineteen inches thick through a cup. Or cup your hands and it would be heard through on the other side.

Most of the time they were interrogating me almost daily. So I paid for it. I dealt with the vice camp commander in the Zoo. The one we called Rabbit and one we called Spot. Then we had Dumb-Dumb. Dumb-Dumb was my menace. Oh, boy. Dumb-Dumb and I went around. He issued more punishment for me than anybody else in the camp. We couldn't be across the desk for five minutes before we'd be at each other's throat. He didn't like me and I didn't like him. So he'd make me hold up the walls for no real reason. Holding up the wall is you put your nose against the wall. You face against the wall. Your body as close to the wall as you can get and you stand there with your arms in the air above your head all day. Nobody could do it or did it because nobody was standing there watching you all day. If one of us did get in that punishing position, the rest of the building would watch for you. Let you know when a guard was coming to keep them from catching you.

I ended up with a punctured lung, for which I had to have surgery to remove my seventh rib. That was because of the ropes and the tying me up. They told me that the bone slipped off my shoulder blade, chipped off and was working its way towards my heart. That's the only time that I felt that I might not make it. I was afraid that they would sedate me and I might not wake up. That was my biggest fear.

WAYNE COE

Chief Warrant Officer
Pilot, Helicopter Assault Company
U.S. Army

Wayne Coe

As a very, very small boy I used to fly on the old Sikorsky P-3s with my dad and the other guys. I have pictures of my dad running me up to Santa Claus getting out of the old 1952 Sikorsky helicopter. I always thought that would be the most fun in the world to fly. But I thought I would have to go through college and become an officer in the Air Force to fly. When I found out that I could go to war in officer training and in a year be flying helicopters, I didn't care about anything else. I went and did that. And I truly loved flying helicopters. I still love flying helicopters.

I loved flying a UH-1D. It was really a truck. We all knew it was a truck and we loaded it to the gills with everything that we could. It would haul about ten combat troops if it was running good, about six if it wasn't. We flew those helicopters all day and maintained them all night. And we lived in them. We hauled troops. We made combat assaults. We did our own medevacs. I thought flying a helicopter was the best job in the entire world. I volunteered to go to Vietnam and volunteered to fly just so I could fly that helicopter.

The D models that we flew came with a gunner who was usually a man that had infantry experience. A lot of gunners came out of infantry outfits and they were men who re-upped to stay longer in Vietnam so they could fly as our gunners. They were the guys that we basically trusted our lives with. We had a crew chief on the helicopters as well. What you really were looking for was a gunner that knew how to fix guns and that was really a crackerjack shot and could work on the helicopter. And a crew chief that not only could work on the helicopter but could also shoot things as well. Then an aircraft pilot, and a peter pilot or a copilot. In Vietnam we called them peter pilots. I don't know why. We just did. I never, ever broke ground in a helicopter in Vietnam without four guys in it as a crew. I never flew a mission over there by myself. One time during a mortar attack I jumped in with a towel and a set of flip-flops on and flew around while the mortar rounds were landing and then brought the helicopter back. I almost couldn't land it without someone clearing me into the revetment. I was used to having guys with me and the men would apprise me of where the tail boom was and what were the instructions. Whenever I heard a gun going off, I knew we were being engaged. My crews didn't ask for permission to fire. They found a target, we trusted them, they got it. Sometimes that split second was the difference between us surviving and being cut up by the machine guns on the ground. We owed more than just maintenance of our helicopter, closing the doors and stuff. These guys were our life line. They kept us alive.

Most of the guys were nineteen years old. I flew in Vietnam for six months before I turned twenty over there. I was shot down five times before I turned twenty years old. The young guys in the crews didn't mind the real dangerous assignments. They were the ones that would fly into the middle of these combat assaults and stuff. I'm sure there was a method of madness in the army of having these young officer pilots who were only specialists. The only enlisted men that we dealt with were our own crew. They didn't call us sir or Mr. Coe. They called me by my first name, Crash. We would rotate helicopters. You wouldn't get the same helicopter because of maintenance or because of scheduling. So you had a chance to fly with different crews and different copilots. Pretty soon you got to fly with everybody. Everyone had to fit the same mold. Everyone had to be absolutely

While most people think of Vietnam as a location only of rice paddies and jungles, this operation is taking place in the Mui Mum mountains in the Central Highlands.

WAYNE COE
CHIEF WARRANT
OFFICER
U.S. ARMY

Wayne Coe

Coe always wanted to fly and volunteered for Vietnam. In 1967 he arrived in Vietnam, fresh out of flight school at age nineteen, as a chief warrant officer. Over the next two years he flew with the 187th Assault Helicopter Company and the 120th Assault Helicopter Company. After leaving the army, he flew for the National Guard. He also returned to school and, when not flying, spent most of his life as an electrical or chemical engineer. He has four sons and today spends most of his time, as he says, "Fishing very hard in Florida and loving every minute of it."

spectacular at their job. Everybody had to be absolutely trustworthy. If they said it was done, it was done. If the gun went off, it was pointed at a bad guy. We really all stuck together.

We really stuck together. It was interesting to see. We had the same kind of stick-together feel with the grunts on the ground. We had one grunt flying in the back already as our gunner, so he could directly relate to the guys on the ground. We lived to support them. That's what we did: we lived to support the grunts on the ground. We fed them and we medevacked them and we did everything that was done for them with our helicopter because there were no roads going in. We picked up recon teams on the top of mountains when they needed to be picked up, whether it was daytime or nighttime. Everything they did we did for them as their vehicle driver. We basically lived in sync with these men. At first I was terrified by the flying in Vietnam because it was at low level and high speed and heavy aircraft at hard turns and bad weather. After a little while we realized that that is really what your job is and that is really what you were sent there to do. Then it starts to become more of a game. So you fly the helicopter harder and you try to do more things with it to learn to push the envelope further and further. By the time I got home from Vietnam, I pretty much flew a UH-1D at the red line all the time. I was most comfortable pushing it real, real hard because I was so used to being in an air combat situation.

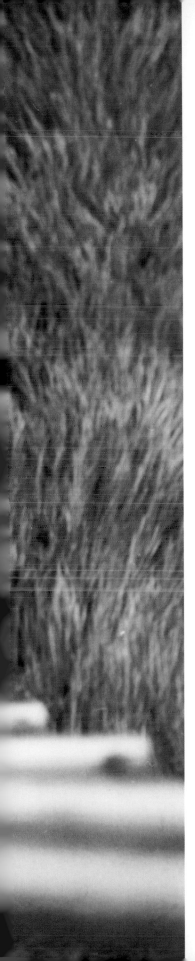

If there was a routine, it would probably be like this. We would usually have a combat assault where we would be inserting troops into a new landing zone. We would get up in the morning early when it was dark and we'd fly to a staging field and pick up troops. Artillery and the Air Force and the Navy guns would hit whatever target it was. We'd take our troops in and insert them. As soon as the troops got on the ground, they'd break up the platoon and they'd say you're attached to so and so and then we'd start flying resupply. Later in the afternoon we'd come back, refuel, rearm, get our helicopters ready, form back up with the platoon. Either resupply the guys for a night defensive position or pull the guys and take them back to the base camp. That was pretty much the daily grind. Some days it would just be resupply and some days just combat assault, but pretty much a mixture of those two.

We actually ate with the grunts, and we ate C-rations most of the time because we would be gone when the mess halls would normally be open. It was a long flying day over there. A lot of guys would fly ten to twelve hours in a day, which is a lot of time in a helicopter when you consider refueling and rearming and down time. The one thing I remember about Vietnam is being tired. We didn't get Saturdays and Sundays off, and we had no time off. You worked twenty-four hours a day.

Flying in a helicopter is a little bit like being on a magic carpet. You can see everything because you can see above you and below you. We flew these things about six inches off the top of the rice paddies. And we flew them in between trees. You'd have to roll them up on the side to get the rotor blades in between the trees. When we would hover down into a resupply and pull out medevacs, our crews would literally clear the tail room down a little tiny slot and we would have to sometimes chop away pieces of tree with the rotor blades. Other times they'd make us go over the top of artillery and they'd run us up sixteen thousand feet so we'd go from hot and steamy down in the jungle to over the top of a shoot somewhere and be way up where it's cold with the doors closed to see if the heater would actually work. The view out of the front of the helicopters was really, really spectacular.

I was shot down with a .50 caliber machine gun. They are real hard on the helicopter. They literally just tear it apart. I had an RPG shoot the tail boom off of a helicopter I was flying, and the helicopter spun in. I just had a little bit of control and got it on the ground. We got hit by mortars in the landing zone. We had problems from the AK-47s. They shot a big bullet and they would get a lot of them in the air at one time. We took a lot of small-arms fire. At fifteen hundred feet you don't get much small arms fire but when we were operating down in the jungle, down in the landing zones, I mean you're a sitting duck. On the 7th of August '67 I lost a tail to them. I landed forward in the landing zone and the guy stepped out of the bamboo that was just off the end of my rotor blades. The rotor blades were forty-eight feet across, so from where I was, it was probably twenty two feet or something like that. He pointed his AK-47 in the windshield of my helicopter and he pulled the trigger and all the bullets came through and passed me and my copilot and into the transmission. We pulled pitch and went

Extraction by 100-foot rope ladder to the back of a CH-47 Chinook helicopter, which is hovering over the area.

over the top of him. My gunner killed him as we went over the top of him while he was putting another clip in. Just as we got over the top of him, a .50 hit us on the side and tore the tail boom clear off. The tail boom folded alongside of the helicopter and we started to spin. I had a little bit of control of my collectives, and I rolled the throttle off and put the collective down.

My instructor in-flight school had told me time and again that some day I would lose a tail boom if I wasn't ready for it. I thought about it so many times that when it actually happened, I did it before I thought about it. So I'm spinning upside down and I can see the rice paddies. I roll the throttle back and I add the pitch to the helicopter and it stopped, and started beating itself to death beside the river. When the plane stopped beating, I was under water and my foot was caught underneath the side of the helicopter. The helicopter was actually on fire before we hit the ground. My crew chief got in there, unbuckled and pulled me out of the helicopter by my helmet. Almost as fast as we got on the ground, there had been a Mayday that all these helicopters were being shot at. As soon as I was on the ground, I looked up and here comes a rescue ship for me wasn't part of our company. It was this guy that heard the Mayday in the air and had come in to help, to see what he could do. He had a chaplain on board and I thought that was kind of amusing. They came to take us out of the wreckage because they thought that we were all dead. The plane was on fire and all beat up but all four of us survived.

I was in the hospital and they were taking Plexiglas out of my face from where all of the bullets had come through the windshield. I had some pretty big hunks embedded in my face because I didn't have my hood down. I was flying outside standard operating procedures, you could say. The colonel came in and he said, "How bad are you hurt." I said, "Well, I've just got this Plexiglas in my face." He says, "Go get in that helicopter, we've got to get stuff out." And so right back on. We didn't really ever take time to lick our wounds over there. We fought hard and we got hit we just got hit and that's the way it was.

We had the best of times in Vietnam. We loved our brothers and we fought together. When someone was hurt, wounded, killed, downed, whatever, we were all on top of it. We were as tight as you could be. It's pretty hard to erase the memories of hauling dead bodies all day long in your helicopter. It's pretty hard to erase that you were covered in blood all day long and the inside of your helicopters was covered with blood because the men you were hauling, it was pumping out of their arteries and was catching a 120-knot slipstream and depositing itself all over the inside of the helicopter. We would come back from these missions and get a water truck and hose out the inside of the helicopters so that we could get in them and fly them back out. It's also pretty hard to forget a guy in the middle of the night calling on the radio saying we're completely surrounded and if you don't come get us when it's daybreak, then we're dead. And you say it's raining and you know, it's kind of shitty out here and then you go, well what do you want us to do. So you find them. You know, you find them however you can find them. One time I had them shoot a parachute flare up in the air so I could see down below me. I went down to follow the parachute flare through the triple canopy jungle and then put ropes down to find the guys. Finally got them all hooked up and pulling them out and by now we're just enveloped with tracers, just completely enveloped with tracers from the bad guys. Those things, like I said, they're a little more difficult to forget.

Opposite: A UH-1D helicopter takes off after completing a resupply mission for Company A, 1st Battalion, 7th Cavalry Regiment, 3rd Brigade, 1st Cavalry Division (Airmobile) during Operation Pershing, a search and destroy mission conducted approximately 50 kilometers northeast of An Khe in Binh Dinh Province.

CHUCK DEBELLEVUE

Captain, F-4 Pilot, Ace
U.S. Air Force

Chuck DeBellevue

Some people want to be policemen, some people want to be firemen. I remember early on seeing airplanes fly overhead and I thought that'd be neat. I don't know where it came from.

The F-4 is a two-seat airplane. In order to fly it well, it takes two people that know what they're doing. The front seat is the pilot and he's the aircraft commander. He flies the airplane and he's in charge. The back seat, when I was in it, was the navigator. Before that it was another pilot, a young pilot who was going to learn how to fly better from the front seat. In the back seat we did the navigation, the setting up of some of the bombing missions, the intercepts if we were going up against another airplane and we have to get involved with him. I did that. It takes two people to fly it well. Right in front of you is the instrument panel. A radarscope that sits down low so you have to bend over to look into it. When you look up you see instruments in front of you. You have a canopy around you. You can look out all around you, but straight-ahead is the instrument panel and the backside of the ejection seat. If you want to look out front you've got to cant your head over to the side so that your helmet is on the side of the canopy and you look out the quarter panel. It has to be on the left side because there's too much equipment, too much junk on the right side.

Acrylic on board, 24"x36" US Army art collection by Bruce J. Anderson.

We were called into the briefing room. Nobody thought anything about it. Just another mission. It was 4:30 in the morning. Everybody's half asleep. The intelligence officers usually joke with us. Today they were very serious. The briefing boards were covered by curtains so nobody knew where we were going. Finally Colonel Gabriel, the wing commander at the 432nd, walked in and sat down. The two captains pulled the curtains away from the board and said, "Gentlemen, your target for today is downtown." It got so quiet in the room you could hear a pin drop. And the room was carpeted. Everybody woke up. I mean, you went from half asleep, to yo, this is something. Everybody woke up, wide awake, started paying attention. They got through with their briefing. Colonel Gabriel got up and said, "Guys we've been waiting for this mission a long time. Let's go do a good job. Take a look at the guy sitting next to you, he may not be coming home." So you're sitting with the guy next to you and he's looking at you and you're thinking, well, that's too bad he's not coming back today, because I know I am. And everybody came home. It did wonders for our morale.

July started out just another Linebacker mission. Before we got west of Hanoi we had to go through refueling, making sure everything was working well. All of a sudden our radar controller says, "Paula," which was our call sign that day,

Two U.S. Air Force McDonnell F-4D-30-MC Phantom II fighters from the 435th Tactical Fighter Squadron, 8th Tactical Fighter Wing, over Vietnam, off the wing of a Boeing KC-135A Stratotanker. Both Phantoms are armed with three SUU-30/B cluster bombs (right wing), three LAU-3 rocket launchers (left wing) and six Mk 82 227 kg bombs (centerline).

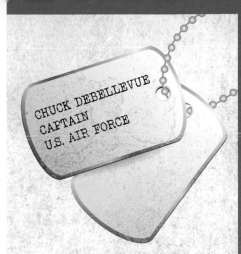

Chuck DeBellevue

As a captain in the Air Force, DeBellevue served in the famed "Triple Nickel," the 555th Tactical Fighter Squadron based at Udorn, Thailand. A weapons systems officer, he completed 220 missions, 96 over North Vietnam. Credited with the destruction of six North Vietnamese jet fighters in aerial combat—four MiG-21s and two MiG-19s—he is the leading ace of the Vietnam War. A command pilot with 3,000 flying hours, 550 in combat, when he retired as a colonel in 1998 he was the last American Ace on active duty. His many decorations include the Air Force Cross, three Silver Stars, three Legions of Merit, and six Distinguished Flying Crosses. He is married with three children.

CHUCK DEBELLEVUE
CAPTAIN
U.S. AIR FORCE

"Paula you're emerged." Which meant on his scope, both us and the MiGs are in the same piece of sky. He can't tell us any information, other than, heads up, they're among you. That scared us because we didn't see anybody. For about two minutes we have eight guys with heads on swivels looking around. You know, where is he? Looking in the radar, nothing there. Looking out, looking at the radar. Nothing. Nobody sees anybody. We're maneuvering around. You never go anywhere in an F-4 in a straight line. So we're moving around. For some reason I have an inkling that the MiG is in front us. I look up and there's a black speck on a white cloud at eleven o'clock. General Ritchie saw it about the same time I called it out. We came left. Now we were aligned with the MiG. The MiG came close. One of the ways our wing men knew that we were getting closer to a fight was when the wing tanks came off the airplane. When we went to the afterburner, the more afterburner we had, the closer we were getting to the fight. General Ritchie started a slice, and the MiG came up on our back. As the MiG came by us we held it because we knew there were two of them. They never flew by themselves. They always flew two ships. There was a high probability that his buddy was somewhere around. This lead MiG came by us, shot a classic Soviet J leg tactic. He wanted us to follow him and his buddy was going to come in and shoot us down. Except we didn't pull. We didn't take the bait. We waited in this slice, just waiting, 175 degrees a bank. Just waiting to pull. The F-4 will go five hundred knots in one direction. You can slice through and seventeen seconds later you're doing five hundred knots in the opposite direction. And it's high G, max power.

The second guy comes through and makes an oval turn and follows his lead. They turned away so they're over here and we're over here. Instead of having to go full circle to get to them, we just cut around the circle and slide into their six o'clock position. Now this is all happening very fast and also it's a high-achieve fight. I mean you're in a lot of pressure, max power, the Gs or whatever it takes to get in behind the guy, the two guys. We rolled out and trailed with the trailing MiG. Because it's going to be a dogfight, I move the radar to a function that allows for the front seater, for General Ritchie to now use a little switch on his throttles to then key the radar. I've bore-sighted the radar, so now the radar is looking wherever the piper is. That allows him to hit a button on his stick, on his throttles, which then lets the radar range out anything it locks onto and you get a full system to lock onto. As soon as that happens, I clarify that it's a full system lock and I start counting because he has to wait four seconds. Two seconds for the radar to settle down and have good information, two seconds additional for the radar missiles to get good radar information. You fire at three, three and half seconds, you have stupid missiles, blind and ballistic missiles. It's thousand one, thousand two, thousand three, thousand—fire. And two M-7s come off the airplane. Squeeze. Ritchie squeezes the trigger. The technique is squeeze, release, squeeze, and you've committed the first missile and as soon as the first missile is gone it automatically steps to the second missile and you've committed that one already. In one minute of time we'll get two missiles off the airplane. The MiG was in a 5G turn so we saw the top of his airplane. We fired at about six thousand feet, one radar a mile or so, and the first radar missile comes out and it's going for the central radar engine, which is right behind the canopy where the wings meet the airplane, just as the wings expand out. That's where the radar energy is concentrated. That's where the missile hit when it cut him in two. The second missile went through the firewall. At that point we rolled out of the flight. We thought the other MiG would blow out of the fight and run us down but he didn't. Instead he stayed.

We got a call from our number 4 man who said they're on me, they've come full circle and they're threatening our number 4 crew. We unloaded to get our air speed back and came back into the fight, locked on the other MiG, the lead MiG now. At this point he's in four thousand-feet range and he's in high-G turn. He has now

Opposite: Captain Charles B. DeBellevue, Vietnam Ace, F-4 D Phantom. The Phantom was a two-seat fighter, with a pilot and a weapons system officer working in tandem. As the WSO, Capt. DeBellevue became the first non-pilot ace during the Vietnam War.

Cockpit of F-4 Phantom II

pulled off the scope. The radar scope in the F-4 is a pie-shaped attack display, plus or minus 60 degrees in the nose. The target, the second MiG when we locked onto it, pulled off the scope and he is about a 70 degrees angle off so he was not on my radar scope. There is no target on the scope. But he is on a side lobe of the radar. This is an old analog radar with a lot of bleed-over and stuff, so he's in the side lobe. Although he wasn't on the scope, the radar missile still got programmed properly. When it came off the airplane what you saw was not a missile coming out straight-ahead because the target was over here, you saw the missile when it dropped off the airplane. What happens is the missile is jettisoned off the airplane. There's a lanyard. As soon as the missiles clear the fuselage, the lanyard pulls free and the missile motor is firing. It's programmed in the autopilot of the missile to do an initial maneuver based on the parameters the radar has told it to expect the target to be in. First time we saw the missile was when it exited the wing tip area. Now this is for a target that wasn't on the scope. The missile's heading right for him. He's at a high-G turn. Again what we see is the top of the airplane pretty much and the radar is concentrating on the top of the airplane. It cuts it in two and burns both ends.

The time it took for the black fly speck on that white cloud until the second MiG 21 blew up was a minute twenty-nine seconds.

That is the longest eighty-nine seconds I've ever spent. Or the shortest, depending on how you look at it. What had to happen, teamwork had to be perfect. Everything had to work as programmed. There was no chance to say, well, you know, you ought to do this, or I'm going to check my checklist. You had to react properly or it didn't matter.

The G forces we felt had to be read on the G meter because we didn't feel any. I never felt any Gs. My adrenaline was always pumping so fast it didn't bother me. I'm paying for that now as I get a little older. From maneuvering around the airplane at high Gs we didn't feel anything then. Getting ready for the fight, you had to be ready for when you saw him to be able to react to him. You didn't know where you were going to see him. Usually the F-4 causes the engines to smoke very badly, especially in those days. Now they use smokeless engines. But when we were flying in Southeast Asia, the engines smoked. You expect to find the enemy behind you. That smoke trail was a big pointer and at the head of every smoke trail was an F-4. We had to maneuver around to make sure nobody got behind our six. The wing men were there as outriggers to make sure nobody saw us and got behind us unobserved. Teamwork was extremely important.

After the kills, there's the elation of being successful, but at the same time you couldn't let your guard down because you're not out of harm's way. You're still deep in the heartland of the enemy. And we were three hundred miles from Udorn. At that time we're closer to Hanoi, so we could glide into Hanoi just about if we had to, we're that close. So the fight is not over yet. This particular battle was over but the fight is not over. We got word later in the mission that there were two sets of MiGs coming, two from the north, and two up from the south. We couldn't let our guard down. You had to say, okay, that's nice, we did good shooting, let's go.

I've had SAMs come through the formation close enough you could read the graffiti on it if I could read Vietnamese. You could reach out and touch it almost. Either of the two missiles would have gotten two of us. They had optically launched and didn't turn off the guidance until after the booster fell off. By then they were almost in on us. Luckily I was heads down in the cockpit at that time. The radar system lit up from nothing to full launch light. It tells us that we had somebody launching at us and you got a rattlesnake sound in your headset that will put fear into you right now. We keep our jammers in standby. Well, I reached down and turned both jammers on before I looked up and then I looked up and saw the missile. Both missiles blew high.

Vietnam was not a target rich environment. They had very few MiGs that would launch against us. We were flying a great general purpose jet. It does everything quite well. We were flying the workhorse of the Air Force, the F-4.

The guys on the ground had a different war. They were living it in the Army and the Marines. Out on patrol they were living in the swamps and we didn't do that. It was just a different war for us. At the end of the mission I could at least get into clean clothes, take a shower and go down to the club and get a bite to eat. Did it mean that it was less of a war for me or more for them? It was different. I had a lot of friends that were full time residents at the Hanoi Hilton, not the chain that has hotels here in the states. The room service at this Hilton was beatings on demand. It wasn't very pleasant. We all knew that if we got shot down and taken prisoner we would be there for a long time. I had lots of friends that were residents there. I had no desire to go to Hanoi as a prisoner of war. But I went to Hanoi everyday.

STEVE RITCHIE

Captain, F-4 Pilot, Ace
Vietnam, 1968–69, 1972
U.S. Air Force

Steve Ritchie

Steve Ritchie arrived in Da Nang, South Vietnam, April Fool's Day, 1968. He volunteered for a new program called FAST FAC. These were reconnaissance missions originally carried out by small, slow-moving propeller airplanes. When the Air Force decided these "slow movers" could not do the job over North Vietnam because enemy ground fire was too intense, they switched the missions to the more powerful F-100 jet, with the call sign of Misty. Soon the program expanded to include the F-4 Phantom jet, and Ritchie became a part of those dangerous missions. By the end of his second tour, Ritchie had become an American ace, one of only two pilots in the Vietnam War to achieve that distinction.

On the 6th of September 1968, we flew the first official F-4 FAST FAC mission in Southeast Asia. These were difficult missions. It involved flying at low altitude over North Vietnam, searching for what we call fleeting and lucrative targets; river traffic, barges on rivers, truck parks, oil storage, resupply concentrations, AAA sites, etc. Trucks didn't operate during the daytime; they operated almost exclusively at night. During the day they would congregate in truck parks. Of course, they were camouflaged and hidden under trees. We searched for those types of targets and when a target was discovered we would perform in a very similar manner to a forward air controller in the South. Other airplanes were called in, generally flights of four, with a variety of weapons. We would describe the target, mark it with a white phosphorous smoke rocket, and direct the strike. The missions were normally four to five hours long, generally requiring four to five refuelings. It was demanding, low altitude, high threat action, and one of the most productive and successful programs of the war.

We worked closely with RF-4s based at Udorn. They took pictures in the afternoon of the targets from our morning missions. Thus, new target photographs were available for the strike fighters the next morning.

Some targets were moving, such as river traffic so these would have to be handled on an individual basis. However, being able to work closely with our RF-4 reconnaissance airplanes and have current film of a variety of types of targets was very helpful.

Ground fire was always a threat as these missions attracted a fair amount of AAA reaction. Our training, tactics, and execution of the missions were planned to minimize the danger. Fundamental common sense was the rule in a high-threat area. When there were a lot of guns, we made only one pass. If a second pass was required, we returned from a different direction, varied the speed and altitude, and used a curvilinear approach to minimize exposure to the ground fire.

Having flown 142 missions without any serious problems, something happened to me that is common in aviation … complacency. I was becoming over-confident. I was in a high threat area over Laos during a FAST

FAC mission and I had directed several strike flights against a line of supplies along the Ho Chi Minh Trail without success. We had a 20mm gun pod, so I decided to strafe the target. As we rolled in to attack, Lieutenant Bob Houge, in the back seat, said, "Steve, I really wish you wouldn't do this." I replied confidently, "No sweat, Bob. We're in out of this sun." This meant the sun was behind us and would blind the gunners.

Just about the time that I was ready to squeeze the trigger, WHAM!

Bob yelled, "We're hit. I told you we were going to get hit."

I pulled off the target, calling "Mayday! Mayday! Mayday!" and headed for the South China Sea about eighty miles away. Our best bet for rescue was to get out over the water. The area surrounding the target was occupied by the Pathet Lao. They were not friendly at all. If they captured us, we would be tortured and killed. This was not an area where anyone wanted to bail out. As it happened, we didn't have to.

Turns out a 37mm had entered the intake of the right engine, gone through the engine, taken out a whole bunch of rotor blades and then exited the rear end. Plus, it was not a high explosive shell. Otherwise we would have been out of business. The chances of the shell being a non-explosive shell and the angle being so perfect as to not cut any fuel or hydraulic lines were extremely slim. We were very fortunate to have lived. Thereafter I always followed the basic rules for survival.

When I returned for the second tour of combat in 1972, I was as ready, as prepared as it was possible to be. And this was the first time I ever saw an airplane that was not like the one that I flew and trained in, the MiG-21 over Hanoi. In other words, training against an airplane that was similar to the enemy that we might expect was not allowed when I was coming along in those early years in the late sixties and seventies. Obviously, this was a serious disadvantage.

As a result of those experiences shortly after Vietnam, we developed the aggressor program. We trained against an airplane that looked, acted like, and flew like the enemy.

We were facing a threat in air combat that we'd never seen before: antiaircraft artillery, the surface-to-air missile, and the MiG-21. That triple threat was a new experience in the air arena. It was integrated and active during the entire mission and presented quite a challenge. The mission of the MiGs was to intercept the inbound strike force and prevent the F-4s with laser-guided bombs from attacking targets in North Vietnam. Our mission, called combat air patrol, flying out in front of, to the side, and to the rear of the combat patrol, was to fly out in front, to the side, and to the rear of the strike force. The task was to intercept the MiGs as they came out to attack the strike force. We ran interference for the Phantoms with laser-guided bombs who were severely

Steve Ritchie

Ritchie was dispatched to Da Nang as an F-4 Aircraft Commander when a captain in the Air Force and was selected to fly the first Fast FAC (Forward Air Controller) mission in Southeast Asia. In 1969 he completed the Air Force Top Gun Fighter Weapons School in the F4 Phantom. He volunteered for a second tour in Vietnam in 1972. He was the only pilot to ever down five MiG-21s and thus became America's last pilot ace. He completed 339 missions and 800 hours of combat. Since then, he has been active in the Air National Guard, the Air Force Reserve, and politics. As a brigadier general he travels around the country recruiting for the Air Force, often flying the supersonic T-38 Talon in air shows. As president of his company, he lectures on leadership, teamwork, achievement, and success.

Major Robert Lodge and Major Roger Locher in the cockpit of their F-4D Phantom II jet. The team had shot down two MiGs when they clashed with MiG-21s and Shenyang J-6 (Chinese MiG-19s) jets on the morning of 10 May 1972 and were shot down. Lodge decided not to eject and was killed. Locher was recovered 23 days later in the deepest search and rescue operation inside North Vietnam.

limited in their ability to counter a MiG-21 at high speed, particularly from the rear.

The 10th of May was a very bittersweet day. It was a mission we had planned for a long time and it worked exactly as we anticipated. We met a flight of 4 MiG 21s, we fired head on, we scored two victories, we converged on the other two MiGs. Chuck and I took the third MiG and Bob Lodge was going after the 4th MiG, which would have been his fourth MiG, total. Unfortunately, again, something happened to him that previously happened to me.

Even though he had Roger Locher in the back seat, and they were the most experienced crew in Southeast Asia—they were on their third tour and had over four hundred missions—they became fixed to the target in front of them. It's called target fixation. Two MiG-19s were hiding behind the flight of four MiG-21s, and were able to achieve a six o'clock position on Bob and Roger. Our frantic radio calls, warning them, that MiG-19s were in the rear quarter, were not heard. We screamed, "Break, break!" Unfortunately, their plane was shot down. It was not until almost a month later that we knew their fate.

We knew that our colleagues, our comrades, and our commanders would do anything that could possibly be done to rescue downed aircrew members. The greatest mission I ever flew was the rescue of Roger Locher who was downed for twenty-three days, some sixty miles northwest of Hanoi. It was the deepest rescue ever attempted. He was shot down on the 10th of May in 1972 and there was no word for twenty two days. We had given up, feeling he had been killed or captured. Then, as we were flying near Yen Bai Airfield, he came up on the radio. We heard this call, "Any allied aircraft. This is Oyster Zero One Bravo," and I remember thinking we don't have an Oyster Zero One Bravo.

Then we realized, "That's Roger Locher!" We answered him. This is exactly what he said, "Guys I've been down here a long time. Any chance of picking me up?"

We went in that afternoon with a rescue effort, but the ground fire was so heavy that we had to back off. We couldn't get him out. The next day the 7th Air Force in Saigon canceled the entire strike mission to Hanoi and dedicated all the resources, over 150 airplanes to the rescue of Roger Locher. We went in for about two hours and we made sure the guns at Yen Bai Airfield were silenced. Then the lead of two Jolly Green Giant helicopters sent the jungle penetrator down through a heavy canopy of trees and were able to snatch Roger Locher as he was about to be captured. The PJ's pulled him out of the jungle and into the helicopter.

We flew cover for the two Jolly Greens and the C-130 refueling tankers. They brought him all the way back to Udorn, Thailand, and, with hundreds of colleagues cheering, he stepped off that chopper after twenty-three days. It was very comforting for all of us to know that if we went down, we would have the same opportunity to be rescued.

Heading inbound we were usually a little nervous knowing that there might be an engagement. When MiGs were up and outbound from Hanoi, and the likelihood of an intercept was pretty high, the adrenaline was pumping. I often compare it to competitive sports. I was a football player at the Air Force Academy. All week before the game, we'd practice, we'd study the opponent, we'd look at the films, we'd review intelligence, we would learn their plays, their tactics, their training. On the day of the big game, we put on our uniforms, take our equipment and go to the arena. I was always nervous, apprehensive. There were always butterflies. That's the way it was as we proceeded to North Vietnam. But once the ball is in the air, once you take the first hit, the jitters vanish. It was the same in combat.

Once in the fight, one has to rely on all the years of training, practice, study, teamwork, communications, and focus. It becomes very intense. We had to react with split-second timing. We had to be disciplined. There are no other choices. There were no other excuses. We spent many hours of study and critique on the ground for every hour in the air.

Think of it as being in an arena where living and dying depends on winning or losing. When you win and you live it is very, very exciting. It's like winning

Captain Steve Ritchie, 555th Tactical Fighter Squadron, pictured beside the aircraft in which he became the first Air Force ace of the Vietnam War.

the Master's, or winning the Super Bowl. Except … this is different. Lives are at stake. Do we like the thought of killing another individual? No, of course not. But, in a situation where one is able to apply everything that he or she worked for, trained for, studied and learned over a period of five, ten, maybe even fifteen or twenty years, and it all comes together and it works … it gels … and it happens, and you are victorious in a very high threat, lethal situation, you can imagine what a tremendously rewarding experience it may be.

RALPH DRESSER

Pilot
Commander
Operation Ranch Hand
U.S. Air Force

Operation Ranch Hand started in the early 1960s using several modified C-123 cargo airplanes. Each plane carried a one thousand-gallon herbicide tank in the back end and on wing booms on the wings. Herbicides, primarily used in defoliation missions, destroyed everything green around Special Forces camps, major air bases, along canals, rivers, highways, and anything that would offer the enemy cover. Crop destruction was part of the mission to deny the Viet Cong and North Vietnamese use of food grown in the areas they controlled. Ranch Hand defoliated every province in South Vietnam, the DMZ between North and South Vietnam, Laos, all of the Ho Chi Minh Trail, and even parts of North Vietnam.

Ralph Dresser

It was the kind of place that you wished you didn't have to come there and do that. You hoped that you could come back sometime in the future and see it under better conditions. But the people were nice to us. The country was literally a beautiful place.

We were in support of the American ground troops. That was our purpose. To help them survive by cutting down surprise or ambushes on them and giving them more of a chance. We had no political purpose at all over there. There was no psychological warfare, although the North Vietnamese tried to claim that's what we were doing. Purely support for the ground troops.

We, of course, didn't have ground troops along the Ho Chi Minh trail in Laos. We were trying to uncover the trail. It wasn't one little trail hidden under the trees. It was hundreds of little trails that connected. We would have to go over there and fly up and down and try to find parts of the trail. We would throw a smoke bomb out, a grenade out on the ground and we'd line a couple of those up and we'd spray it and we'd go look for it someplace else. We frequently got surprised over there. With that milling around we've seen .50 caliber guns mounted on the back of elephants. But that was kind of a mission for us; to search out the trail and to uncover it and highlight it and make it appear like a super highway so the other guys in the C-130 gunships or forward air controllers could come over there and observe the traffic up and down the trail in Laos.

Once we sprayed this stuff on the foliage in about three days the foliage would change color from green to brown. The trees all shriveled up. It really accelerated the growth of the tree or the plant and it like gave it a heart attack. When the leaves shriveled up then it took some physical force like wind or rain or something like that to hit the leaves and knock them off. And it would give an increase in vertical visibility of up to 85 to 90 percent, depending on the foliage and whether it was only one layer of canopy. You could see down to the ground with visibility of 85 to 90 percent. You could tell where their camps were. You could see the people. They couldn't move around unobserved. That was the reason it was used and asked for.

Defoliant spray run, part of Operation Ranch Hand, during the Vietnam War by UC-123B Provider aircraft.

We used different kinds of chemicals. The first one we used was called Agent Purple. Where did they get these color names? They came with a purple band around the fifty-five-gallon drum that came into the country on ships. The most notorious chemical that we used was called Agent Orange. It came in country in a fifty-five-gallon tank with an orange band around it. We used Agent White and Agent Blue. We had a one thousand-gallon tank in the back of our airplane.

We had a GI sitting in the back of the airplane in an armored box. He had a little ten-horsepower gasoline engine back there that gave us a pump. It pumped it out of the tank and into spray booms in the wings and the tail. But the control of those booms was strictly the pilot. He had a little toggle switch up on his control column. The pilot in the left seat flew with both hands and worked the controls over the boom. The guy in the right seat, the copilot, maintained the throttles and monitored the engine and maintained the air speed. No matter what the pilot did, he kept the air speed safe. We frequently in the lead airplane would have a navigator straddling a parachute over a radio panel, sitting between us and who would navigate using a stopwatch and a regular terrain map. We flew at 150 feet normally on target. We flew at 150 knots, just like a state-side crop-duster, except we would rarely go back and forth over a field because the environment was not conducive to our safety. We always flew with a minimum of two airplanes or in a formation of maybe as many as ten or twelve airplanes, depending on what the target would allow us to do.

At 150 feet and 150 knots we were low enough to see the muzzle flash and to hear the muzzle report. We could smell the cordite. When we would get those factors we would tell the forward air controller who was flying with us that we were taking ground fire. We had fighter cover going along with us and they would come in and strafe or whatever they had to do to suppress the fire. Sometimes they would come in and pre-strike. That is, they would strafe in front of us or lay down ordnance in front of us. A few times where they strafed over the top of the airplane we had to ask them to stop that because the empties would come out and hit our airplanes when they'd go by. We had fabric control surfaces on the wings and they were tearing up the fabric when the casings would get hit from our own friends. But the fighters were important to us.

I flew 350 defoliation missions in my year's tour there as commander of Ranch Hand. And I had to make emergency landings on 87 of those 350 missions with battle damage on the airplane. I don't mean just a little hole. I mean a hole that caused me to doubt the structural integrity of the airplane, the landing gear or something like that. Getting serious damage done to the airplane where it warranted an emergency landing. We were recognized as the most shot at and hit aircraft in South Vietnam. Better than half of the pilots and crew members while I had been there had been wounded at least once, some two or three times.

We would get up probably an hour and a half, two hours before sunrise, eat breakfast, report for final crew briefing, have our intelligence, and go get our airplane. We would get off the ground before sunrise to be over the target right at first daylight, meet our forward air controller, meet our fighter escort, and hit our target with as much surprise as we could. We would come off target, go back to our base, either Tan Son Nhut or Da Nang, refill with herbicide, get the maps for the second target and take off and do the same thing all over again. We did not intentionally spray over any of our troops. We would spray around the perimeter of

Soldiers sleeping during transit, by Ed Bowen, Vietnam 1969

314

Special Forces camps. If they were inside, the wind drifts that stuff in and out. We had to get the target usually at sunrise and we had to fly our mission while the temperature was below 85 degrees. Above 85 degrees, the stuff rose up instead of settling down. If we got shot down early in the morning and had to crash land, our survival rate of getting picked up would be better but it was mostly because of the temperatures. The temperatures would allow the defoliant to settle into the ground. We were through with our mission by one o'clock. The rest of the day was taken up with planning the next day's or the next week's mission. Taking off and going out and flying at high altitude over future targets with both the Army people and spotting the targets, selecting the route we wanted to take into the target, where we wanted to avoid. Or we would, in the case of some of our missions, we would have to fly into the province capitals with our Army Chemical Corps people and meet with the province chief and the South Vietnamese Army people in those places and find out what they wanted and how they wanted it.

We were asked to categorize our targets as A, B, C, and D. A targets we had to have fighter suppression where they went in and hit the target. We went in and killed the trees and got out. B targets were where we would go in first with surprise and the fighters would be there with us to make sure that they could come in and suppress fire if we got heavy fire while it was going on. C targets were very few. Only about two or three in the country we would go on that we thought we could go on and not take fighters along with us. Just have them sitting alert on the pad. The D targets were training targets, and we had one area that we used to train our people when they first came in country for one or two flights. That was the Saigon River between Saigon and down to the coast. We would go down there without fighter escorts and one airplane and we would continuously spray this area along the riverbanks. Well, as a result of that continuous spraying we did affect new growth out of the soil. You didn't see anything growing out of the soil. It was a devastated wasteland. And interestingly, when people want to paint the defoliation mission in a very dark picture, they go to that section of the river that we purposely did this to. No other section of the country was this way. But they point to this as typical to what it did to the countryside, and that is not so. It was just this thirty-mile strip of riverbank that had nothing else going on there.

We slept in the airplanes just like the GIs slept on the ground. We didn't have protective gear. We wore white shirts, a purple scarf and a flak vest. We were more concerned about getting shot down than we were about problems with the chemicals. I've had about five or six medical tests. We want to know the facts, not using emotion or rumor. We want the facts. We're waiting to find out what the medical data and the science is, to prove whether or not this stuff hurt our families, hurt us, or anything else.

THE AIR WAR

In the Vietnam War, the air war was exciting, dangerous, and controversial, thus making it difficult to measure and to appreciate its role.

In the Vietnam War, fighter planes or highflying B-52 bombers or helicopter gunships were important and powerful weapons used by American forces against their Communist enemy. Though unrelenting bombing raids hurt the Viet Cong, the North Vietnamese Army, and North Vietnam itself, it did not stop them from fighting.

The Air Force flew its missions from Udorn and Korat in Thailand, and from Tan Son Nhut, Bien Hoa, and Dang in South Vietnam. Fighter aircraft and fighter bombers attacked enemy troops on the ground and gave close air support to troops during combat. Highflying, powerful machines such as F-105 Thunderchiefs, F-4 Phantoms, and F-5 Freedom Fighters, along with many other fixed-wing planes flying for the Air Force, the Navy and the Marines, roared out of the sky to attack enemy troops and their positions on the ground in South Vietnam. F-105s and F-4 Phantoms also engaged in frequent dogfights over North Vietnam, often against Russian and Chinese MIG fighters piloted by North Vietnamese. In time a new breed of American jet jockeys developed-- "aces," a pilot who had destroyed more than six enemy planes in the air during high speed, hi-tech dogfights.

Among the Navy and Marine airplanes that launched from aircraft carriers on the coast were the A-7, the A-4 Skyhawk, and the A-6 Intruder. These fighters regularly hit enemy traffic in the South China Sea, usually junks, small fishing boats, and even small freighters carrying arms and munitions for North Vietnam. These ships often plied the waters along the Vietnamese Coast in shipping lanes that constantly changed.

Marine aircraft flew from Da Nang and Chu Lai to protect and aid the grunts on the ground, especially during their firefights along the DMZ in I Corps, in northern parts of South Vietnam. Close air support by fighter jets helped troops on the ground, especially during close combat. Spotters flying aerial reconnaissance usually in single seat, single engine O-1 Bird Dog planes bravely circled enemy positions. These were the Forward Air Controllers (FACS) who also flew in OV-2 Skymasters or even twin-engine Broncos. From their post in the sky, they identified enemy targets, allowing fighter planes to bomb and strafe enemy soldiers, sometimes only yards from American troops.

In many ways, the pilots in the Vietnam War were carbon copies of the pioneering pilots of World War I. Then, for the first time, we first saw single-wing and by-wing aircraft fighting against German planes. They were

Huey Medical Evacuation (Medevac)

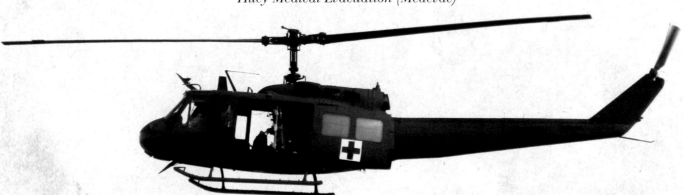

locked in life and death combat in the sky. Air battles did much to change the nature of modern war. In 1917, those bold young pilots often cruised so low to the ground that they could see the face of their enemy as they tossed bombs and grenades by hand from their tissue-thin airplanes hoping some would hit their target. Clumsily mounted machine guns strafed German forces in their trenches and shot at German planes in the sky in what were the first dogfights. If enemy fire hit a plane, it tore apart the fuselage or wings, often blowing the plane apart and causing it to fall to the ground in flames.

In the Vietnam War, most of the pilots were just as young, brave, vigorous, and as daring as those pioneers from the First World War. All of them loved to fly. Some dreamed of being in the air from the time they were children. Their frequent flights into the unknown over Hanoi and Haiphong in North Vietnam were dangerous; the danger became a thrilling way for them to live. Still, as they maneuvered through the air in their massive, sophisticated, powerful, multimillion-dollar machines, they depended on each other; in that way, they were no different from soldiers on the ground.

We witnessed this when American pilots shot down over North Vietnam did everything they could to evade capture. Jolly Green Giant helicopters went on search-and-rescue missions looking for downed pilots. Usually

The B-52, designed as a nuclear strategic bomber in the 1950s, was widely used for tactical conventional bombing over both North and South Vietnam. A weapon of amazing strength and versatility, it is still in use today by the U.S. Air Force.

U.S. Navy F-4 Phantom, originally designed for fleet defense against a possible threat from Russian bombers, was so versatile that it was used in Vietnam for air support and ground attacks.

A-4 Skyhawks, a primary strike aircraft widely flown off of air craft carriers.

A-6 Intruder, a two-seat Naval attack aircraft, designed for all weather conditions.

enemy flak, rather than North Vietnam's fighter planes, shot them from the sky. Other fighter planes and smaller Huey helicopters went on daring rescue missions in enemy territory. They searched the jungles and rice paddies to find and rescue downed pilots, but they were not always successful. These men formed a close-knit fraternity that only gave up searching when it became fruitless.

The unfortunate pilots and crew who were not rescued became prisoners of war. More than five hundred of them spent the war, however long that might have been, behind bars. They lived under subhuman conditions where guards beat them, where they had poor medical help and barely edible food. Most of these prisoners were held in Hanoi, in a prison dubbed The Hanoi Hilton, where they did their best to stay alive. Now Senator John McCain, then a navy pilot shot down over North Vietnam, gives moving testimony in these pages of his long captivity—how he suffered at the hands of his guards, and how he survived to become a major figure in American politics. Yet, no matter how much these men suffered, nor how much indignity they experienced, they pulled together and they endured. It is a testimony to the human spirit and a powerful will to survive.

As we delve more deeply into the war in the air, it is worth noting that the United States flew 5,250,000 sorties (a sortie for airplanes is one flight by one plane) over South Vietnam, North Vietnam, Cambodia, and Laos. America lost at least 10,000 planes, mostly fixed-wing aircraft. Those loses, though high, never deterred the spirit of the men who flew their planes and helicopters into action every day of the war.

An EA-6 Prowler refueling in front of Marine composite reconnaissance squadron.

Vietnam was as much a helicopter war as it was a ground war. Because Hanoi's troops did not have choppers, it often, but not always, gave American forces an advantage before, during, and after battles. Helicopters transported troops to and from military operations and provided firepower during fighting with enemy troops. Helicopters flew nearly 500,000 missions. Communist forces, sometimes armed with new ground to air missiles, shot down as many as 4,865 helicopters. It is difficult to determine an exact number because there were also choppers that crashed because of mechanical failure or bad weather.

It is little known that each type of helicopter, the hardest working vehicle of the Vietnam War, has the name of a Native American tribe attached to it. Over the years, some opponents of the practice thought it defamed American Indians, but the tribes whose names adorned helicopters in Vietnam supported the practice. The Bell H-13 is the Sioux. The Bell OH-58 is the Kiowa. The Hughes OH-6 is the Cayuse. The Bell UH-1, the famously named Huey, one of the hardest working machines of the war, proudly carries the Iroquois name. And, the big Boeing CH-47, an important transport helicopter carries the name of the Chinook tribe. Interestingly, the Bell AH-1 Cobra gunship does not carry a tribe's name because the military chiefs thought the Cobra would be associated with too much violence during the war, as was the case. On occasion, a Native American tribe even christened a helicopter, giving it its blessing. For good luck, some pilots carried a feather associated with the tribe's name in the cockpit of their helicopter.

The Boeing KC-135 was used for in-flight refueling which was required for the distances flown by both Air Force and Navy Strike forces against North Vietnam.

Boeing CH-47 Chinook, a cargo helicopter with greater lift capacity than the Huey, it is still in use today. It could carry 33 to 55 troops.

Medevac helicopters, also called "Dustoffs," the universal call sign for all medevac missions, were the whirly birds that brought the wounded from the battlefield, usually under dangerous conditions. Those who flew them and worked in them may well be the unsung heroes of the Vietnam War. The Huey was the main medevac bird. Each chopper had a crew of four: two pilots, a medic, and a crew chief. The pilots rotated but the medics usually stayed the same, flight after flight. Treatment on the wounded started immediately in the air and continued at one of the 18 field hospitals throughout Vietnam. Though many casualties suffered serious wounds, the mortality rate was the lowest of any war up to that time, a tribute to the speedy work done by the medics on Dustoff flights and the doctors and nurses in the field hospitals. In Vietnam, the casualty survival rate was 90.6 percent compared to World War II when it was only 80.9 percent.

When measured in numbers, air power is usually effective and deadly in destroying enemy positions. But numbers never tell the whole story. Bombing helps disrupt the enemy but it rarely serves to deter him from reaching his goals. From North Vietnam's perspective, the goal was to achieve victory against the United States and its client, South Vietnam. The more the United States bombed North Vietnam, and North Vietnamese positions in South Vietnam, its leaders in Hanoi were that much more determined to keep fighting. The resolve to continue the war grew stronger as more bombs fell on the cities and countryside of North Vietnam.

Some of the military and political leaders in the United States understood Hanoi's attitude; many in the American government did not accept Hanoi's will to keep fighting. In Operation Rolling Thunder, America's air war over North Vietnam and Laos, the Air Force dropped about 643,000 tons of bombs over those two countries from March 1965 through October 1968. The United States lost almost 900 airplanes in Rolling Thunder, which was halted by President Lyndon Johnson because of intense pressure on him to end the bombing. In hindsight, military experts doubt that Rolling Thunder had much effect on how the North Vietnamese conducted the war.

Throughout the war, the United States Air Command sent hundreds of silent and deadly flights of B-52s from Guam to drop huge amounts of bombs on the usually unsuspecting enemy below. The ground shook and rumbled when the bombs landed, as if it was an earthquake and not an ordinary bombing raid. In North Vietnamese cities, B-52 bombings destroyed buildings and bridges and caused numerous civilian casualties. In South Vietnam, enemy troops died under the bombing assaults. It was normal for enemy troops to suffer severe nosebleeds from the falling bombs. Headaches from the explosions lasted for hours. In the end, B-52's dropped 7,662,000 tons of explosives on all of Vietnam, more than three times the 2,150,000 tons dropped during all of World War II.

Often bad weather, dense jungle terrain in the South, and heavy anti-aircraft fire, called flak, around Hanoi and Haiphong, meant that the bombing raids were not always on target. Assessing the damage caused by the bombings, especially in North Vietnam, was almost impossible. Whenever possible, American planes pounded the Ho Chi Minh Trail that coursed its way through the jungles and mountains of North and South Vietnam carrying ammunition and food to the Viet Cong and North Vietnamese regular soldiers. All those bombing runs were somewhat effective but not decisive. It is now common knowledge that bombing German cities in World War II and firebombing Japanese cities, though effective to a degree, had less to do with the outcome of that war than bombing advocates want us to believe. The Vietnam War is further evidence of that.

★ CHAPTER 6 ★

THE FALL OF SAIGON

That Saigon fell at the end of April 1975 surprised no one. That South Vietnam fell so quickly, with almost no resistance, shocked the aggressive North Vietnamese Army and the world as well. Hanoi's original plan called for capturing Saigon sometime in 1976. Hanoi started its attack in the northern provinces of South Vietnam and in the Central Highlands. Its army moved rapidly south. Hanoi wanted to cut the country in half, as the Viet Minh wanted in their war with the French and as North Vietnam wanted since the battle of Ia Drang Valley. Hanoi's leaders believed the rest would be easy once the country had been divided in two.

South Vietnam's leadership, never any good in the best of times, crumbled as Hanoi's forces advanced unchecked. President Thieu became passive, providing no leadership and issuing orders to his military that were as bizarre as they were foolish. Consequently, Thieu's army fell apart, its leadership fled, and its troops deserted in droves, throwing down their arms and discarding their uniforms as they retreated. The general population panicked in the wake of the army's collapse, and hundreds of thousands of people also ran away, clogging the roads and rivers and jamming the ports. With the irrational flight of the population and their so-called protectors, the inevitable end was near. It was all over for a country that had been living on borrowed time ever since the United States pulled out in 1973. The South Vietnamese feared the unknown as much as they feared the end of the tenuous lifestyle they had been leading. Soon after the start of their campaign, North Vietnam's leaders realized they would reach their goal one year earlier than planned.

PROVINCIAL MAP OF VIETNAM

NORTH VIETNAM

SOUTH VIETNAM

Hanoi

DMZ

Khe Sanh

Ia Drang Valley

Saigon

Hanoi's forces moved aggressively down the coast, and by April 1975, had Saigon surrounded. America's last ambassador, Graham Martin, resisted planning the final evacuation from Saigon. He did not want to show the South Vietnamese that the United States had given up, but everyone knew it was the end of the line. The evacuation of the remaining Americans and those Vietnamese closely associated with the United States momentarily stalled. Evacuation plans were underway, anyway. Ships from the 7th Fleet filled the South China Sea off the coast of South Vietnam. Helicopters were ready to fly in a hurry during an assumed last-minute evacuation. American citizens and South Vietnamese departed on special flights in the last weeks of April. A task forced designated meeting points everywhere in Saigon where last-minute evacuees would board buses or get on helicopters to leave the country. The American embassy was under siege as thousands of frightened Vietnamese banged on the gates and climbed the walls, seeking a way out of their defeated country.

Then the word came from Washington to start the final evacuation. Helicopters ferried evacuees to the 7th Fleet. Unauthorized and equally frightened Vietnamese flew out to the waiting ships. Some crashed into the sea. Those who landed safely saw their helicopters pushed over the side to make room for new arrivals. Not much more than twenty-four hours later the evacuation abruptly ended when Washington pulled the plug, still leaving thousands behind, many of whom sat patiently waiting at the American embassy. Fighting off desperate Vietnamese civilians and army deserters, the last eleven Marines made their way to the top of the American embassy. There they watched the North Vietnamese march triumphantly into Saigon while waiting for a helicopter to carry them away. When it came, on April 30, 1975, their departure spelled the end of the American presence in South Vietnam.

WALTER SPARKS

Sergeant
Security Guard, Da Nang, Saigon
U.S. Marine Corps

It is early March 1975. The North Vietnamese Army is moving rapidly down the western coast and through the eastern mountains, heading towards its ultimate goal, Saigon. The South Vietnamese Army breaks and runs. Hoardes of panicked people flee the onrushing Northern troops. South Vietnam is clearly on the way to defeat. Marine security guard Walter Sparks decides to take a last look around the countryside where he had been serving.

Walter Sparks

knew a lot of Vietnamese there from having been there before. I knew an ARVN lieutenant. He and I jumped on the Honda and went back out to the old 1st Marine Division Headquarters or Freedom Hill, they used to call it. I could tell from the ARVN that were out there that they were getting antsy. All the huge bases that the Americans had out there were gone. All of the huts and the buildings, as high as those Vietnamese could reach, were gone. The plywood. The light fixtures. You name it. I went out there and was talking to a village chief that was a friend of mine who was a VC. Even during the war we knew which villages were. Here's old pop out there in the middle of the rice paddy. He hasn't got anything anyhow. And here the Americans come. Put a gun upside his head and said you're going to deal with us or the Vietnamese Army. Here comes Charlie at night, puts a gun beside his head. You're going to deal with us. So what's he going to do? He ain't got anything. When I was talking to the village chief, I said, "What do you think?" And he says, "You better leave." He said, "Now we've become Vietnam." I said, "Is this what you want? Communism?" We got into these philosophical discussions and he said, "Yeah. Yeah," he said, "haven't got anything now. When the Communists get here the peasants can't have it any worse." I thought, well, you're probably right. But there was panic in this village. I asked, "Is there going to be retribution?" And he says, "Oh, yeah. We know." He was talking about senior military officers, political people.

We went through other villages and just talked. Once again life was going on. But you could see the panic. Because everybody else was running, I'm going to run too. Charlie wasn't going to hurt them. Even a lot of soldiers would throw their uniforms away and their weapons. Put on their black pajamas and go home. Unless somebody had him on a list, there wasn't anybody going to really mess with you. Especially the old people. Or the women and children.

The army just kind of busted up and the Vietnamese took their families with them. So they crowded Highway One, which is coming into Da Nang, coming south. I went up with an Air America pilot, and we could see what they called the Hai Van Pass coming out of Highway One. It was just thronged. I said to myself then, he and I both, "This is all she wrote." As the soldiers started coming in, probably the twenty-seven or so, they were panicking and mad at the same time. And the way they treated their own people. I saw them slapping them, hitting them with rifles, shooting them. Breaking into stores, doing whatever they felt like they wanted to do.

That last night in Da Nang we were down at the Consulate General's home. It was total, utter chaos. Soldiers coming in. Shooting. Just a mess. But they weren't bothering us. Da Nang was swelled to, gosh, a million plus

A section of Da Nang with small shops and merchandise.

Walter Sparks

Raised in the small Mis
sissippi Delta town of
Inverness, Sparks spent
three tours as a Marine in
Vietnam before the evacu
ation in 1975. He was first
in data processing and
then a platoon sergeant
in the infantry, his "first
love." After retiring from
the Marines, he went into
trucking. Single, he plans
to soon retire as an inde
pendent trucker.

people. There weren't that many Americans or Europeans walking around, I walked back to a little apartment I had. We left everything except for a little briefcase I had with some stuff in it. We didn't have much. All our clothes. All our uniforms and my boom box. I remember walking down the street. And it had gotten quiet. This is late at night. This is midnight. As I walked along there were little fires going and people chit-chatting and walking around. It was kind of like a low hum but kind of far out. Occasionally you'd hear artillery impacting out there. You'd hear a pistol shot or a rifle shot but no screaming. So I went to my little old apartment. Kind of looked around for the last time. There were a lot of people in the compound. I remember walking out onto the thoroughfare there and there was an old papa-san there that had a little cart next store. In the mornings I'd always stop and we'd solve the world's problems and talk a little bit. He'd make coffee and we'd drink a little coffee. He's just an old man.

I said, "I left my apartment open. Why don't you go, get whatever you need out of there." My clothes wouldn't fit him, and he said, "No." He said, "Now we go back to Vietnam. No longer American." I thought, you're right, partner. There were other people around. I remember a young man sitting there kept looking at me with a hard look. I had a pistol but I had it under my shirt. I don't know what I would have done. Shot myself, I guess because there was too many folks. But he was real hard-looking. Young guy. Kind of cocky-looking. First I thought he was a cowboy. That's what we call a thug. The more I thought about it, I looked, sitting down beside him. He had a pith helmet, an NVA pith helmet, and there was an AK laying down there. He just looked at me and he said, "That's okay," in pretty good English. He said, "We'll be here tomorrow.

Yes, sir." And walked off back to the consulate's home. All along there were people, and I'd nod. I stopped. Talked to people. I'm sure there were hundreds of VC in the city. Probably NVA, too. But nobody bothered me. That was the thing that got me. I felt, well, stupid out here by yourself. What do you think you're doing? Yet nobody bothered me. They talked to me. I had the feeling as long as they saw Americans were still here, I guess their feeling was they're going to get us out.

Soldiers were telling me, you come back. And I kept saying to myself, no way, slick. By then those soldiers were walking those streets with guns. They were killing people right there. They'd kill an officer. They'd kill somebody that had more than they had. They were raping women. They were just doing tough stuff. Wasn't anything we could do about it. It's their country. That's their people but they had the guns. I've got the gun, you give me the Honda. You give me that bread or water or whatever.

There were some consulate officials at the airport trying to get most people out. We Marines still at the consulate had to destroy all the classified material, which was an impossibility. There was too much paperwork. I went back out toward the airport and it was so crowded, I couldn't get out there. So I got what they call a cowboy, that's a gal on a Honda and just jumped on the back of the Honda motorcycle. It was just chaos. Just a mess. That evening I got a call from a colonel in Thailand talking about trying to send some Army or Air Force helicopters to get the civilians. It wasn't going to work. He said, "Son, it's looking bad and we can't help." I went, "Ah, hell." They had a plan to send a bunch of barges, tugboats, and ships, and put any of the Americans and any third-country nationals that wanted to go on these barges and just push them out into the bay and try to get to those ships. And it was so chaotic that there were people throwing babies at the barges and missing and the babies were falling in the water and the Vietnamese were shooting other Vietnamese. It was a real mess.

Some agency people and consulate people had this radio equipment, this classified equipment. We brought that on the barge and got all the Marines and civilians and got them on the barge and just pushed the thing out into the bay. There were people hanging on anything that would float. It was just a mob. You could hear gunshots and artillery kind of far out, probably at Da Nang Air Base in the outskirts of the city. We got on out to the bay and eventually the ship Pioneer Contender came along and a tugboat pushed the barge over there. On our barge, somebody later said, were four thousand-plus people, from soldiers to civilians to women and children, third country nationals, embassy people. We got the Marines up the ladder and we kind of lined the little passageway coming up there. We were not going to let armed people on the ship. So a couple of us went back down to the barge and we're letting some of the old people first, then the women up with the babies. We take the babies, put them in a water bucket and then pull them up to the side of the ship. In the meantime, their mammas would get up the side and we'd have to beat back some of the other people and this is going on for quite awhile. Realized that a lot of those folks had probably not had any food or water all night. And now it's daytime, and it's hot, and they're in panic, and they really started rushing that gangway. They were afraid we were going to leave them. We had to kind of push them back and get kind of tough with them. There were other barges coming up and small boats. These guys were armed, and they were shooting a couple of rounds over our heads. Like, we want to come, too. Late in the afternoon we got most of the folks on there and the ship was starting to move.

We had taken the Americans and the third-country nationals and got up on the bridge level. We were armed and not going to let the rest up there. Some more Americans came out from the embassy in speed boats, we

Opposite: Troops frequently walked through rice paddies to protect themselves from booby traps. The price they paid was jungle rot on their feet, also called tropical ulcers. They would not remove their boots for fear of not getting their boots back on.

A typical Saigon street. Note South Vietnamese flags in middle of the scene.

got them aboard, so we had more people that were armed. A lot of the Vietnamese were down in the holds. They were coming up, if I remember this right, and saying, "We're not going back to Vietnam." And we were saying don't worry about that. The ship's people went down in the holds and opened the water spigot so they could drink. There was no food. At least give them some water. I know there were people dying down there, but there wasn't anything we could do about it. Nha Trang was falling, but we wound up going there, so the Americans and third-country nationals could be off-loaded and catch an Air America flight to Saigon. So that was the end of the Da Nang evacuation for me and my Marines.

I remember when we landed in Saigon. Everything was kind of normal. Life was going on. From the airport to the embassy, a pretty good little drive, I didn't see any panic. All the shops were open. Stores were open. Traffic as usual. At the embassy there were people at the swimming pool, children swimming, sitting around eating supper, drinking a cold drink. And I kind of got a little excited and I said, "Hey folks, don't you understand that, you know, all the bad guys in the world are coming this way?" And they just wasn't concerned. Da Nang had fallen. It wasn't a day later, Nha Trang fell. It's starting to move into Saigon and we're still going downtown. This thing is coming unglued. Yet, there still was no panic. The embassy hadn't ordered evacuation. I just kept saying that if I was you, I would leave. As Marines we were never in Saigon. We were up in I Corps. So I kind of played tourist. All the restaurants, the shops, the upper-class lounges and bars, and things, everything's open for the reporter-types at the Caravel Hotel. Downtown was normal.

ANTHONY "TONY" WOOD

Anthony "Tony" Wood

Special Planning Group
Final Evacuation of Saigon
U.S. Marine Corps

Anthony "Tony" Wood

As the Vietnam War was winding down, Wood, a career Marine officer, was "executing clandestine operations with the Special Forces in Laos, Cambodia, and Vietnam." In the spring of 1975, as the North Vietnamese began their final advance, Wood was detached to Saigon to form a small unit called the Special Planning Group, working with General Homer Smith on the final evacuation of Saigon. Wood retired from the Marine Corps in 1998.

In early February of 1975, I was detached from my job, which was executing clandestine operations with the Special Forces in Laos, Cambodia, and North Vietnam. We were waging fewer and fewer operations, and finally we were waging no more of these operations because of the North Vietnamese advance. Major General Homer Smith who was the defense attaché in Saigon at the time formed a small group called the Special Planning Group and ordered us to begin planning for the final evacuation of Saigon. We were to report only to him initially to prevent rumors in a city that was already panicked and very sensitive. So began the process. Mostly in the very early days, a process of who did we have to evacuate, how many were there. No one really knew. We actually put hundreds and hundreds of pins on a map on the wall and using taxi records and even the records from the Circle Sport, which was a social club, we identified about twenty-five thousand people for which the U.S. had responsibility to evacuate from Saigon. What followed was called the Black Evacuation and the unreported evacuation in which that actual community was reduced to about fifty-eight hundred or somewhere close to that for the final evacuation. That was the number we thought we might be able to get out in twenty-four hours. But certainly not twenty-five thousand under North Vietnamese pressure on a short notice evacuation. Our concern in Saigon was that you cannot predict the rate of collapse, and the city was so large and the population so intense at this point that we thought we would only have at best twelve hours after we began, in order to complete our actions.

There was a secret evacuation that had to do with people that we were certain would probably not survive a North Vietnamese victory. And there was a flight from the country of many wealthy Vietnamese businessmen during that period as well. All of our planning, all of our execution and training, and our preparations had to be performed in secret. We fully assumed after about the 20th of April, that it could come at any time. We were literally sleeping an hour or so at a time from that day on because of the tense situation in the country. General Smith personally would give the order and we knew it would not come from the ambassador, at least not directly.

We purposely had learned as much as we could about how cities implode. How they collapse on themselves when they are panicking. We had selected a dozen or so buildings in Saigon where we tried to concentrate most of the

American air crews aiding child refugees, as the war was ending.

remaining American official mission population. Secretly we put in special doors that could be closed so that the mobs, which we anticipated, would not be able to get up the stairwells. They were essentially fireproof. Then they had the opportunity to allow for helicopter evacuation from the roof. The whole concept here was to try to bring out as many people as possible on the evacuation route using armored buses, which we had armored inside so they didn't show. We had trained volunteers in secret. We had to make do with the American citizens, not military personnel, who would volunteer to perform the evacuation of the American mission because the ambassador would not permit any active evacuation planning or training. The bus driver's average age was over fifty. None of them had ever driven a bus before in their lives. As it turned out, they didn't get a chance to practice driving a bus even once before they had to drive them into a collapsing city and cycle through mobs with no armed escort of any kind, only a bluff that looked like armed escort. Civilians driving fake police cars were leading the convoys. Bogus national police cars that were painted with Venetian blinds to look exactly like Vietnamese national police cars were guiding the convoys through the city. That worked, as it turned out, pretty well. We had routes and the routes were all named after American western trails: Chisolm, Oregon, California, and so forth. The inside of the buses had flak jackets and other things to protect them and mesh on the windows.

When the balloon went up and General Smith ordered us to start evacuating, it was about seven in the morning. We had prepared the parking lot. Demolition charges on all the light poles were blown. The light poles went down automatically, were pushed to one side, and the parking lot became a helicopter landing zone for the evacuation. We immediately used the radios whose antenna was inside of the water tower, which had been drained and turned into an antenna to control the convoys throughout the city in secret. The convoys started moving and picking up people on their assigned routes. Got lost several times. It wasn't hard to get lost in the confusion of Saigon that day. There was a lot of shooting going on. Most of it in the air, but you couldn't tell. We had a bus flipped over by a mob. You don't know the power of a mob until you see a bus picked up and thrown over. Eventually they picked up my jeep and threw it over so we had to get off and find our way to a bus. The last convoy came in about five o'clock in the afternoon. I was with it. It was a very slow convoy that had taken a long time to get in. The last bus had been shot up. The engine had been shot up and it was over. We couldn't get back in and out of the city another time. We still brought about twelve hundred people off the roofs of these four to five buildings, which also had radios and C-rations and water placed on the roofs well in advance.

Not a single volunteer ever left. They all stuck; while the others left Vietnam in the aircraft, they stayed and they all had reserved seats to leave. But they all stayed not knowing what was going to happen. Many were secretaries. One was an auditor. Others simply American civil servants. Boy, when the chips were down, your average American did a great job and it was an evacuation which literally rested on their shoulders. Between the American citizens who went into the city and brought out the rest of the mission and the Marines at Tan Son Nhut, that's how Saigon was evacuated.

We never really thought that the North Vietnamese were interested in harming Americans. Because we were leaving the country and interfering or harming Americans would result in a suspension of the evacuation and the introduction of combat forces. Nor did we think that they really wanted to interfere with the thinning of the mission or the Vietnamese leaving the country because effectively, all future troublemakers from the North Vietnamese point of view were leaving the country. It was helpful to them. But we did think it was possible that they would seize the capital quickly, that we would not have completed the evacuation and a sizable American community would remain captive. We were prepared to sustain a population of ten thousand for ten days— everything, including babies.

HOMER SMITH

Defense Attaché to the Republic of South Vietnam
U.S. Army

Homer Smith

The bulk of my effort went toward maintaining the material flow in support of the South Vietnamese armed forces. When the protocols were signed in Paris, the U.S. agreed to continue to support the South Vietnamese in their fight for full liberty of their country against the Viet Cong. And that's what my job was.

I was out at the old Mac V headquarters at Tan Son Nhut. As early as January 1975, when the North Vietnamese attacked Phuoc Long Province and took it, the United States did not respond. And from then on, everything went downhill. It was inevitable. I used to be the Commander up in Da Nang during '69 and '70. When the first region began to crumble, why, from then on, it was just a roll-up.

We had a situation where people were fighting, but at the same time their families were probably uppermost in their minds, and sometimes when push came to shove the Vietnamese went for their families to help them out. I knew that was happening. But I also asked myself, if the same circumstances had occurred in Germany, as a result of the Russians, during that period of time, with all the dependents we had over there, although we had plans to get them out and all that sort of stuff, I asked myself, would it have been repeated to a certain extent? I mean, the South Vietnamese are humans. And, it was unfortunate as it was, but it was not surprising. The First Infantry Division of the South Vietnamese army was probably their best division, and they were up there and it happened. Disaster. It was a disaster. Some people came out by helicopter, some came out by fixed-wing earlier, and some came out by Vietnamese navy ships.

On April 2, 1975, Ed Daley, the owner of World Airways, a small airline with a few big jets, decided to evacuate 58 Vietnamese-American orphans, potentially forgotten when Saigon finally fell. Various agencies in the United States waited for the orphans to arrive. Without the fall of Saigon looming, their departure would have been orderly and not rushed. A great deal of publicity surrounded the flight. In reaction to Daley, the White House ordered the evacuation of as many orphans as possible. The first flight would carry 226 orphans and 70 civilians.

The fourth day of April, 1975. I'll never forget it. It was probably the longest day of my life.

I received a message that morning from the Department of Defense asking me, or suggesting, or ordering me, to evacuate a significant number of American-Vietnamese orphans that were there in Saigon, and gave me the authority to take the first aircraft I wanted. Well, the first aircraft was a C-5. The C-5 has seventy-five passenger seats on the second deck. The cargo area is the biggest area. The decision was made that we would deck load orphans as well as load them on the C-5, and that meant you had to have adults. So I directed my division chiefs to identify X number of women employees who could go on the flight. I was in reduction of force posture so I could do that. So people came to work that day, didn't know they were leaving that day. It was just like that. So we had about forty, and then there some other members of the staff or another couple of smaller staffs that were elected to go. Some of them had dependents. They took their dependents out. The Air Force had sent some medics, nurses, because of the number of children. The plane took off loaded to the gunnels.

Got out over the South China Sea, about twenty thousand feet, and the rear ramp blew off. When it did, it damaged the control surfaces on the tail. It also sucked, I don't know how many, but a few of the load masters. The young captain who was flying it, turned it around, brought it back to land, and he lost … lost it short of the runway, short of the Saigon River. Jumped the river, crashed, and that was it. I recall my exec telling me, coming in and saying, "Boss, we have a disaster. The C-5 just crashed out toward the air base." And you could look out and you could see the smoke coming. We had a group of people there who were the ones that were searching for remains from the war. So we sent them out to work the situation. We set up a morgue over at the Seventh Day Adventist Hospital and brought bodies over there. We had a few survivors. They were taken to the hospital. But it was a shattering, shattering experience.

One hundred thirty-eight orphans, thirty-nine civilians and eleven crew members died in the crash. Despite the tragedy, the flights continued and military airplanes carried thousands more orphans to the United States before Saigon fell. By the middle of April, General Smith and his staff are already handling the evacuation of American and Vietnamese civilians.

Most of the evacuation plans were done by my staff. We were the ones that were interfacing with the Marines and the Navy. In fact, the Ambassador was not overly enthused about an evacuation. He had a great, great respect for the Vietnamese people, and he just did not want to abruptly pull everybody out. He delayed the evacuation of people in the embassy almost up to the last minute.

We just started moving people out. We had a lot of aircraft. We had some aircraft bringing in material and weapons from Taiwan that belonged to the South Vietnamese. The biggest problem we had with getting people out of Vietnam was paperwork. The United States required a passport and a visa for every Vietnamese civilian. The Vietnamese were very slow about issuing passports. We started out evacuating as few as two hundred a day and built up to seventy-five hundred the day before the 29th by fixed-wing aircraft. The Vietnamese authorities were down in Saigon. Our people were at Tan Son Nhut. We finally got the Vietnamese to move out to our place. Then we had fewer long lines and not the time differential. Plus we had Americans who had Vietnamese dependents. There were instances where the male and female were not married, so we married them on the spot. The thing that really helped us was an agreement with the ambassador that the United States would accept a single paper where an American citizen signs that, "I will guarantee that these people will be taken care of in the United States." Once we got that, we began to move people.

There was no television. You were down to radios. There were no newspapers, so the only words they got were though the grapevine. I think they were principally concerned about continuing to live. Saigon just ballooned with people. The Vietnamese never panicked under those circumstances. They had

Homer Smith

A Texan and graduate of Texas A&M with a degree in chemical engineering, Homer Smith served in the army as a 2nd lieutenant in England, Germany, and France during World War II. After leaving the army in 1946 he operated a small fishing resort in Oklahoma until he returned to active duty in 1948. Over the next thirty-one years he served in the Pentagon, Korea, and twice in South Vietnam, the last tour as the Defense Attaché to the Republic of South Vietnam. As South Vietnam was falling, General Smith and his staff planned and managed the evacuation. After serving as commander of the U.S. Army Logistics Center, he retired from active duty in July 1979 as a major general. He then joined NATO as Director of Logistics. He still lives in Texas where he serves on several charitable organizations.

to wait three or four days before we could get them. They weren't allowed to take out very much with them. There were no complaints. It went smoothly. Maybe there were tears. But I saw none.

The flights went to the Philippines and then the Philippine government got upset. So we started evacuating to Guam, which increased our flight time and therefore narrowed the number of aircraft. We had an evacuation control center set up running twenty-four hours a day. We were bringing refugees in by busloads, and we had facilities to put them up in our gymnasium. We had food to feed them. Based on what our population was we would order in so many aircraft so it just became a sort of routine thing. We had built up to five thousand a day and we expected to take ten thousand out the day of the "evacuation." That's what the ambassador wanted. That's what we were going to meet.

The CH-47 Chinook helicopter was first introduced in Vietnam. It is so versatile that it is still widely used by the American armed forces today.

On April 29 the North Vietnamese sent rockets onto Tan Son Nhut. Well, one of those rockets blew my wife and me out of bed. It got our attention. I'll put it that way. I heard them coming in. I woke. It shook us up. We were not hurt. We got up, we got dressed, and we went to our operation center. My wife and another lady who worked there began shredding documents. They spent the whole morning from about three o'clock on until I finally sent them to the fleet at about 10:30 in the morning in an Air America helicopter. The unfortunate thing was we lost two Marine guards who were killed by the rocket that landed just before the one that hit us. Fortunately I was living in the quarters that General Abrams had had when he was there. It was a prefabricated hospital wing that had been reworked. There was a bombproof wall about a foot thick right in front of the bedroom window, and the rocket hit right at the base of that. So we were lucky. It wasn't our time. Behind me in another part of the building, a rocket went in there and it blew an Air Force colonel out of his bed. He wasn't hurt, but it also blew in his air conditioner.

After the rockets there was no way we could continue the fixed-wing evacuation. We had a build-up of people. I called the ambassador and I said, "I don't think we're going to be able to go out there by fixed-wing." He insisted on coming out and seeing for himself. After he departed, nine, ten o'clock, time was running out. I called the ambassador and I said, "Mr. Ambassador, there's no way we can get out of here except by rotary-wing aircraft," and he said, "OK, that's your judgment." I said, "It is. I'll stake my reputation on it." He agreed that we would go out by rotary-wing.

The first elements of the evacuation force landed in Huey's at 1:30 in the afternoon. It wasn't until 3, 3:30 that the first Marine security force landed and then we started. In five hours, by 8:30 that evening, we had moved five thousand people out by rotary wing aircraft and we didn't have any more to move. There was no evidence of any overt nervousness. I think the people completely counted on us to do what had to be done. We had no problems whatsoever out of Tan Son Nhut. No crying mothers. No screaming grandmothers. We had a little bit of consternation that morning because two more rockets landed and wounded a couple of people. We had a birth during that period of time. These people had one little bag with everything that they could carry out in it. They just were good strong people that trusted us to do what we said we would do.

We didn't have the capability or the capacity to go out and knock on Americans doors and say, "Hey, by the way you're supposed to be leaving." We didn't know where people were. I knew where my employees lived. I didn't have problems with them. One individual showed up the morning of the evacuation—no shirt. I suspect that he was probably a deserter. I made arrangements for the military police to meet him when he got to Guam. I don't know what happened there. But there were just people crawling out of the woodwork there on the last day. We got out, as far as I know, all the Americans. We did not get out every Vietnamese and others that wanted to get out, but all in all it worked far better than I think anybody ever expected.

I've been told that the best were down, that it would be a disaster. The fact that it wasn't a disaster was a wonderful thing. We didn't need a disaster. We already had a series of disasters. But I will tell you that I was just totally surprised that it went off as well as it did. Time passed fast and everything clicked.

That's when I left with the remnant of my staff. When I got on the helicopter that night, and we were flying out, my operations officer was sitting across from me crying. And I said to myself, I still feel that way, this is the saddest day of my life.

STEVE HASTY

Commander
Security Guard Detachment
Can Tho, Vietnam
April 1975
U.S. Marine Corps

Steve Hasty

I've always been of the philosophy that you could never have too many weapons or too much ammunition. So I would take the vehicle and drive north to Saigon to start policing up all the weapons, communications gear, supplies that I could find and drive back down to Can Tho and increase our stockpile. I happened to be on one of those police runs and I was out at Tan Son Nhut. As I was driving by the Air America terminal in Tan Son Nhut, I saw ambulances starting to pull in and other vehicles starting to pull in and a lot of activity. We got out, made our way to the front of the crowd, and that was when the helicopters started landing with the dead and wounded. So I spent the next few hours hauling body parts out of the helicopters, taking them to the ambulances after the crash of the C-5, the inauguration of Operation Baby Lift. The helicopters would land and we would run toward them with stretchers and basically just scrape the body parts off the deck of the helicopter and onto the stretchers and cover them with a sheet. The husbands of some of the Defense Attaché Office wives who volunteered to take care of the children on the flight were still in the terminal, so we were doing what we could to try to spare them their horror there.

The helicopters would come in and they would land, the rotors still churning. We would run up. I have a vision of the guy and the team ahead of me, you know, a white-haired guy. I don't know who he was. He may have been in fact the husband of one of the women that died on the plane and he was reaching in with his arms and scraping out the chunks of meat, because that's all they were, onto the stretcher that two people were holding and he was vomiting as he did it, onto the body parts. We tried to cover the bodies with sheets, but the rotor wash from the helicopter blades would sometimes blow the sheets away. To me it was kind of just a fitting image of the end of the whole war. Kind of a fitting image for something that started out with such good intentions and ended up so badly for so many.

The very last trip I made back from Saigon I was driving between Vinh Long and My Tho, and I saw people passing in a panic and crowds of people coming across the front of the road from my right to my left, fleeing something, so I stopped. They were going, "VC. VC." And there's a platoon of VC coming out of the tree line about three hundred yards away. So I had about fifty yards worth of distance to decide whether you want to keep on the road before they cover that last fifty yards and get in effective range of AK-47 fire. In about thirty seconds I decided that I'd rather get out of there than stop and engage in a firefight on their terms. At that point it was no longer feasible to do the road trip anymore. Before it was random sniper fire. When you get enemy units moving in daylight, then you know you got a problem.

Consul General Francis Terry McNamara in May, 1975 boarding a Navy aircraft at Subic Naval Base after evacuating from Can Tho.

Our Consul General in Can Tho was a Foreign Service Officer, Francis Terry McNamara. An interesting character. Very inspirational leader. He loved his Marine security guards and his Marine security guards loved him—fierce loyalty both ways. This was Terry McNamara's third tour in Vietnam. He had a great sense of loyalty to the Vietnamese. He did not want to risk leaving behind those Vietnamese that had worked for Americans and that might face the same fate that was befalling those Cambodians in Phnom Penh. So Terry McNamara decided that by any way that's possible he was going to get those people out. The city of Can Tho a couple of weeks before the evacuation was shelled pretty heavily one night by the enemy. No American casualties, fortunately, although it was a close-run thing because they were dropping shells within a hundred meters of the consulate. A lot of civilian casualties, of course, and burned a good chunk of the city from the fires that started there. That was the first heavy artillery attack against the city in some years. I think an indicator of things to come. I think the CIA decided at that point that they would do what they could to accelerate the evacuation of their people and themselves, and not without reason. Had they ended up as prisoners, it would not have gone well for them. Terry McNamara and I had done a helicopter reconnaissance in an Air America helicopter earlier of the route that we might have to take. We were aware of the intelligence reports that showed the disposition of enemy forces, and the river runs through enemy territory. The potential for fire fights, ambushes, was very great and we recognized that risk and took whatever measures we could to arm ourselves to be able to counteract it.

McNamara had arranged to have four Air America helicopters ready to assist in the evacuation that came sooner than expected.

It was then decided we would make contingency arrangements to go down the Bassac River and out to sea if necessary. While a more dangerous course of action, it was one that would enable us to bring a lot of our Vietnamese with us in case they could not get out earlier. So we had two boats which were basically old landing craft and we also got a wooden boat used for fishing or rice hauling or what have you and we staged all of those just in case they would be needed. It was a very wise choice to do so, because as events turned out that was how we made it out. The times kind of blend together in my mind now. But, early that morning of April 29 the city was rocketed again, at about 4 A.M. Word came from Saigon to launch the evacuation. Consul General McNamara made the determination to launch the helicopters to Saigon to help evacuate the Americans there, and that we would take the boats out. Unfortunately, the agency personnel assigned to Can Tho decided to take the helicopters, and instead of going to Saigon, flew out to navy ships in the China Sea. When they did, they left behind their communicator at the embassy and several of their Filipino employees, the third-country national employees. And we were able to bring them out with us when we came. It was a sore point at the time. We crammed a couple hundred people easily into those boats. If they're Vietnamese, they're smaller than Americans. Whatever we could cram on the rice barge. Total number of Americans that bought down the river that day was I think about eighteen Americans and probably about three hundred or so Vietnamese refugees.

Steve Hasty

Hasty started his third tour of duty in Vietnam in 1974 as commander of the Marine Security Guard detachment at the U.S. Consulate in Can Tho. He helped evacuate three hundred Vietnamese employees and their families by small boat and then to the 7th Fleet as South Vietnam was falling to the North Vietnamese. Although he entered the Marines as a high school dropout, he later graduated magna cum laude and was elected Phi Beta Kappa from George Washington University, and is now a lieutenant colonel. He served in and commanded intelligence operations in the Gulf War, Somalia, Haiti, and Bosnia. Currently he is a Master's degree candidate at the Naval War College in Newport, Rhode Island.

A barge crammed with refugees is towed to the SS Pioneer Contender to be evacuated in 1975.

South Vietnamese refugees arrive on a U.S. Navy vessel.

We got the word by radio from the compound to get out there immediately. We got there, the agency had taken their small speed boat the Marines had planned on using for the river evacuation. It was to be close-in fire support as the first line of defense between us and the boats full of the refugees. Unfortunately, they had already taken that boat and their machine guns back to their compound for the helicopters so that kind of left us holding the bag. Fortunately I still had another machine gun, a BAR, and a lot of other weapons, but we would have appreciated the extra range that an M60 gives you. When we got to the compound, pretty much everybody had boarded. We got on board, and found that the Vietnamese crew of the boat had deserted. They had changed their mind. They didn't want to go. But Terry McNamara was a former submarine sailor in World War II and naval officer in Korea so we figured he could figure out how to operate the landing craft. And he did. We were going to cast off. As we were pulling away from the little pier you could see some of the Filipino employees, agency employees which we thought had already been evacuated, come running down the gang plank and the Vietnamese starting to come into the compound. I and one of my Marines jumped ashore and started throwing them on board, and we hopped back aboard and took off. Got out in the center of the river, joined up with the other boat, and the rice barge that we had with us. We then proceeded to head downriver and out to sea.

There had been arrangements made earlier in case we went the river route. There was supposed to be a Navy ship at the mouth of the Bassac River to pick us up when we came out. So, we set sail, so to speak, and headed down the river. There were six Marines, twelve U.S. civilians. We'd gone a few miles downriver when we were stopped by South Vietnamese patrol boats who fired a couple of shots across our bow, and we were surrounded by several of the boats. The Vietnamese government had passed the word that no military-age, Vietnamese males would be allowed to evacuate or get out as evacuees or refugees. We had some aboard. They were family members or employees, whatever the case may be. So the order had been given by Commodore Tang to stop us and search the vessels. Terry McNamara had been very astute early on in meeting with Commander Tang, making arrangements to get his family to safety. As a result Commodore Tang's boat showed up alongside us. He and the Consul General talked back and forth. Commodore Tang says, "Do you have any military-age males on board?" And Terry said, "Oh no, we wouldn't do that." Commodore Tang said thank you very much, and that was that. It was an interesting moment there because as the Vietnamese gunboats were leaving, one of the young sailors jumped aboard our boat just briefly because his father was one of the refugees that we were taking out. They embraced and said good-bye, I think probably knowing they would never see each other again. So it was a human element too, you know, something that's really indeed overwhelming at the time.

So the Vietnamese gunboats left, leaving us free to go downriver and we set sail again and about an hour later, we came under attack from enemy positions on the bank of the river, the North bank of the Bassac River. They launched 8-40 rocket fire at us and they missed. We opened up with everything we had. We weren't sure if we hit them or not but we suppressed the fire and that was the idea behind it. We managed to get through with no casualties, but we knew worse times were coming because we were starting to enter the portion of the Bassac River that narrows dramatically into small channels before it widens out again. And if we were going to get hit and taken out that's when it was going to really happen, but just as we started to enter it, a rainstorm broke, just a driving rain, so hard, so thick that from the stern of the little boat you could not see the bow. It was that heavy. And it must have rained for twenty-five to thirty minutes, hard.

Well, the sound of the water, the force of the water hitting the river muffled the engine of the boats and the thickness of the sheets of rain masked us visually from enemy positions on the shore. We made it through the most dangerous part of the river under cover of the rain. By the time it ended we were through the narrow channels there, and opened out again into the wider part of the river. No more firefights after that. We were approached several times by boats, fishing boats, who knows, maybe river pirates. It was common there, but any time a boat came close to us, the Marines would just stand up with the weapons and so forth. Whoever they were they decided that they could find more productive use of their time and they'd immediately veer off and head elsewhere.

It was about sunset when we reached the mouth of the Bassac River and headed out to sea. No ship in sight. We tried contacting everybody on every radio that we had but none of the frequencies that we were given seemed operable. About the only thing we could pick up when we went through the dials was Vietnamese. The South Vietnamese under attack or North Vietnamese attacking. We basically hoped to be out of the mouth of the river far enough from shore to be out of range of fire but within sight of the shore and we remained there for an hour or two, attempting radio contact. Then we had to make a decision of what we were going to do. We could see on shore tracer fire and explosions and one of the towns or base camps was under attack. That obviously was not a choice option, so we decided that we'd head out to sea and take our chances.

So we set sail, headed south. About two in the morning we saw a light. Couldn't tell what it was, knew it wasn't land, probably had to be a ship of some sort. We had flares that we would periodically fire off and try to attempt to make radio contact asking them to fire a flare in return, if they acknowledged our signal. Never did, but we kept heading for them and finally when we moved into view it was the SS Pioneer Contender, a merchant vessel which several weeks before played a very big part in the evacuation of Da Nang. It was operated by the Military Sealift Command and had a platoon of U.S. Marines on board for security. We got within sight of the vessel and hailed it. They answered back and we told them who we were. First they wanted us to throw our weapons in the water. They were used to pulling aboard Vietnamese refugees and didn't want any problems but about that time we said we were Marines and we were coming aboard with our weapons or we weren't coming aboard.

Well, once they heard that they perked up and said we could come on board. We did in fact board and came to find out that in fact, they were not waiting for us. They were there by chance. We were so damned tired at that point. I mean I hadn't had any sleep in well over twenty-four hours. None of us had had much sleep in the days preceding that. We were sunburned. We were tired. We were just happy to be aboard a bigger vessel. One that we didn't have to try to sail ourselves.

South Vietnamese soldier carrying machine gun ammunition runs for cover.

RUSSELL THURMAN

Gunnery Sergeant
USS Okinawa
April 29, 30, 1975
U.S. Marine Corps

Russell Thurman

The remarkable thing that morning was the number of ships that had joined our task force. It was incredible. We were there by ourselves. Four ships. Then all of a sudden, it was just like there was ships everywhere. Then once we launched, the sky filled with helicopters and most of them weren't ours. They were Vietnamese flying every conceivable helicopter that they could get their hands on. So there was a lot of drama going on. The sky was like black with helicopters. Needless to say, tensions were kind of high because those helicopters were trying to land on our ship, the primary ship for taking refugees off and going back in. The evacuation was supposed to end in daylight. Of course, they just kept going and going and going. A lot of children. A lot of women came aboard the Okinawa.

U.S Navy helps South Vietnamese refugees who are fleeing Vietnam as the country is falling to the North Vietnamese.

I had come back with a load of evacuees. As I was getting ready to go back on another helicopter to go back in, this helicopter landed and all these people came off. They were going to push the helicopter over the side because we had just maxed out deck space, And one woman went berserk. We had Vietnamese interpreters with us. We got one of them to find out why she had gone hysterical because they were pushing the helicopter over the side. And she finally got it known. She went over and pulled a baby out from underneath the seat. It was a moment of immense emotions. That said a lot to us. There was a lot of desperation at the moment. A lot of confusion about what would happen if you stayed behind. It was—we're going to get everybody we can out. It was supposed to be a quick, daylight-type thing. It turned into—we're going to do it until we can't do it anymore.

Most of the people were somewhat in shock. A lot of fear. A lot of tears. A lot of confusion. Most did not get out with entire families. Once they were brought aboard the ship, they were brought down below into the hangar deck and processed. Rather rapidly. Medical checks were done. We had babies born aboard the Okinawa. A lot of trauma, but more than anything they were just in shock. A lot of relief. Some were very, very happy to get out. Some of them worked with the Americans for so long that they were very grateful that they did not stay behind because they felt that they would be subject to some fairly significant punishments.

We were supposed to be out before dark. At the DAO compound (Defense Attaché Office) at Tan Son Nhut there was increased artillery in the distance. Explosions fairly close. Continuous small-arms fire from the South Vietnamese soldiers who were trying to intimidate us and let them come into the compound. We were receiving truckloads of refugees being brought in from other points. There's a lot of tension at Tan Son Nhut because a lot of these families were huddled together. Some of them would lock their arms because they were afraid that when we got them to the helicopter we would separate them. Or that we would only take the kids and women and force the men to stay behind. So they would lock their arms together. Some are old women and older men. At one point a truck came up and a Vietnamese officer got off. He sent his family in and he stayed behind. They wouldn't leave the fence line. They were all locked—their hands through the fence.

Some of these people didn't want to leave anything because it was all they had in their lives. There was a lot of valuables. Money. Things they felt they needed to take with them. They were given options. You don't want to leave your bags? You don't go. There was a point where you got to get tough. It eventually got down to whatever you could carry in your hands without it being too big or something you could set on your lap. So a lot of these people were separated from their life belongings. Usually it was jewelry or gold or something that they felt they could at least get a start when they come to the United States. A lot of people just left large stacks of stuff, entire bags.

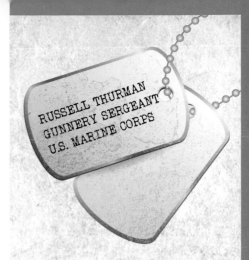

Russell Thurman

Thurman first went to South Vietnam in 1966 as a Private 1st Class in the Marines. He was a combat correspondent for two years with the 1st and 3rd Marine Divisions. In 1975 he returned to Vietnam as a gunnery sergeant to take part in the evacuation of Saigon. He retired as a captain after twenty-one years in the Marines and worked in Hollywood as a military technical advisor on films such as HBO's Vietnam War Story and Born on the Fourth of July. He is now a magazine editor in California.

Got very, very tense as dark came on because just like in any combat situation, the night time is the most tense. The city was still lit up, which was almost an irony. The city looked like a city. All the lights were on. It was just like business as normal. Yet this enormous thing was happening. I don't think really the fact that the war was like over was really the feeling at the moment. It was, are we going to be able to finish this and when are we going to finish this? The frustration was, there were still thousands of people that needed to be evacuated. Plus helicopters were getting well used. Pilots had to be rotated because of the number of hours that they had in the air. Some of these pilots were way over the safety mark, yet they continued to make those runs. And there were a number of bad boys, bad guys, cowboys, trying to assert their authority and try to run their gang that they had run in the streets of Saigon aboard ship. That was shut down quick. As soon as these people come off they were met with Marine security guards and naval boarding guards with rifles making sure that those people understood that you're now on a U.S. ship and you might as well forget about playing any games. Finally at a point we started shutting down LZs.

The fact that the Marines kept their heads I think is a real tribute to them. Never fired one shot. The fact that they flew the number of hours. That we lost just one bird. It went in the water. There were no crashes. There was no disasters, air to air. We didn't lose any Vietnamese in the evacuation. We didn't kill anybody coming out of there. There was not a guy that we had ever served with, not a guy that died, that I saw die or that I fought alongside of or that I knew died there whose name is on the Wall that I didn't think about on that day. It was a very emotional time. It was like we did the right thing. We did one hell of a job. We did what we were supposed to do, the largest helicopter evacuation in the world. And we pushed it. We pushed the envelope. The day afterward there was a group of Vietnamese huddled around a small radio trying to catch a broadcast from Saigon to find out what was going on. Of course, the city fell that morning, and it was no longer Saigon. It was just very much of a depressed time, especially in the days following the evacuation. It was very quiet aboard the ship.

The fall of Saigon for those of us who had been in Vietnam before was very emotional. It didn't really hit at that moment. The evacuation is going on. You've got responsibilities. You're helping out where you can. It was the days afterward when it got very quiet. Most Marines amongst Marines are very talkative. Very active. It was very quiet. Especially officers and staff NCOs. Very moody. We went through the motions of getting the job done. But not a whole lot of getting together and chatting. We had made significant investments of our lives in Vietnam. Everybody just kind of pulled back for themselves, and it was absolutely the saddest day that none of us wanted to come to.

Opposite: Refugees disembarking from an American helicopter. Republic of Vietnam Air Force personnel and their families arrive aboard USS Blue Ridge, 29 April, 1975. This helicopter was one of 15 that landed that day on the U.S.S. Blue Ridge.

GERRY BERRY

Captain
CH-46 Pilot
Flight Leader
April 30, 1975
U.S. Marine Corps

Gerry Berry

We did not think that there was going to be a very large evacuation from the embassy. In fact, my very first mission was called Embassy Snatch. I was supposed to bring the ambassador out as early as probably one thirty, two o'clock in the afternoon, the 29th of April. That was all I was supposed to do. I had four airplanes. Two CH-46 helicopters to bring him and his staff out. Then we had two others that were loaded with Marines in case anything went wrong. There was a rescue team there, if we went down, to protect the ambassador and the downed planes. That was our primary mission. Of course, when we got to the embassy, it was just crammed full of people. We weren't going to get the ambassador right away because he simply wasn't coming out. It was just decided that we would try to evacuate as many people as we could from the embassy. I mean we had all the third-country nationals. We had Vietnamese. We had some Americans. It was very confusing, very fast and your time goes relatively fast. We carried out a bunch of third-country nationals to the 7th Fleet ships. Those four airplanes then were dedicated exclusively to the evacuation of the embassy.

Marines of Company A, 1st Battalion, 3rd Marines Regiment waiting to load on a
CH-46 for Operation Scotland at landing zone.

You start to get discouraged. I think we made two, three, four trips. This is absolute chaos. The crowd is not getting any smaller. If anything, it's getting larger. And it's kind of like a bottomless pit. Every time you land, there's more people than there were before. And you're using a lot more helicopters than you were using before. What is the end? No one has really figured out what the end is. This thing kept getting bigger. We were supposed to evacuate, but the more helicopters you put into it, the bigger the crowds got. The kind of look on somebody's face would be kind of forlorn, a little bit. You knew all these people were connected. Everybody that wanted out, wanted out for a reason. They didn't want to be there when the Communists took charge. I think for the Vietnamese, you're giving up your country. That's very difficult. For Americans, you were finally admitting some kind of failure because we were committed to this point. We made a lot of promises and that was, I think, for third country nationals probably the same thing but maybe more than anything else, I would say across the spectrum—relief. It was finally over. It was finally done.

Because the evacuation started so late in the day, Berry and his crews did most of their flying at night.

Nighttime is a bit more difficult than daytime. We also had weather involved here. There's a lot of storms along the coast and some pretty heavy clouds. We had two options of coming into Saigon. We were originally supposed to come in high because we were worried about the antiaircraft artillery and things like that. Up above a certain level you don't have to worry about that as much. But as the weather comes in, you're pushed down because there's no real navigation aids to allow to land on the embassy roof. It's almost very difficult to plan where you're going. Of course, when you've got far enough up the Saigon River, then you have to maneuver from there. But it became very stressful to maneuver back and forth, in and out of Saigon. A radio station played all night long. Pretty good American music, in fact, about maybe a couple of hundred yards from the embassy. But that was not commonly known. We found that only because we were bored and looking for some music. We were able to navigate back and forth about two blocks from the embassy off that radio station. So that worked out pretty well. During the day it was very hectic. The streets were absolutely packed with people.

The nighttime was definitely more difficult. There's no radar separating all these helicopters flying around Saigon. You have at any one time probably forty or fifty during parts of the day and the early parts of the evening going in and out of one place, the embassy in Saigon. That's kind of stressful when you're kind of moving in and out of the clouds, and it's starting to get dark and it is dark. And because we didn't have anybody to shoot at us, we'd have the number two guy often turn his lights off so he's running with lights out which is dangerous in its own self with the other choppers. But also a little safer because nobody shoots at you.

You're landing on anywhere between eight and ten different ships along the coast of South Vietnam. A flight one way would be anywhere between thirty

Gerry Berry

Born in Lewiston, Montana, Berry graduated Simpson College before being commissioned a 2nd lieutenant in the Marine Corps in 1968. He completed flight school in 1969, flew in Vietnam for a year, and returned home to Marine training and command positions. During Operation Frequent Wind, the evacuation in 1975, by then a captain, he logged the most hours in the air flying helicopters on that last day. After twenty years in the Marine Corps and three Distinguished Flying Crosses, he retired as a colonel and invented a Visual Identification System now used by the U.S. Air Force. Married with three children, he lives in Florida.

Vietnamese refugees boarding a Sea Stallion helicopter to safety as the war was ending.

to forty minutes. If you left the USS Denver, it might be thirty minutes into the embassy. Never much time at the embassy whether you loaded behind the embassy or on top of the embassy. In no more than a half minute or a minute max, they're ready. The Marines were in charge of this thing. They'd just run them on the back and then you'd fly out. You got to the carrier, you drop your load, you need to refuel. About every four or five hours, you'd have to shut down and check out your helicopter, like a ten minute stop. They would hand you food through the window. That would be the only delay.

Of course, you were very, very sad about this whole thing. Then you got a little antsy over how this thing was going to end, because it still was not making progress. You got a little frustrated. You started getting a little tired probably about the ten o'clock mark because that's very exhausting. At ten o'clock at night there were still more people in there than when we started. We have six-and-a-half hour limits on us to fly. About every time we landed on the command ship, USS Blue Ridge, General Carey would usually come up and say, "Do you have the ambassador?" That was my original mission and I'd say, "No, I don't have the ambassador."

There was a lot of dialogue back and forth. But finally at three o'clock we realized there was really nobody else flying. The conversation went that we should bring the ambassador out on the next run. Under whose authority? I always felt that he had direct contact with the president. I thought, why would we tell him to come out. Why wouldn't the President of the United States say, "Hey, Ambassador Martin, it's time." Somebody had to make a decision. At 3:30 in the morning General Carey decided that we should definitely try to bring the Ambassador out on the next pass.

We land on the roof. We actually loaded up a group of Vietnamese and I had to get hold of the side radio and say, "It's not going to work. We're not leaving the rooftop until the ambassador's on board." Well, they unloaded the Vietnamese and it was an amazing thing. Couldn't have been more than a minute and the ambassador and his whole entourage are on top of the roof getting ready to get on. I think involved in there somewhere, we told him the president sends orders or the president demands something like he get on this helicopter. I always felt years later all he wanted was the guidance, you know, center stage to do this, and he was happy to do it. And that was really the end of it. The Marines are now in charge and they closed off all the doors, started up the stairways and sequestered themselves on the roof.

The admiral and the general came around the side of the airplane. You have a side door on the CH-46 and that's usually where your VIPs get out. They don't go down the back ramp with everybody else. I'd already made the call, "Tiger, Tiger, Tiger," like we really had the ambassador on. Then they come around and I see them scuttling back around the front of the airplane like he's not here. And I thought, maybe it wasn't the ambassador. I have no idea what the ambassador looks like. Maybe it wasn't him. But fortunately he was getting off the back ramp and they connected. When he came around the side, he was just absolutely a very haggard, very tired guy that had obviously been in a very stressful position for a very, very long period of time. As one would expect. You know, I didn't envy him his position, either. I think it was very difficult.

Then General Carey came back on the airplane and said, "You know, we still have Marines left in the embassy. Can you go one more time?" Of course. We'd been out pretty close to seventeen hours at that time but then we made one more round, came in and policed the rest of them up. It's daylight. You can see absolutely everything. You can see the North Vietnamese tanks roll into town. If you look far enough you could make out the troops coming in. My biggest fear was the well-armed army of South Vietnam. They're not going anywhere, they've lost, you're leaving them. These individuals may decide to take you out with them. That was my biggest fear.

It's very strange to ask a generation of young men to go fight for you and then determine later that it really didn't matter. I'm not sure we ever had a plan. I'm not sure that anybody really knew what we were doing over there. Somebody had to tell somebody that this was a bottomless pit just like the embassy was during the evacuation—that it wasn't going to work. I don't think it was ever that hard to figure out. I thought those who fought in that war and those who did the evacuation of Saigon, a lot of the same people, I thought they did a tremendous job. If you thought about who did the best, whether it was the soldier in the field or the Marine or the sailor or the Air Force guy or your politician in Washington, D.C., I think the scale of balance would be far on the side of those who went and fought. Those politicians made some really poor, poor decisions. I think that's something that America has to kind of think about once in a while. I think we owed these people an obligation. I think the politicians somewhere are going to take a tremendous hit when history writes against this thing, if they haven't already.

TED MURRAY

Security Guard
Defense Attaché Office
Tan Son Nhut Airport
U.S. Marine Corps

Ted Murray was a Marine security guard at the United States Embassy in Saigon until he was reassigned to the Defense Attaché Office at Tan Son Nhut Airport before Saigon fell. He and other Marines presided over the evacuation of American civilians and those Vietnamese afraid of reprisals who wanted out of Vietnam.

No photo available

Ninety percent were Vietnamese that I saw. I don't know what their status was with regards to should they be going. I know there were some people that had no links with the American government that were going out probably because their families had some links. If one went, they all went. Some probably had gotten married within that short period of time and were sent out that way. It's a question of who you know, too, that helped get them out.

USDAO COMPOUND SAIGON 30 APR 75

As the situation worsened, probably the last week, the last couple of days, when people saw what was going on around Saigon, the paperwork quickened. People weren't really concerned towards the end with who was getting out. Just sign them, get them on a plane and get them out. A lot of people just didn't care who was getting out. Just get them out. They were all grateful to be going. Everybody has a fatalistic attitude about this is the end. Let's get out of here.

Aerial reconnaissance photo of the destroyed American headquarters, Saigon, Vietnam, 30 April 1975.

Everybody knew from the past couple of weeks that it was just a question of time. How much time do we have? How much time is left? How many people can we get out? Everybody wanted to get out. I had been asked by Vietnamese soldiers how do we get out. Can you get us out? When are you leaving? I couldn't answer and I couldn't do anything to help them. There were stories about people offering people money to help get them out. And those that could went.

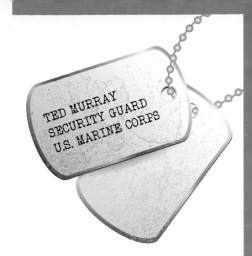

It was pretty much twenty-four hours a day. The Marines were catching whatever hours of sleep they could. We always looked tired but we were always upbeat. At the time it was kind of surreal. The reality hadn't quite set in yet. It was kind of like, okay, people are leaving the country. We process them. They get on the bus. They go to the airplane. Reality hadn't hit us yet. But it was done in a quiet and orderly manner so that it didn't look like we were bugging out and leaving everybody behind. What was important was to save face and to not cause a panic. I felt we were letting the Vietnamese people down. We had promised to back them against the Communists in the North. We did feel like we were leaving and that we were giving the Vietnamese people up to the North. We felt that way ever since the North started their offensive.

USMC CH-53s at LZ 38.

On the last day, April 29th, myself and two other Marines were at the tennis court. That was our post at the final evacuation. Four Vietnamese soldiers came up in the morning to the chain link fence that surrounded the DAO compound and asked to go in. Now these are fully armed ARVN soldiers. The two Marines that I was with were in a ditch behind me. I walked up and was talking to the soldiers. I could feel the animosity, the "you're leaving us behind, you cowards." It upset me because I knew that we were leaving them behind, that we couldn't do anything, that we were turning tail. At the same time I was scared because here I was with nothing around me. All they had to do was unsling their weapons and take out an American Marine who was leaving them behind as a symbol of their frustration and their hatred of what we were doing. I think I was more scared of the ARVN at that time than the NVA because the ARVN were all around us. The main gate of the DAO compound and Tan Son Nhut Airport up the street had at least one tank. I kept thinking, "What are they gonna do with the tank if they see us bugging out?" They could just come down here and take revenge.

9th MAB intelligence photo of the DAO Compound with LZs marked.

So many thoughts going through our heads. We felt the NVA was going to take the airport first, after bombing it for so long. I figured that was their target and we were in their way. Many times during the late afternoon and during the night we could hear artillery or tanks or whatever going off. The shells going off overhead and landing and we kept saying to ourselves, are they that close? If they are, then are they going to let us go, or you know, are we going to be able to get the last helicopter? As night fell, it got scarier. So much time had gone by and we didn't know what our fate was going to be.

Vietnamese evacuees board a CH-53 at LZ 39.

Marines boarding a Sea Knight helicopter.

Ambassador Graham Martin arrived at the air base to inspect the serious damage to the runways.

So we prayed when he left that the decision to finally get on with the evacuation, get all the people out that needed to get out, or as many people as possible, and then get us out. I knew that we were going to be the last ones out, so let's get everybody out as quick as possible so we can get out of here with all our skins. I can't say what the feeling was at the embassy. Being there I would have liked to have said, "Hello, wake up. It's time to leave." We just felt like Ambassador Martin was holding back.

The evacuation started late morning. The helicopters would fly in and the majority of them were the big CH-53s. We only put fifty on in the beginning but as the day progressed, we started putting more people, fifty, sixty, seventy, eighty, ninety on the helicopter that normally holds fifty people. As many people as we could on the helicopter. Everybody had to leave their luggage behind. Either you stay here with your luggage or you go out. We put them on a quickly as possible and got them out as quickly as possible.

We knew we were in artillery range, rocket range of the NVA. It was just a question of when they would start lobbing shells into us.

At four o'clock in the morning of April 29th, North Vietnamese rockets slammed into Tan Son Nhut Air Base killing Corporal Charles McMahon, Jr., and Lance Corporal Darwin W. Judge, the last two Marines to die in the Vietnam War.

I heard the first rocket in the distance. The second rocket closer. Then the third rocket right outside where we were sleeping. I grabbed my M16, ran outside the bunker and after a couple of minutes it was quiet. We were wondering where the last rocket had hit and somebody yelled from the gate that it had hit at the crossroads. So we all ran out there and the image of Judge laying there is indelibly etched into my mind. I had expected after seeing, growing up watching all the war movies, the huge crater but where the rocket hit was a little tiny hole. It wasn't that deep. It was probably three or four inches wide by a couple of inches deep. But I guess that's the way it was made to explode. Looking for McMahon and finally finding him. The Vietnamese ambulance drivers that came to get them having a kind of lackadaisical attitude. I guess you'd have to do, though, doing their job. It upset us at the time because they were Marines that we had known. Friends. It brought home the fact that what could happen to all of us. The reality and the severeness of the situation and the fact that this wasn't a game. This was something that finally touched us. Two of our own had died and it kind of sobered us up. It took a while for us to let the reality sink in.

When all the helicopters had taken off with all the other personnel we were kind of sitting around. We had all been gathered together and told that we had done a good job. It was now our turn to go, but we'd have to wait for a helicopter. I guess the waiting, watching the starlight flares going off, hearing guns going off, artillery still going on overhead, there was the question of let's hope he's not too late. When the helicopter finally did come in, we could see the lights. There was a CH-46. I'll never forget that as long as I live. I could have kissed the pilot. He set it down in the main parking lot. We all took a last look around and then walked to the helicopter, got on it and as were taking off, I looked out the back and looking down seeing tanks moving just outside the Vietnamese Air Force barracks. I think to myself, in another half hour who knows what would have happened if this pilot hadn't come. It was a scary thought because they were that close.

On an aircraft carrier out at sea, a Marine escorts an old woman to safety who just landed from the mainland.

COLIN BROUSSARD

Staff Sergeant
Bodyguard to Ambassador Graham Martin
U.S. Marine Corps

America's last ambassador in Vietnam, Graham Martin, had Marines guarding him around the clock in Saigon. He could do nothing alone or go anywhere without an armed escort. Colin Broussard was Ambassador Martin's bodyguard on April 29, 1975.

Colin Broussard

Everybody felt that there would be an evacuation at the embassy. The North Vietnamese were going to encircle the city of Saigon. I think that specifically Ambassador Martin didn't want to let on that there was going to be an American evacuation. I personally think he helped a lot of people in Saigon by keeping their nerves a little bit less. We did know and feel that we were going to evacuate Saigon. Ambassador Martin did not share any details like that with me or to my knowledge outside of his inner circle.

On April 29 Ambassador Martin told me that he wanted to go to his residence and he wanted to leave in fifteen minutes. I radioed Major Kean, the commanding officer, and I informed him the ambassador wanted to go to his residence. Major Kean protested. All the political officers protested the ambassador going to his house. He looked at me, and he says, "We're going. Get the car ready." I notified the staff sergeant to get the vehicle. I notified Major Kean. He was at the gate with about five Marines. There must have been ten thousand people outside the gate. I drove the vehicle slowly to the gate. Major Kean was trying to keep the people out at the same time trying to let me get outside. There was no way, and I just put the car in reverse and went back to the embassy.

Ambassador Martin waited about ten minutes. He was pretty frustrated. He wanted to go back to his residence. He didn't tell me why. There was a secret entrance between the American embassy and the French embassy. The Ambassador called the French Ambassador and we went through that little secret entrance between the two embassies. We went through the French embassy and we walked two blocks, two major country blocks to the ambassador's residence. We had an old gray-haired man and two young Marines in civilian clothes, mind, with two machine guns. There were Viet Cong on the streets. Artillery going off. The fall was happening right then and there and we're bringing this man, walking this older man down the road. We were stopped at one time by a motorcycle with what they called cowboys, Vietnamese with rifles shooting them up in the air and what not. They stopped us. Jim jumped in front of the motorcycle, and the two Vietnamese sped off. We walked the ambassador into the residence. He went upstairs and he brought down classified information. We burned it in the house. We used fragmentation grenades and thermal grenades to destroy all classified materials.

Ambassador Martin was extremely fatigued. He hadn't slept in like seventy-two hours. He knew that he needed to get that information out of that house. He didn't want that to go to the enemy if we did evacuate. I respect him for doing that. He put Jim's and my life and his life in danger by doing this. We didn't want to walk the ambassador back so I radioed Major Kean and requested permission to secure the two sentries at his residence and we tried to start a backup Pontiac that we had in the garage. It didn't start the first time. I jiggled around with the cables, got it to start. I radioed Jim to get the ambassador outside. I got the two Marines. We all got inside the car. Jim lay on top of the ambassador's body. The two Marines with their M16s on each window. I was driving. We rammed the gates and headed straight to the French embassy, where we got the Ambassador safely back to the American embassy.

Ambassador Martin wanted to see what's going on at Tan Son Nhut. I guess he just didn't believe it. So he got us and told us he wanted to go out. We protested to go out there because it was too dangerous. We already lost our two Marines. We drove. I was in the backup car. On the streets at that time we didn't know who was friend or who was foe because the Viet Cong was in the city. So we locked and loaded our rifles and machine guns and went down the main street to Tan Son Nhut Air Base. We were stopped by some ARVN guards at the gate, and we persuaded the ARVN guards to allow the ambassador to go inside. At that time artillery rounds were landing on the base. Smoke was coming up from some of the destroyed aircraft. We brought the ambassador down to General Smith's headquarters and he could see firsthand what was going on. After he finished talking, we put him back in the cars and we took him back to the American embassy. We got back to the embassy and the evacuation started. Within four hours, the first helicopters started coming into the embassy. The ambassador didn't want to be that far away. He wanted me to go out and check on the situation. I went to the roof. We had machine-gun emplacements up there. I checked things out and brought back information to Ambassador Martin. He was absolutely exhausted. But you had to respect Ambassador Martin. You know, he kept his cool. He knew the awesome thing that was happening, not only to himself but America as a whole and I think he carried out his duties quite well.

At around two in the morning the other three bodyguards came aboard. They were out helping other people in the embassy. The ambassador told him and I that our duties in Vietnam were over and he ordered us to board the next helicopter. As the ramp was closing, as we were taking off, there was a lot of fires. There was a lot of tracers going through the air. I started shaking. I hadn't had a cigarette in about three weeks and the Marine corporal gave me Marlboro cigarette and lit it with a Marine Corps Zippo®. That's what I remember about taking off from the embassy.

I landed on the USS Midway. Ambassador Martin landed on the USS Blue Ridge. He had somebody call and get Jim and I to fly to be with him. His mood was still tired from all those days without sleep.

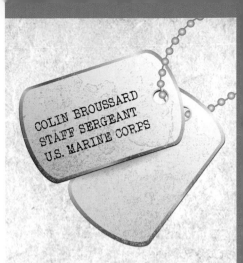

Colin Broussard

Originally from Deerpark, Texas, Broussard joined the Marines in 1969. Stationed in Saigon during the war, he was part of the Personal Protection Security Unit, assigned to Ambassador Graham Martin as his bodyguard. After service at the American Embassy in Nicosia, Cyprus, and Brussels, Belgium, he retired from the Marines in 1989 as a master sergeant. In civilian life he became a computer programmer and is currently back to work for the Marine Corps, this time as a program analyst. He has one daughter in college.

American embassy personnel arrive on an aircraft carrier after being evacuated from Saigon.

TOBY HAYNSWORTH

Supply Officer
USS Midway, South China Sea
7th Fleet Evacuation Force
U.S. Navy

Toby Haynsworth

The USS Midway normally docked in Yokuska, Japan. The ship had arrived in Subic Bay, the Philippines for exercises but instead took on a squadron of Air Force helicopters. Soon the USS Midway joined a growing number of ships sixty to seventy miles off the coast of Vietnam waiting for the air lift of Vietnamese from Saigon once the evacuation started.

The first I knew it was going to happen was the 29th of April in the middle of the day. The Air Force helicopters were all launched in the afternoon. Overnight on the 29th and 30th we probably had one thousand refugees left on board out of over two thousand brought on board that day. We didn't have one thousand bunks so they were sleeping down on the hangar bay underneath the aircraft. The sailors were magnificent in trying to make them as comfortable as possible. They really went all out to give what hospitality they could. They would take things from their own possessions. They made toys for the kids. They tried to entertain people as best they could. They worked very, very hard to get an appropriate meal for these people.

The Air Force helo pilots were highly professional. It was very orderly. We had these teams set up to escort the refugees out of the helos and over to a holding area. It went very smoothly. Some were brought down to the mess decks where they were fed. Some were processed in the hangar bay. The people were very subdued. They were quiet. It seemed to me there was a mixture of relief that they had gotten out; fatigue, because many of them had traveled many miles to get to Saigon in hopes of getting out one way or the other; and sadness, at having left home. There was no untoward activity of any kind. Everybody was very cooperative.

The next day there was a flood of helicopters with South Vietnamese pilots flying out. They had just left South Vietnam within the two or three days before to an island where the South Vietnamese Air Force had a runway. A large number of South Vietnamese aviators and their families concentrated on that island trying to figure out what was going to happen because they didn't know how the end would come. Fixed-wing aircraft were able to load up families and friends to fly around the coast of Vietnam to Thailand. But the helicopters and one small Cessna didn't have enough fuel to fly to Thailand. It was just amazing to see them flying out in hopes of finding the fleet and in hopes of being rescued. They had no guarantees. There was mostly no radio communications. They were just hoping to get away and be saved by the American Navy. They came out in droves. At points the sky was literally filled with helicopters. It was nerve wracking for the people up on the flight deck. It was a very dangerous operation. The people up in the tower had a devil of a time trying to make sure everything was done safely. The landings were not always so orderly. Many of them were low on fuel. They weren't familiar with carrier operations. The carrier personnel had no way to communicate with most of them. It became a contest. Could we get the helos down, the people out? Sometimes there were two or three of them trying to land at the same time and if they could, avoid having to ditch in the water. Many of them had lots of women and children on board. Some of those aircraft configured to take loads of up to a dozen fully equipped soldiers were bringing fifty people out. Women, children, old grannies. It was really something, to see them get off of those helicopters in such a mixed bag of humanity. Then the sailors were pushing the helicopters over the side to make room for the next group to come in. You've seen helos with the slide-like runners. Well, they didn't roll, so they had to get thirty, forty, fifty sailors and throw them over the side.

The third wave consisted of literally hundreds of small boats filled with refugees just trying to find a way out. And they came out and were picked up both on the 30th and in the next two or three days by the surface ships that were still there. One of these boats of refugees came up alongside the Blue Ridge. One of the officers on the Blue Ridge was sort of trying to coax them to go away. And Admiral Whitmire came down to the ship and he said, "Son, there are days when we go by the book. There are days when we don't go by the book. Give them what they need so they have a chance to get away." So they were given supplies from the Blue Ridge. That was a manifestation of the attitude that most people had. We wanted to do whatever we could to save as many people as we could. There was a feeling of having let down the South Vietnamese people, promises that were made that weren't kept. We wanted to do what we could to try to at least salvage that group which could get out to sea.

On the first or second of May while anchored in a bay off of Thailand, a boat of eighty-four Vietnamese refugees came alongside. The executive officer, Larry Grimes, went over to the side of the ship where the boat was tied up. It was in sad shape. Larry called the captain up to the bridge and said, "We've got this boat with eighty-four refugees aboard. I would like permission to bring them aboard." And the Captain said, "Well, just a minute, I've got to check with the admiral." And the admiral said, "Just a minute, I've got to check with Hawaii." And Hawaii said, "Just a minute, I've got to check with Washington." And in the meantime, much to his credit, as far as I am concerned, Larry Grimes said, "This is ridiculous." We had an officer down in the boat who happened to have an ax with him. Larry Grimes said, "How about chopping a hole in the bottom of the boat?" Which they did. And then he called up to the bridge, "Sorry, Captain, we've got to bring them aboard. Boat sinking. We have no choice." And so we did get some refugees from the boats aboard our ship. We made room for them and took them back to Guam with us. And the crew of cooks would sort of challenge each other to see who could be the best cook to prepare for the group of eighty-four refugees. They went out of their way to do it and they did a wonderful job, trying to make them feel at home and boost their morale.

It was a salvage operation at that point. Save as many people as you can. I felt that my shipmates had just done a wonderful job in giving their all to get as many people out safely as they could. It was a very heartwarming thing to have a chance to participate in something good in a warship. We weren't killing people. We were saving people. And that was a good feeling.

Opposite: So many helicopters fled to the fleet to escape the Communists, that the aircraft carriers could not accommodate them all. Here, a Huey, one of many that last day, is pushed off the carrier into the sea, to make room for other incoming helicopters.

HARRY SUMMERS

U.S. Chief of Negotiations
Four Party Joint Military Team
U.S. Army

Harry Summers

We were stationed at Tan Son Nhut Air Base to negotiate with the Vietnamese and the Viet Cong on the question of U.S. prisoners of war and missing in action. As part of our duties, I went back and forth to Hanoi every week or two. At the very end I was in Hanoi a week before the fall of Saigon, and got the terms for the U.S. withdrawal. On April 30, we moved from our headquarters at Tan Son Nhut to the embassy with the idea we were going to stay in country after the fall. So that's how we happened to end up at the embassy on the morning of the 30th.

What was left in country were three officers, Colonel Madison, Captain Harrington, and myself, and three hundred commissioned officers. A Marine gunnery sergeant and an army master sergeant and an army special 7th class. I was a lieutenant colonel at the time. We assisted in the evacuation of Tan Son Nhut. We helped get the people together and run them through the processing lines. We had taken all of our own civilian employees and evacuated them early on, because we thought if we stayed in country, we didn't want them to be hostage to the North Vietnamese. My family was with me in Saigon, and they went out the third of April, the day before the C-5 crash. My secretary as a matter of fact was on that plane that crashed, and she was killed. So we were fairly busy. I had the feeling, and this was in considerable dispute … that there was a faction at least that wanted a negotiated settlement. That wanted to come to some terms temporarily with the South Vietnamese government. Then of course the South Vietnamese government faded away. But there was another faction that wanted a victory parade down the main street in Saigon. And that faction won out. And it cost them dearly. You know, it took what? Ten, fifteen years for them to reestablish negotiations with the United States. That's in considerable dispute. The CIA station chief William Polgar believed that that was a possibility. Kissinger in Washington didn't believe that at all. I guess it will never be known. So there was a feeling at the end that there could be a negotiated settlement rather than a military victory.

I think there's a perception in some American minds that the Vietnamese war was a guerrilla war waged by guerrillas. That was not true the last seven years of the war. The guerrillas had almost nothing to do with the Vietnam War after the Tet Offensive in '68. The last seven years it was almost exclusively the North Vietnamese regular army affair, but that's part of the misperceptions, I think, of the Vietnam War.

So we could see the ring tightening as the North Vietnamese moved more and more divisions down to encircle Saigon. We knew they were there, but again, from my conversations in Hanoi, I had the feeling that they were not going to launch an all-out attack on Saigon. It didn't make much sense; they didn't have to. I mean, the South Vietnamese army was collapsing, there was reason to destroy the very prize they'd been working to gain for the last thirty or so years, so I didn't really think that a direct assault on Saigon was in the making. And I said to them, "You know, I hear all you're saying, but look what's happened in Phnom Penh," which had fallen earlier. I said, "the blood bath that took place there." And they went up like a skyrocket. They said, "We're not Khmer's for Christ's sake, we're not Cambodians, we're not savages." The animosity between the North Vietnamese and the Cambodians, who they look down upon, as sort of sub-human. And they said, "None of that's going to take place, there will be no blood bath." Although I don't know how you term seventeen years in re-education camp, but it wasn't a blood bath at least. So in that sense, I think they were very sensitive to world public opinion on that particular point.

The traumatic experience for us was not Hué, was Da Nang. My older son, a West Point cadet at that time, was visiting us over Easter in '75. And he was at the airport the day the planes came in from Da Nang with people actually in the wheel wells, who died trying to hang on in the wheel wells of these planes, and we were very happy to put him on the airplane to get out of there. And my wife left. My younger son left the next day. So Da Nang was the specter that hung over the evacuation of Saigon. That things would get out of hand, that we would have to fight our way out, that we would have to turn on our own allies in order to get out, and that panic would set in and it would be impossible. Thank God that never happened, but that was always the sort of sword of Damocles hanging over our head. The South Vietnamese airborne division, one of their better divisions, was at Tan Son Nhut, right on the base. And they could have stopped the evacuation in a heartbeat. They let it proceed, which I think is a great testimony to them, that is not normally spoken of. But they had the ability to stop it anytime they chose.

The South Vietnamese troops had their families on their battle positions, so when the North Vietnamese cross border invasion began, this wasn't anything to do with guerrilla war, by the way. This was the fall of France in 1940. This was thirty some divisions coming south from four corridors with heavy air, tanks, and artillery, so that when they suddenly hit these South Vietnamese positions, the soldiers had a choice, do I take care of my family, or do I stay and fight? And unfortunately the families won out. I think this is very significant. Because we faced that very potential problem with our own military in Europe during the Cold War, because we had our families in Europe with our front line forces, and what would have happened if the Russians attacked? Would people take care of their families first or would they take care of their job? So anyway, I think that explains the collapse of the ARVN, which I think most people don't understand. It wasn't cowardice as much. The units that didn't have their families on their battle position, the Marine brigades and the Marine division and the airborne division, fight very well.

Again, as with the South Vietnamese, the North Vietnamese could have stopped the evacuation anytime in their choosing, very simply, especially at the end when we were evacuating the embassy. One gunshot would have stopped the evacuation. We left at their sufferance I guess is what I'm saying.

Our chain of command came directly from the office of the Secretary of Defense. So we were getting all these calls from Washington saying get this person out, get that person out, get the other person out. They had lists of people they wanted evacuated, and to get a person on to Tan Son Nhut Air Base was very difficult because the South Vietnamese wouldn't let any people on unless they had the proper credentials. We ran a lot of, I guess, what could

Harry Summers

A combat infantry veteran of the Korean and Vietnam Wars, Summers was twice wounded on the battle field and twice decorated for valor. As a captain in 1966–67 he served as op erations officer of the 1st Battalion, 2nd Infantry in the 1st Infantry Division. He returned to Vietnam in 1974–75 as the negotiator on the POW/MIA issue and was among the last to be evacuated from the roof of the U.S. Embassy in Sai gon when the city fell on April 30, 1975. Retired in 1975, he is the author of the classic On Strategy and the more recent Histori cal Atlas of the Vietnam War. A Distinguished Fel low of the Army War Col lege, Colonel Summers is now a syndicated colum nist and editor of Vietnam Magazine. Summers died in 1999.

be called, black operations, of picking people up, specific people, and evacuating them. So we were so busy during that period that, we didn't really have a lot of time to worry too much about the military situation. But I never had the feeling that we were about to be attacked, I'll put it that way.

There was a panic at first, and then there was almost a sort of fatalism that took over. That the end was inevitable, and there was nothing they could do about it. So there wasn't the kind of panic that took place in Da Nang. I think what happened in Da Nang, there was an obvious way out. If you could get to Saigon, you'd be safe. But in Saigon, where would you go? I mean, there's just no place to go from there. That kind of panic that overtook Da Nang never happened. There was some quasi panic at the U.S. Embassy probably, people trying to get into the embassy, but the rest of the town was quiet. I mean, very quiet as a matter of fact, strangely quiet. I mean, by that time the end was inevitable.

The people who worked for the United States, the people who worked some of the covert operations against the North, the information agency people for example, who made the clandestine broadcasts, and CIA people, and military officers who had served in combat against the North Vietnamese. Most of them, of course, ended up in re-education camps. Most of them did not get out. My counterparts on the South Vietnamese delegation, the Four Party Joint Military Team, evacuated their families, but they stayed to the very end and ended up in re-education camps, by and large, after the takeover.

I sent my wife and younger son out on a Pan Am flight on the third, and it cost me $1,700. I mention that, only that the next day the C-5 left, and it was free. And I was bitching that, well, you know, if I had just waited a day, we could have put them on the C-5 and I could have saved all that money, and then when the plane crashed, I felt like I'd been brushed with the wings of death. I mean … you know … it came that close. My wife and son could've been on that plane, and in fact my secretary was on that plane, and Bill Bell, who was my chief translator, his wife and three children were on a plane, and were all killed except one daughter. So it was a very traumatic experience for us when that plane crashed. It really put just a pall over everything that followed. Because most of the secretaries from the Defense Attaché office, and Four Party Joint Military Team, and the embassy were on that plane.

Well, again, I'm a combat veteran of the Korean War and the Vietnam War. So as far as combat goes, it certainly wasn't. That certainly put a pall over everything and the final evacuation, you know, which we'll get to, was the only time in thirty-eight years of military service I ever felt ashamed to be an American. So that was part of it. But the crash of the C-5—the rest of it was almost anti-climactic. We set up processing stations at Tan Son Nhut, and several thousand people got out during that particular period. Everybody got out of Tan Son Nhut. There was nobody left. Everyone was in the process of going finally got out. That's not true at the embassy, but it was true at Tan Son Nhut. Everybody that was there was evacuated. When the last lift took off at Tan Son Nhut there was no one left to be evacuated. In part of my conversation in Hanoi, they kept saying to me, you know, "Everything's going to be okay. There's not going to be any bloodbaths," and this, that, and the other. Sort of reassuring in that sense.

Washington put a lot of pressure on, they had names they wanted out, people they wanted out. We were constantly getting lists from Washington. Of course the Agency had people they wanted out for their own reasons. But after that it sort of it became more of the common people. Americans with their Vietnamese families, Vietnamese families themselves. There was a prohibition against evacuating any military people, military officers or NCOs. And we violated that in at least two instances. One of the waitresses at the Defense Attaché mess was about eight-months pregnant, her husband was a Marine sergeant who had been missing in action for a while and had finally got back to Saigon. We bundled him and his wife off and put them on an airplane and got them off although it was illegal to do it, we did it anyway. And one of the South Vietnamese members of the Four Party Joint Military Team was evacuating his wife and family, and in tears as he was

O 191801Z APR 75
FM THE WHITE HOUSE
TO AMEMBASSY SAIGON
ZEM
~~TOP SECRET~~ SENSITIVE EXCLUSIVELY EYES ONLY
DELIVER AT OPENING OF BUSINESS VIA MARTIN CHANNELS WH50728

APRIL 19, 1975

TO: GRAHAM MARTIN

FROM: SECRETARY KISSINGER

  1. THANKS FOR YOUR 0715.

  2. MY ASS ISN'T COVERED. I CAN ASSURE YOU I WILL BE
HANGING SEVERAL YARDS HIGHER THAN YOU WHEN THIS IS ALL OVER.

  3. NOW THAT WE ARE AGREED THAT THE NUMBER OF AMERICANS
WILL BE REDUCED BY TUESDAY TO A SIZE WHICH CAN BE EVACUATED
BY A SINGLE HELICOPTER LIFT, THE EXACT NUMBERS ARE COMPLETELY
UP TO YOU. THAT HAVING BEEN DECIDED, I WILL STOP BUGGING
YOU ON NUMBERS, EXCEPT TO SAY THAT YOU SHOULD ENSURE THAT THE
EMBASSY REMAINS ABLE TO FUNCTION EFFECTIVELY.

  4. YOU SHOULD GO AHEAD WITH YOUR DISCUSSION WITH THIEU.
IN YOUR SOUNDINGS RELATIVE TO HIS POSSIBLE RESIGNATION,
HOWEVER, THE MATTER OF TIMING IS ALSO OF GREAT SIGNIFICANCE.
IN ANY EVENT ANY RESIGNATION SHOULD NOT TAKE PLACE PRECIPITATELY
BUT SHOULD BE TIMED FOR MAXIMUM LEVERAGE IN THE POLITICAL
SITUATION. YOU SHOULD KNOW, ALTHOUGH YOU SHOULD NOT INTIMATE
THIS TO THIEU, THAT WE THIS MORNING HAVE MADE AN APPROACH TO
THE SOVIET UNION. WE SHOULD NOT BE SANGUINE ABOUT ANY RESULTS
BUT, IF THERE ARE ANY, THEY COULD EASILY INVOLVE THIEU AS ONE
OF THE BARGAINING POINTS.

  5. YOU SHOULD ALSO KNOW THAT THE FRENCH HAVE APPROACHED US
WITH THE IDEA OF RECONVENING THE PARIS CONFERENCE. WE
TOLD THEM WE WERE OPPOSED AND FELT IT WOULD BE COUNTERPRO-
DUCTIVE.

  WARM REGARDS.

(196)

*Cable from Henry Kissinger, Secretary of State, to Graham Martin, Ambassador to South Vietnam,
Concerning the Evacuation of Saigon.*

putting them on an airplane, and Captain Harrington went up to him and said, "Get on the plane." And he said "I can't do it." And he said, "Get on the plane, President Tu's already left, you're a fool to stay here, get on the plane." Well, President Tu hadn't left and he knew it, but he thought it was either then or never, and really jumped on Harrington for putting him in that kind of a position, where he had to choose between his wife and his children or his family and his country. But that was really the hard choice, and it was probably best that he that he did it. I mean, it was a terrible position to put anyone in, and I was very unhappy with Captain Harrington for doing it, but in retrospect it was the right thing to do.

Well, I remember one old man saying that it was the third time that he had been evacuated. He was evacuated when the Japanese came in, in the 1940s, then he was evacuated from North Vietnam to South Vietnam when the Communists took over, and this was his third evacuation. Of course the Asians are somewhat more stoic, I think, than we are, in a sense. They accept fatalism, I suppose. They were certainly sad to leave, but in fact, some refused to leave. I mean, quite a few refused to leave. But they just understood that you know, that this was a chance to make a new start, and of course America has an attraction around the world. It's sort of, Americans don't see it that way, but it's almost a "Let's take a trip to Utopia," because everything is perfect here, at least from their viewpoint. Unfortunately for some of them, they believed us. So we were able to move the people out of the embassy proper into the next door compound and then clear the landing zone so the helicopters could begin coming in. And, we were putting about sixty to seventy Vietnamese on a helicopter, and about twenty Americans, that's the difference in weight and in size. And we began the evacuation. It proceeded all during the day and into the night, into the next morning. The evacuation at Tan Son Nhut went as planned. It went very smoothly. The Marine helicopters came in, picked the people up, got them out of there. By dark, almost everyone was gone from Tan Son Nhut.

The plan had called for the evacuation of I don't have the exact number, people from the embassy, who would be picked up from the roof of the, moved out to Tan Son Nhut by helicopter, and then evacuated. By this time Graham Martin was, I guess best described in a daze. I mean, his world had collapsed, he'd lost a son in Vietnam. I have a lot of respect for Graham Martin, but he was in an exceptionally difficult position. Because he couldn't order the evacuation too early, otherwise it would have triggered a Da Nang, and it would have been all over. And he couldn't wait too late, or nobody would get out. So he had to make some decisions that were very, very difficult and he's gotten an awful lot of criticism by people who don't know what the hell they're talking about. He certainly didn't have an easy time of it. Anyway by this time, he was just, almost in a state of physical collapse. And Wolfgang Lehman, his deputy, was sort of running the show. So he asked my boss, Colonel Jack Madison, who was the head of the U.S. delegation, to give him a hand in trying to organize this evacuation. That became our mission. That became the mission of the three of us, the three officers and three NCOs of the Four Party Team, to organize the embassy, and break the people down into helicopter loads. Clear the embassy itself, so the helicopters could get in. That was going to be the main evacuation form. But in the morning of the 30th, there was thousands of people jammed within the halls of the embassy. Totally unplanned for. And the embassy had no idea whatsoever what to do with them.

We got through the gate, and it was just chaos. There was just wall to wall people inside the wall of the embassy. And it just total confusion. We had people from the various embassies, we had a large delegation from the Korean embassy, for example, who were there, some Korean CIA people. We had a German priest with a bunch of refugee children. We had the families of U.S. citizens, Vietnamese families of U.S. citizens. We had people who had worked for the government before, low profile. The high profile people had been taken out earlier. So just a little bit of everything as a matter of fact. Very hard to categorize. The famed tamarind tree was still in the center of the courtyard. There was no way they could get a helicopter into the courtyard itself. All of the evacuations would have to take place off the roof, which was the plan. The plan was fifty to one hundred people off the roof. That was beginning to take place, and of course that was stirring up the crowds who saw some people leaving and you could just feel the uneasiness in the air. Part of the first problem was to clear a landing zone, so that the helicopters could get into the embassy courtyard itself. And second, was to clear the people out of there so the helicopters could land. And it was a thing called the C.R.A., the Community Recreation Association area, adjacent to the embassy. A swimming pool and a small club, and the plan was in place to move them out of the embassy courtyard itself, and move them next door so we could get helicopters into the landing zone. We started doing that and at the same time the Marine guards and some of the embassy staff cut down the tamarind tree and got that out of the way. There was some guy clearing the LZ, landing zone, and there was also some radio guy-wires that were blocking the, the landing zone, so we had those cut. And for a while you couldn't get anybody to make a decision. Because to cut the radio wires meant cutting the communications. But there was no way you could get a helicopter in with those with those guy-wires across the landing zone.

So finally Wolfgang Lehman made the decision to cut them and that cleared the LZ. We took a lot of the people inside the embassy and they were evacuated off the roof, just to clear the LZ. And then the rest of them were herded from the embassy courtyard into the next door compound. That occupied our time for the next 24 hours. And Captain Harrington, in particular, spoke Vietnamese, was able to reassure the crowd, and one of the things that still sticks in my craw, we said, "Honestly, we believe that everyone will be evacuated," that no one would be left, that we would be the last ones out. Trying to calm this mob which, if it got out of hand, of course, would have stopped everything. We were down to six helicopter loads left, of about three hundred or four hundred people. And they canceled the lift. We had to abandon them on the LZ. And that still sticks in my craw.

We abandoned the firemen who had volunteered to stay until the very end in case there was a helicopter crash. We abandoned this German priest with his refugee children. We abandoned the CIA people from the Korean embassy who were all executed later. It was just a very distasteful thing, and it was done by accident. It was done not by design, but because there was a breakdown in communication. It was the Vietnam War in microcosm. Great intentions and poor performance, you know. It was the only time in my life I've ever been ashamed to be an American, in those final moments when we had to leave the people, that we would take care of them and then didn't. It violated every precept of the plan.

I had thirty-eight years military service, ten years enlisted man, and twenty-eight as an officer. The only time I have ever been lied to in thirty-eight years on an operational matter was in the evacuation of Saigon. When a foreign service officer who was assistant to Graham Martin, came down and looked us in the eye and lied to us, knowing it was a lie, that the evacuation was going to continue, that the helicopters were en route, that we should just stay there and wait for the helicopters to come, knowing that the president had canceled the lift. And that was the most disgraceful thing that has ever happened to me in my, as I said, almost four decades of government service, and again, something that is absolutely unforgivable. So for a while, at least, we ... you know, we sat there thinking that the evacuation was going to continue. And only then, later, did we find out that, it had been canceled, and were told to sneak off the landing zone, to leave the people to their fate, and, again, a very disgraceful performance.

We went up to the rooftop of the embassy. I was the second-to-last Army guy off the roof. Stu Harrington deliberately, I think, was the last army guy. The Marine guards were still there, and were there for some time later, but we were the last Army people off the roof of the embassy. And we flew from there out to Okinawa, to the evacuation ship.

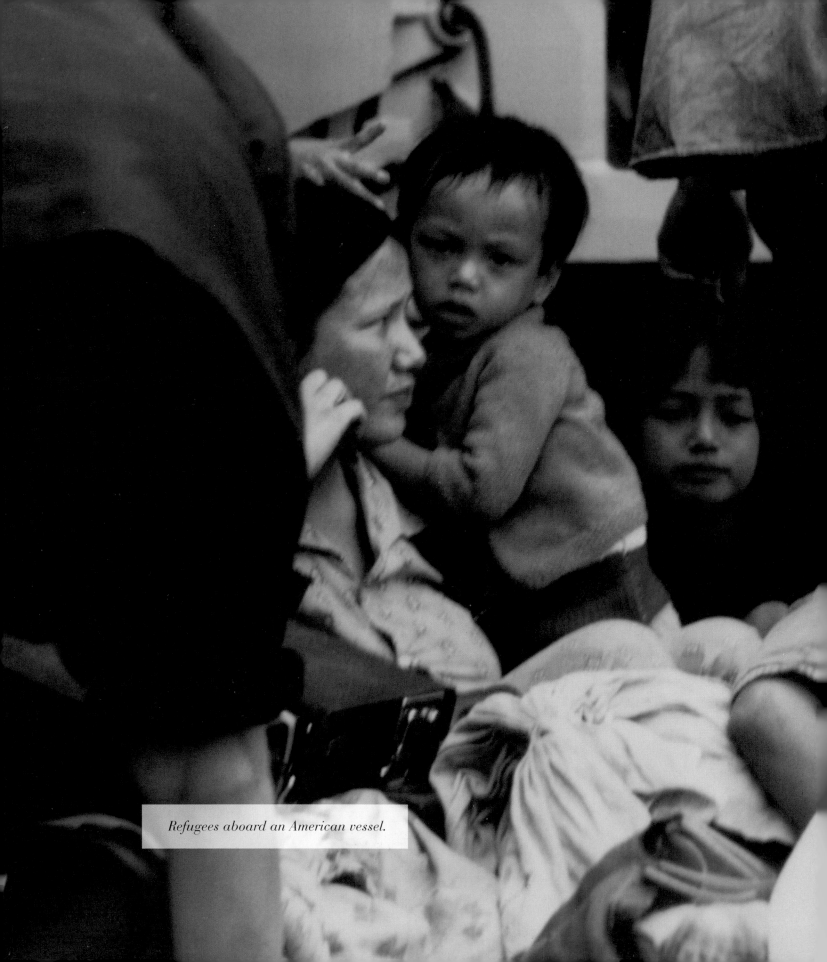

Refugees aboard an American vessel.

JOHN VALDEZ

Master Sergeant
Detachment Commander
U.S. Embassy, Saigon
Marine Security Guard

John Valdez

The 15th of April is when it became apparent that things were deteriorating in Saigon. We were told that we had to pack our personal belongings. The Marines had to leave Marine House and move into the embassy. From that day on, we never left the compound itself. Around April 20th we were getting reports that the North Vietnamese main goal was to encircle Saigon and get the Americans out. It wasn't total chaos yet, but you could see more activity on the outside. Some people were starting to come to the gates of the embassy. Just standing there. Just looking inside of the embassy. A lot of them stayed there. They never left. The lines got bigger and bigger but there was no panic.

The final days was pretty much total chaos. There were people all around all the gates of the embassy. People trying to get out. There was a lot of traffic. Which made it very hard for some of the vehicles that were still evacuating people to Tan Son Nhut or even the buses to move. A lot of people were raising their children up in the air, like to get the children out. They didn't care about themselves, as long as they got their children out of there. For a while we were opening the gates but every time we did that, masses of people kept pushing the gates and then we had to push them back out. At the end we just kept the gates closed and if somebody pointed a Vietnamese that had to be evacuated, we would just jump on each other's shoulder, reach the top of the gates, and yank them inside the compound. We could no longer open the gates, because we couldn't control them. We couldn't control the people any longer. Some people had jewelry, money. They tried bribing some of the Marines because the Marines were the ones that were doing the security at the gate, but the Marines didn't take any bribes.

We had very little sleep. Catnap here and there whenever we could. It's had to say how many hours we were without sleep because we were dead tired by the time of the final evacuation, the last hours before we got out of there. Our Marines had to stay awake. We couldn't afford to go to sleep. The actual evacuation started around 12 noon and they were around the clock until almost seven the following day. The crowds got bigger and bigger, larger and larger. More people wanted to get out. We didn't stop once the people were pretty much panicked. They all wanted to get out of there and we're rushing them to the choppers. Putting them on. The choppers taking off. Another one's landing. We're getting sixty more people out of there. So it was pretty much continuous, chaotic. Then you could hear in the streets a lot of cowboy shooting. It was never directly at us. It was just people firing in the sky. Mostly South Vietnamese soldiers that had weapons.

Major Kean finally approached Sullivan and myself, you know, the ambassador's gone. This is it. We're not taking any more people. We got to evacuate. The word was passed to the Marines in the different locations to start making plans for leaving. We kind of carefully try to make it appear we were not leaving but the people determined we were all leaving.

I kind of passed the word to the Marines to sort of make a semi-circle and gradually start breaking themselves away from the gates. Start moving back cautiously. Not trying to cause any more panic than was already there.

It worked successful until we got about halfway. We were getting blank stares from all the people on the outside of the compound. Then, all of a sudden, they just started climbing the gates. We looked at each other and I said, "This is it. We have to run for it." So we all ran, all going through only one door. We had to rush. Just as the last Marine got in we pressed the button, the doors closed and we slammed the blockade on the inside. Then we could hear the people slamming on the door, trying to push it in. But those doors were pretty thick. We were pretty confident they would hold.

Then we climbed and took the elevators to the top and locked them. Some Marines went through the ladder well. Each ladder had gates. Steel gates. And we locked those. That was pretty much it. Looking over the side we were able to see the people from the top of the embassy. Masses of people by this time. In the compound. Rushing towards the gates. Then we saw people take some of the vehicles and drove them off, jolly riding around there inside the embassy. We started evacuating the Marines who came in to assist us. Chopper landed. We got them out of there and eventually there was only a few of us left. Then for some reason the flights stopped. Out of the clear blue sky, everything stopped. There were no more choppers. We just sat up there. We were wondering … maybe the pilots are taking a break. As long as the Vietnamese could see some Marines, they didn't panic. They knew somebody was still out there and there was a chance they could be evacuated.

Finally two choppers showed up, a Cobra gunship and a CH-46. The Cobra hovered around in a circle while the CH-46 landed on the roof to get the last Marines out of there. The pilot was pretty anxious. He wanted to get out of there. As the chopper starts taking off with the ramp still down, one of my Marines inside the chopper still had a smoke grenade. He decides to take the pin out of that grenade and drop it down the compound just to get rid of it. The grenade starts smoking. The heli blades pick up all the smoke which blinds the pilot. I'm stepping my foot on the ramp. The chopper's lifting off. The pilot gets blinded by the smoke and sets the chopper down real hard … so I fall off. He gains his composure and he started to take off again. I'm climbing back on the roof and Solomon and one of the other Marines just kind of grab me and yank me inside the chopper. And the chopper takes off. He put up the ramp. We were airborne.

We could still see the chaos going down there. Confusion in the embassy compound. By this time you could see North Vietnamese tanks on their way to the presidential palace. We are exhausted. Relieved. Relieved that they hadn't forgotten us because for a moment we thought they'd really forgotten us. I kept saying to myself, it's finally over, you know. We're finally getting out of here and going back home.

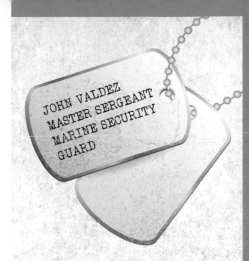
JOHN VALDEZ
MASTER SERGEANT
MARINE SECURITY
GUARD

John Valdez

A native of San Antonio, Valdez enlisted in the Marines in 1955. Trained as an assault amphibian crewman, he served in Hawaii, Okinawa, and in Vietnam. In 1973, then a master sergeant, he completed Marine Security Guard School and assumed command of the Marine detachment at the U.S. Embassy in Budapest. In 1974 he was in charge of the Marine Security Guards at the American Embassy in Saigon. He was the last Marine to board the last helicopter to leave Saigon the morning the country fell to North Vietnam. Promoted to master gunnery sergeant in 1976, he commanded Marines at embassies in Vienna and Brussels before retiring in 1985 after thirty years. After retirement, he enrolled in college, earned two associate degrees, and now works for the government as manager of base housing for general officers at Camp Pendleton.

MAJOR JIM KEAN

Commander, Security Guards
U.S. Embassy, Saigon
April 1975
U.S. Marine Corps

Major Jim Kean was in charge of all security in South Vietnam and at the American embassy from April 17, 1975 until Saigon fell on April 30, 1975. He said, "Seventy-five turned out to a very interesting year."

Major Jim Kean

Sometime after the 19th of April they took this emergency evacuation plan that had been written by a security officer in 1973, dusted it off, and said this is horse manure. That's how I got involved immediately. I got asked to help. What are we going to do if have to leave from here? If we got sealed off. Nothing made sense other than the embassy itself, which was a labyrinth of walls. The outer walls and then the inner walls, and a huge old tree. If it hadn't been for that huge old tree, we could make a decent landing zone in the parking lot of the embassy which would hold the big, heavy lift helicopters. Hence, the joke about the tree. You know, feeling frustrated, take a whack. But Martin called me and said, if anybody touches the that tree until I give the word … It had been there for a couple of hundred years. It dominated this massive parking lot on the interior of the compound. The more important people got to park in the shade of the tree so their cars would be cooler when they left. We finally got the word from Martin at eleven o'clock on the 29th of April and it took no more than twenty minutes to have that tree down, chopped up, and the logs and all the debris removed. One of the Seabees came up with a can of luminous paint and we painted a big H in the parking lot for the helicopters.

We had twenty-five hundred evacuees already inside the compound. Then we had an embassy staff of several hundred. This was roughly noon on the 29th when the emergency evacuation was given and there was a lag time. The helicopters started flying later in the afternoon and they were going to Tan Son Nhut. I started talking to them. We got a problem over here. We're going to have to divert some, so on a case by case basis, a helicopter would land on the roof of the embassy and we would fill them up. We used all twenty-two helicopters to take Vietnamese out. We were loading as many as we could. I swear, I actually counted eighty-three Vietnamese on one of those CH-53's and it was enormously problematic. Everybody flying those airplanes should have been given some sort of medal because they had to come in and hover over the embassy and really helicopters don't hover, they move around. They had to then drop seventy feet. It's a vertical descent into this compound and then we would start stacking people on. Sitting target. And the pilot has to keep lifting to see if he can get it off the ground with that many people. He'd say, okay, that's it, he can get it up. He had to pick up and come straight up seventy feet, and there were a bunch of goons—we called them cowboys—that were deserters and were armed and shooting at the helicopters. We could see the tracers and from time to time I would yell at Sergeant Valdez and he would send some Marines to find these guys and clean them out. I never did ask what they did and I didn't care. But it stopped.

A lot of helicopters were shot, had holes in them and it was very disconcerting, because one crash and it would have been all over. I mean they were coming in after midnight at four-minute intervals. I mean it was fast. It was like a train station. Once the tree came down, we had taken all the embassy vehicles, fueled them, and parked them in a circle and turned on the lights to create a lighted LZ. It was a good place for me to be so that the fleet Marines in to help could all see me. It was important because they didn't know who I was. They had never seen me before in their life. I just was the major, and I wasn't even wearing a uniform. I was wearing an Arnold Palmer golf shirt and a pair of blue slacks.

In preparation for this night I had twenty-four hours before brought to the embassy all the Marines from the hotel called the Marine House the embassy owned in Saigon. We put them on cots in the recreational compound, the dressing room for the swimming pool at the embassy. I said, if push comes to shove and this thing goes to hell in hand basket, we may have to defend this building. From who? We don't know. North Vietnamese. South Vietnamese. But we might have to defend it. We had an enormous amount of ammunition. We had a full complement of combat weapons. We set up some machine gun positions inside the compound so that grazing fire—in other words, knee high—could fire down in a flat trajectory and create a wall of steel. We told everybody when push comes to shove and it's time to go, we'll fire a red star cluster and that will be the signal to start moving towards the huge mahogany doors at the embassy. We would back in a semi-circle towards that door. On the inside of the walls we put sodium nitrate burn barrels that you could throw a match into and they would burn for a long time. These things were used to destroy classified material.

I was very proud of the guys that worked for me, of what they did at great risk. There were these power cables that stretched across the embassy compound. In order to get the helicopters into the landing zone, they all had to come down. We weren't sure which of them were alive and there wasn't any technician around to tell us. And this Sergeant Hargis climbed up this power pole. And he had a big pair of bolt cutters. And this one last cable had to come down. Had that been live, he would have electrocuted himself. He goes, "Fifty-fifty." I said, you crazy? It wasn't. You know, just absolute nuts. I ended up writing him for a medal. Same guy two days before he went down to Tu Do Street, the red light district, with a bread truck and picked up twenty-six hookers and sent them all to Guam. Signed for every one of them. I held non-judicial punishment on him. I fined him five dollars. I said, "What the hell did you do that for?" He said, "They're all personal friends."

When twenty-two helicopters had flown, there weren't any more. There was dead silence. I talked to the ships and made a point to explain that there were 450 people still waiting down there with their suitcases to get out. They said, let me repeat, "The President directs." And with that I went down to Martin. Martin looked like death warmed over. His eyes were sunken in his head. He was a chain smoker anyhow, and he was just beat down. We were scared to

Jim Kean

Kean enlisted in the Marine Corps 1961 and received his commission from the ranks in 1965. As a 1st lieutenant in Vietnam in 1966, he served as a forward observer for Marine infantry, then, in 1967, he served as a captain and battery commander of artillery. Wounded twice during his tours, his combat awards include two Bronze Stars and two Purple Hearts. In 1975, Major Kean commanded all Marine security guards in Asia. He presided over the evacuation of American embassies and consulates in Cambodia and Laos. In Saigon he was one of the last eleven Marines to leave the American Embassy as Saigon fell. Married and the father of four children, Kean retired as a lieutenant colonel after twenty-two years in the Marine Corps.

death that this guy that we served, we were going to have to pick him up and carry him on the helicopter at some point in time, kicking and screaming. Once the person gave him the order, and I was the one that brought it to him, one of his aides said that I was histrionic. I came in and I said, "The president directs that you leave." And he looked up, and he had these glasses on and he looked up over his glasses, and he had this stare that he could freeze people with, and he said, "All in good time, young major." And then he looked at Wolf Lehmann, his deputy chief of mission, and he said, "Wolf, I guess it's time we leave." He got up and he asked me if we should pull the flag. We lowered the flag and put it in a brown paper sack and gave it to him. With that he went out and got on the helicopter about four o'clock in the morning.

During the night we had evacuated five thousand people and there were only supposed to be twenty- five hundred. People kept coming over the walls.

Early in the morning of April 30, the North Vietnamese Army had surrounded Saigon. Crowds of frightened Vietnamese jammed the capitol. It was chaotic on the streets surrounding the American Embassy.

There were not enough Marines to man the whole perimeter. It was literally like the Alamo. There were great gaps between the individual Marines. There were people trying to pay off the Marines on the wall. A Chinese businessman had a brown paper sack full of uncut gems. He handed it up to the Marine and then he handed a baby up. All he wanted to do was send the baby up. The Marine just handed him back his sack and the child and said, "I can't do it." It was just going on all over the place around the walls. The people outside of the walls were afraid of these guys because they were in full combat gear. They all have automatic weapons and enormous fire power, so they weren't pushing too hard, even though they were panicked. The people inside the compound had been lulled into a sense that we're here. We're free, free, free. We made it inside. We got our luggage. We got boat space. So they didn't make a fuss.

Then a semicircle formed around the door. And I could see it coming. You could see the punch coming. All of a sudden it was going to break and all hell was going to break loose. The people were going to come over the walls and the people in the parking lot were going to start running. There's a great big Seabee. Big man. He grabbed the timber for the door and put it behind his back, with his arms locked around it. And he stood out in front of the semicircle at the gate and just started spinning in a circle. Fortunately everybody was afraid of that. They got hit with the timber and it knocked them senseless. That allowed the Marines to start grabbing people and throwing them inside. We got everybody in. We brought him in. Bolted the doors. The electronic gate froze halfway down. Inside, we sent the elevators up and locked them on the upper floors. Then there were two floors, the second floor and the fourth floor on the stairwell that that had steel gates and screened fences inside the embassy. Heavy-duty stuff. We locked those behind us as we proceeded up. There was a fire truck full of water inside the compound. The people drove it right through those mahogany doors and came in after us. Then they started chasing us up floor by floor. At the same time the helicopters were coming in and the people were leaving from the roof. The last access to the roof there was a burn machine for burning classified material. The helicopter zone was like a square box of a building that was raised and the landing zone was on top. There was a little zigzag stairway that went up there. The last barricade we crammed with one-hundred-gallon capacity fire extinguishers and a wall locker behind two steel fire doors, one on each end before you went out on the roof. We put Corporal Stephen Bauer in there, the youngest and smallest Marine because he fit, and gave him some tear gas and some mace. The people immediately beat through and they were reaching through, trying to get out and he would jump up and mace them.

The next-to-the-last bird left and we told the crew chief, don't forget us. There were eleven of us left. The president had already given the word that it was over when the announcement was made that the "tiger," the ambassador was out. People in Washington, D.C., went to sleep. Kissinger was on his way to a black-tie dinner.

All of a sudden somebody came back and they discovered this crew chief got word to people that there's eleven guys sitting back there. We waited two and a half hours. We watched the sun come up. We saw Big Minh and his motorcade come down the street. The national police shooting at the looters and we were going to get to see the invasion of Saigon. There was a huge sun. It looked like that advertisement for Miss Saigon. And then this lone CH-46 comes in out of the sun. The Marines, of course, all along had said, "They're coming aren't they, Maj ?" And I said, "Sure, they're coming." I had no idea but I was wondering, where were they? I mean, the stupid fact was that here we were. We put ourselves at the top of the tree, like a kitten, and you know it was going to be grim. And of course all the kids were just feistier than hell. This helicopter shows up. Steve Bauer set off a tear-gas grenade. Of course, we didn't have any gas masks so we gassed ourselves. It was a classic final act of Vietnam.

Now the helicopter sat down. Poor captain that was flying the airplane got a whiff of tear gas, and he tried to lift off and he had to set it back down, ever so gently and then try again. When the gas hits you at first, it makes you choke and it scares the hell out of you. You don't know what it is. We went in and sat down inside the helicopter, and then he lifts off.

We were up there for a couple of hours. We had seen this sun come up in the morning. Saigon looked like On the Beach. People had been driving cars all over and wrecking them. We had been throwing all the weapons in the swimming pool and the bottom was just carpeted with machine pistols, all those weapons of war. Then there were these people sitting around, these poor folks sitting down in the parking lot on their suitcases, wondering why they had missed the bus. I don't think there was anybody that wasn't touched emotionally.

On the helicopter we started heading southeast down to where the fleet was off the Bassac River. Before we got to the USS Okinawa, the right fuel-cell light came on, and then the left fuel light. Because the helicopter had been circling off the coast, they had not been prepared to get us. It was a fifty mile trip down to the boats, and we almost ran out of gas before we made it to the ships. When we hit the ship, they shook us down, took our weapons away from us, and we just jumped into bunks and slept for two or three hours.

Top: Evacuees from the American military headquarters are offloaded onto the U.S. Navy aircraft carrier USS Midway.

Bottom: A Huey loaded with Vietnamese evacuees on the deck of the U.S. aircraft carrier USS Midway.

THE NAVY IN VIETNAM

If you were in the Navy during the Vietnam War, chances were you spent little time on land. Most likely, you were aboard ships at sea, as a fighter or bomber pilot, or a member of the inland Riverine Force—the Brown Navy. As a Seabee or SEAL, however, you did spend time on land, and with your fellow combatants. The Navy was everywhere on the sea, in the air, and on land. It had a profound and important effect on the war.

One of the Navy's longest-running, and biggest, roles in Vietnam was Operation Market Time, an effort to blockade, as best it could, the 1,000 mile coastline of both North and South Vietnam. Market Time's purpose was to interdict enemy vessels and suspect ships of all types. These included junks, other small boats, and even the big freighters that often carried supplies from Russia, East Germany, and other Iron Curtain countries to North Vietnam. Operation Market Time continued throughout the war. Men aboard United States Navy ships boarded and searched thousands of suspected, and often real, enemy vessels in the South China Sea. The Navy had many successes, but it could never completely stop the never-ending flow of supplies to the major North Vietnamese ports, such as Haiphong.

The Navy fleet had guided missile cruisers and destroyers. The Navy also operated armored troop carriers to land Marines on beaches, usually in I Corps. And Navy ships worked closely with Coast Guard boats that also patrolled the length of the Vietnamese coastline. Even a battleship saw duty in the Vietnam War. The USS New Jersey was in combat off the coast of Vietnam from 1968 to 1969. In that time, it expended more rounds at enemy positions than it did in World War II. The New Jersey was what the Navy called its "last all-gunned battleship to see combat."

From its aircraft carriers based in the South China Sea, the Navy F-4 Phantoms, also flown by Marine pilots, and A-6 Intruders, among others, participated in Operation Rolling Thunder, the constant bombing of targets in North Vietnam and the parts of Laos and Cambodia that bordered South Vietnam. Navy planes attacked and destroyed bridges, roads, supply depots, and the few operating railroads that ran through North Vietnam. The Navy flew thousands of sorties over these countries during the war.

The Navy had its own fleet of Huey, UH-1B, helicopters usually heavily armed with machine guns and air-to-surface missiles. These choppers supported boats patrolling the coast, and engaged in firefights to aid Marine and Army actions. Often they went on daring missions to rescue downed fighter pilots over South Vietnam, and they even flew north of the DMZ into rough parts of North Vietnam. In South Vietnam, Navy choppers went on many medevac missions to help wounded troops.

In addition, the Navy operated hospitals in Da Nang and Saigon, as well as two hospital ships off the coast at sea, the Sanctuary and the Repose.

In Operations Linebacker and Linebacker II, Navy planes helped to stall North Vietnam's Easter Offensive against the South in 1972. The Easter Offensive was a successor operation to the 1968 Tet Offensive, one of Hanoi's failed attempts to defeat South Vietnam. That defeat would come years later under entirely different circumstances.

Mining enemy harbors in war is always controversial. Some experts believe that ships from sympathetic countries which enter and dock in an enemy harbor should not fear attack. American military chiefs believed that any country delivering goods to North Vietnam, even if it was innocent supplies and equipment, if such things exist, were fair game for attack in North Vietnam's territorial waters. To that end, the Navy, in Operation Pocket

Big capital gun ships, better known as a battleships, were not widely used in Vietnam. When they were, it was generally for shore and inland bombardment.

The U.S. Navy aircraft carrier USS Constellation (CVA–64) underway with
Carrier Air Wing Nine (CVW-9), 1971-1972.

Left: A Swift Boat used during Riverine inland waterway operations.

Center left: USS Midway (CVA-41) in the western Pacific. Various aircraft are visible on deck.

Center right: USS Newport News (CA-148) firing her forward turret in 1972 during the Vietnam War.

Right: USS Garrett County (AGP-786, patrol craft tender) at anchor in the Mekong Delta, South Vietnam.
On deck are two U.S. Navy Bell UH-1E Hueys

Operation Deckhouse IV - USS Thomaston.

Fast Patrol Crafts (Swift boats) operating up a river in Vietnam, in background monitors and landing crafts.

*A U.S. Navy McDonnell F-4B Phantom II of Fighter Squadron VF-111 Sundowners drops 227 kg
Mk 82 bombs over Vietnam during 1971. VF-111 was assigned to Attack Carrier Air Wing 15 (CVW-15)
aboard the aircraft carrier USS Coral Sea.*

Money, mined key North Vietnamese ports. Despite the dangers of entering the mined harbors, countries supporting North Vietnam continued to their ships at their own risk. To defend itself against the mines set in its waters by the U.S. Navy, North Vietnam operated its own coastal and oceangoing minesweepers.

On land, Navy Seabees built and maintained many port facilities, mainly at Da Nang and Saigon. If there was a need for a well-built facility, Seabees, continuing a long tradition through many wars, were the ones to build it.

The United States Navy soon realized that the Mekong River, the 12th largest river in the world, with its mouth in the South China Sea, provided many problems for American forces in Vietnam. The enemy, mostly local Viet Cong units, usually moved with impunity over and through the Mekong's many branches, the smaller rivers it fed, its canals, creeks, streams, and swamps, including the complex and dark Rung Sat mangrove quagmire south of Saigon. Exceptionally important because of its abundant fishing, the river's flow helped irrigate the country's wide-ranging rice paddies, especially in the southern delta. It was said that the North Vietnamese were jealous of their southern enemy because all he had to do was to put a line in the water, take a nap, and wait for the fish to come, and when planting rice he just waited for the water to come to fertilize his crop. This was in contrast to what many experts considered a harder life in North Vietnam.

To overcome the usually trouble-free movement of enemy troops who used the many and varied inland waterways, the Navy and the Army got together and created the Mobile Riverine Force, known as the Brown Navy. As part of Operation Market Time, the 31 foot long Patrol Boat Riverine, popularly called the Swift

Troops wading ashore from L.C.V at the mouth of Tau Viet river two miles north of Dong Ha.

Boat, armed with machine guns and mortars and carrying a five or six man crew, became the mainstay of the inland Navy. The Riverine Force served to land small troop units into combat zones along the river, into rice paddies, and in the swamps. Even with somewhat limited firepower, the boats helped support the troops in a continuing effort to keep the waterways open. Many of the boats also had chains attached to the front of the hull to drag the waterways, sweeping for mines placed by Communist forces.

The Riverine Force also used the Alpha Boat, a smaller vessel, designed for coastal missions. Along with training the Vietnamese Navy to be self-sufficient, the force also included support vessels that carried supplies and munitions, and salvage boats.

The Navy SEALS—Sea Air Land teams—played a strong and, still in many instances, secret role in Vietnam, going on special operations not only in North and South Vietnam, but also in Cambodia and Laos. Their bravery is unmatched. The successes of the SEALS missions are still untold. But they did their job quickly, efficiently, and never complained about the danger that accompanied the work they did and continue to do.

A POSTSCRIPT

Hearing from readers is gratifying. It means you are reaching people. It says you do not work alone. If there is anything that has become clear over the years about *The Soldiers' Story*, it is that people want to connect with each other. And they sometimes look to me to help with those connections. To my surprise and gratitude, I keep receiving letters, e-mail, and notes from new readers. Regularly there is a message from someone about the book. These readers tell me that they feel a part of the stories, as they seek to understand the Vietnam War, which, for many, is slipping into the shadows. These notes come from the sons, daughters, wives, brothers, and sisters of the men who served in that war. They ask questions. They present new facts.

In an e-mail not long ago, I learned that retired Marine Lt. Colonel Jim Kean, a defender at the American Embassy at the end of the war, had recently died. I also learned that Steve Hasty is retiring from the Marine Corps after more than forty years of active service, and others, such as John Valdez, Ted Murray, and Walter Sparks, are doing well. One day a question came to me from a woman wondering if I knew her father, an information officer in Vietnam during my time there. I sent her a note to tell her I think I knew him. Then, this from an editor working on a Vietnam memoir: her author "writes of a Mr. Anthony 'Tony' Wood." She says she is trying to find him for possible inclusion in the book she is working on, and she wonders if it is the same person as in my book. Most likely, I tell her, but I lost contact with him many years ago. In any case, whether I can provide precise information or not, I answer each question that comes my way. If a person spends time trying to connect with me because of the book, they deserve a reply.

Then there was this recent note from a mother in Oregon who blogs and teaches her kids at home.

"I wanted to let you know that I just finished reading *The Soldiers' Story*. Thank you for compiling these stories and writing this book. I have been working my way through the major American war histories of the 20th century, and this book was so insightful as to what happened in Vietnam. I sincerely appreciate the work you did to bring this work to fruition. I am also a homeschooling mom, and this book will be a mandatory read for my kids when they study this time period. Thank you again for your efforts. I really do appreciate them."

I remember doing a book signing and a reading in a small, independent bookstore on Long Island. The room, to my surprise and satisfaction, was full, which is rare for most signings. When the session ended, a hulking man in his forties with short blond hair and a ruddy face approached the desk where I sat. I looked up at him. Tears streamed down his rugged face. He tried to speak but he could not get out any words. The store was mostly empty by then so the two of us were practically alone and face to face, me with nothing to say but recognizing that he could have been one of the men in my book. He, knowing, too, that he fit perfectly among those on the pages in the book. He struggled to say something. I stayed silent and waited for him to find himself. Finally he spoke, haltingly and almost in a whisper, the tears still streaming down his face. "Thank you for telling my story," he said. And with that and with great dignity he turned neatly on his heels and walked slowly from the store.

The notes I receive and the people I meet, remind me that the war has not ended for those who fought in it and survived it, and for the relatives who are looking for answers about their loved ones— often a father or brother—who were in Vietnam during that time. Some sons and daughters, anxious to know about their father, use the book as a template in an attempt to understand the mind of the Vietnam veteran. I have a suspicion this will always be case. The stories these men tell will continue to resonate, helping those who were not there to understand the war and allowing those who were in the war to better understand their place in i.

PHOTO CREDITS

p. 1: Copyright Lukiyanova Natalia, used under permission from used under permission from Shutterstock 124702435, throughout

p. 3: National Archives, 127 GVC-44, Photograph by Cpl. G.W. Wright, Defense Dept. Photo (Marine Corps), A371932

p. 6: National Archives, 36-2933M

p. 7: National Archives, 127 GVC-43, Photograph by Cpl. A. V. Huffman, Defense Dept. Photo (Marine Corps) A371630

p. 9: National Archives, 127 GVC-75, Defense Dept. Photo (Marine Corps), A192818

p. 10: Copyright by Keith Tarrier; used under permission from used under permission from Shutterstock 144525857

p. 12: National Archives, 111-CCV-557, 45991, Photograph by SP6 Samuel L. Swain, US Army Sp Photo Det. Pac.

p. 14: National Archives, 91-14, Interior of Ward #5 (Medical) - 91st Evac Hosp (Chu Lai)

p. 15: National Archives, 127-GVC-6, Photograph by Ssgt Osterma, Defense Dept. Photo (Marine Corps), A189114

p. 17: National Archives, 111-CCV-93, Photography by SP5 H. Walls, SC 659121

p. 18-19: Copyright Michael Hero, used under permission by used under permission from Shutterstock_105410135

p. 20-21: Copyright Keith Tarrier, used under permission by used under permission from Shutterstock_167984732

p. 22: Top image: copyright RCPPHOTO; used under permission from used under permission from Shutterstock_29588542

p. 22: Bottom image: CC, Wiki Commons, uploaded by Harald Hansen, US_M18a1_claymore_mine

p. 23: Top image: copyright Carol Guzowski, Charles Snyder Private Collection

p, 23: Bottom image: copyright Carol Guzowski, Charles Snyder Private Collection

p. 24: Top image, copyright Militarist; used under permission from used under permission from Shutterstock, 101235115

p. 24: Bottom left: copyright Carol Guzowski, Charles Snyder Private Collection

p. 24: Bottom center: CC, Wiki Commons, uploaded by Ironmonger

p. 24: Bottom right: copyright Epic Militaria, http://www.epicmilitaria.com

p. 25: Top images: copyright Carol Guzowski, Charles Snyder Private Collection

p. 25: Middle and lower images: copyright Carol Guzowski, Charles Snyder Private Collection

p. 26-27: Copyright Carol Guzowski, Charles Snyder Private Collection

p. 29: Image copyright Lee Koh Lang, used under permission used under permission from Shutterstock 189694184

p. 30: National Archives, 111-CCV-255, Photograph by Spec. 4 Burt W. Peterson, CC 50434

p. 32: National Archives, Defense Dept. Photo (Marine Corps), A185205

p. 33: National Archives, 127 GVC-42, Photograph by Sgt. Dickman, Defense Dept. Photo (Marine Corps), A370495

p. 34: National Archives, 111-CCV-527, CC-50499

p. 35: National Archives, Defense Dept. Photo (Marine Corps) A372279

p. 36: National Archives, 127 GVC-43, Defense Dept. photo (Marine Corps) A191150

p. 38: National Archives, 127 GVC-44, Photograph by Milo, Defense Dept. Photo (Marine Corps), A192759

p. 39: Marine Corps University, Defense Dept. Photo A187837

p. 40: National Archives, 127 GVC-43, Photograph by Sgt. Dickman, Defense Dept. Photo (Marine Corps), A370616

p. 41: National Archives, 111-CCV-554, Photograph by Sgt. 1st Class Jack H. Yamaguchi, U.S. Army photo, CC 32242

p. 43: National Archives, 127 GVB-158, Defense Dept. (Marine Corps), A372842

p. 44: National Archives, 111-CCV-270, Photograph by SPh. Childs, Dept. of the Army, CC 64703

p. 45: National Archives, 111-531457, Dept of Defense (Army), SC-651408

p. 46, Bottom image; copyright Carol Guzowski, Charles Snyder Private Collection

p. 48: National Archives, 111 KV, Photograph by Carl F. Schneider, USAPA, CC 40689

p. 49: National Archives, CC 112428, Photograph by Garner

p. 51: National Archives, A192442, Photograph Cpl. R.S. Walden, Defense Dept. Photo (Marine Corps)

p. 53: National Archives, 111-C-CC34613, Defense Dept. (Army), 530610

p. 54: Alamy, Copyright Keystone Pictures US / Alamy, E0XF6H

p. 55: National Archives, 111-CCV-529, Photograph by PFC Talmadge B. Harbison, USAPA, CC 48683

p. 56: National Archives, 127 GVC-41, Defense Dept. Photo (Marine Corps), A371275

p. 57: National Archives, 111-CCV-555, Photograph by SSG Lyle V. Boggess, Photo Det, Pacific, CC 033247

p. 58: National Archives, 127 GVC-89, Photograph Sgt. A.V. Huffman, Defense Dept. Photo (Marine Corps), A372102

p. 60: Copyright by John Gomez, used under permission from used under permission from Shutterstock, 201243965

p. 61: National Archives, 127 GVC-93, Photograph by LCpl Brumley, Defense Dept. Photo (Marine Corps), A190670

p. 62: National Archives, 127 GVC-132, Photograph by A.V. Huffman, Defense Dept. Photo (Marine Corps), A371627

p. 63: National Archives, 111-CCV-554, Photograph by Spec. 5 James I. Hatton, U.S. Army Photo, CC 32293

p. 64: National Archives, 127 GVC-43, Photograph by Pfc Eshbach, Defense Dept. Photo (Marine Corps), A191807

p. 65: National Archives, 111-CCV-268, Photograph by SP5 Clyde Delk, Jr., USAPA, CC 47124

p. 66: National Archives, 111-SC-650555, Defense Dept. Photo, (Army), 531455

p. 69: National Archives, 127 GVC-42, Photograph by Sgt. F. Lee, Defense Dept. Photo (Marine Corps), A188473

p. 70, Bottom image: National Archives, 127 GVC-158, Photograph by Cpl. R.L. Pearson, Defense Dept. Photo (Marine Corps), A373985

p. 71: National Archives, Photograph, description not available

p. 73: National Archives, Photograph by SSgt J.T. Purcell, Defense Dept. Photo (Marine Corps), A190715

p. 74: National Archives, 111-CCV-270, Photograph by SPh . Childs, Dept of the Army, CC 64703

p. 75: National Archives, 127-N-A188522, Defense Dept. (Navy), 532446

p. 76: Top left image: National Archives, 127-GVC-152, Photograph by Tilson, Defense Dept. Photo (Marine Corps), A190153

p. 76: Top right image: National Archives, 111-CCV-134, Photograph by SP5 Robert G. Lafoon, Photo Det (U.S. Army), CC44069

p. 77: Top left image: Wikimedia Commons, Photograph by Starry, Donn A, Defense Dept. (U.S. Army), ACAV and M48 Convoy Vietnam War

p. 77: Top right image: Wikimedia Commons, Photograph by SPC5 Brian K. Grigsby, Defoliation agent spraying

p. 77: Bottom image: Image copyright by Militarist; used under permission from used under permission from Shutterstock 216918370

p. 78: Top left image: Wikimedia Commons, Defense Dept. (U.S. Air Force), Boeing B-52 dropping bombs

p. 78: Top middle image: Wikimedia Commons, USMC-111101-M-KU932-059

p. 78: Top right image: Wikimedia Commons, Photography by Dwight Burdette, Flak Jacket

p. 79: Top image: National Archives, description not available

p. 79: Lower left image: National Archives, 127-GVC-134, Photography by Cpl. L.F. George, Defense Dept. (Marine Corps), A190596

p. 79: Lower right image: National

Archives, 127-GVC-29, Photography by Cpl. Patrick L. Schackman, Defense Dept. (Marine Corps), A192031

p. 81: Image copyright Lee Koh Lang, used under permission used under permission from Shutterstock 189694184

p. 83: National Archives, 342-AF-109171USAF, Defense Dept. (Air Force), 542312

p. 84: National Archives, 342-AF-100513USAF, Defense Dept. (Air Force), 542300

p. 87: National Archives, 111-CCV-97, Photograph by SP4 Richard S. Durrance, USAPA, CC 41854

p. 88: National Archives, A193281, Defense Dept. Photo (Marine Corps)

p. 90: National Archives, 127-GVC-98, 20

p. 93: National Archives, Photography by Ray W. Stubbe, Defense Dept. (Marine Corps), A800207

p. 94: National Archives, 127 GVB-158, Photograph by J.E. Thorton, Defense Dept. Photo (Marine Corps), A374458

p. 97: National Archives, 127 GVC-90, Defense Dept. Photo (Marine Corps), A199200

p. 98: National Archives, 127 GVB-363, Photograph by I / Cpl. Hildreth, Defense Dept.

p. 99: National Archives, 111-C-CC64305, Photograph by Signal Corps Activity, Department of Defense, 530627

p. 101: National Archives, Photograph by LCpl D.C. Moore, Defense Dept. photo (Marine Corps), A189650

p. 102: National Archives, 127 GVC-107, Photograph by PHI Elder, USN, Defense Dept. Photo (Marine Corps), A800247

p. 103: National Archives, 127 GVC-71, Photograph by LCpl Del Vecchio, Defense Dept. Photo (Marine Corps), A371332

p. 104: National Archives, 127 GVC-43, Defense Dept. Photo (Marine Corps), A191311

p. 105: National Archives, 127-GVC-11, Photograph by LCDR Ray W. Stubbe, Defense Dept. Photo (Marine Corps), A800187

p. 107: National Archives, 127

GVC-135, Photograph by Shearer, Defense Dept. Photo (Marine Corps), A191791

p. 108: National Archives, 127 GVC-43, Photograph by LCpl D. Moore, Defense Dept. Photo (Marine Corps), A374591

p. 110: National Archives, 111-CCV-97, Photograph by 2LT Thomas H Wilson, U.S. Army SP Photo Det, Pac, CC-43380

p. 112: Bottom image: National Archives, 127 GVC-43, Photograph by LCpl Stelson, Defense Dept. Photo (Marine Corps), A191302

p. 115: National Archives, 127 GVC-132, Photograph by Cpl. Philip R. Boehme, Defense Dept. Photo (Marine Corps), A193316

p. 117: National Archives, 111-CCV-97, Photograph by SP4 Jacob E. Hawes, US ARMY Sp. Photo Det, Pac CC 54783

p. 119: National Archives, 111-CCV-104, Photograph by SGT Virgille Rodriquez, Photo Det, PAC, CC 41406

p. 121: National Archives, 127 GVB-158, Photograph by Cpl. Pearson, Defense Dept. Photo (Marine Corps), A374145

p. 122: Wikimedia Commons, L'homme venteux, http://goo.gl/SQFOOg

p. 123: Wikimedia Commons, L'homme venteux, http://goo.gl/6SftXU

p. 124: National Archives, 111-CCV-97, Photograph by PFC Wendell D. Garrett, USAPA, CC 43245

p. 127: National Archives, 111-CCV-134, Photograph by SP4 Roland Spriggs, USAPA, CC 65806

p. 128: National Archives, 127-N-A 187335, Photograph by Flle of the U.S. Marine Corps, Department of Defense (Marine Corps), 532444

p. 129: Top image: National Archives, description not available

p. 129, Bottom image: National Archives, 127 GVC-42, Photograph by G.L. Foster, Defense Dept. Photo (Marine Corps), A189900

p. 131: National Archives, 127 GVC, Photograph by Sgt. Behrens, Defense

p. 132: National Archives, 342-AF-104326USAF, Photograph by U.S. Air Force, Department of Defense, 542306

p. 134: National Archives, 127 GVC-29, Defense Dept. Photo (Marine Corps), A193631

p. 135: National Archives, 127 GVC-135, Defense Dept. Photo (Marine Corps), A190631

p. 137: National Archives, 127 GVC-29, Photograph by G.L. Foster, Defense Dept. Photo (Marine Corps), A190785

p. 138: National Archives, 127 GVC-100, Photograph by Sgt. E.H. LeBlanc, Defense Dept. Photo (Marine Corps), A191579

p. 139: National Archives, description not available

p. 140: 111-CCV-556, VN-Div. 1st Cav (air), CC 36836

p. 141: Top image: National Archives, Photograph by Cpl. McDonald, Defense Dept. Photo (Marine Corps) A369979

p. 141: Bottom image: National Archives, Defense Dept. Photo (Marine Corps) A191147

p. 142: National Archives, 127 GVB-158, Photography by Cpl. A.V. Huffman, Defense Dept. Photo (Marine Corps) 4372687

p. 143: Top image: National Archives, 111-CCV-555, Photograph by SFC Peter P. Ruplenas, US Army Sp Photo Dat, Pacific, 6442-B-698C

p. 143: Bottom image: National Archives, 127-N_A192611, Defense Dept. Photo (Navy, U.S. Marine Corps), 532462

p. 144: Alamy, Copyright INTERFOTO / Alamy, DE1A04

p. 146: Image copyright Tzubasa, used under permission used under permission from Shutterstock 185343743

p. 148: National Archives, 111-CC-529, Photograph by SPC Samuel L Swain, USAPA, 45771

p. 152: National Archives, 111-CC-529, Photography by Spec. 5 James Newlin, CC-45840

p. 153: National Archives, 127 GVB-158, Defense Dept. Photo (Marine Corps), A191870

p. 154: National Archives, 111-

CCV-529, Photography by SP4 J.P. Fitzpatrick, Jr, USAPA, CC-48599

p. 156: National Archives, 111-CCV-529, Photography by SP4 Bryan K. Grigsby, USAPA, 48673

p. 158-159: National Archives, 127–GVC-74, Photography by Eshbach, Defense Dept. Photo (Marine Corps), A190261

p. 160: National Archives, 127–GVC-75A, Photograph by Cpl. G. J. Vojack, Defense Dept. Photo (Marine Corps), A372287

p. 161: National Archives, 127–GVC-43, Photography by Cpl. L.F. George, Defense Dept. Photo (Marine Corps), A190597

p. 163: National Archives, 127–GVC-27, Defense Dept. Photo (Marine Corps), A370528

p. 164: National Archives, 127–GVC-42, Photography by PFC McDowell, Defense Dept. Photo (Marine Corps), A190034

p. 166: National Archives, Photography by Cpl. G.J. Vojack, Defense Dept. Photo (Marine Corps), A372285

p. 167: National Archives, 111-CCV-529, Photography by SP5 J. V. Fitzpatrick, Jr., CC-48593

p. 168: National Archives, 111-CCV-529, Photography by SP4 Richard S. Durrance, CC-46600

p. 171: National Archives, 127 GVC-42, Photography by Sgt. W.F. Dickman, Defense Dept. Photo (Marine Corps), A370629

p. 172: National Archives, Photography by SSgt Upton, Defense Dept. Photo (Marine Corps), A370997-A

p. 175: National Archives, 111-CCV-529, USAPA, CC 45830

p. 176: Bottom image: National Archives, 111-CCV-529, Photography by SP4 Bryan K. Crigsby, USAPA, CC-48671

p. 178: National Archives, 111-CCV-529, Photography by Sfc K.C. Uchima, USAPA, CC-32355

p. 180: National Archives, 68 CCA-186-8, Photography by Carl F. Schneider, US Army Photographic Agency, CC-051133

p. 182: National Archives, 127 GVB-158, Photography by Cumming, Defense Dept. Photo (Marine Corps), A189961

p. 183: National Archives, Photograph by Sgt. W.F. Dickman, Defense Dept, Photo (Marine Corps), A371481

p. 184: National Archives, 127-GCV-107, Photograph by LCpl. G.W. Wright, Defense Dept. (Marine Corps), A371884

p. 186 National Archives, 111 CCV-529, Photograph by SP4 Samuel L. Susie, USAPA, CC-45770

p. 189: National Archives, 111-CCV-256, Photograph by SP5 J. F. Fitzpatrick Jr., USAPA, CC 48595

p. 190: National Archives, Photograph by Sgt. J. Ryan, Defense Dept. Photo (Marine Corps), A189813

p. 192: National Archives, 127 GVC-42, Photograph by Sgt. J. Ryan, Defense Dept. Photo (Marine Corps), A189812

p. 194: National Archives, 127 GVC-42, Photography by Sgt. Ryan, Defense Dept. Photo (Marine Corps), A189520

p. 196: National Archives, 111-CCV-529, Photograph by SP5 Edward Worman, USAPA, CC-49923

p. 198: National Archives, 127 GVC-28, Photograph by Sgt. R. Woltner, Defense Dept. Photo (Marine Corps) A186042

p. 199: National Archives, 127 GVC-43, Photograph by Sgt. W.F. Dickman, Defense Dept. photo (Marine Corps), A371144

p. 201: National Archives, 127 GVC-6, Photograph by GySgt. Duncan, Defense Dept. photo (Marine Corps), A191020

p. 202: National Archives, 111-CCV-529, Photograph by SP5 Anthony B'recht, USAPA, 48578

p. 204: National Archives, Photograph by Cpl. L.B. George, Defense Dept. Photo (Marine Corps) A190599

p. 205: Left image: National Archives, Photograph by Cpl.

Philip R.Boehme, Defense Dept. Photo (Marine Corps) A193314

p. 205: Middle image: National Archives, Photograph by Cpl. L.B. George, Defense Dept. Photo (Marine Corps) A190598

p. 205: Right image: National Archives, Photograph by Sgt, L.R. Green, Defense Dept. Photo (Marine Corps) A25644

p. 206: National Archives, Photograph by Cpl. L.F. George Defense Dept. Photo (Marine Corps) A190592

p. 207: Left image: National Archives, Photograph by Sgt. Burch, Defense Dept. photo (Marine Corps) A191250

p. 207: Middle image: National Archives, 111-CCC-40384, Defense Dept. (Army), 530614

p. 207: Right image: National Archives, 11-CCV-527, Photography by Sp4 A Hill, CC-067774

p. 208: National Archives, Photograph by LCpl R.J. Smith Defense Dept. Photo (Marine Corps) A371117

p. 210: Alamy, Copyright Cindy Hopkins / Alamy, CP128R

p. 216: Wikimedia, Battle of Lima Site 85.US, Lt. Col. Jeannie Schiff, USAF

p. 217: National Archives, 111-CCV-97, Photograph by PFC Wendell D. Garrett, USAPA, CC 43089

p. 219: National Archives, 127 GVB-158, Defense Dept. Photo (Marine Corps), A371611

p. 220: WikiCommoms, Jeannie Schiff, LS85 Phou Pha Thi.

p. 223: National Archives, 111-CCV-104, Photograph by SP4 Rockoff, USAPA, CC70608

p. 224: National Archives 111-CCV-97, Photograph by SP4 Robert C. Lafoon, Photo Det, Pacific, CC- 33827

p. 227: National Archives, 111-GVB-158, Photograph by LCpl Fisher, Defense Dept. Photo (Marine Corps), A370409

p. 229: National Archives, 111-CCV-527, Photograph by SSG Miguel A. Perez, USAPA, 66574

p. 230: National Archives, 111-

CCV-97, Photograph by SP5 Lawrence J. Sullivan, USAPA, CC50483

p. 232: National Archives, CC-112307, Photograph by Garner, USAPA, CC112307

p. 235: National Archives, 127 GVB-158, Photograph by SSgt D.L. Shearer, Defense Dept. Photo (Marine Corps) A191947

p. 237: National Archives, 127 GVC-145, Photograph by Lt. Cpl. Bruch, Defense Dept. Photo (Marine Corps), A370972

p. 238: National Archives, 111-CCV--270, Photograph by SP5 James F. Sullivan, USAPA, CC 59218

p. 240: National Archives, 111-C-CC47777, Defense Dept. (Army), 530621

p. 243: Bottom image: National Archives, 127 GVC-41, Photograph by SSgt. Brown, Defense Dept. Photo (Marine Corps), A187317

p. 244: National Archives, 127 GVC-131, Photograph by LCDR Ray W. Stubbe, Defense Dept. Photo (Marine Corps), A800197

p. 245: National Archives, 127 GVC-13, Defense Dept. Photo (Marine Corps), A25883

p. 246: National Archives, 111-CCV-529, Photograph by SP4 Wendell D. Garrett, USAPA, CC 46602

p. 251: National Archives, 111-CCV-536, Photograph by Spec. 4 James Harmon, U.S. Army Photo, CC 53148

p. 252: National Archives, 111-KV, Photograph by Carl Schneider, U.S. Army photographic agency

p. 254: National Archives, 111-CCV-255, Photograph by PFC Talmadge B. Narbison, Photo Det. Pac. CC 48679

p. 256: Top image: National Archives, 111-CCV-529, Photograph by SP5 Samuel L. N., USAPA, CC 43717

p. 256: Bottom image: National Archives, 111-CCV-557, Photograph by SP6 Samuel L. Swain, US Army Sp Photo Det. Pac.

p. 257: National Archives, 111-CCV-529, Photograph by SP4 John Budac, 2 February 1968, USAPA, CC46030

p. 258: National Archives, 127 GVC-89, Defense Dept. Photo (Marine Corps), A193605

p. 259: National Archives, 111-CCV-105, Photograph by SP4 Vest, USAPA, CC 62795

p. 263: National Archives, 127 GVC-42, 1967, Defense Dept. Photo (Marine Corps), A421831

p. 265: National Archives, 111-KV, Photograph by Carl Schneider, U.S. Army photographic agency, CC 043843

p. 266: National Archives, 342-AF-95673USAF, Defense Dept. (Air Force) 542296

p. 269: National Archives, 111-CCV-97, Photograph by SP4 John Atkinson, SC 658869

p. 271: National Archives, 111-CCV-104, Photograph by SP4 Steven B. Ford, USAPA, CC 75726

p. 272: National Archives, 306-MVP-14(28), U.S. Information Agency, 541859

p. 275: National Archives, 342-AF-93093USAF, Defense Dept. (Air Force), 542293

p. 276: National Archives, 127-GVC-71, Defense Dept (Marine Corps), A371443

p. 279: National Archives, 111-CCV-93, Photography by SP5 H. Walls, 659121

p. 283: National Archives, 111-CCV-97, Photograph by SP5 Darrell L. DuRall, C-20806

p. 286: Wikimedia Commons, Photography by Thomas J. O'Halloran, John McCain interview on April 24, 1974

p. 289: National Archives, 111-CCV-529, Photograph by SP5 Wilson Elsson, CC-46622

p. 291: National Archives, 111-CCV-554, Photograph by SP5 Lawrence J. Sullivan, Photo Det. Pacific, CC 36383

p. 292: Wikimedia Commons, Photography by USAF, Republic F-105D cockpit 060901-F-1234S-009

p. 294: Wikimedia Commons, Photography by USAF, Republic F-105D-30-RE (SN 62-4234) in flight with full bomb load 060901-F-1234S-013

p. 295: Wikimedia Commons,

Photography by U.S Military photograph, HanoiHilton1973

p. 297: National Archives, 111-CCV-97, Photograph by AP4 Seller, SC 658844

p. 298: National Archives, 111-CCV-105, Photograph by SP5 Robert C. Lafoon, Photo Det, Pac, CC 38275

p. 301: National Archives, 111-CCV-97, Photograph by SSG Howard C. Breedlove, USAPA, CC 40277

p. 302: National Archives, CC 112038, Photograph by Garner

p. 303: 110224-F-XN622-006, USAF ; F-4Ds over Vietnam

p. 304: 1960's Capt. Charles B. DeBellevue, U.S. Air force photo (McDonnell Douglas) ; McDonnell-Douglas-F-4-Phantom-II-055

p. 306: Wikimedia commons, Photograph by Public Domain, Cabinacaza, goo.gl/xwT4xJ

p. 310: Wikimedia Commons, Photography by USAF, Maj lodge locher F4D

p. 311: Wikimedia Commons, Photography by Defense Dept. (Air Force), Capt. Richard S. Ritchie, in South Vietnam - 1972

p. 313: National Archives, 111 C-CC59950, Defense Dept. (US Army), 530626

p. 314: National Archives, CC 112872, US Army Photo

p. 316: Copyright Olivier Le Queinec ; used under permission from Shutterstock 16526386

p. 317: Copyright Steve Mann, used under permission from used under permission from Shutterstock 57944419

p. 318: Top image: National Archives, 127 GVC-20, Photograph by Sgt. Carl Frickson Jan69, Defense Dept. Photo (Marine Corps) A422408

p. 318: Middle image: National Archives, 127 GVC-18, Defense Dept. Photo (Marine Corps) A422395

p. 318: Bottom image: National Archives, 127 GVC-19, Defense Dept. Photo (Marine Corps), A422128

p. 319: National Archives, 127 GVC-19, Photograph by LCpl G. A. Martinez, Defense Dept, Photo (Marine Corps)

p. 320: Top image: Copyright IanC66 ; used under permission from Shutterstock 179517689

p. 320: Bottom image: used under permission from Shutterstock 95943844

p. 323: Image copyright Lee Koh Lang, used under permission used under permission from Shutterstock 189694184

p. 325: National Archives, 111-CCV-529, Photograph by SF3 Lawrence J. Sullivan, USAPA, CC-57458

p. 327: National Archives, 127-GVS-158, Photograph PFC P. Shaekman, Defense Dept. Photo (Marine Corps), A190238

p. 328: National Archives, 111-CCV-529, CC-45843,

p. 330: Ron Steinman Private Collection, USN 711642

p. 334: National Archives 111-CCV-105, Photograph by SP4 Vest, USAPA, CC 62795

p. 336: Wikimedia Commons, Photography by Sciacchitano, Terry at Subic

p. 338: Left image: Wikimedia Commons, Operation Frequent Wind, USS Pioneer Contender

p. 338: Right image: Wikimedia Commons, Operation Frequent Wind, Uploaded by Jbarta, 1970s decade montage.png

p. 340-341: Ron Steinman Private Collection

p. 342: Ron Steinman Private Collection, USN 1162139

p. 345: Photograph from the Naval Historical Centers "L" File

p. 346: National Archives, 127 GVC-89, Photograph by Sgt. E.H. LeBlanc, Defense Dept. Photo (Marine Corps), A191576

p. 348: National Archives, 127 GVC-90, Defense Dept. Photo (Marine Corps), A191489

p. 350: Wikimedia Commons, Photograph by United States Navy, CC-PD-Mark, goo.gl/X3lFdF

p. 351: Top image: Wikimedia Commons, Photograph by USMC , Dept. of Defense Photo (Marine Corps), PD US Marines, goo.gl/Uo7huA

p. 351: Middle image: Wikimedia Commons, Photograph by 9th MAB, Marine Corps Historical Collection, PD US Marines, goo.gl/dllXQz

p. 351: Bottom image: Wikimedia Commons, Photograph by USMC, U.S. Marine Corps, PD US Marines, goo.gl/DJLBII

p. 352: National Archives, 127 GVC-43, Defense Dept. Photo (Marine Corps), A190897

p. 354-355: Ron Steinman Private Collection

p. 358: Ron Steinman Private Collection

p. 361: USN 711644 ; pushing helicopter to make space.

p. 365: Wikimedia Commons, National Archives, Dept. of State U.S. Embassy, CC-PD-Mark, goo.gl/pvIheE

p. 368-369: Ron Steinman Private Collection

p. 375: Top image: Wikimedia Commons, Photograph by USN, U.S. Navy Photo, CC-PD-Mark ; http://goo.gl/qhlxJO

p. 375: Image bottom: Wikimedia Commons, Photograph by USN, U.S. Navy Photo, CC-PD-Mark ; http://goo.gl/6OtFCe

p. 377: National Archives, 127 GVC-127, Photograph by Sgt. R.W. Nelson, Defense Dept. Photo (Marine Corps), A373475

p. 378: Top image: Wikimedia Commons, Photograph by USN, U.S. Defense Imagery, PD US Military ; http://goo.gl/SNhYSd

p. 378: Bottom left image: Wikimedia Commons, Photograph by USN, Naval War College Museum, CC-PD-Mark ; http://goo.gl/uApkUt

p. 378: Bottom middle-left image: Wikimedia Commons, Photograph by USN, U.S. Navy Photo, CC-PD-Mark ; http://goo.gl/Dsci2S

p. 378: Bottom middle-right image: Wikimedia Commons, Photograph by PH2 Elvin House, U.S. Navy, CC-PD-Mark ; http://goo.gl/Pi24y9

p. 378: Bottom right image: Wikimedia Commons, Photograph by McHennessey, U.S. Navy, CC-PD-Mark ; http://goo.gl/GSUYkl

p. 379: Top Image: National Archives, 127 GVC-127, Photograph by J. Johnston, Defense Dept. Photo (Marine Corps), A704379

p. 379: Bottom Image: National Archives, Photograph by GySgt. Duncan 24 March 1968, Defense Dept. Photo (Marine Corps), A191020

p. 380: Wikimedia Commons, Photograph by U.S. Navy, 25 November 1971, U.S. Navy National Museum, CC-PD-Mark, goo.gl/H9z5DZ

p. 381: National Archives, 127 GVC-30, Photograph by SSgt: J.L.Harlan 19 September 1967, Defense Dept. Photo (Marine Corps), A190005

p. 382: Top image: National Archives, 127 GVC-43, Photograph by Sgt. Dickman, Defense Dept. Photo (Marine Corps), A371943

p. 382: Lower left image: Wikimedia Commons, Photograph by PH2 Phil Eggman, Defense Imagery, CC-PD-Mark , goo.gl/lBp246

p. 382: Lower right image: Wikimedia Commons, Processed Vietnamese refugees

p. 383: Top right image: National Archives, Photograph from the Naval Historical Center's "L" File

p. 383: Lower right image: Ron Steinman Private Collection

p. 384: Copyright Jimmy Tran, used under permission from used under permission from Shutterstock_168038441

p. 390: Used with permission from used under permission from Shutterstock

p. 391: Copyright Carol Guzowski, Ron Steinman Private Collection

p. 399: National Archives, 127-GVC-107, Defense Dept. (Marine Corps), A193088

p. 400: Copyright Eileen Douglas, by permission

HỘI NGHỊ QUỐC TẾ ĐOÀN KẾT VỚI NHÂN DÂN VIỆT NAM CHỐNG ĐẾ QUỐC MỸ XÂM LƯỢC

VIỆT NAM DÂN CHỦ CỘNG HÒA

12 xu

MIỀN BẮC BẮN RƠI 4181 MÁY BAY MỸ

ĐẢNG LAO ĐỘNG VIỆT NAM QUANG VINH MUÔN NĂM

2 xu

ĐẠI HỘI ĐẢNG LẦN THỨ IV

VIỆT NAM

TEM QUÂN ĐỘI

VIỆT NAM

BẢO VỆ TỔ QUỐC

BƯU CHÍNH

VIỆT NAM DÂN CHỦ CỘNG HÒA

TEM QUÂN ĐỘI

ĐÁNH MẠNH
DIỆT GỌN
PHÁT TRIỂN NHANH

BƯU CHÍNH

BƯU CHÍNH

VIỆT NAM

12 xu

VIỆT NAM
DÂN CHỦ CỘNG HÒA

40 xu

BƯU CHÍNH

BƯU CHÍNH

12 xu

VIỆT-NAM

DÂN CHỦ CỘNG HÒA

VIỆT NAM BƯU CHÍNH   UNE DES PREMIERES CARTES   200d

CERAMIQUE PEROU

1989

50 NĂM CÁCH MẠNG THÁNG MƯỜI
1917-1967

VIỆT NAM

DÂN CHỦ CỘNG HÒA

BƯU CHÍNH

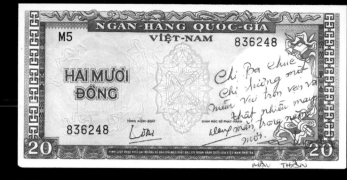

INDEX

Ron Steinman

Ron Steinman, with NBC News for 35 years, was a writer and field producer for Chet Huntley Reporting, a writer on the Huntley–Brinkley show and worked on documentaries before going to Saigon as bureau chief for NBC News in 1966. After leaving Saigon, he served as South East Asia bureau chief based in Hong Kong. He went to London as bureau chief, where among many other stories, he covered the Troubles in Northern Ireland from 1969 to1973. On returning to New York, he became general manager of special programs during Watergate. He then went to Washington as producer for Today. Returning to New York had senior producer positions on the Today Show where he helped create and produce Early Today. He was a senior producer for specials and a producer for Sunday Today. As ABC News Productions, he produced documentaries for A&E, The History Channel, and the documentary series, "*The Soldiers' Story*" for The Learning Channel. He has been a writer and executive editor for the digital magazines, The Digital Journalist and The Digital Filmmaker. He is currently a partner, producer, and writer at Douglas/Steinman Productions where he directed the documentaries, "*Luboml: My Heart Remembers,*" and "*My Grandfather's House*" and "*The Dance Goodbye.*" He is the author of "A Saigon Journal: Inside Television's First War," "The Soldiers' Story, " "*Women in Vietnam*" and a novel, "*Death in Saigon.*" He has written political and media commentary and photography criticism for various Web sites.

Acknowledgments

The new edition of *The Soldiers' Story* would not have been possible without the vision of Michelle Faulkner, an editorial director at Quarto Publishing Group USA Inc., who came to me with the idea of turning the original version of the book into an illustrated edition. Special thanks go to Maria Tubil, Hourglass Press' Karen Matsu Greenberg, and Carol Guzowski at Coral Communications & Design, for their work in making the illustrations, photos, and new text come to life on the page. Thanks to Jason Chappell for his general assistance on the project. Without being specific, I want to thank the many Web sites, too numerous to name, often run by veterans who know whereof they speak, who supplied much of the hard information for the new chapters in this, the illustrated edition of my book. Special thanks as always to Eileen Douglas for her sharp eyes in reading my copy and her strong support and faith in what is, in many ways, a new book.